Films and British national identity

From Dickens to *Dad's Army*

JEFFREY RICHARDS

Manchester University Press
Manchester and New York

distributed exclusively in the USA by St. Martin's Press

Copyright © Jeffrey Richards 1997

Published by Manchester University Press
Oxford Road, Manchester M13 9NR, UK
and Room 400, 175 Fifth Avenue, New York, NY 10010, USA

Distributed exclusively in the USA by
St. Martin's Press, Inc., 175 Fifth Avenue, New York,
NY 10010, USA

Distributed exclusively in Canada by
UBC Press, University of British Columbia, 6344 Memorial Road,
Vancouver, BC, Canada V6T 1Z2

British Library Cataloguing-in-Publication Data
A catalogue record for this book is available from the British Library

Library of Congress Cataloging-in-Publication Data
Richards, Jeffrey.
    Films and British national identity : from Dickens to Dad's army /
Jeffrey Richards.
        p.   cm.
    Includes bibliographical references and index.
    ISBN 0-7190-4742-0 (C).—ISBN 0-7190-4743-9 (P)
    1. National characteristics. British, in motion pictures.
    2. Great Britain in motion pictures.   I. Title.
    PN1995.9.N352R53   1997
    791.43'658—dc21   96-53007

ISBN 0 7190 4742 0 hardback
      0 7190 4743 9 paperback

First published 1997

01 00 99 98 97   10 9 8 7 6 5 4 3 2 1

Typeset in Great Britain
by Northern Phototypesetting Co Ltd, Bolton

Printed in Great Britain
by Redwood Books, Trowbridge, Wilts.

For
Scott Jones

STUDIES IN POPULAR CULTURE

General editor's introduction

There has in recent years been an explosion of interest in culture and cultural studies. The impetus has come from two directions and out of two different traditions. On the one hand, cultural history has grown out of social history to become a distinct and identifiable school of historical investigation. On the other hand, cultural studies has grown out of English literature and has concerned itself to a large extent with contemporary issues. Nevertheless there is a shared project, its aim, to elucidate the meanings and values implicit and explicit in the art, literature, learning, institutions and everyday behavioiur within a given society. Both the cultural historian and the cultural studies scholar seek to explore the ways in which a culture is imagined, represented and received, how it interacts with social processes, how it contributes to individual and collective identities and world views, to stability and change, to social, political and economic activities and programmes. This series aims to provide an arena for the cross-fertilization of the discipline, so that the work of the cultural historian can take advantage of the most useful and illuminating of the theoretical developments and the cultural studies scholars can extend the purely historical underpinnings of their investigations. The ultimate objective of the series is to provide a range of books which will explain in a readable and accessible way where we are now socially and culturally and how we got to where we are. This should enable people to be better informed, promote an interdisciplinary approach to cultural issues and encourage deeper thought about the issues, attitudes and institutions of popular culture.

Jeffrey Richards

Contents

List of illustrations

Acknowledgements

I am indebted to the following friends and colleagues for advice, assistance and information: Dr Anthony Aldgate, Dr James Chapman, Mr John Clegg, Dr Stephen Constantine, Professor Hugh Cunningham, Dr Sue Harper, Dr Kevin Gough-Yates, Dr Rob Humphreys, Professor Alain Frogley, Dr David Kershaw, Professor John M. MacKenzie, Ms Pat Robinson, Professor Dai Smith, Mr Derek Smith, Mr Anthony Slide, Mr Peter Stead, Professor John K. Walton, Dr Michael Winstanley and Ms Susan Waddington. Thelma Goodman and her staff at Lancaster University Inter-Library Loans Department worked tirelessly to summon up rare volumes. The National Film Archive Viewings Service (Ali Strauss and Bryony Dixon) kindly arranged the showing of many rare films. Thanks are also due to Hazel Bell for compiling the index.

Earlier versions of individual chapters appeared in Charles Barr (ed.), *All Our Yesterdays* (London, BFI, 1986), Philip Taylor (ed.), *Britain and the Cinema in the Second World War* (Basingstoke, MacMillan, 1988); and Bart Moore-Gilbert and John Seed (eds), *Cultural Revolution?* (London, Routledge, 1992). I am grateful for permission to reuse the material.

Stills were provided by the British Film Institute Stills Department and the author's collection. They come from films originally distributed by United Artists, 20th Century-Fox, Gaumont British, British Lion, Warner Bros., British National, Republic Pictures, RKO Radio Pictures, Metro-Goldwyn-Mayer, Columbia Pictures, Rank Film Distributors, Mancunian Films, Ealing Studios and General Film Distributors, to whom thanks are due.

Introduction

It became unfashionable in the 1960s and 1970s to talk about national character and national identity because of their ninteenth-century overtones of race, empire and hierarchy. The Left, who dominated British intellectual and cultural life in the 1960s and 1970s, believed that such things as nationalism and patriotism were dead or dying. They operated from an internationalist perspective, believing in decolonization and in a continuing class struggle as the dominant themes of society. They were therefore shocked to their roots by the widespread popular support for the Falklands War in 1982 and ever since that war there has been a massive and continuing academic interest in the questions of national identity, national character and patriotism. This has taken the form of an unending stream of conferences, articles, books and collections on Britishness, Englishness, national identity and so forth. It has resulted in some extremely good and some dismayingly shallow work.

This academic interest in national identity has been accompanied by a more populist interest resulting in newspaper and magazine articles, radio and television programmes, debates, discussions and phone-ins. The academic interest has been sharpened, widened and enhanced by Britain's uneasy relationship with Europe, the continuing struggle over the status of Northern Ireland, the rise of nationalist and Home Rule movements in Scotland and Wales, criticism of traditional British institutions such as the monarchy, the law and the Church of England and the ideological dominance over the past eighteen years of Thatcherism with its nationalist rhetoric. This combination of circumstances has undoubtedly resulted in an intellectual and emotional crisis of national identity.

Culture, in particular popular culture, is the battleground for identity. Cinema and latterly television have played a vital role in defining, mythifying and disseminating national identity. This volume consists of a series of linked essays on various aspects of the national identity, the creation of a British identity, the development of alternative identities and the interaction of cinema and other cultural forms. Its aim is to contribute to a wider understanding of the cultural construction of the national identity, to contextualize the crisis and to examine the options for future development.

National identity

Each individual has a set of multiple identities which operate at different times and under different circumstances. People define themselves by gender, family, religion, ethnic group, class, status, city, region, nation. But as Anthony Smith observes in his admirable book on national identity:

> Of all the collective identities which human beings share today, national identity is perhaps the most fundamental and inclusive ... other types of collective identity – class, gender, race, religion – may overlap or combine with national identity but they rarely succeed in undermining its hold.[1]

The nation is the population that collectively occupies a defined territory. The governing powers in that territory invariably seek to socialize its members into identifying with it by education, culture, ceremonial and ritual. For the nation is, above all else, in Benedict Anderson's felicitous phrase, 'an imagined community', a focus of loyalty and a source of identity, providing a sense of belonging to something bigger than oneself.[2] It is pre-eminently, therefore, a cultural artefact.

The history of a country in the modern world is a matter of continual renegotiation between the nation (the officially designated and sanctioned cultural form embracing all) and the people (the masses, the working classes, the majority segment of the population); between the state (the governing institutions of the country) and the citizenry (the collective membership of the country); between the centre and the localities; between the city and the countryside; between the majority and minorities; between official and unofficial culture.

There is, however, always a dominant ideology, a dominant image; otherwise there would be nothing to contest or negotiate with.

Every nation has a set of national values, desirable qualities that derive from the national identity and the national character, phenomena which are linked but not identical. The concept of national identity, first articulated in the seventeenth century, had, according to Smith, by the eighteenth century become a commonplace.[3]

Herder argued that every nation has its peculiar 'genius' and that this must be recovered – hence the vital importance in the eighteenth and nineteenth centuries of etymology, history, philology, antiquarianism, archaeology, all of which were deeply involved with the new 'science' of racialism.[4] These disciplines flourished because of an overpowering desire to discover the roots of the national identity. All of this was the product of a particular intellectual moment in history – a moment which experienced simultaneously the rise of Romanticism, the Industrial Revolution and the French and American revolutions. Taken together, they resulted in the known world and its governing assumptions being turned upside down, and precipitated the need to define and locate, preserve or restore the national identity.

Once the national identity has been defined, it can be promoted and spread by a whole range of institutions, events, symbols and ceremonies. Smith lists flags, anthems, parades, coinage, passports, war memorials, folklore, museums, oaths, popular heroes and heroines, fairytales, national recreations, legal procedures, educational practices and military codes.[5] An agreed national identity also tends to underpin the whole range of mass-produced popular culture, which seeks to maximise its profits by appealing to broad common denominators.[6] The practitioners of both elite and popular culture, and later the mass media, therefore play a central role in defining and disseminating national identity, values and character.

The study of a nation's self-image is crucial in understanding its actions both at home and abroad. I take the same view of national character/national identity as Sir Ernest Barker, who in 1927 declared that national character is a cultural construct:

> Not only is national character made; it continues to be made and remade. It is not made once, for all, it always remains modifiable. A nation may alter its character in the course of its history to suit new conditions or to fit new purposes.[7]

I believe that we are in the midst of one of those periods of change and what may emerge is as yet unclear.

The classic English gentleman (1): Sir Percy Blakeney in *The Scarlet Pimpernel* (1935) with Leslie Howard and Merle Oberon.

It is a truism that foreigners are best able to define the true character of a nation. As one foreign observer noted:

> Since the concept of a national character arises out of the comparison of nations one with another, the best self-portrait is likely to be less valid than the pictures painted by foreign observers.[8]

For many foreigners the terms British and English are interchangeable. How then have foreigners traditionally seen the English/British? The Frenchman

Jules Verne, who disliked the English, created his typical Englishman in Phileas Fogg, hero of *Around the World in 80 Days* (1873). Fogg is depicted as phlegmatic, methodical, well balanced, anti-intellectual, sporting, chivalrous and with a deadpan sense of humour. The Hungarian Baroness Orczy, who liked the English, created her perfect Englishman Sir Percy Blakeney in *The Scarlet Pimpernel* (1905). He was sporting, chivalrous, cool, daring, patriotic, aristocratic, and with a notable sense of humour. The Home Secretary Sir William Joynson-Hicks told Baroness Orczy: 'You have put your finger on what is best and truest in English character.'[9] These two characters have much in common. Both are gentlemen. Both are heroic individualists. Both have a strong sense of humour and a deep sense of duty. Both act decently, sportingly and with restraint. And both, of course, were translated from the page to stage and screen. Phileas Fogg was played by David Niven in Mike Todd's 1956 extravaganza *Around the World in 80 Days*, and Sir Percy Blakeney by Leslie Howard, Barry K. Barnes and David Niven in successive cinematic retellings of the story of *The Scarlet Pimpernel* (1934, 1937 and 1950). It is important to stress, however, that this image was neither gender nor class specific, but highlighted characteristics shared across the culture. Such key female icons of Englishness as Mrs Miniver and Mrs Dale, Anna Neagle and Gracie Fields, embodied them too.

The worldwide amazement at outbursts of English hooliganism abroad, whether by drunken louts on the Costa Brava who kick Spanish taxi-drivers to death simply for being foreign, or by violent thugs using football matches as cover for their psychotic jingoism; and the genuine astonishment with which the Italians greeted the sight of footballer Paul 'Gazza' Gascoigne belching into a microphone during an interview, or with which the Indians reacted to the sight of unshaven, track-suited, lager-swilling English cricketers rubbishing Indian food and Indian culture are in part due to a century's worth of conditioning of the world by popular culture, and in particular by the cinema. Popular culture has portrayed the English as the inventors of good sportsmanship, as the upholders of the tradition of playing the game, being a sporting loser, not letting the side down, keeping a stiff upper lip, doing the decent thing. The Scarlet Pimpernel, Phileas Fogg, Beau Geste, Bulldog Drummond, Rudolph Rassendyll, Richard Hannay, Robin Hood, the Knights of the Round Table and all the rest have gone round the world doing just that. Popular culture has created an expectation of certain characteristics and attitudes. A recent study surveyed groups of forty to fifty students in the first year at university or the last year in secondary school in England, France, Germany, Italy, Austria, Fin-

The classic English gentleman (2): Phileas Fogg in *Around the World in 80 Days*   **2**
(1956), David Niven with Cedric Hardwicke, Ronald Colman and Cantinflas.

land, Greece and the Philippines. They were asked to mark various nationalities on a range of characteristics. The British came out as reserved, practical, peaceful, serious, calm, sceptical and self-controlled.[10] Apart from the absence of a sense of humour, which tends to confirm the oft-repeated view that foreigners do not understand the English sense of humour, the picture conforms to the traditional image of the phlegmatic, stiff-upper-lipped English gentleman, and can only be the product of cultural conditioning. But how did the British get this character?

There seems to be agreement among many leading authorities that something remarkable happened to the national character in the second half of the eighteenth century and the first half of the nineteenth century. As the great social historian Harold Perkin wrote:

> Between 1780 and 1850 the English ceased to be one of the most aggressive, brutal, rowdy, outspoken, riotous, cruel and bloodthirsty nations in the world and became one of the most inhibited, polite, orderly, tender-minded, prudish and hypocritical.[11]

In fact Britain only became a nation as such in the eighteenth century. It was the Act of Union of 1707 that linked England, Wales and Scotland and created a single geographical entity – the United Kingdom of Great Britain. Ireland was only incorporated in 1800 and most of it was unincorporated in 1921.

In her brilliant book *Britons*, Linda Colley has demonstrated how a sense of specifically British nationality was forged in the eighteenth century by the combination of a set of historical forces.[12] The unity of the United Kingdom was strongly reinforced and underpinned by a shared Protestantism, a factor often underrated by historians. As David Vincent has shown, the common culture of Britain in the eighteenth and nineteenth centuries was rooted in the key texts of popular Protestantism – the Bible, Milton, Bunyan and Foxe.[13] This pervasive Protestantism, celebrated in a succession of mythicized victories against Catholicism (the Armada, the Glorious Revolution, the Jacobite rebellions), led the British to see themselves as a chosen people, with a tendency to equate the Israel of the Bible with the Britain of the present day.[14] Thus the most popular British composer of the eighteenth and most of the nineteenth century was George Frederick Handel whose oratorios, particularly *The Messiah*, could be seen as celebrations of Protestant Christianity and, by extension; of the British as God's chosen people, whether or not they went to church. As Colley notes:

> Protestantism, broadly understood, provided the majority of Britons with a framework for their lives. It shaped their interpretation of the past and enabled them to make sense of the present. It helped them to identify and confront their enemies. It gave them confidence and even hope.[15]

It was not the divisions within Protestantism but the division between Protestantism and Catholicism that was crucial in the 18th century. This popular Protestantism and its view of Britain was resoundingly confirmed by the military events in the eighteenth century.

The succession of successful wars against France had the effect of emphasizing and consolidating British nationality and drawing a pointed contrast between Britain – defined as Protestant, democratic, parliamentary, commercial and progressive – and France – defined as Catholic, aristocratic, absolutist, agrarian, backward and poor. For Britain, the result was the acquisition of a vast overseas empire – India, Canada, the West Indies – into which the Welsh and the Scots enthusiastically opted as rulers, generals, traders and missionaries. Glasgow and Cardiff each became as much an imperial city as London. Britain, then, as it emerged in the eighteenth century, was the product specifically of Protestantism, empire, war and international trade.

In the unending debate about what it means to be *British* and what it means to be *English*, it is worth remarking that whereas many people slip in conversation from one to the other casually enough, three institutions are referred to consistently as British and not English: the British Empire, the British Army and the British Constitution, all of which include and transcend England, Wales and Scotland. As Keith Robbins points out, during the nineteenth century there remained considerable diversity within the British Isles.[16] Scotland retained its own legal, educational and banking systems, for instance. The Anglican Church was the established Church of England and Wales, though Dissent dominated within Wales; in Scotland, the Presbyterian Church was dominant. Even within England, there was a north–south division, as indeed there still is, and London remained a huge, unique, separate entity, almost another world. Regional dialects were spoken in different parts of the country, so much so, for instance, that Geordie music-hall comedians could not be understood in the south and Cockneys had problems in the north partly because they spoke too fast and switched their *v*s and *w*s.

Nevertheless, a British unity emerged that was perfectly compatible with diversity. Pride in local dialect literature, in local regiments, in local, regional, civic and provincial identity, not only survived but flourished, and was perfectly consonant with pride in the British nation and Empire, because of the Britishness of key elements. The political system was national. The political parties (Liberal and Conservative, later joined by Labour) were specifically constructed and projected as national British parties. Successive Scots led the Liberal Party (Gladstone, Rosebery, Campbell-Bannerman) and the Tories (Balfour, Bonar Law). Wales became a bastion of Liberalism and later Labourism, channelling its sense of identity not into political separation but into official opposition and, indeed, government when a Welshman, Lloyd George, became Prime Minister. Parliament was the embodiment of the Whig theory of history, of the gradual and inexorable evolution of democracy, the recognition and incorporation of Catholics, Jews, the working classes and women into the body politic and the operation of political parties that were cross-class and transnational.

In the nineteenth century the railways unified Britain as never before, imposing a national time standard and making possible a national diet, national newspapers, national sporting leagues. The Empire transcended national differences and became supranational, with the English, Irish, Scots, and Welsh alike serving in the British Imperial Army, Ireland providing colonial viceroys and governors, and the Empire being seen as distinctively British rather than specifically English. The monarchy came to embody the whole nation. Queen Victoria and Prince Albert shared a well publicized love for the Highlands, building Balmoral Castle and spending summer holidays there, and the royal princes wore kilts. The eldest son of the monarch became known as the Prince of Wales, and Lloyd George devised a fake antique ceremony for the installation of the future Edward VIII as Prince of Wales in order to emphasize the Welsh identity within the imperial British context. All the royal princes were given titles that emphasized Britishness – Queen Victoria's sons were the Prince of Wales, the Dukes of Edinburgh and Albany representing Scotland, and the Duke of Connaught representing Ireland. Regular royal visits to all parts of the British Isles stressed the role of the monarch as a unifying factor.

A genuinely British culture emerged. Many of the leading Victorian gurus – Ruskin, Carlyle, Samuel Smiles, Edward Irving – were Scots. Scots were nationally prominent in journalism, publishing, medicine and science. At the same time, all parts of the British Isles revered Dickens, Scott and Shakespeare.

Not only did a unified culture emerge but a strongly structured and regulated society – orderly, law-abiding and deferential. There were a number of contributing factors: the growth of the factory system which instilled punctuality, regularity and discipline and of large-scale organizations like the railways and the Post Office which enforced military-style discipline and uniformed their employees; the work of the police force and the courts; a general improvement in the quality of life (health, housing, transport, civic amenities); the socializing effects of schools and Sunday schools on the young and of chapel, trade unions and adult education movements on their elders; and, above all, the pervasive power of the doctrine of respectability at all levels of society.[17]

Because England was the centre, the seat of power, the hub of the Empire, the character of the new *Britain* was provided by *England,* which is why Britain and England are still often spoken of interchangeably by the English and by foreigners though never by the Welsh and the Scots. There could be no successful countervailing Celtic identity for *Britain* because the other parts of the United Kingdom were divided among themselves in a way that England was not: Scotland between Highlands and Lowlands, Wales between north and south and later between Welsh and non-Welsh speakers, and Ireland between Catholics and Protestants. A Celtic identity was constructed but it was deliberately constructed to be opposite to the perceived qualities of the English. Where the Anglo-Saxon was prosaic, the Celt was poetic; where the Anglo-Saxon was phlegmatic, the Celt was emotional and spontaneous, and so on.

But the overriding fact of the eighteenth, nineteenth and twentieth centuries was that both Anglo-Saxon and Celt could be, and were, accommodated within the British Empire, making Britishness perfectly compatible with Englishness, Welshness and Scottishness.

Gerald Newman, in an important book which reinforces Colley's interpretation, has explained how the British national identity came to be created and defined by England.[18] Newman's focus is specifically the rise of English nationalism and consequently he undervalues both the wider Britishness and the pervasive Protestantism highlighted by Colley. Nevertheless, he persuasively argues that Britain underwent a profound identity crisis during the second half of the eighteenth century and that this provided the context for the emergence of a defined national identity. The crisis was precipitated by a violent reaction against the Enlightenment. The Enlightenment, by virtue of its belief in reason, was internationalist and cosmopolitan in flavour, as was the aristocratic elite which ran most Western European countries. But because France was its central intellectual powerhouse, the English aristocratic elite was characterized by an extreme Francophilia, which embraced fashion, manners and literature, and by a slavish admiration for French ideas. This provoked a strong nationalist reaction, particularly among the the English bourgeois intelligentsia which saw France and Frenchification as the enemies. They linked alien cultural influence, the military and colonial rivalry with the French empire and domestic, moral and political corruption and located them in a Francophile English aristocracy. Newman traces a whole range of parallel cultural and intellectual developments which can clearly be seen as responses to the nationalist reaction.

First, there was a great upsurge in scholarly activity – the writing of strongly nationalist histories and a proliferation of philological, ethnological, literary and antiquarian studies. Dr Johnson published his *Dictionary* in 1755 with an explicit warning against the danger of Gallicization of the language. The first histories of English painting (1762), music (1776) and poetry (1774) appeared. These were all self-consciously national ventures, seeking to reclaim the national English past and often making invidious comparisons with France. Avowedly British rather than English in their scope, however, were, the British Museum (opened in 1769), the Royal Academy (founded in 1768) and the *Encyclopaedia Britannica* (begun in 1768).

Second, there was a search for national literary heroes. Great writers of the past were revived and reappraised, and portrayed as masters of the native language, representatives of the national spirit and embodiments of the English genius. Shakespeare in particular became *the* great English writer, but there were cults, too, of Geoffrey Chaucer, Edmund Spenser, John Milton and Dr Johnson. From the 1750s onwards, essays began to appear seeking to define and analyse the 'national genius'.

Third, there was a rise in the 'science' of racialism and with it new works on the racial origins and racial virtues of the English, whose origins were variously traced to the ancient Trojans, Teutons, Saxons or Goths. There was a crucial linkage between racial history and constitutional development. The rediscovery of an ancient and pristine past led to an idealization of pre-Conquest constitutional arrangements, destroyed by the imposition of the so-called 'Norman yoke' which had replaced democratic government with aristocratic tyranny. In the eighteenth-century context this was updated to mean French aristocratic domination of native English society and institutions.

Fourth, iconographical images of the national personality were developed, in particular John Bull and Britannia. Originally invented in 1712, John Bull was eventually to be identified with, and retain the appearance of, a sturdy and robust early-nineteenth-century country squire in swallow-tail coat, waistcoat and boots, and carrying a riding crop. He became the epitome of bluff, decent, commonsensical Englishness. The popularity in the nineteenth century of such fictional characters as Samuel Pickwick and Sir John Falstaff is partly due to their assimilation to John Bull. Britannia had a broader role. Established in the 1750s, she was the iconographic personification of the nation, a symbol of the virtues relevant to national life – patriotism, dedication, honesty, selflessness, discipline and simplicity.[19]

Lastly, national virtues were endlessly paraded in fiction, poetry and drama. The dominant character ideal to emerge in the eighteenth century was 'sincerity', the direct result, according to Newman, of the resurrection of the old English authors like Shakespeare and Chaucer. Sincerity was seen to comprise innocence, honesty, originality, frankness and moral independence and was manifested in 'an uncompromising commitment to duty – the subordination of the self to some general good'. Sincerity was embodied in the popular characters of prints, plays and novels – Oliver Goldsmith's Doctor Primrose in *The Vicar of Wakefield* (1764), Smollett's *Humphry Clinker* (1771), and Fanny Burney's *Evelina* (1778) for instance. By the 1780s the British had been so thoroughly indoctrinated with the idea of 'sincerity' – or, as it later came to be called, 'decency' – as the basis of the true national character that it had become a 'given'. It was the literary and cultural matrix from which the powerful ideological force of Evangelicalism was to take off in the first half of the nineteenth century. Newman seeks to play down the importance of Evangelicalism on the Victorian code in favour of the preceding cult of sincerity, but this is both unnecessary and misguided in view of the weight of evidence on the cultural and ideological importance of Evangelicalism, whatever its matrix.

The definition of the national character was completed, in the nineteenth century, by the fusion of two powerful creeds. The first was Evangelical Protestantism, the dominant social ethic of the first half of the nineteenth century described by historian G. M. Young as follows:

> By the beginning of the 19th century, virtue was advancing on a broad invincible front … The Evangelicals gave to the island a creed which was at once the basis of its morality and the justification of its wealth and power, and with the creed, the sense of being an elect people, which, set to a more blatant tune, became a principal element in Late Victorian imperialism. By about 1830, their work was done. They had driven the grosser kinds of cruelty, extravagance and profligacy underground. They had established a certain level of behaviour for all who wished to stand well with their fellows. In moralizing society they had made social disapproval a force which the boldest sinner might fear. By the beginning of the Victorian age the faith was already hardening into a code … The Evangelical discipline, secularized as respectability, was the strongest binding force in a nation which without it might have broken up.[20]

The Evangelicals, characterized by an intense seriousness of purpose, immense industry and enthusiastic missionary spirit, censorious highmindedness and a puritanical abstention from worldly pleasures, mounted a full-scale and successful assault on every level and aspect of society, promoting philanthropy, religion, education, duty and hard work, and attacking cruelty, frivolity and vice in all its forms.[21]

It was Evangelical activists who ensured the civilizing of a violent, disorderly society by banning the slave trade and public executions, outlawing cruel sports like bull-baiting, cock-fighting, and bare-knuckle prizefighting, by restricting gambling and drinking, by abolishing the national lottery, by imposing a puritanical code of sexual conduct and inculcating the ideas of duty, service and conscience, thrift, sobriety and personal restraint. Taught in schools and Sunday schools, promoted in literature and enshrined in law, these ideas became the British national values while the predominant Protestantism of Wales and Scotland ensured that they were accepted there as much as in England.

At the same time, there was a revival of chivalry which became all-pervasive in the nineteenth century.[22] Inspired by Sir Walter Scott's idealizations of the

Middle Ages, chivalry was deliberately promoted by such key figures of the age as Ruskin and Carlyle to provide a code of life for the young, based on the virtues of the gentleman: courtesy, bravery, modesty, purity and compassion, and a sense of responsibility towards women, children, the weak and the helpless. It permeated the literature and painting of the period, was advocated by youth organizations like the Boy Scouts and Boys Brigade, enshrined in the codes and regulations of sports like football and cricket and embodied in the public school ethos (fair play, team spirit, modesty, loyalty) absorbed not just by public schoolboys but by schoolboys everywhere through popular fictions from *Tom Brown's Schooldays* to the Greyfriars stories in *The Magnet*.[23] 'The idea of the gentleman is *not* a class idea,' wrote Sir Ernest Barker in 1947, identifying it as a key component of the national identity, 'it is the idea of a type of character … a mixture of stoicism with medieval lay chivalry, and of both with unconscious national ideals, half Puritan and half secular.'[24] The idea of the gentleman was an integrative image for the ruling elites of Great Britain, once again transcending the boundaries between England, Scotland and Wales, and percolating down from the elite to the rest of the population through popular culture. It was seen as a counterweight to the selfishness, greed and individualism of capitalism, and as a vehicle for service and social concern. Evangelicalism and chivalry thus became the distinctive shaping social and ideological forces of the nineteenth century. Each fed into a political party: Evangelicalism into Liberalism, chivalry into Conservatism.

The two ideologies cross-fertilized to provide a justification for an empire that had been acquired for economic, strategic and political reasons. The Evangelical missionary impulse, the desire to bring the heathen to the light of God, and the Calvinist idea of the elect, the British as the greatest nation in the world obliged to provide justice and good government for inferior races, intertwined with a chivalric vision of empire as a vehicle for young Englishmen to demonstrate the virtues that made them gentlemen. This confluence inspired a continuing theme in imperial writing, the idea that the British ran their empire not for their own benefit but for that of those they ruled. It was Lord Curzon, the Viceroy of India, who summed it up when he wrote that in Empire 'we had found not merely the key to glory and wealth but the call to duty and the means of service to mankind'.[25]

What these ideologies had in common was the overwhelming importance of the ideas of personal restraint and concern for others, of duty and service. Merged together, they helped form the national character. Both these traditions seem to have been grafted on to older ones, specifically English rather than British. First there is the sense of humour, considered a characteristic of the English since at least the Middle Ages. In 1140 Pope Eugenius III declared that, 'the English nation was fit to be set to anything it would handle and one to be preferred to others, were it not for the impediment of levity.'[26] The second is the ineffable sense of English superiority. The Venetian ambassador observed in 1497:

> The English are great lovers of themselves and of everything belonging to them. They think there are no other men like themselves and no other world but England and whenever they see a handsome foreigner, they say he looks like an Englishman and it is a great pity he should not be an Englishman and whenever they partake of any delicacy with a foreigner they ask him whether such a thing is made in his country.[27]

This sense of superiority can only have been increased by the acquisition of the British Empire, and by the fact that Britain, unlike virtually the whole of continental Europe, had not been conquered and occupied by foreigners since 1066.

The idea of English superiority to foreigners is inculcated in its citizens from an early age and is embodied in the juvenile literature to which the British young have been exposed since the arrival of mass literacy in the nineteenth century. As George Orwell noted in his celebrated essay on boys' weeklies, published in 1939, foreigners in boys' papers conformed to stereotypes that had not changed since before World War One. They were as follows:

Frenchman: Excitable. Wears beard. Gesticulates wildly.
Spaniard/Mexican etc.: Sinister. Treacherous.
Chinese: Sinister, treacherous, wears pigtail.
Italian: Excitable. Grinds barrel organ or carries stiletto.
Swede/Dane etc.: Kindhearted, stupid.
Negro: Comic, very faithful.[28]

This one-dimensional stereotyping is now carried on by the British tabloid press, which regards all foreigners as subhuman and habitually refers to them by such opprobrious epithets as frogs, krauts, dagoes, nips and chinks, claiming in defence that it merely uses the language of the pub, as if great issues of state should only be discussed in terms comprehensible to people who are half-cut. Thus, its contribution to the Maastricht debate was summed up in the *Sun*'s urging of its readers to go about with two fingers raised chanting 'Up yours, Delors'. It is not surprising, then, that when they see the car plates GB, the French now mutter to themselves 'Les grandes bêtes' Little, indeed, has changed since the Middle Ages when the French called the English 'les god-dems' because the English soldiers marauding around during the Hundred Years War constantly said 'God-damn'; the French now refer to the English as 'Les Fuckoffs' for much the same lamentable reason.[29] British ignorance of 'abroad' fuels the nation's mindless anti-Europeanism and is deeply damaging to good relations within the European Union.

War always brings the question of national identity into sharp focus and World War Two was no exception. In 1940 the British Council issued a series of eleven essays on various aspects of British life, published as a collected volume in 1941 under the title *British Life and Thought.* The author of the essay called 'The Englishman' was Earl Baldwin of Bewdley, who, during the 1930s as plain Stanley Baldwin, had been projected as an archetypal Englishman, a Conservative John Bull, bluff, honest and commonsensical, a pipe-smoking, cricket-loving, detective-story-reading combination of country squire and paternalist managing director of an old-established family firm. He began his study with the fact that Britain was an island, from which he traced the nation's insularity, its measure of complacency and sense of superiority to 'foreigners'. But alongside those qualities he saw tolerance and compromise, a strong sense of duty, a mistrust of logic and a pervasive anti-intellectualism, a spirit of 'dauntless decency' and a broad and good-hearted sense of humour. The Englishman, he believed, was above all an individualist, given to grumbling certainly but in the main considerate and easy-going. He was sentimental, a lover of home and garden, animals and sport. But,

> he will not be interfered with by his employer, by his neighbour or on a greater scale by another nation. He is apt to resist at a point and when his mind is made up and his tenacity … is … acknowledged even by his enemies. You can lead him a long way; you cannot drive him an inch. He will neither cringe nor be bullied.[30]

At perhaps the other end of the political spectrum from Stanley Baldwin was George Orwell, the Old Etonian, who consciously re-created himself as a Socialist John Bull. Orwell had hobbies and hobby-horses, was given to praising such English institutions as suet pudding, red pillar boxes and comic seaside postcards, and liked to vituperate what he called 'the pansy left', most notably for their lack of patriotism. In his memorable essays *The Lion and the Unicorn* (1942) and *The English People* (1944), Orwell saw the common people of England as law-abiding, considerate, gentle, decent, patriotic, insular, private, anti-intellectual, sentimental, given to compromise and class-ridden, as lovers of home and garden, sport and animals. He believed that the gentleness of English civilisation was 'perhaps its most marked characteristic'.[31]

It is a picture that is almost identical with the one painted by Lord Baldwin, with the notable and characteristic addition of 'class-ridden'.

J. B. Priestley was another Socialist John Bull and in his novel *Let the People Sing*, published in 1939 and filmed in 1942, he put into the mouth of his Czech professor Krolak a similar definition of the English:

> The great traditions of this country ... are these. First, the liberty of the individual. So long as they do no harm to others, men must be allowed to develop in their own way. Second, that which goes with liberty – toleration. Third, voluntary public service. Fourth, a very deep love, a poetical love, rooted deep down in the unconscious, of England and the English way of life, of the fields and the woods, flowers and birds, of pastimes, of the poets and storytellers. Fifth, which you find everywhere among the common people, humour and irony and along with these a profound depth of sentiment.[32]

The liberal centre preached the same view as the left and right. The Liberal philosopher and historian Sir Ernest Barker, who wrote regularly on the national character in such books as *National Character* (1927), *Britain and the British People* (1942) and *The Character of England* (1947), saw it as comprising tolerance, individualism, balance, compromise, a sense of humour, equanimity, social homogeneity, amateurism, eccentricity, class consciousness, a tradition of voluntary work. Occupying a similar place on the political spectrum was Leslie Howard – not just a film star but, after J. B. Priestley, the most popular and important broadcaster on the overseas service of the BBC. In his regular broadcasts to the USA he highlighted the qualities that had emerged in the English during the war,

> qualities which seem to me to represent the best there is in human nature: the qualities of courage, devotion to duty, kindliness, humour, coolheadedness, balance, common sense, singleness of purpose ... and idealism.[33]

In a later broadcast he added:

> the one thing we have contributed to the civilisation of the world which is new and our own, something which the Germans have never known the meaning of, something called tolerance.[34]

All the comentators so far mentioned are English. But the view from abroad was much the same. Leland DeWitt Baldwin (no relation to Stanley) was an Anglophile American who, in *God's Englishman* (1943), set out to write a history of Britain that would explain the emergence of the English character, in which he distilled the views of a host of British and foreign commentators from the previous half-century, including Wilhelm Dibelius, George Santayana, Esmé Wingfield-Stratford, W. M. Dixon, Price Collier and Rebecca West. Leland Baldwin detected that the Englishman was distinguished by insularity and a sense of superiority, a distrust of logic, a facility for tolerance and compromise, a capacity for moral indignation, a sense of humour ('never more apparent than when he is confronting a terrible crisis, particularly a war') and an 'unparalleled reverence for the law'. The English, he concluded, were hopelessly sentimental, class-ridden, sports-loving, anti-intellectual, courteous, endowed with a gift for understatement, respect for privacy and an indomitable sense of fair play. At the root of the English character was 'respect for the individual'.

These were essentially impressionistic accounts, of course, but they achieve a remarkable unanimity, whether from domestic or foreign commentators, whether on the left or the right politically. This national persona was faithfully projected in wartime cinema, where the same characteristics come through time and again. There is the sense of humour. There is the sense of tolerance. In a nation with more than its fair share of individualists and eccentrics, tolerance is the only feasible policy to adopt. For, as the philosopher George Santayana wrote, 'England is the paradise of individuality, eccentricity, heresy, anomalies, hobbies and humours.'[35] Mutual tolerance as a basis for political consensus had been a principle of British life since World War One and was to remain so until 1979 when it was summarily abolished. Stoicism or emotional restraint is the third quality, the essence of the much parodied British fondness for understatement, reserve and the stiff upper lip. It was seen at the time as a central and admirable characteristic of the nation. Lastly, there is the sense of duty and service, evident on the mobilization of the nation for action both in the front line and on the home front. There is an additional piece of evidence that was not for publication and is probably as near to being objective as is possible to get. This was the report by Dr Stephen Taylor in 1941 of the first year's work of the Home Intelligence Unit, set up to monitor national morale and which reported to the Cabinet. It made some generalizations and conclusions about the national character:

> The British public as a whole shows a high degree of common sense ...
> The British public are pragmatic. They are little influenced by immaterial, ethical or theoretical considerations. There are three main exceptions
> i) a determination not to be 'put upon' or 'messed about' except by their
> own consent ii) a determination not to allow others to be 'put upon' iii)
> a sense of fair play. The British public has a basic stability of temperament

with a slightly gloomy tinge. Arising from this i) a tendency to voice grumbles loudly ii) a delight in 'knowing the worst' iii) a tendency to doubt rather than believe any new information and particularly a suspicion of 'newspaper talk'. The public has a great capacity for righteous indignation when things go wrong. Gratitude is rarely exhibited. A fundamental tenet of the British public creed is that all in authority, above all 'officials', are inefficient. The public is unimaginative. The English public is basically lazy with in consequence a very large reserve and capacity for effort on the rare occasions when it considers this vitally necessary ... This innate laziness leads secondarily to a high degree of tolerance.[36]

With but a few differences of emphasis and omissions and a few less flattering home truths, this conforms remarkably with the picture painted both in books and films about the British character.

What is interesting about the British national characteristics is how many of them relate to elements of the national identity: from parliamentary democracy come the values of tolerance, compromise, law-abidingness; from Empire a sense of superiority; from Protestantism, individualism, anti-intellectualism, duty and service. Interesting, too, is the way in which continual exposure to images of Britishness provokes a corresponding reality. George Orwell noted:

Myths which are believed in tend to become true, because they set up a type or persona which the average person will do his best to resemble. During the bad period of 1940 it became clear that in Britain national solidarity is stronger than class antagonism. If it were really true that 'the proletarian has no country', 1940 was the time to show it. It was exactly then, however, that class feeling slipped into the background, only reappearing when the immediate danger had passed. Moreover it is probable that the stolid behaviour of the British town populations under the bombing was partly due to the existence of the national 'persona' – that is, to their preconceived idea of themselves. Traditionally the Englishman is phlegmatic, unimaginative, not easily rattled, and since that is what he thinks he ought to be, that is what he tends to become. Dislike of hysteria and 'fuss', admiration for stubbornness, are all but universal in England, being shared by everyone except the intelligentsia. Millions of English people willingly accept as their national emblem the bulldog, an animal noted for its obstinacy, ugliness and impenetrable stupidity. They have a remarkable readiness to admit that foreigners are more 'clever' than themselves, and yet they feel that it would be an outrage against the laws of God and Nature for England to be ruled by foreigners.[37]

During the Blitz, people behaved exactly as they had been taught British people should behave – courageously, stoically and good-humouredly. This 'persona' was one of the reasons why the Home Intelligence Unit could report in 1941: 'There is at present no evidence that it is possible to defeat the people of Britain by any means other than extermination.'[38]

E. M. Forster wrote in 1920: 'The character of the English is essentially middle class.'[39] But what he calls 'middle class' values were in fact shared, as sociologist Geoffrey Gorer confirmed in his 1955 study *Exploring English Character*, by a large section of the working classes. Indeed, crucial to any understanding of British social and cultural history is the great divide within the working classes between what the Victorians called 'the rough' and the 'respectable. The 'respectables' cultivated what have been miscalled 'middle-class values' but are in fact merely civilised values: self-improvement, education, restraint, thrift, good manners. The 'roughs' lived a life of immediate gratification, particularly in sex, drink and violence. This always provided a potential alternative image for Englishness but it was largely kept underground until the 1960s when a social and cultural revolution occurred, and a world that had remained in all its lineaments substantially Victorian was overturned by a range of fundamental social, cultural and economic changes of seismic significance. These allowed a highly structured society 'consciously or unconsciously related in a ... general way', as Harold Perkin put it, 'by the bonds of language, inherited ideas and beliefs and all the common experiences of a shared community' to unravel.[40]

The background to this cultural revolution was the affluence, full employment and materialism of the 1950s and 1960s which released people from the immediate disciplines of survival and turned their attention to their 'expressive' needs – self-discovery, self-assertion, sensation. In a delirious upsurge of Romanticism similar to that which overtook early nineteenth-century culture, the rebel and the deviant became heroes, the self was exalted, spontaneity was encouraged and rules, restrictions, conventions and traditions in both life and art were ditched. The old structure, old values and old certainties (notably the doctrine of respectability) were increasingly derided and rejected. The legal framework designed to contain the forces of disorder was dismantled. Violence, profanity and sexuality, hitherto rigorously suppressed, became prominent both in high culture and low. Personal style, cool, chic, cynical and consumerist, became the ideal: self rather than service, immediate gratification rather than long-term spiritual or intellectual development.

In the 1960s it became fashionable for the first time in British history to be young and working class. This emphasis on youth with its desire to be free from restraint and on the working class of the 'rough' rather than 'respectable' variety, plus the promotion of the philosophy of the self, preached by the fashionable pundits of the 1960s, completely undermined the two shaping creeds of the national character and the social structure, both of them based on the idea of the subordination of the self for the greater general good: evangelical religion and chivalry. The rigorous social controls applied to society during the Victorian era by the forces of evangelical religion were virtually simultaneously scrapped: capital punishment was abolished, censorship of the arts was greatly reduced, abortion and homosexuality were legalized, divorce was made easier, the contraceptive pill became widely available, restrictions on gambling and drinking were relaxed. Many of these developments were long overdue and greatly to be welcomed in their recognition of individual rights, dignity and freedom. But the new social and sexual freedoms were not exercised with the sense of responsibility that their advocates might have wished, if the statistics are to be believed. During the 1960s crimes of violence doubled, convictions for drunkenness rose by three-fifths, there was a tenfold increase in drug addiction. Vandalism spiralled. Football hooliganism, previously virtually unknown, blighted the national game. All these anti-social acts have gone on rising inexorably.

Freed from the shackles of restraint, the counterculture, polar opposite of evangelicalism, flourished. Its credo was summed up by Richard Neville in his book *Playpower* (1971). All roles, boundaries, continuity, structures, forms and certainties must go. Childhood was the goal of life – no responsibility, all play. Everything was based on immediacy, emotional reaction rather than cerebral response, on flux, movement, noise and uncontained sexuality. Sex and drugs were crucial to the defining of the new identity. Obscenity was important too for as Neville wrote: 'The deflowering of language, rendering it obscene and useless, is part of structuring a new age.'[41] Sex, drugs and obscenity were explicitly a rejection of the culture of control. What began as a fringe movement was recycled into mainstream popular culture, as rock music and films fed the affluent young a diet of anti-authoritarian and pro-liberation messages which have continued to be a staple of these mass media. It heralded the birth of what Christopher Lasch dubbed 'the culture of narcissism'.[42]

The mirror image of the stress on self-gratification was the rejection of all doctrines and structures of control. Notions of honour, duty, service, decency, selflessness were rejected either as outdated bourgeois conceits, or as oppressive patriarchal constructs. Notions of right and wrong, good and evil, punishment and retribution have been increasingly abandoned in favour of moral and cultural neutrality, of the idea imported from America that everyone is a victim

3   The classic English gentleman (3): Rudolph Rassendyll in *The Prisoner of Zenda* (1937), Ronald Colman with Douglas Fairbanks Jr.

and no-one is responsible for anything.[43] This inevitably meant the rejection of that chivalry and sportsmanship which had been so integral to British popular culture and to the national image as portrayed in film and books. In sport, this has led to the progressive abolition of amateurism (a key element of sportsmanship), culminating in the falling of its last bastion – Rugby Union in 1995.

Chivalry and sportsmanship were rejected in the 1960s on the grounds that they inhibited free expression and were class-based. But as the Victorian guru Samuel Smiles put it:

> Riches and rank have no necessary connexion with genuine gentlemanly qualities. The poor man may be a true gentleman – in spirit and daily life. He may be honest, truthful, upright, polite, temperate, courageous, self-respecting and self-helping – that is, be a true gentleman.[44]

Successive generations of Britons of all classes grew up believing and practising that. Many brought up before the 1960s still do. But the generations brought up since the 1960s have had no such instruction. Quite the reverse. Instead of modelling themselves on such graceful and stylish gentleman heroes as Ronald Colman and Leslie Howard, today's young Britons choose as their cinematic role models the muscle-bound thugs Arnold Schwarzenegger and Sylvester Stallone. Indeed, the very notion of heroism has been devalued and anti-heroes have become the order of the day. Culturally and socially there has come to be greater interest in, and sympathy with, criminals than victims; and the mad have come to be regarded as more sane than the sane. As time passes, the cultural heroes of a generation are more likely to be the cannibals, rapists, psychopaths and sadists celebrated in such films as *Silence of the Lambs*, *Cape Fear*, *Taxi Driver* and *Nightmare on Elm Street* than the saints, statesmen, thinkers and writers revered in previous ages.

At the same time as popular culture was transformed by the counterculture, all the other traditional control structures that had created the tightly regulated, structured and deferential society of Victorian Britain began to break down, creating a much more fluid, mobile and ultimately unstable society. The traditional family began to erode. The community structure which had exerted its own unofficial sanctions since the rise of industrial society collapsed as the misguided redevelopment of the old Victorian cities in the 1960s destroyed the closeknit inner-city working-class communities and replaced them with bleak and heartless high-rise estates which rapidly became breeding grounds for alienation, criminality, violence and drug abuse. The collapse of the factory system and the rise of permanent mass youth unemployment removed another important structure of constraint: the discipline of the workplace. In education, the school had for a century operated a curriculum aimed at instilling as moral values hard work, discipline and thrift, and as cultural values decency, duty and gentlemanliness. In the 1960s this was rejected in favour of 'child-centred' learning where the emphasis was on individual self-expression and the quest for personal fulfilment free from moral and cultural prescription which was condemned as elitist, paternalist, patriarchal and hegemonic. Protestant religion, which had been in decline since World War One, continued to decline, so that Britain is now one of the most secularized countries in the world. All that is now left of it is that combination of prurience and sanctimonious censoriousness which characterizes the tabloid press and which goes along with a widely preached and culturally celebrated sexual permissiveness. The police force and the legal system were discredited after a long and continuing series of miscarriages of justice. Teachers, clergymen, policemen, judges, politicians, once seen as repositories of wisdom and authority, lost status and came to be regarded with suspicion, even mistrust and hatred. The Americanization of the youth culture, underway since World War One, was completed – and the British young now go round in baseball caps, eating Macdonalds, using American slang, watching American films, idolizing macho American stars, and supporting a culture that advocates the virtues of extreme individualism, violent self-assertion and total sexual freedom.

Perhaps the most significant developments have been the decline in the traditional family and the rise of violence. The traditional family, long one of the building-blocks of society, and marriage, which since the Middle Ages has been one of the primary agencies for taming young men, have collapsed, undermined by a rocketing divorce rate – Britain has the highest divorce rate in Europe, with nearly half of all marriages now ending in divorce – the rise in illegitimacy, single-parent families and living together – the product of an ethic in which individual emotion and self-gratification rather than duties and responsibilities often, though not always, take first place. In parallel with this erosion of family bonds, violence has spiralled both in reality and in cultural representations.

Crime fell in the nineteenth century. Between 1857 and 1901 there was a decline of 50 per cent in the rate of indictable offences per head of the population. A steady rise in crime began in the 1920s, but its largest rise came in the period 1955–91. By 1991 the rate of indictable offences was ten times what it had been in 1955, and forty times the rate in 1901.[45] The statistics for reported woundings are revealing of the increased levels of violence in society.[46] In 1920, there were 791; in 1930, 5,177; in 1960, 14,142; in 1980 95,044.

Violence is integral to the self ethic. The instant resort to violence for 'the buzz', the demonstration of power, the physical expression of frustrations and angers of various kinds is a logical corollary of the gratification of the self in all its moods. It has led to a situation in which it is now statistically more likely that young men under thirty will die violently than at any time this century during peacetime. Much of the violence is drink-related. In 1932 the Home Secretary was able to say that the British had largely got rid of drunkenness as a major national vice. It is now rampant again, particularly among the young.

The social context of these value changes is the victory of consumerism. The consumer society emerged in the 1950s – average weekly wages rose by 130 per cent between 1955 and 1969, and Harold Macmillan memorably said: 'Most of our people have never had it so good.' In 1956, 8 per cent of households had refrigerators; by 1971 this figure was 69 per cent. In the early 1950s only 10 per cent of the population had TV; by the 1970s only 10 per cent of the population did *not* have TV. Car ownership rocketed. In 1950 there were just over two million cars and vans in Britain; by 1970 nearly twelve million and it has gone on rising.[47] But the downside of the affluent society is that an expectation is created, a desire to possess and this has two results: in boomtime, hectic spending, much of it on credit; and in recession, collapse, disillusionment, debt and the 'feel bad' factor. But it also creates a norm in terms of possessions which the underclass cannot attain and so they steal – and the corollary of a dominant consumerist ethic is burglary, mugging, car theft and shop lifting on a grand scale. It is significant that during the great recession of the 1930s there was nothing like the crime rate there is now. Why? Because there was no dominant consumerist ethic. People merely wanted to survive rather than to survive and possess car, television, videos. Also the family and the community were strong and provided discipline and structure to people's lives.

There was a positive side to the 1960s – an outpouring of youthful idealism that inspired movements for peace, the protection of the environment, Third World development and minority rights. But its dark side was the exaltation of the self, the validation of a rootless, self-indulgent individualism – and it was the dark side that ultimately prevailed.

In the 1960s sex, drugs and rock 'n' roll represented the route chosen by the new individualism. But with the recession of the 1970s, the self took a new direction – the aggressive pursuit of wealth which came to incorporate a contempt for those who had not got it. This aggressive individualism found its cultural heroes in Rambo, Rocky, Conan the Barbarian, Gordon Gecko and 'Loadsa Money,' and its cultural validation in drinking twenty-two pints of lager, playing loud music, buying big dogs and fast cars, and knocking seven bells out of anyone whose face does not fit.

Thatcherism was the political expression of this mindset. Thatcherism was not the cause of the changes, it was the logical consequence of the social and cultural changes of the 1960s, the ultimate political philosophy of self-gratification, the elevation of individual desire above the good of society. Mrs Thatcher promoted the first dominant political ideology in modern times not to have the ideas of selflessness and public service at its heart. She promoted a crude 'let the people have what they want', lowest-common-denominator populism; she let the free market rip and dismantled regulations left, right and centre. For all her talk of Victorian values, Mrs Thatcher came to embody that aggressive and uncompromising individualism which glories in combat and which rejects consensus and concern as wet and wimpish – she once talked about people 'drooling and drivelling' about the plight of the homeless. She even more memorably said: 'There is no such thing as society.' So what was her vision? – it was a mass of struggling individuals each out for what they could get. Her Utopia was a nation of families, each in its own car, driving up and down motorways visiting shopping malls on a Sunday – the ultimate consumerist and individualist Nirvana. So the government set about dismantling all controls, abolishing the nationalized industries, disparaging and denigrating all ideas of public service, and systematically undermining, emasculating and destroying those embodiments of the older ethic of public service: the BBC, the universities, local government, the trade unions, the Church of England, even the monarchy. The symbol of the new age was Britain's best-selling newspaper the *Sun*, a sinister cocktail of chauvinism, racism, sexism, anti-intellectualism, illiteracy and prurience, which panders to all that is worst, most base and most reprehensible in human nature. Victorian Britain, the heyday of Britain's commercial and industrial pre-eminence, believed quite the opposite of the idea that there was no such thing as society. It believed that economic individualism and capitalist endeavour must always be tempered, moderated and constrained by social need and communal concern. It was this belief which fuelled the Evangelicalism and chivalry that underpinned the national character. The counterpart of the aggressive Thatcherite economic individualism is a self-absorbed social individualism whose emblems are the ghetto blaster, the pit bull terrier, the crack addict, the video nasty and the football hooligan, all of them virtually unknown before the 1960s and all the direct consequence of the absorption of the idea that there is no such thing as society, that you should do what you like when you like and that all restraint and regulation are bad.

What has been the effect of all this change? A five-year survey of the young published by Academia Europea, a European academic think-tank, has uncovered a 'substantial' increase in psychosocial disorders among the young since the 1950s. The suicide rate among the young, particularly young males, has risen in Britain by 70 per cent in the last twenty years. There has been a massive increase in drugtaking and crime among the young – one in three young men under thirty in Britain has a criminal record. The survey attributes such disorders to widespread family break-up and bad parenting, the promotion of anti-social attitudes in youth culture and the consumerist ethic which has created expectations of attainment that cannot be met in an era of widespread youth unemployment.

Such massive, wide-ranging social and cultural changes and value shifts cannot but affect the national character and the national identity. Almost all of the elements that went to make up British identity have been eroded since

World War Two. The Empire has gone, taking with it the sense of duty, service and chivalry it inspired and leaving behind only the racism it also engendered. Parliamentary democracy is increasingly despised. Protestantism is dying. The Methodist Church has predicted its own extinction by the next century.

True, one or two of the elements have remained but they are the negative ones. We are still at war with the French. In 1995 when French seamen block-aded ports preventing English ferries from leaving, irate English holidaymakers were interviewed by the BBC. One of them declared: 'They're rubbish the French. They've never forgiven us for the Armada.' This one sentence encapsulates the insularity, sense of superiority and sheer pig ignorance which have made the English abroad such an appalling spectacle for civilized foreigners. The English are still anti-intellectual to the point of philistinism. They are still insular and feel superior to foreigners, a feeling which lies at the heart of the knee-jerk anti-Europeanism and the sinister undercurrent of racism that regularly bursts forth in acts of savagery against coloured immigrants. There is still a sense of humour too, but it is now all too often cruel, sour and spiteful, with the gentle and affectionate humour of the Ealing comedies, of Joyce Grenfell and Flanders and Swann, giving way to the savagery of *Spitting Image*, Jack Dee and *Viz* magazine.

When a third of young men under thirty have criminal records it is hard to see the gentleness and law-abidingness that Orwell so praised. The culture is steeped in violence and images of violence, and where violence rules, tolerance, fair play and restraint go out of the window. As an ever nastier yob culture swirls around us, the national character inexorably changes. Britain is currently undergoing a crisis of national identity as profound as that of the eighteenth century which produced the new sense of Britishness. Evidence of this can be found in a recent Gallup poll which revealed that 48 per cent of the British population would like to emigrate. For national character is not innate, it is learned, the product of the world around it. It may be that a historian of the future, reversing the words of Perkin, will write that 'between 1960 and the year 2000, the English *ceased* to be one of the most inhibited, polite, orderly, tender-minded, prudish and hypocritical nations in the world and became once again one of the most aggressive, brutal, rowdy, outspoken, cruel and bloodthirsty.'

One of the sources from which national character is learned is the mass media. Cinema and latterly television, as the pre-eminent mass entertainment media of the twentieth century, have functioned as propagators of the national image, both in reflecting widely held views and constructing, extending, interrogating and perpetuating dominant cultural myths. It is instructive, therefore, to look at films for evidence of the promotion of images of both the national character and national identity. In the discussion, I will refer both to British and American films because American cinema has been just as great an influence on British culture as its British counterpart.

I have begun this study by charting in the wider culture the creation during the eighteenth and nineteenth centuries of a distinctive British national identity, strongly shaped and influenced by England and Englishness. In turning now to look at how cinema has participated in this process, I have adopted both a chronological and a thematic approach. The period covered is roughly from the 1920s to the present, but I have also concentrated on some of the individual identities which fit into each other like a set of Chinese boxes creating that multiple set of identities which everyone carries withing them. Thus, I examine in turn the imperial identity, the national identity and regional identities through an analysis of groups of key films, assessing how they change over time and how they relate to the dominant image outlined above. In each case, there is an alternative to the dominant image, a minority image constructed of different styles, values and beliefs, and the dialogue between these dominant and alternative images is one of the continuing strands of British cultural history. Thus a discussion of white imperial heroes is followed by an account of a black hero (Paul Robeson) operating in the same cultural milieu. The social realist semi-documentary war film is contrasted with the flamboyant Gainsborough melodrama. An examination of the changing face of the English/British dominant image is followed by an examination of Scottish, Welsh, Irish and Lancastrian cinematic images, which underline the ethnic and cultural diversity of Britain. Such images of diversity, while they may enrich and reinforce the Union when Britain is a major world power, are potentially divisive at a time of national decline when pride in the whole is dented and distinct alternatives are sought to replace the tarnished whole.

While I have called this last section 'Region', I am aware that Wales, Scotland and Ireland would all insist on themselves as countries and nations. Nevertheless, I am here concerned to examine them in their relation to – how they negotiate with and construct themselves against – the perceived dominant Anglocentric vision of the United Kingdom of Great Britain and its Empire. In that context, region seems a more appropriate term, particularly since the majority of Scots, Welsh and Lancastrians have been for much of this century as wholeheartedly British as they have been Scots, Welsh and Lancastrian.

I end by examining the rich and productive interaction between film and other cultural forms, thus extending the debate about the national identity into the wider culture. The case studies chosen for this purpose are the music of Vaughan Williams, the novels of Charles Dickens and the long-running television series *Dad's Army*. I hope that the result will illuminate some of the complexities, ambiguities and continuities involved in the ongoing process of the creation, evolution and promotion of Britain's national identity.

Notes

1   Anthony D. Smith, *National Identity*, London, 1991, p. 143.
2   Benedict Anderson, *Imagined Communities: reflections on the origin and spread of nationalism*, London, 1983.
3   Smith, *National Identity*, p. 75.
4   Smith, *National Identity*, p. 75.
5   Smith, *National Identity*, p. 77.
6   Richard Maltby, *Harmless Entertainment*, Metuchen, New Jersey and London, 1983.
7   Ernest Barker, *National Character*, London, 1927, p. 8.
8   R. Virtanen, quoted in Dean Peabody, *National Characteristics*, Cambridge, 1985, p. 124.
9   Baroness Orczy, *Links In The Chain Of Life*, London, n.d., p. 98.
10 Peabody, *National Characteristics*, pp. 95–108.
11 Harold Perkin, *The Origins of Modern English Society, 1780—1880*, London, 1969, p. 280.
12 Linda Colley, *Britons*, New Haven and London, 1992.
13 David Vincent, *Literacy and Popular Culture: England 1750–1914*, Cambridge, 1989.
14 Howard Weinbrot, *Britannia's Issue: the rise of British literature from Dryden to Ossian*, Cambridge, 1995.
15 Colley, *Britons*, p. 54.
16 Keith Robbins, *Nineteenth Century Britain: integration and diversity*, Oxford, 1988, and *Nineteenth Century Britain: the making of a nation*, Oxford, 1989.
17 F. M. L. Thompson, *The Rise of Respectable Society*, London, 1988 and F. M. L. Thompson, 'Social Control in Victorian Britain', *Economic History Review*, 34 (1981), pp. 189–208.
18 Gerald Newman, *The Rise of English Nationalism 1740–1830*, London, 1987.
19 Mike Taylor, 'John Bull and the Iconography of Public Opinion in England *c.*1712–1929', *Past and Present*, 134 (1992), pp. 93–128; Madge Dresser, 'Britannia', in Raphael Samuel, (ed.), *Patriotism*, volume 3, London, 1989, pp. 26, 49.
20 G. M. Young, *Victorian England: portrait of an age*, Oxford, 1977, pp. 4–5.
21 Ian Bradley, *The Call to Seriousness*, London, 1976.
22 Mark Girouard, *Return to Camelot*, New Haven and London, 1981; Alice Chandler, *A Dream of Order*, London, 1971.

23   Jeffrey Richards, *Happiest Days: the public schools in English fiction*, Manchester, 1988.

24   Ernest Barker (ed.), *The Character of England*, Oxford, 1947, pp. 566–7.

25   Jeffrey Richards, *Visions of Yesterday*, London, 1973, p. 12.

26   Barker, *National Character*, p. 8.

27   Ralph Waldo Emerson, *English Traits*, London, 1903, pp. 85–6.

28   George Orwell, *Collected Essays, Journalism and Letters*, Volume 1, Harmondsworth, 1973, p. 517.

29   Geoffrey Pearson, *Swearing*, Oxford, 1991, p. 1.

30   The British Council, *British Life and Thought*, London, 1941, p. 458.

31   Orwell, *Collected Essays,*, volume 2, p. 79.

32   J. B. Priestley, *Let the People Sing*, London, 1939, p. 384.

33   Leslie Howard, 'Shopkeepers and Poets', broadcast 14/15 October 1940, BBC Written Archives, Caversham, Talks Script Microfilm 234.

34   Leslie Howard, 'New Order in Europe', broadcast 23/4 December 1940, BBC Written Archives, Caversham, Talks Script Microfilm 234.

35   George Santayana, *Soliloquies in England*, London, 1922, p. 30.

36   Dr Stephen Taylor, *A Review of Some Conclusions Arising Out of a Year of Home Intelligence Reports*, INF 1.292. Public Record Office.

37   Orwell, *Collected Essays*, volume 3, p. 21.

38   Dr Stephen Taylor, *A Review of Some Conclusions Arising Out of a Year of Home Intelligence Reports*, INF 1.292.

39   E. M. Forster, 'Notes on English Character', *Abinger Harvest*, London, 1936, p. 3.

40   Harold Perkin, *The Structured Crowd*, Brighton, 1981, p. ix.

41   Richard Neville, *Playpower*, London, 1971, p. 65.

42   Christopher Lasch, *The Culture of Narcissism*, London, 1980.

43   Robert Hughes, *The Culture of Complaint*, Oxford and New York, 1993.

44   Samuel Smiles, *Self-Help*, London, 1911, p. 470.

45   Gertrude Himmelfarb, *The Demoralization of Society*, London, 1995, pp. 224–226.

46   A. H. Halsey (ed.), *British Social Trends Since 1900*, Basingstoke and London, 1988, p. 637.

47   Arthur Marwick, *British Society Since 1945*, Harmondsworth, 1982, p. 121.

Part I

Empire

2

British
imperial heroes

Empire was one of the major component elements of British national identity and its principal justification was the superiority of British character. Good conduct and sound character were more than just desirable, they were essential. They were the Empire's *raison d'être*. It was British character which set the British, and particularly their imperial administrators and soldiers, apart from other peoples and justified their ruling a quarter of the globe. *The Times* declared in the mid-nineteenth century:

> That which raises a country, that which strengthens a country, and that which dignifies a country – that which spreads her power, creates her moral influence, and makes her respected and submitted to, bends the heart of millions, and bows down the pride of nations to her – the instrument of obedience, the fountain of supremacy, the true throne, crown and sceptre of a nation; this aristocracy is not an aristocracy of blood, not an aristocracy of fashion, not an aristocracy of talent only: it is an aristocracy of character.[1]

It is impossible to overestimate the significance of character for nineteenth-century Britain. Stefan Collini argues that 'the ideal of character ... enjoyed a prominence in the political thought of the Victorian period that it had apparently not known before and that it has arguably not experienced since.'[2]

It was more than just an ideal; there was a religion of character. It was rooted in moral certainties, was promoted enthusiastically by Evangelicalism, and incorporated into the teaching of the public schools which turned out a ruling elite for nation and empire. It stood at the heart of the chivalric revival. Books were written arguing that Britain's industrial pre-eminence, imperial achievement and parliamentary democracy were all based on character. Samuel Smiles devoted one of his best-selling moral guidebooks to *Character* just as he had to *Self-Help*, *Duty*, *Thrift*. There was seen to be a causal connection between certain character traits and national achievement. As Emil Reich in *Success among Nations* (1904) declared: 'The Englishman's idea is that the world is ruled by character, by will, and in order to secure himself that domination, he applies himself to the development of those qualities.'[3]

Both pessimistic and optimistic social commentators pointed to the centrality of character. The influential and widely read Benjamin Kidd argued that given the inevitability of competition in human affairs, progress could only be achieved by social efficiency and social efficiency depended on the development of a character type that emphasized energy, resolution, application, self-control and a single-minded devotion to duty. It was, he believed, the responsibility of the socially efficient nations, notably Britain, to administer the rest of the world. This could only be done by subordination of the self to the greater good of the race and the development of the necessary characteristics to rule. Essentially these late-Victorian commentators were applying to empire the concept of character expounded by Smiles who argued that, 'Character is human nature in its best form, it is moral order embodied in the individual ... the strength, the industry and the civilization of all nations – all depend on individual character.'[4] The characteristics he defined as essential to character were restraint, duty, courage, honesty, self-reliance and perseverance.

H. John Field in his valuable book *Towards a Programme of Imperial Life* has demonstrated the centrality of the concept of character to late-nineteenth-century discussions of empire both for the elite and the masses:

> Among many diverse sources – journalistic accounts of imperial activity, memorials to slain imperialists, books of self-instruction and schoolbooks, topical review articles, works in social theory or social prophecy – a common denominator can be found in the general preoccupation with individual character and its wider ramifications.[5]

The whole mass of formal and informal propaganda popularized the ideas of British character to the public. Citizenship classes in the Board Schools were geared to generating the character and attributes needed to sustain British pre-eminence – duty, discipline and good conduct. Juvenile literature complemented and supplemented formal teaching, setting similar moral instruction in a palatable fictional format.[6]

The Empire was seen and promoted as a vehicle for the operation of British

character at its best, a character that was a cross between evangelical commitment, strength of purpose and hard work and chivalric ideals of leadership, service and sacrifice. It was force of character that was seen to enable a handful of
Englishmen to rule entire provinces and informed the lives and legends of such
imperial heroes as John and Henry Lawrence of the Punjab, Sir John Nicholson (who was proclaimed a god in 1848 and worshipped by Nikalsaini fakirs),
Gordon of Khartoum, James Brooke 'The White Rajah' of Sarawak and
Lugard of Nigeria. The dying Henry Lawrence asked that his epitaph read:
'Here lies Henry Lawrence, who tried to do his duty'; while Gordon wrote to
his sister: 'I am quite happy, thank God, and like Lawrence, I have tried to do
my duty.'[7]

It was force of individual character and its power that justified the system of
indirect rule in Africa. The eminent critic of imperialism, E. D. Morel, after a
visit to Nigeria in 1910, wrote of the British district officer:

> When one sees this man managing, almost single-handedly, a country as
> large as Scotland, when one sees that man, living in a leaky mud hut,
> holding by the sway of his personality the balance even between fiercely
> antagonistic races, when one sees the marvels accomplished by tact, pas-
> sionate interest and self-control, with utterly inadequate means, in con-
> tinuous personal discomfort, short-handed, on poor pay, out here ...
> then one feels ... that the end must be good.[8]

It was this concept of British character that was projected in the imperial films
made both in Britain and America during the 1930s. One of the reasons
Alexander Korda produced his notable trilogy of imperial dramas, *Sanders of
the River*, *The Four Feathers* and *The Drum*, all of them directed by his brother
Zoltan, was, as his biographer Karol Kulik put it, because he was a confirmed
Anglophile who saw the Empire builders as 'the embodiment of all the most
noble traits in the English character and spirit'.[9]

'Character and spirit' are at the heart of Korda's imperial vision. The tone
and theme of *Sanders of the River* are set by the prologue, which declares:

> Sailors, soldiers and merchant adventurers were the pioneers who laid the
> foundations of the British Empire. Today their work is carried on by the
> civil servants – the keepers of the King's Peace.

Then over a map of Africa is imposed the legend:

> Africa – tens of millions of natives, each tribe under its own chieftain,
> guarded and protected by a handful of white men, whose work is an
> unsung saga of courage and efficiency. One of them was Commissioner
> Sanders.

So from the outset the heroic individualism of the lone British officer is established.

Commissioner Sanders, admirably played by Leslie Banks, is established as the ideal colonial administrator, and the film is constructed to demonstrate his attributes. Quiet, pipe-smoking, good-humoured, stoical and authoritative, Sanders has virtually single-handedly brought law and order to the River territories over the previous ten years. He has banned slavery and the running of gin and guns, 'the most dangerous gifts of civilization to the natives'. Having brought peace and order, he now seeks to maintain it, a direct reflection of the situation in the contemporary British Empire.

Backed as he is by only a handful of white officers and a single regiment of native troops, he rules by force of personality and character. The key sequences in the film are predicated on Sanders's charismatic strength. When he summons the troublesome King Mofalaba to palaver, Mofalaba comes with his warriors who outnumber the British forces by ten to one. Yet Sanders curtly reads the riot act to the king, warning him to behave, and then dismisses him with an abrupt: 'The palaver is finished.' Mofalaba and his men could easily have fallen on the British and slaughtered them. Instead they go home obediently. The rapid crumbling of the situation when Sanders goes on leave and war and revolt flare up indicate just how essential the personal charisma of Sanders is to the government. The missionary priest Father O'Leary cables the Colonial Office: 'Send four battalions or Sanders.' Sanders returns from leave, descending godlike from a plane, and puts down the unrest. But he expects no thanks. He does the job out of a sense of duty, telling Lieutenant Tibbetts at the start that he is in for 'tramping through swamps and jungles, your only decoration – mosquito bites'. It should be noted, however, that although it is never mentioned, this moral authority is underpinned by Western technology in the form of an airplane, a paddle steamer and machine-guns.

The characteristics that Sanders embodies are entirely in line with the criteria actually employed to select colonial administrators. The selection was virtually controlled from 1910 to 1948 (with the exception of the period covering World War One) by one man – Sir Ralph Furse. Furse selected his men specifically on the basis of character and recruited them mainly from the public schools. He wrote: 'We could not have run the show without them. In England, universities train the mind; the public schools train character and teach leadership.'[10] Experience as a public school prefect, and thus an exemplar of the ideas of character instilled by the system, Furse regarded as perfect training for colonial administration. After a prefect, the next best qualification was a university rugger blue, preferably a captaincy. Indeed, Sudan was once described as 'a country of blacks run by blues'.

Robert Heussler, in his book on the Colonial service, gathered together some of the testimonial letters used to make selections, which include such statements as, ' He would be capable of dealing with men. His mind is well-balanced, his manner agreeable and in every respect he is a perfect gentleman'; and 'He would maintain the best traditions of English government over subject races … He is a gentleman, a man of character.'[11] This could well be a description of Sanders. For Edgar Wallace had indeed created his hero as 'a mixture of Harry Johnston and the other West African commissioners of whom he had heard such romantic and bloodcurdling tales', and had established an archetype which had a long life in popular culture.[12] Although Leslie Banks became the definitive Sanders, there was an earlier incarnation. In the now-forgotten Edgar Wallace adaptation *The River of Stars* (1921) Commissioner Sanders appears as a supporting character, played by H. Agar Lyons. Appropriately brusque and authoritative, he pops into the narrative in time to hang a witch doctor who has been holding a white man prisoner. As late as the 1950s, District Commissioners in *Tarzan* films and other Hollywood African adventures conformed to the Wallace archetype.[13]

The message of *Sanders of the River* is reinforced by the other two main characters, the archetypes of the 'Good African' and the 'Bad African'. The British govern the River Territories through nominated chieftains, an accurate dramatization of the policy of 'indirect rule' operated in West Africa. Sanders's particular favourite is Bosambo, chief of the Ochori, with whom he has a headmaster–pupil relationship.

The 'Bad African' is King Mofalaba, who is sly, cruel and overbearing. He murders Commissioner Ferguson, kidnaps Lilongo and conducts slaving raids against neighbouring tribes. Where Bosambo loyally serves the British, Mofalaba plots against them. But he does not do so in the interests of the Africans, of freedom or principle. He seeks to get rid of the British because they prevent him tyrannizing over the people. The British stand between him and the despotic exercise of absolute power that he seeks. At the end of the film, he is killed and replaced by Bosambo, who will rule under the British in peace and justice and will not seek to destroy his people with war or tyranny.

The film gives every indication that the tribes will carry on as they always have under British protection – 'at peace in their primitive paradise' as the film puts it. The consent of the governed is implied by the scene in which Sanders, about to go on leave, asks Bosambo if he will still be a popular chieftain when

Sanders returns. Bosambo replies: 'I have learned the secret of good government from your lordship. It is this, that a king should not be feared but loved by his people.' 'That,' replies Sanders with a knowing smile, 'is the secret of the British.' The inescapable conclusion is that British rule is changeless and timeless.

For the second film in his imperial trilogy, Korda turned to India, the obvious choice in that he had under contract the young Indian boy Sabu, who had scored a great hit in *Elephant Boy* (1937). The script for *The Drum* was based on a story written directly for the screen by A. E. W. Mason and subsequently issued as a novella. Unlike *Sanders*, *The Drum* was a military film, drawing freely on the heroic scarlet-and-gold imagery of the Indian army and the exhilarating literary and filmic tradition of adventure and excitement on the North-West Frontier, stirring regimental ceremonial and the Kiplingesque concept of 'The Great Game', dangerous secret service work in the defence of the Empire. All these ideas are evoked as the credits unfold over Technicolor reproductions of romantic paintings of British military engagements to the uplifting strains of John Greenwood's Elgarian score. A globe spins slowly, the splashes of red indicating the territories of the Crown, and the familiar cadences of *Rule Britannia* are heard. The imagery, visual and aural, is unquestionably one of pride in the imperial achievement.

The British hero of *The Drum* is Captain Carruthers (Roger Livesey). Blood-brother to Sanders, he is quietly spoken, dedicated, wise and good-humoured. The twinkle in his eye when dealing with recalcitrant natives is something else Carruthers shares with Sanders. It demonstrates both his superiority and his humanity. Carruthers knows and loves India and the Indians. The film deals with his successful establishment of a British protectorate in the key border state of Tokot. In order to ensure British rule, Carruthers is prepared to risk his life by going to a banquet which he suspects may well be a trap. He tells his wife: 'A not unusual preliminary to our establishing law and order is the murder of one of our representatives.' He cites the examples of the murders of Sir Lewis Cavagnari at Kabul and of Gordon at Khartoum, which led directly to the British occupation of Afghanistan and Sudan. 'Our establishing law and order' is the key phrase. The reason why British control in Tokot must be established is not so much in the interests of the Empire as of the Tokotis. Carruthers's decision to attend the banquet, and the reasoning behind it, is one of the emotional high points of the film, the counterpart of Sanders's decision, when racked by malaria, to sail up to the Old King's country to rescue Bosambo. In both cases, the British representatives scorn their numerical inferiority, entertain the possibility of martyrdom and place their trust in their strength of character and their moral superiority.

As in *Sanders*, the moral of the story is pointed up by the presence of a 'Good Native' and a 'Bad Native'. The good one in this case is Prince Azim (Sabu), son of the Khan of Tokot. Where Sanders and Bosambo had a headmaster–pupil relationship, Carruthers has an even closer, almost father–son relationship with Azim. When Azim's own father is murdered, Carruthers and his wife become surrogate parents of the boy. It is Azim who gives the warning signal to save the British from massacre at the banquet, overruling the suggestion of his followers that they allow the massacre to take place because that will lead to punitive British action against Azim's usurping uncle. Azim duly ends up on the throne of Tokot, pledged to the policy articulated by his father at the beginning: 'If England is our friend, we shall have peace.'

The Bad Native is Ghul Khan, in a compelling performance by Raymond Massey. The anti-British Ghul murders his pro-British bother and usurps the throne of Tokot. He tries to murder his nephew Azim, tortures his fellow countrymen and seeks help from the Russians. He is in short a mad fanatic who, like Mofalaba, dreams not of freedom for his people but power for himself. His massacre of the British garrison at Tokot is intended to be the signal for a tribal uprising, which will culminate in the invasion of the plains and an orgy of pillage, rape and murder. Significantly, he is finally killed by Mohammed Khan, one of his fellow countrymen whom he has hideously tortured.

The third, and in many ways the best, film of the trilogy is *The Four Feathers* (1939), one of the finest British films of the 1930s. Two years in the making, it was filmed in Technicolor partly on location in Sudan, with the full cooperation of the Governor-General and the British Army. There can be no doubting the popularity of A. E. W. Mason's novel, which had already inspired three film versions (1915, 1921, 1928). Korda's version, however, topped them all. It was greatly helped by an excellent R. C. Sherriff script, which made several changes in the story in the interests of narrative cohesion and injected a welcome note of humour in the entirely new character of the comically pompous old bore General Burroughs (C. Aubrey Smith).

Once again character is the centre of the film's story. The central theme is the triumph of character, training and breeding, over baser instincts. The imperial context is set precisely by the opening, in a foreword which tells us that in Sudan the Khalifa and his cruel army of dervishes enslaved 'thousands of defenceless natives', in other words a situation ripe for British intervention in the interests of law and order and the underdog. There is a montage of natives attacking Khartoum, killing General Gordon and hauling down the Union Jack. The framework of the action and the narrative drive of the picture then is geared towards the raising of that flag once again.

Within the framework, the action is built around the trials and tribulations of Lieutenant Harry Faversham (John Clements), the roots of whose dilemma are demonstrated in the introductory section of the film. Old General Faversham confides in his friend Dr Sutton that he is worried about his son Harry, whom he has sent to one of the finest military schools in England but whom he has recently discovered reading a volume of Shelley. The implication is obvious. The boy is a weakling and possibly a coward. The effect of these worries on the boy himself is demonstrated when he attends a dinner of old Crimean War Veterans, hosted by his father. The old men regale each other with tales of past glories and heroic deeds and the cautionary tale of a coward's expiatory suicide. 'There's no place in England for a coward,' says the General, looking pointedly at his son, who lowers his eyes in embarrassment. As he retires for the night, young Harry walks down a long, shadowy corridor hung with portraits of his heroic ancestors. He pauses and looks up at them. The portraits dwarf him. It is a powerful and effective metaphor for the weight of military tradition and family pride already hanging heavy on the boy's shoulders.

Ten years later, Harry is a lieutenant in the East Surreys. The regiment is ordered to sail for Egypt to join Kitchener's army which is preparing to march into Sudan and avenge Gordon. Harry resigns his commission, telling his commanding officer that he only joined the army out of duty to his father and that duty ended when his father died. He tells Ethne, his fiancee, that he has resigned because of all the things they have often discussed – 'the futility, madness, ghastly waste of time' that war involves. He talks of the devotion of his family to seeking glory overseas while the ancestral estates and the tenants' livelihood go to rack and ruin.

Both reasons are, objectively speaking, sound and logical. But they are in fact excuses. For as he eventually confesses to Dr Sutton he is afraid, not of fighting or even dying, but afraid of being afraid and therefore letting down the family name. This qualification avoids the opprobrium of cowardice for which a bullet in the brain is the only answer and instead throws attention on the question of the burden of duty and responsibility.

The commanding officer answers Harry's initial plea of a discharged duty to his father with the question: 'Have you no duty to your country?' and this is elaborated by Ethne in what is the key ideological scene of the film. Ethne, the one person he had expected to understand, expresses her horror at his decision and explains that they are not free to act as they might wish. They were born into a tradition, a code which they must obey because the pride and happiness of everyone around them depends on it. She allows him to take a white feather from her fan to add to the three feathers, the symbols of cowardice, that his fellow officers have sent him.

The rest of the film details Harry's redemption, as he goes to Sudan, determined to return the four feathers and prove himself. He rescues Captain John Durrance, blinded and lost in the desert, and enters the prison at Omdurman, frees the prisoners (who include the other two fellow officers), raises them in revolt, seizes the arsenal at the height of the battle of Omdurman and hoists the Union Jack. Thus both the overall political theme – the restoration of British rule and all it implies in terms of law, order and justice – and Harry's personal redemption are completed in a final symbolic act.

Interestingly, on his arrival in Egypt, Harry tells his story to a native doctor and receives the casual answer: 'Be a coward and be happy.' This is the fatalistic Eastern way. If Harry were to follow it, there would of course be no film and no story. The entire action of what is on one level a rip-snorting adventure film is based on the acceptance of a concept of British character involving duty, stoicism, courage and perseverance. A reporter at the film's premiere wrote disbelievingly:

> From what he said on the stage at the premiere, A. E. W. Mason seems to take an unexpectedly serious view of this lusty schoolboy yarn of his. He finished on a rather jingoistic note about 'British character'.[14]

But the reporter missed the point. This serious view of British character was what the film was all about.

Harry learns to accept his duty, wins fame and the hand of Ethne. But what makes the film more complex, profound and tragic than either *Sanders* or *The Drum* is the subplot, the story of Captain Durrance, who is in a sense the real hero of the story and is superbly played by Ralph Richardson in one of his finest screen performances. For where Harry wins everything, Durrance loses everything (Ethne twice over and his army career) and demonstrates the strength of his character.

Durrance, a simple, straightforward career soldier with none of Harry's doubts and sensibilities, is from the outset a potentially tragic figure. We first meet him as the announcement of Harry's engagement to Ethne is made. As the other officers crowd round Harry offering congratulations, Durrance turns to the window to conceal his distress. But he rallies and joins in the congratulations. Another officer, knowing of his feelings for Ethne, consoles him with 'There are plenty of other women.' He replies sadly: 'Plenty of other women – for other men.' Blinded by sunstroke on the Sudan campaign, he is rescued by Harry, of whose identity he is unaware and returns to England. There he gradually adjusts to his blindness and becomes engaged to Ethne, who believes Harry to be dead. But he learns the truth and in a moving renunciation scene quietly dictates a letter to Ethne, telling her he is going abroad indefinitely to seek treatment for his condition. In fact his blindness is permanent and he is releasing Ethne to marry Harry. The pain that this decision causes and his stoical acceptance of it demonstrate even more effectively than Harry's desert adventures the strength and nature of British character.

In each of the Korda films, the man is the message. The films offer no political, economic or constitutional justification for the Empire. Its justification lies in the strength and nature of British character and the moral superiority of the British to everyone else by virtue of their commitment to a code of behaviour which involves the preservation of law, order and justice for love of those qualities. The exercise of power by the British is supported by the consent of the governed and defined by the opposition of self-seeking, power-hungry native despots.

The same distinctively British virtues were shared by the real-life heroes of the Empire in their cinematic manifestations. The nineteenth century was an age of heroes and hero worship. Edmund Gosse said of the Victorians that 'they carried admiration to the highest pitch. They marshalled it, they defined it, they turned it from a virtue into a religion and called is hero-worship.'[15] Thomas Carlyle wrote the classic exposition of it in his published series of lectures *On Heroes and Hero-Worship*:

> Universal History, the history of what man has accomplished in this world, is at bottom the History of the Great Men who have worked here. They were the leaders of men, these great ones; the modellers, patterns, and in a wide sense creators, of whatsoever the general mass of men contrived to do or to attain; all things that we see standing accomplished in the world are properly the outer material result, the practical realisation and embodiment, of Thoughts that dwelt in the Great Men sent into the world; the soul of the whole world's history, it may justly be considered, were this history of these ... We cannot look ... upon a great man, without gaining something by him. He is the living light-fountain, which it is good and pleasant to be near.[16]

Imperialism naturally had its own pantheon of heroes: Gordon of Khartoum,

Clive of India, Rhodes of Africa, Raffles of Singapore, Lugard of Nigeria, the Indian Mutiny generals.

The great heroes of Empire were heroic individualists who embodied the national character in its noblest form – stoicism, service, duty. Almost all of them died, making the ultimate sacrifice and becoming effectively the gods and martyr saints of an imperial religion, representing a potent fusion of Protestant Christianity and British imperialism. As John MacKenzie has written:

> Imperial heroes developed instrumental power because they served to explain and justify the rise of the imperial state, personified national greatness and offered examples of self-sacrificing service to a current generation.[17]

Their myths were established in popular biography, poems, statues and paintings. All these media were used to establish and then perpetuate their cults for succeeding generations. MacKenzie has identified at least a hundred biographies of David Livingstone between the 1870s and the 1950s and seventy of General Gordon. The pattern for imperial heroes was set by Clive, Wolfe and Nelson, the last two of whom died in the hour of their triumph. But they also presented problems for the Victorians: Nelson was vain, over-emotional and openly kept a mistress; Clive was financially self-serving, depressive and a suicide. It was the Mutiny heroes who provided better examples and could be more easily promoted in both knightly and Christian terms: Sir James Outram ('The Bayard of India'), John and Henry Lawrence, Sir Colin Campbell, Sir John Nicholson, Sir Henry Havelock. Havelock was a devout evangelical who died at his moment of triumph, having relieved Lucknow. He became the epitome of the Christian soldier, emerging in mid-Victorian England as a moral exemplar. Thereafter the great heroes like Livingstone and Gordon were cast in this approved mould. It is the martyr's death that makes them gods of Empire, whereas Wolseley, Kitchener, Roberts and Milner who did not experience premature death were merely heroes and received no biopics.

During the heyday of the cinema, most of the great imperial heroes received celluloid apotheosis. All their film biographies were inaccurate and distorted. But that is unimportant. The cinema does not deal in precise historical accuracy. It deals in drama, dreams and myths. So the imperial heroes inevitably lose their three-dimensional human reality and are stylized into ideals. They also become epitomes of the national character.

On the other hand, the heroes of the Mutiny did not make it to the cinema screens for political reasons. Plans were announced in 1938 for an epic film called *The Relief of Lucknow* which would feature the Mutiny heroes. It was banned by the British Board of Film Censors (BBFC) whose president, Lord Tyrrell, announced:

> The B.B.F.C. has been advised by all the authorities responsible for the government of India, both civil and military, that in their considered opinion, such a film would revive memories of the days of conflict in India which it had been the earnest endeavour of both countries to obliterate with a view to promoting harmonious cooperation between the two peoples.[18]

Nevertheless, a heroic biographical film was made of *Clive of India* (1934). Produced in Hollywood by Darryl F. Zanuck's 20th Century Pictures and directed by Richard Boleslavski, it was based on a British play by W. P. Lipscomb and R. J. Minney which had enjoyed a successful run in the West End of London, with Leslie Banks as Clive. It was one of a series of films celebrating the British Empire that Hollywood produced in the 1930s. Ronald Colman was perfectly cast as Clive. He believes himself a man of destiny ('India is a sacred trust. I must keep faith'). He is conscious always of what he is about ('We play for an Empire,' he declares before the Battle of Plassey). His overriding characteristic is his devotion to duty, to which he sacrifices everything: the life of his child, the love of his wife, his honour and his reputation. But he succeeds in establishing British rule over Southern India – and this means peace, order and freedom to trade. When Suraj-ud-Dowlah, Nawab of Bengal (Mischa Auer), threatens this control, Clive marches against him and defeats him at Plassey. Suraj is depicted as a half-mad tyrant, whipping his dancing girls as he perpetrates the Black Hole of Calcutta. Plassey is thus contextualized as a just and necessary victory that will benefit both Britain and India. 'What happened at Plassey will live forever as a monument to one man's courage, and revenge for the Black Hole of Calcutta,' says a title.

But Clive's work in India is threatened by a regime of corruption and extortion, sanctioned by the greedy and self-interested officials of the East India Company, and he seeks to stamp out these abuses, thus offending vested interests who mount a campaign against him at home. In Parliament, he defends himself against his enemies' charges in a moving speech: 'I have done what I have done for India and for my country. It has cost me what I hold most dear. This action is unworthy of the British people. When they come to decide on the question of my honour I trust they will not forget their own.' But the vote goes against him. He returns home alone, an ill and broken man. But the film ends on an upbeat note. His wife, Margaret, who had refused to go back to India with him, returns to him and the Prime Minister, Lord Chatham (C. Aubrey Smith), arrives to tell him that, although Parliament has passed a vote of censure, 'King George desires me to tell you that he remembers with gratitude that you have added a great new dominion to the Empire.' This makes everything worthwhile, and the film ends with *God Save the King*.

Clive is thus idealized as a paladin of Empire, a heroic individualist who in pursuit of his destiny disobeys orders from over-cautious or corrupt superiors and commits forgery, but who always acts in the interests of the higher good. He does battle against native tyrants who oppress their own people and against vested interests which offend against the basic imperial principles of disinterested and just administration. It is all done in a spirit of stoicism, duty, dedication and good humour.

The facts of Clive's life needed considerable manipulation to make them fit the imperial stereotype as it emerged in the nineteenth century. In the published version of their play, Lipscomb and Minney felt the need to acquit Clive of several serious charges. The fact that he accepted large sums from Mir Jaffar, the man he elevated to the throne of Bengal, is justified by being put into the context of accepted East India Company practice. His suicide is discounted and his death attributed instead to an accidental overdose of opium, which he had been taking to alleviate pain. The forging of Admiral Watson's signature on a bogus treaty is justified as the means of saving thousands of lives and being retrospectively approved by Watson. Finally, Clive is vindicated by his advocacy of altruistic imperialism:

> If for no other reason, we must remember Clive for one great thing. Up to this time, the Spanish, Dutch, French, Portuguese – indeed all the colonisers – had but one idea: to get rich quickly by any method possible, and we know to some extent how ruthless those methods were. Clive was the first man to advocate openly that if you come into a country as a conqueror you must give as well as take. His view was that if we accept the responsibilities of India, we must give them colour by governing for the benefit not only of ourselves, but of the people of the country.[19]

Far less manipulation was needed with the life of General Charles Gordon, the perfect 'Christian soldier' of imperial myth. A heroic individualist, campaigner against slavery, a devout Christian, a dedicated philanthropist who rescued street Arabs in Gravesend, a charismatic and successful general who led the armies of the emperor of China to victory during the Taiping Rebellion, armed only with a swagger stick, he died in Khartoum refusing to abandon his post in the face of overwhelming odds. He was, according to the biographies that proliferated after his death, the perfect Christian knight, who united 'all that is noble and chivalrous in man'. 'Doubtful indeed it is if anywhere in the past we shall find figure of knight or soldier to equal him.'[20] Gordon was etched indelibly in Victorian consciousness by the painting *General Gordon's Last Stand* by G. W. Joy (1885), in which Gordon stands at the top of a flight of steps, one arm across his chest, the other at his side holding a revolver. The dervishes are swarming up the steps and one of them aims a spear at his heart.

The image was 'realized' with interesting variations in two of the notable films of the 1930s. In *Sixty Glorious Years* (1938), Queen Victoria declares her emphatic support for Gordon ('The great Christian soldier means something to the world as well as to us'). In a brief scene in Khartoum, Gordon, speaking in a Scottish accent that is not historically correct but which reminds audiences of his Scottish ancestry, toasts the Queen. Then, during the final assault, he lays aside his revolver, picks up his swagger stick, kisses the Bible, goes out onto the steps and is killed in a re-creation of Joy's staging. *The Four Feathers* (1939) opens with the storming of Khartoum and the death of Gordon on the steps (although this time he carries only a Bible), followed by the lowering of the Union Jack and the raising of the rebel flag. This sets the context within which the rest of the story unfolds, culminating in the avenging of Gordon's death as Sudan is reclaimed for the Empire. The elimination of the revolver from the scene makes Gordon's martyrdom all the more Christlike.

It was not until 1966 that Gordon received his own biopic, the splendid *Khartoum*, directed by Basil Dearden from a script by Robert Ardrey. Charlton Heston gave a superb performance as Gordon, the mystic patriot, the Christian idealist, the heroic individualist who knows no fear and acts strictly according to his notion of his duty. His individualism is stressed. Gordon tells his aide Colonel Stewart: 'I regard myself as a religious man but belong to no church; I am an able soldier but I abhor armies; I have been introduced to many women but I have never married.' This being the 1960s, the film does not attribute imperial ambitions to him. Instead it stresses his devotion to Sudan and its people ('I am not a loving man but I love this country'), his opposition to slavery and oppression, his stoicism and his sense of duty and service. Nor does it attribute imperial ambitions to Gladstone ('I will not undertake a British obligation to police the world.'). It also simplifies the Sudanese political situation. In reality, Egypt was the colonial power in Sudan, Khartoum was an alien settlement and the Mahdi was backed by slave-trading tribes and was

Imperial heroes in action (1): General Gordon's last stand in *Khartoum* (1966) with Charlton Heston.

4

seeking to free Sudan from Egyptian interference in the trade. None of this is discussed. Instead it universalizes, suggesting the similarity of Gordon and the Mahdi, as visionaries, mystics and military geniuses, each with a sense of mission, each loving the people and the land.

The film opens spectacularly with the massacre of Colonel Hicks and his Egyptian army in Sudan. The government of W. E. Gladstone in London is confronted with popular demands for vengeance. But Gladstone is adamant.

He will not send a British army down the Nile. But a solution is offered. He will satisfy public opinion by sending one man – General Gordon, 'a hero to the Sudanese, to the English, to the anti-slavery people, to the churchmen and to Her Majesty herself'. Although Gladstone has reservations about Gordon, he sends for him, ordering him to go to Khartoum, evacuate the Egyptians and retire. He warns him that he will receive no official backing. Gordon travels to Khartoum, fortifies the city but refuses to leave the anti-Mahdist Sudanese to their fate. He sends appeal after appeal for aid, but Gladstone refuses to act until it is too late. Sir Garnet Wolseley's expedition arrives two days too late. Gordon dies in a re-creation of the Joy painting, this time clutching his swagger stick and not a revolver. Gordon dies but his legend lives on, and his death is the prelude to eventual British occupation of Sudan and the establishment of law and order. As Gladstone observes with heavy irony: 'When I think how history will record some day that the decisions of an empire were made by greedy businessmen, scheming generals, and conniving politicians.'[21]

The other great Victorian who caught the popular imagination was Dr David Livingstone, who became in effect a Protestant saint. He was a largely self-made working-class Scot who was able to be simultaneously a Scottish hero, a British hero (the opening up of Africa for the Empire), a Christian hero (Protestant missionary), a scientific hero (explorer) and a humanitarian hero (doctor). He also died at his post, thus achieving the necessary martyrdom.[22] A silent film devoted to his exploits, *Livingstone*, directed by and starring M. A. Wetherell, was released in 1925. Dean Rapp and Charles Weber call it 'an important expression of popular imperialism which in the 1920s continued to be widely upheld throughout British society' and see it as a product of the concern that Britain's cultural identity was being threatened by the dominance of Hollywood and the promotion of sexual permissiveness and lawlessness.[23]

Wetherell's film was financially supported by the London Missionary Society and a variety of businesses and *backed* by clergymen and members of parliament. The aim of the film was explicitly to portray Livingstone as an epitome of 'British character' and to instil in the young courage, perseverance, devotion to duty, self-sacrifice, patriotism and pride in empire. Wetherell shot the film on the actual locations of the story, basing his script on Stanley's and Livingstone's own writings and on the classic Victorian biography of Livingstone by W. G. Blaikie. The filming expedition was widely covered in the press, and Henry Walton, who played Stanley, wrote and published in 1925 an account of the expedition.

The film re-created key episodes from Livingstone's life: his Scottish boy-

Imperial heroes in action (2): 'Dr Livingstone, I presume', in *Stanley and Livingstone*   **5**
(1939) with Cedric Hardwicke and Spencer Tracy.

hood; medical training; departure for Africa as a missionary; his marriage and
raising of a family; his encounter with the slave trade and return to England to
campaign against the trade; audience with Queen Victoria; return alone to
Africa and rumours of his death; his discovery by Stanley; his continued explo-
rations; his death in the service of the people he loved and served. The heroic
image of explorer and missionary is coupled with the idealism of his opposition to of the slave trade, whose horrors are graphically shown. He receives the
blessing and backing of Queen Victoria. He is shown as a devoted and loving
husband and father. His dedication, devotion to duty, stoicism, modesty, perseverance are stressed throughout. The critics praised the film as an 'all-British
masterpiece', 'a triumph for the British kinema [sic] industry' and as 'the most
notable film ever made by British enterprise', with idealism seen as 'typically
English' (Livingstone was, of course, Scottish).[24]

The film was reissued in 1933 with a soundtrack. But in 1936 a British
sound film, *David Livingstone*, a respectful but episodic and generally unin-
spiring film, with Percy Marmont in the title role, recounted the same story
with the same episodes. The 1936 film, however, was completely eclipsed by

20th Century-Fox's lavish and professional *Stanley and Livingstone* (1939), directed by Henry King. Safari sequences were shot by second-unit director Otto Brower in British East Africa, in stunning locations with spectacular native and animal footage. This was then integrated with footage of the actors shot at the Fox Studios in Hollywood.

Stanley and Livingstone had a completely different emphasis from the British films. Here, the American reporter Henry M. Stanley is the leading figure and the film emphasizes his centrality by adding a fictional romantic subplot (Stanley unrequitedly falls in love with the daughter of the British vice-consul in Zanzibar whose memory sustains him on his safari) and by giving him a garrulous western scout (Walter Brennan) as sidekick. According to his latest biographer, Frank McLynn, Stanley was in reality a pathologically cruel schizoid egotist. The film, though, turns him into a flawless hero.[25]

The film is constructed entirely from an American standpoint but also from the need to promote Anglo-American friendship. It opens in Wyoming territory in 1870 with Stanley obtaining an exclusive interview with Comanche chief Satanta while US peace commissioners prepare to conclude a treaty. This at once establishes the fact that the United States has its own imperial problems with native peoples. Stanley is sent for by his employer, James Gordon Bennett, of the *New York Herald* and asked to find Livingstone, and succeed where the *London Globe*, run by monocled English aristocrat Lord Tyce, Bennett's hated rival, has failed. Stanley has not heard of Livingstone and Bennett defines his appeal to the public: a Christian missionary converting the heathen, an anti-slavery campaigner and great adventurer/explorer in 'Darkest Africa'. All these aspects of his career are highlighted in the film.

Stanley goes and, having survived fever, native attacks and wild animals on an expedition which is the centrepiece of the film, finds Livingstone. As played by Cedric Hardwicke, Livingstone is an English gentleman characterized by stoicism, dedication, duty, sense of humour and with no trace of a Scottish accent. Stanley accompanies Livingstone on his work, medical, missionary and exploratory, and is inspired by him.

Back in England, the Royal Geographical Society reject Livingstone's claims and maps as false and Lord Tyce leads a campaign to discredit him. Stanley makes an impassioned speech in his defence, which is the key ideological moment of the film. He explains how he was born in England at St Asaph Workhouse (actually in Wales), how he grew up in poverty and learned to hate England and emigrated but how finally his faith in his native country had been restored by Livingstone. The Society vote against him, but news arrives that

Livingstone's body has been brought to the coast with letters mentioning Stanley and asking him to carry on his work. Lord Tyce makes a fulsome apology and Stanley takes up the work.

The story of Stanley and Livingstone in fact highlights the wider British dimension of the Empire, since Livingstone is Scottish and Stanley is Welsh/American; the American filmmakers typically see them both as English. It also highlights an American view of England. England is represented by aristocratic Lord Tyce, a disbelieving gaggle of knighted geographers, and the poverty and hardship of Stanley's workhouse youth. But it is all redeemed by Livingstone's dedication and mitigated by Stanley's love for the Englishwoman Eve Kingsley and the unwavering support for Stanley by Lord Tyce's son, Gareth, whom Eve marries.

Stanley, wonderfully played by Spencer Tracy, starts out as a tough, go-getting, singleminded, cynical American reporter, who is spiritualized by his meeting with Livingstone and finally takes up his mission. Friends remark on how much he looks and sounds like Livingstone. Livingstone's life's work has been to map Africa. 'White men have seen Africa only though eyes of ignorance and that means fear,' he says. He wants to remove that fear with maps, so that doctors, teachers and pioneers will come and slavery will be abolished: in other words, the white man will fulfil his humanitarian mission. This is given a clear Christian dimension. In an inspiring, if anachronistic, scene, Livingstone is shown animatedly conducting his African choir in Sullivan's *Onward Christian Soldiers* (only composed in 1871). Later, the same music accompanies Stanley as he marches across the map of Africa, discovering rivers, waterfalls and lakes, all of which are named after him. Both Tracy's and Hardwicke's acting is inspired and their portraits memorable: sincere, idealistic, stoical, dedicated, animated by a spiritual fervour that is as real as it is undemonstrative.

The myth-makers were on rather more difficult ground with the life of Cecil Rhodes because of his deep involvement in power politics and profit-making, both activities beneath the contempt of genuine idealistic imperialists. But in the British film *Rhodes of Africa* (Berthold Viertel, 1936), a reasonably successful attempt was made to deify Rhodes, though the result lacks the sweep and conviction of its Hollywood counterparts like *Clive* and *Stanley* and the film is flawed by the miscasting of an imported American star, of whom James Agate tartly remarked: 'It is a pity that Mr. Walter Huston's Rhodes should look so exactly like Mr. Ramsay MacDonald. As he also makes him act like President Lincoln ... I for one must vote this impersonation a failure.'[26]

6   Imperial heroes in action (3): Cecil Rhodes plans to extend the Empire from the Cape to Cairo in *Rhodes of Africa* (1936) with Walter Huston.

The film is a classic case of cinematic whitewashing. It plays down the disreputable elements and plays up the heroic ones to create the image it seeks. The titles indicate what these elements are, proclaiming before the film begins that it is:

> The drama of a man who set out singlehanded to unite a continent. He spared neither himself nor others. Hailed by some as an inspired leader, by others as an adventurer. To the Matabele he was a royal warrior, who

tempered conquest with the gift of ruling and who gave him at his death the royal salute *Bayete*. They came close to understanding him.

The film constantly emphasizes his dream – an Africa united under British rule and peopled by British settlers. He is guided by it in times of triumph and sustained by it in times of stress. In pursuit of this dream he acquires the De Beers Diamond Mines and once in charge explicitly rejects the directors' obsession with profit in favour of his own expansionist plans, including the Cape to Cairo Railway. The film also emphasizes his love of the native. The natives love him, calling him 'Great White Father' and saluting him on his death with the royal Matabele valediction. In return, he loves and cares for them. The film acquits him of responsibility for the Jameson Raid and the Matabele and Boer wars. He emerges as a heroic figure, constantly ailing and battling with Death ('so much to do, so little time') to make his dream a reality. At the end, he achieves the immortality accorded to all the great men of Empire. 'Living he was the land,' declares the narrator, 'and dead his soul shall be her soul.' His character is stoical, dedicated, devoted to duty.

The twentieth century produced two authentic imperial heroes – Scott of the Antarctic and Lawrence of Arabia. G. A. Henty, the premier boys' writer of the late nineteenth century, had perfected a formula in which his boy hero accompanied a *bone fide* British imperial hero on his expeditions, producing a stream of books with titles like *With Clive in India*, *With Kitchener in the Soudan*, *With Roberts to Pretoria*. Subsequent boys' writers imitated the style, for example, Colonel F. S. Brereton (*With Allenby in Palestine*, *With Wolseley to Kumasi*, *With Roberts to Kandahar*). So common did it become that the humorist Arthur Marshall coined the all-purpose boys' story title *With Wilkinson to Nairobi* for the genre. Fascinatingly, this convention was echoed by myth-making lecturers, giving us a clear indication of the romantic and heroic terms in which they were presenting their subjects. Lowell Thomas's illustrated lecture which helped to mythologize T. E. Lawrence was called *With Lawrence in Arabia* and Herbert Ponting's illustrated lecture of the ill-fated 1910–13 polar expedition was initially called *With Captain Scott R.N. to the South Pole*.

Herbert Ponting was the official photographer of the Polar Expedition and the film and still photographs he brought back still take the breath away with their sheer beauty. Ponting's filmed record was originally shown by the Gaumont Company in 1913, but Ponting purchased all the rights to it and included it in his illustrated lecture given in 1914 and 1917. He subsequently turned the lecture into a silent film, *The Great White Silence* (1924), which was, however, heavily weighed down with intertitles containing Ponting's lecture text. However, in 1933 he re-edited it once again with music and voice-over commentary into a much more artistically satisfying film, *90° South*. The film traces the voyage of the expedition ship *Terranova* from New Zealand to the Antarctic; it shows the Great Ice Barrier and there are beautifully composed shots of ice-scapes, glaciers and the changing Arctic weather, as well as much footage of the animals both natural to the region and imported by the explorers (seals, whales, penguins, dogs, ponies).[27]

While *90° South* is thus in part a nature and wildlife documentary, it is also a celebration of an imperial hero. It is dedicated to 'the undying memory of Captain Scott and his four companions' and it opens with a picture of Scott. The film is introduced by Vice-Admiral E. R. G. R. Evans, who as Lieutenant Evans was Scott's second-in-command and later a World War One naval hero – 'Evans of the Broke'. Dressed in an evening suit with his hands thrust into its pockets, and looking distinctly uneasy, Evans introduces Ponting – they call each other by their expedition nicknames 'Ponto' and 'Teddy'. Ponting, also in evening dress, then begins his lecture. The stress throughout is on imperial values. Scott, accompanied on the soundtrack by *Hearts of Oak*, appears and Ponting announces 'his enthusiasm for achievement for the honour of his country set a fine example for all'. Ponting subsequently comments on the stoicism of Evans as he endures the cold while studying the Antarctic stars through his telescope out of doors.

The camaraderie of the men on the expedition is stressed: their games (boxing, football) are shown; their communal meals; officers and men working together on the ropes of the *Terranova*. The tragic final push of Scott and his companions to the Pole is recounted using maps and a few still photographs because Ponting, of course, did not accompany them. He reads extracts from Scott's journals which highlight Oates' death ('a brave and gallant gentleman'); the men's character, their cheerfulness, perseverance and stoicism. Scott's final entry concludes that they have no cause for complaint: 'They had shown that Englishmen can endure hardship, help one another and meet death with as great a fortitude as in the past.' Ponting concludes that they perished 'happy in the knowledge they died for the honour of their country'. He also notes that the most inspiring sight in the entire expedition was a lone cross on an icy headland, erected in memory of an earlier British seaman who died in the performance of his duty. Duty, service, stoicism, sacrifice, nobility in defeat are the prevailing values stressed.

When Ealing Studios came to make its Technicolor dramatization of the expedition, *Scott of the Antarctic* (1948), Ponting's film was studied in detail and several of its most celebrated sequences re-created (the departure of the *Terranova* from New Zealand, the magical view of the ship from the inside of an ice cave). Ponting himself was played by Clive Morton in the film. Ealing, too, laid stress on British character and achievement. As producer Michael Balcon later recalled, director Charles Frend had long sought an epic subject and found it in this story, being 'especially inspired by Scott's last written message "Had we lived, I would have had a tale to tell of the hardihood, endurance and courage of my companions which would have stirred the heart of every Englishman".'[28] The film treatment and dialogue were prepared by Major Walter Meade, 'born in the same year as Captain Oates and himself a widely travelled pre-1914 Indian cavalry man'.[29] Meade was later joined by Ivor Montagu who shaped the material dramatically and by Professor Frank Debenham, director of the Scott Polar Institute in Cambridge and a survivor of the expedition, who provided technical advice. But the tone of the Ealing version remained that of Scott's journals and Ponting's film.

The Ealing film is narrated by John Mills as Scott. Scott sets out to reach the South Pole partly for the purpose of scientific investigation but principally for patriotic reasons ('I think an Englishman should get there first'). He raises an expedition of like-minded souls, mostly naval personnel, some with imperial connections (Bowers arrives from the Persian Gulf, Oates from India, Day from Australia). They pit themselves against the terrifying forces of nature. They soldier on even after learning that the Norwegian Amundsen has decided to go south, although he had told everyone he was going north ('Damned unsporting'). Scott records in his diary: 'Among ourselves we are unendingly cheerful but what each man feels in his heart I can only guess.'

But what is most interesting about Scott is that he is in the tradition of Englishman as gallant loser. It is perhaps significant that many of the great mythic events in British history have been heroic defeats (Dunkirk, the Charge of the Light Brigade, Gordon at Khartoum), or have seen the victorious commander die at the moment of victory (Nelson at Trafalgar, Wolfe at Quebec). Balcon noted wryly that the film was not a success in America: 'The American public has no interest in failure, even if it is heroic failure, and certainly they do not easily accept other people's legends.'[30]

Scott is the archetypal gallant loser, and he and all his team display characteristic British attitudes under adversity – quiet determination, understatement, restraint, self-deprecating humour, the stoical acceptance of defeat and disappointment. There is also the eternal boyishness of japes in the mess which is also an integral part of British imperial heroism.

Scott sees himself in the heroic tradition of great explorers (Cook, Ross) and judges his companions in terms of the public school code of chivalry – the dominant British code of masculinity, referring to Bowers as 'an undefeated little sportsman' and Oates as 'a brave man and a gallant gentleman'. It contains classic episodes of heroic understatement. Petty Officer 'Taff' Evans, suffering agonies from gangrene and frostbite, will only say 'It's alright, sir, quite well' even when he is dying. Captain Oates, also enduring great agonies, quietly and without fuss goes out into the blizzard, famously saying, 'I'm just going outside. I may be away for some time.' Each setback is met with a smile, a joke and a stiff upper lip. A scene in which Lieutenant Evans, broken-hearted at not being chosen for the final push, broke down and wept was shot but cut, presumably because it was not thought in keeping with the stiff upper lip spirit of the film.[31]

Ealing took immense pains to establish authenticity, using Ponting's film as a guide, shooting on location in Norway and Switzerland with establishing footage taken in Graham Land, Antarctica, and selecting actors who resembled as closely as possible the original participants. The film graphically charts the expedition through to its tragic finale with John Mills reading Scott's last diary entries on the soundtrack and the camera focusing on the faces of the explorers, fever bright and etched deep with suffering. The final shot of the film is of the cross marking the place where the bodies were found, inscribed with the words 'To strive, to seek, to find and not to yield'.

Charles Barr notes accurately that the film is a story of failure and that Scott makes a series of mistakes which the film records without comment.[32] He does not use dogs exclusively as the Norwegians do but a combination of dogs, ponies and mechanical sledges, even though Nansen tells him to use dogs, dogs and only dogs; Amundsen gets to the Pole first by using dogs. The mechanical sledges break down almost at once and have to be abandoned. Scott makes the final assault with a party of five men instead of four and on insufficient rations. No-one in the film questions his decision. They are presented as being made in the right spirit. He does not want to overtax the dogs ('We look on them as friends') and is committed to technological progress (hence the sledges). The film is entirely on his side, viewing him uncritically as a classic British hero. Barr notes that 'all this could have been presented with unconscious irony'. But the film entirely lacks this dimension, emerging as 'a strange dreamy elegiac film'. In retrospect, John Mills shared Barr's reservations, writing in his autobiography: 'It was a good film but if we'd been allowed to delve more deeply

into the characters of the men themselves, it could have been a great one.'[33]
Criticism, however, was inherently unlikely because as Balcon observed:

> We ... had much help from some of the survivors, particularly Frank
> Debenham but we thought it only proper to obtain the general approval
> of the script from each and every survivor ... We naturally intended to
> avoid anything which might prove hurtful to living people.[34]

'Teddy' Evans, now Admiral Lord Mountevans, demanded payment which
was reluctantly made and Apsley Cherry-Garrard, author of the classic account
The Worst Journey in the World, withdrew his permission, on the advice of
George Bernard Shaw, to his being portrayed, and therefore appeared only
minimally in the film. But Debenham, the first person to see the finished film,
was too overcome with emotion to speak at the Technicolor re-creation of his
comrades' fate.

Reviews of the film were mixed and Paul Dehn in the *Sunday Chronicle* was
moved to criticize the lack of enthusiasm shown by some of his colleagues. He
pronounced himself 'shocked and bewildered' that some critics had remained
unmoved by what he thought a fitting memorial to the expedition. Several critics thought the characters underdeveloped, and Richard Winnington in the
News Chronicle (30 November 1948) thought it lacked both poetry and
tragedy. 'We must make do with gentlemanly courage and gentlemanly pathos
from characters who do not really come alive', he wrote. But 'gentlemanly
courage and gentlemanly pathos' were precisely what the film was about. The
Daily Worker (4 December 1948) – of all papers – admired the 'gentleness and
reticence' of the film which it found 'more powerful and gripping than the hys-
terical heroics of the usual adventure films' and felt 'the overwhelming effect of
the film is to arouse our admiration and pride in the fortitude of the human
spirit in that old conflict between man and nature'. But several papers saw it
squarely in an imperial context. The *Sunday Graphic* (5 December 1948) said,
'it is always an inspiring and noble film, and one that every man, woman and
child in the British Empire must go and see', while The *Sunday Dispatch* (5
December 1948) declared:

> Such a film as *Scott* is welcome at a time when other races speak dis-
> paragingly of our 'crumbling Empire' and our 'lack of spirit'. It should
> make those who have listened too closely to such talk believe afresh that
> ours is the finest breed of men on this earth. And so it is.[35]

Scott and his expedition were of course a team. But the other great imperial
hero of the twentieth century was another heroic individualist. T. E. Lawrence

was not a national celebrity during World War One but became one after Thomas's lectures in 1919. He was an immensely complex individual, whose reputation has undergone continual re-evaluation since his death in a motorcycle accident at the age of forty-six in 1935 and who remains the subject of intense debate. Initially, however, he was presented in uncomplicated terms as an imperial hero in the mould of Gordon of Khartoum, someone whose charisma and courage had enabled him to understand and to lead armies of natives. After the publication of *The Seven Pillars of Wisdom* in 1926, film makers became fascinated by the Lawrence story, and when an abridged version, *The Revolt in the Desert*, became a bestseller their interest only increased.[36]

From 1934 until 1939 Alexander Korda made repeated attempts to film the story of Lawrence. Several scripts were prepared showing the heroic individualist welding the Arab tribes into a fighting force and defeating the Turks, while at the same time defying the High Command in Cairo and shortcircuiting the normal chains of command. Although at various times Leslie Howard, Walter Hudd and John Clements were announced as potential stars, with William K. Howard, Brian Desmond Hurst and Zoltan Korda as directors, the film was never made. Political unrest in Palestine led to filming being postponed on several occasions but principally the Foreign Office brought pressure to bear on Korda after protests from the Turks who objected to being portrayed as villains.[37] A fresh attempt was made to film the story in 1957 with Anthony Asquith directing from a script by Terence Rattigan and Dirk Bogarde as Lawrence, but Rank cancelled the project because the budget was too high. Rattigan turned his script into a stageplay *Ross* starring Alec Guinness. Finally *Lawrence of Arabia* reached the screen in 1962 with David Lean directing Robert Bolt's screenplay and Peter O'Toole making his electrifying screen debut as Lawrence, and Alec Guinness playing Feisal. Lean's film, with its breathtaking vistas, swirling action and complex character interplay, remains a landmark in epic filmmaking. Lean's Lawrence is an imperial hero for a post-imperial age: a heroic individualist who loves Arabia ('God, how I love this country') but who is a strange mixture of idealist, exhibitionist, masochist, with a view of himself as a man of destiny. Feisal explicitly compares him with Gordon, but unlike Gordon he is far from serene. The dramatic hinge of the film is Deraa where after his savage flogging Lawrence's view of his invulnerability is destroyed, he gives way to ferocious bloodlust and alienates former friends. Not only is he a flawed hero, but this version also projects him as an Arab nationalist, desiring freedom for the Arabs and self-government from Damascus, a plan which breaks down, leaving the Allied politicians to carve up the liberated lands. In fact Lawrence was no nationalist, but envisaged the liberated lands as the British Empire's 'first brown dominion'.[38]

The death of the god king is one of the recurrent elements in all mythologies. Be he Christ or Osiris or Dionysus, the god king dies that his people might live. The gods of Empire have common characteristics (dedication to duty, loneliness, the inspiring dream) and a common destiny (death). Clive's metaphorical death with his vote of censure leaves him a broken man. In reality, he committed suicide, worn out by the attacks upon him. Gordon is murdered. Scott dies after reaching the Pole. Lawrence is killed in an accident, though he too, it is implied, had a death wish. Livingstone and Rhodes wear themselves out and die in the service of their countries, native and adopted. Their blood and their strength are subsumed into the living, growing body of the Empire. They have become one with the ideal they served.

The gods of Empire were British archetypes, embodying the values and virtues of Britishness. They were produced in Britain and in America, where the chivalric values and the Protestant evangelical values that underpinned Britishness could appeal equally.[39] As Margaret Farrand Thorp put it in 1939, explaining the popularity of British imperial epics with Americans: 'The American public too, seemed to be stirred with admiration for British Empire ideals. Loyalty as the supreme virtue ... courage, hard work ... *noblesse oblige*'.[40] But most of all they celebrated that heroic individualism that made the British imperialist what George Santayana called 'the sweet just boyish master of the world' and provided an archetype of British manhood.

In her interesting study of some interwar women writers (Agatha Christie, Daphne du Maurier, Jan Struther), Alison Light argues that

> the 1920s and 30s saw a move away from formerly heroic and officially masculine public rhetorics of national destiny and from a dynamic and missionary view of the Victorian and Edwardian middle classes in 'Great Britain' to an Englishness at once less imperial and more inward-looking, more domestic and more private – and in terms of pre-war standards, more feminine.[41]

The box office popularity of the imperial epics, together with the continued literary and cinematic success of the works of imperial thriller writers such as John Buchan, Sapper and Edgar Wallace, suggest that such an interpretation is overstated. Empire and imperial values remained central to interwar culture.

Notes

1 Samuel Smiles, *Self-Help*, London, 1911, p. 449.
2 Stefan Collini, *Public Moralists*, Oxford, 1993, p. 94.
3 H. John Field, *Towards a Programme of Imperial Life*, Oxford, 1982, p. 39.
4 Smiles, *Self-Help*, p. 450.
5 Field, *Towards a Programme of Imperial Life*, p. 26.
6 On this subject, see in particular J. S. Bratton, *The Impact of Victorian Children's Fiction*, London, 1981; Jeffrey Richards (ed.), *Imperialism and Juvenile Literature*, Manchester, 1989; Kirsten Drotner, *English Children and their Magazines, 1751–1945*, New Haven and London, 1988.
7 Kathryn Tidrick, *Empire and the English Character*, London, 1990, p. 47.
8 Tidrick, *Empire and the English Character*, p. 204.
9 Karol Kulik, *Alexander Korda: the man who could work miracles*, London, 1975, p. 135.
10 Robert Heussler, *Yesterday's Rulers*, Oxford, 1963, p. 82.
11 Heussler, *Yesterday's Rulers*, pp. 19–20.
12 Margaret Lane, *Edgar Wallace*, London, 1939, p. 225.
13 Jeffrey Richards, *Visions of Yesterday*, London, 1973, pp. 114–23.
14 Unidentified newspaper cutting, BFI *The Four Feathers* microfiche.
15 Edmund Gosse, 'The Agony of the Victorian Age', *Edinburgh Review*, 228 (1918), p. 295.
16 Thomas Carlyle, *On Heroes, Hero-Worship and the Heroic in History*, London, 1912, pp. 1–2.
17 John M. MacKenzie, 'Heroic Myths of Empire', in John M. MacKenzie (ed.), *Popular Imperialism and the Military 1850– 1950*, Manchester, 1992, pp. 114–115.
18 Jeffrey Richards, *The Age of the Dream Palace*, London, 1984, p. 144.
19 W. P. Lipscomb and R. J. Minney, *'Clive of India'*, *Famous Plays of 1933–34*, London, 1934, pp. 15–16.
20 Mark Girouard, *Return to Camelot: chivalry and the English gentleman*, New Haven and London, 1981, p. 229.
21 See the interesting discussion in Gerald Herman, 'For God and Country: *Khartoum* (1966) as history and as "object lesson" for global policemen', *Film and History*, 9 (1979), pp. 1–15.
22 John M. MacKenzie, 'David Livingstone: the construction of the myth', in Tom Gallagher and Graham Walker (eds), *Sermons and Battle Hymns: Protestant popular culture in modern Scotland*, Edinburgh, 1990, pp. 24–42.
23 Dean Rapp and Charles W. Weber, 'British Film, Empire and Society in the Twenties: the *Livingstone* film, 1923–25', *Historical Journal of Film, Radio and Television* 9 (1989), pp. 3–19.
24 Rapp and Weber, 'British Film, Empire and Society', p. 8.
25 Frank McLynn, *Stanley: sorcerer's apprentice*, London, 1991, p. 128.
26 James Agate, *Around Cinemas* (second series), London, 1948, pp. 391–7.
27 On Ponting and his film, see Kevin Brownlow, *The War, the West and the Wilderness*, London, 1979, pp. 425–34.

28 Michael Balcon, *A Lifetime of Films*, London, 1969, p. 171.

29 David James, *Scott of the Antarctic: the film and its production, London*, 1948, p. 36. This volume contains a complete account of the filming.

30 Balcon, *A Lifetime of Films*, p. 174.

31 Kenneth More, *More or Less*, London, 1978, pp. 153–4.

32 Charles Barr, *Ealing Studios*, second edition, London, 1993, p. 78.

33 John Mills, *Up in the Clouds, Gentlemen, Please*, London, 1980, pp. 205–6.

34 Michael Balcon, *A Lifetime of Films*, p. 172.

35 For dated and undated reviews, see BFI *Scott of the Antarctic* microfiche.

36 John M. MacKenzie, 'T. E. Lawrence: the myth and the message', in Robert Giddings (ed.), *Literature and Imperialism*, London and Basingstoke, 1991, pp. 150–81.

37 Jeffrey Richards and Jeffrey Hulbert, 'Censorship in Action: the case of Lawrence of Arabia', *Journal of Contemporary History*, 19 (1984), pp. 153–70.

38 Tidrick, *Empire and the English Character*, p. 228.

39 John Fraser, *America and the Patterns of Chivalry*, Cambridge, 1982.

40 Margaret Farrand Thorp, *America at the Movies*, New Haven, 1939, pp. 294–5.

41 Alison Light, *Forever England: Femininity, Literature and Conservatism Between the Wars*, London, 1991, p. 8.

3

The black man
as hero

The concept of a British national identity compounded of Protestantism, empire, parliamentary democracy, monarchy and a particular conception of the national character was widely disseminated and widely shared. It was not, however, universal. There were sections of the community which were deliberately excluded by the majority because they were in some way different, in appearance or religion, in origin or language, and not only excluded but the object of hostility and sometimes violence from the majority population.

In Britain since the Industrial Revolution three groups in particular have borne the brunt of popular prejudice within the majority population – the Irish, the Jews, and black and Asian Commonwealth immigrants. They have arrived in Britain in successive waves, have occupied the same geographical areas and have been subject to the same prejudice for the same reasons. This means that ethnicity is at least as important as class in people's definition of themselves. For not only do you define yourself as part of something (a family, a class, a region, a nation). You define yourself as not part of something and against something which is different, what anthropologists call 'the other', the outsider. What is interesting in the case of prejudice is that the same slurs have been attached to each immigrant group in turn: that they are dirty and carry disease and are therefore a health threat; that they are promiscuous and sexually potent and hence a moral threat; that they are disproportionately involved in crime and hence a threat to law and order; that they take jobs and houses and money from the British population or are a drain on state funds and hence an economic threat; and that by diluting the native culture with alien practices they are a cultural threat. Immigrant groups function as scapegoats both in general for the social and economic problems of society and in particular at times of national crisis.

Before World War Two in Britain the black population was tiny, largely confined to the seaport towns where blacks worked as dockers and seamen. There were a number of black students, some of whom, Jomo Kenyatta for instance, were later to earn world prominence. There were celebrated black entertainers, such as the pianist 'Hutch' and the cricketer Learie Constantine. The great increase in Commonwealth immigrants occurred in the 1950s, the symbolic starting date being 1948 when the *S.S. Empire Windrush* brought 492 Jamaicans to England to start a new life. West Indians were deliberately recruited by London Transport and the National Health Service. The overall numbers remained small (less than a million in 1971 out of a population of 54 million) but they were visible and were concentrated in the old industrial working-class areas.[1]

The new immigrants encountered a host population already steeped in the racist attitudes and assumptions that were the legacy of Empire. The Empire was inextricably bound up with the question of race. Belief in the God-given duty of the British race to rule the world was deeply ingrained. Joseph Chamberlain was expressing the view of many when he said:

> In the first place I believe in the British Empire and in the second place I believe in the British race. I believe that the British race is the greatest of governing races that the world has ever seen.[2]

The nineteenth century saw the growth and development of the science of racialism, which sought to explain racial and ethnic differences and the variable levels of civilization in the world. One result of this was the construction of a racial and cultural hierarchy with white Western civilization at the top, the brown and yellow races of the East next and black Africans at the bottom. History was seen in terms of both explanation and justification for this fact.

The innate inferiority of the blacks could be seen in their failure to attain the essential prerequisites of civilization as represented by the British. Their political inferiority was evidenced by their preference for tyranny or anarchy over parliamentary democracy, their religious inferiority by their primitive paganism, their economic inferiority by their practice of primitive communism or a haphazard system of plunder rather than the implementation of an ordered and regularized system of trade, commerce and industry. By contrast, British superiority was seen to lie in their possession of all the key elements of civilization and in their ability to rule a vast empire with only a handful of men.[3]

Douglas Lorimer has convincingly related the intensification of racial feeling to the emergence of a fully formed class system in the mid-Victorian period. Earlier views had been conditioned by the romantic eighteenth-century image of the 'noble savage', the emotional appeal of the anti-slavery movement and the missionary image of the 'native' as a wayward child needing to be led to the truth of Christianity. But by the mid-nineteenth century the situation was changing. The anti-slavery impetus slackened after the American Civil War ended that institution in the United States. The traumatic experiences of the Jamaica Revolt (1865) and the Indian Mutiny (1857) engendered fear of the potential for violent uprising among subject peoples. The failure of the freed slaves of the West Indies to embrace wholeheartedly the Protestant work ethic and Western sexual mores lessened liberal faith in their ability to progress under their own auspices. The science of racialism and the work of men like Robert Knox and James Hunt established the view that biological inheritance governed an individual's physical, intellectual and psychological attributes and therefore determined his place in the natural and social order. The popularization of Darwin's ideas – the nearness of man to apes, the struggle for survival – and the loss of faith in the literal truth of the Bible reinforced the idea of the racial hierarchy by stressing the low ranking of blacks in the evolutionary scale and the triumph of the British as the survival of the fittest.[4]

All this was happening at the same time as class differences in Britain were hardening. Until the 1860s the British responded to the social status of blacks, accepting black rulers as gentlemen, and seeking to create a black middle-class elite in the West Indies. But after this period, with the emergence of a rigid racial hierarchy, race superseded class and gentlemanliness was no longer possible for blacks. All blacks were classed along with the lower orders.

Lorimer noted that 'while racist assumptions were common in the mid-nineteenth century, as yet systematic works on race had a limited readership among a well-educated minority.'[5] But popular fiction promoted, spread and entrenched the assumptions and images emerging from the scientific works. Dr Robert Knox resoundingly declared: 'Race is everything: literature, science, art – in a word civilization depends on it.'[6]

As Philip Curtin has shown, the popular image of Africa was clearly established by the 1850s:

It was found in children's books, in Sunday School tracts, in the popular press. Its major affirmations were the 'common knowledge' of the edu-

cated classes. Thereafter, when new generations of explorers or administrators went to Africa, they went with a prior impression of what they
would find. Most often they found it, and their writings in turn confirmed the older image.[7]

The image was largely based on the accounts of travellers, explorers, traders
and missionaries in the late eighteenth and early nineteenth centuries. They
tended to stress the colourful and exotic aspects of native life, to report
rumours and fables, to stress the aspects of African life most alien to Europe
(human sacrifice, polygamy) and to pay little attention to the detailed structures of society or belief. In the 1830s and 1840s a new generation of explorers began writing and tended to conform to a pattern. Their accounts were
much less interested in scientific or cultural matters than those of their prede-
cessors had been:

> They wrote to give their fellow countrymen a vicarious enjoyment of
> their adventures … vignettes of life on shore were introduced for light
> amusement or sensationalism. Human sacrifice in Ashanti, the female
> army in Dahomey, the 'humorous' attempts of the emancipated Africans
> in Sierra Leone to re-educate themselves in the ways of the western world
> – all this was standard fare.[8]

The most common view of blacks, a view shared by among others Sir
Richard Burton, David Livingstone and John Speke, was that they were childlike. Mr Goodenough a character in G. A. Henty's novel *By Sheer Pluck* (1884)
summarized the view:

> They are just like children. They are always either laughing or quarrelling.
> They are good-natured and passionate, indolent, but will work hard for a
> time; clever up to a certain point, densely stupid beyond. The intelligence
> of the average negro is about equal to that of a European child of ten years
> old … They are fluent talkers, but their ideas are borrowed. They are
> absolutely without originality, absolutely without inventive power. Living
> among white men, their imitative faculties enable them to attain a con-
> siderable amount of civilization. Left to their own devices, they retro-
> grade into a state little above their native savagery.[9]

Henty himself adds later:

> The natives of Africa are capable of extreme exertion for a time, but their
> habitual attitude is that of extreme laziness. One week's work in the year
> suffices to plant a sufficient amount of ground to supply the wants of a
> family … For fifty-one weeks in the year the negro simply sits and
> watches his crops grow. To people like these time is of absolutely no value.

Their wants are few … Such people are never in a hurry. To wait means to do nothing. To do nothing is their highest joy.[10]

Variations within African tribes were acknowledged. The negroes of Sierra Leone are said in *By Sheer Pluck* to be 'the most indolent, the most worthless and the most insolent in all Africa', while the Houssas are 'the best fighting negroes on the coast.' But in general the Africans were grouped into stereotypes of which the most common were the gallant enemy and the faithful servant.

The gallantry of enemies was regularly appreciated. As V. G. Kiernan notes:'A rough and ready but tenacious habit grew up of classifying peoples … as 'martial' or 'non-martial' and of paying more respect (or less disrespect) to the first.'[11] Throughout popular fiction, there are admiring references to the courage and fighting spirit of the Zulus, the Ashantis and the Sudanese 'Fuzzy-Wuzzies'. The faithful servant, the role stressing what blacks are best suited for and equating race and class, recurs regularly from Robinson Crusoe's Man Friday onwards.

While the dominant theme of the cinema in the 1930s was the celebration of the glories of British imperial rule and the concept of 'The White Man's Burden', there was an alternative view and this was to be found in the British films of the black American Paul Robeson.

Robeson declared: 'There is no such thing as a non-political artist. The artist must elect to fight for freedom or for slavery.'[12] He became a 'political artist' during the years in which he lived and worked in Britain from 1928 to 1939. He was by any definition a remarkable man. Born in Princeton, New Jersey, he won a scholarship to Rutgers University and succeeded not only in becoming an All-American footballer but also in graduating with honours. He had intended to study law but drifted into acting and singing, for both of which activities he had a huge natural talent. He established himself on the American stage, particularly in Eugene O'Neill's plays *All God's Chillun Got Wings* and *The Emperor Jones*. But he increasingly found the strict racial segregation in American society a restraining influence on his career. When he went to England to appear in the London production of *Showboat*, he found the atmosphere there freer and decided to settle in London. He became a celebrity in London, hailed by the *Daily Express* as 'a negro genius', lionized by the social and cultural elites.[13] He starred in *Othello* opposite Peggy Ashcroft. But he was also enormously popular with the mass audience as a singer in concerts, on records and on the radio. He was widely praised in profiles and interviews as sincere, modest and unselfconscious. There was a celebrated incident in which he and his wife were refused entry into the Savoy grill on account of their colour. This was taken up both in the press and in Parliament. Interestingly, it was ascribed to the influence of American race prejudice on Britain rather than seen as a by-product of Empire, and thus part of a deplored trend of Americanization of British life.[14]

For the most part Robeson loved London. His wife, Eslanda Goode Robeson, wrote:

> The calm, homely beauty and comfort of London, the more leisurely and deliberate pace of life as compared to the general rush and hustle of New York, the whole-hearted friendliness and unreserved appreciation of audiences and of the public at large appealed to him, and inspired him to his best work. He felt even more at home in London than he had in America. There were few inconveniences for him as a negro in London. He did not have to live in a segregated district; he leased a charming flat in Chelsea near his friends; he dined at the Ivy, a delightful restaurant with marvellous food, directly across from the theatre where he was playing; he ate at many other restaurants in town with his white or coloured friends without fear of the discrimination which all Negroes encounter in America. He was a welcome guest in hotels at the seaside places where he spent many weekends. This was important for his general well-being. In New York ... unless he dined with friends or in the Village itself, he could not get a meal in any good restaurant or hotel – except the Pennsylvania – from Tenth Street to One Hundred and Thirtieth Street; at none of the innumerable first-class eating-places could he be served as a negro guest. This was a great practical inconvenience. In travelling he could not secure good seats in a Pullman train. At hotels outside of New York it was almost impossible for him to secure accommodation: 'We do not take Negroes,' they would say firmly. In places where he knew no one, this was an intolerable inconvenience. So here in England, where everyone was kind and cordial and reasonable, Paul was happy.[15]

Latterday black American writers have criticized Robeson's roles as too integrationist or too individualist to represent the aspirations of his race, but there can be little doubt about his standing during his heyday.[16] His wife wrote of him in 1930:

> Paul Robeson was a hero: he fulfilled the ideal of nearly every class of Negro. Those who admired intellect pointed to his Phi Beta Kappa key; those who admired physical prowess talked about his remarkable record. His simplicity and charm were captivating; everyone was glad that he was so typically negroid in appearance, color and features ... He soon became Harlem's special favourite, and is so still, everyone knew and admired and liked him.[17]

There was criticism at the time from black writers that the roles he was play-ing were too narrow a range of stereotypes, that Joe in *Showboat* was 'a lazy, good natured, lolling darkey' and that Brutus Jones in *The Emperor Jones* was a vicious and cowardly tyrant.[18] Robeson was conscious of the criticism and began to talk to the press about his desire to play 'positive black roles'. He declared himself anxious to play famous blacks from history (Pushkin, Dumas, Hannibal, Menelik, Chaka, Toussaint L'Ouverture, the composer Samuel Coleridge-Taylor, the boxer Joe Louis). He praised Rider Haggard's *Allan Quatermain* for containing 'an excellent negro part in Umslopagaas'. He told the *Daily Express*:

> We are a great race, greater in tradition and culture than the American race. Why should we copy something that's inferior? I am going to pro-duce plays, make films, sing chants and prayers, all with the view in mind to show my poor people that their culture traces back to the great civi-lizations of Persia, China and the Jews.[19]

According to Robeson's biographer Martin Bauml Duberman, who has analysed Robeson's statements and writings, he rejected both that form of black nationalism that sought salvation in a literal (as opposed to spiritual) return to Africa and the assimilationist option by which blacks lost their dis-tinctiveness. In the early 1930s he was advocating the idea of cultural plural-ism in which blacks retained a strong racial identification. But by the end of the 1930s, after his exposure to the Spanish Civil War and the Soviet Union, he tilted more to revolutionary internationalism, stressing the overriding importance of human values and the solidarity of the workers of the world. But for the most part he sought to balance the ideas of black cultural distinctive-ness and international unity.[20]

The formulation of his views began when, in his own words, he 'discovered Africa' and became an advocate of blacks returning to their 'roots'. He studied and wrote about African culture and languages. He and his wife Essie became honorary members of the West African Students' Union and friends of such future black leaders as Kwame Nkrumah and Jomo Kenyatta. As he recalled in 1953:

> I 'discovered' Africa in London, that discovery back in the twenties – pro-foundly influenced my life. Like most of Africa's children in America, I had known little about the land of our fathers. But in England, … I came to know many Africans … and spent many hours talking with them …
> As an artist it was most natural that my first interest in Africa was cultural.
> Culture: The foreign rulers of that continent insisted there was no culture

worthy of the name in Africa. But already musicians and sculptors in Europe were astir with their discovery of African art. And, as I plunged with excited interest into my studies of Africa at the London University and elsewhere, I came to see that African culture was indeed a treasure-store for the world ... I now felt as one with my African friends and became filled with a great, flowing pride in these riches, new found to me. I learned that along with the towering achievements of the cultures of ancient Greece and China there stood the culture of Africa, unseen and denied by the imperialist looters of Africa's material wealth. I came to see the root sources of my own people's culture, especially in our music which is still the richest and most healthy in America.[21]

The corollary of this was a return to African roots. In an article entitled 'I want to be an African', written in 1934, Robeson argued the need to rediscover the African heritage and in particular African culture: 'In my music, my plays, my films, I want to carry always this central idea: to be African.'[22] He argued strongly that Africans should master European technology but retain their own cultural identity.

He also came to believe in the solidarity of the working classes of the world, both black and white. In his autobiography, he wrote:

It was in Britain ... that I learned that the essential character of a nation is determined not by the upper classes but by the common people and that the common people of all nations are truly brothers in the great family of mankind ... This belief in the oneness of humankind ... has existed within me side by side with my deep attachment to the cause of my own race.[23]

The final element in his political philosophy came with his discovery of the Soviet Union which he visited for the first time in 1934. He found there a workers' state that outlawed racial prejudice and he promptly sent his son there to be educated. In an interview with *The Daily Worker* in 1935 he declared:

I was not prepared for the happiness I see on every face in Moscow. I was aware that there was no starvation here, but I was not prepared for the bounding life; the feeling of safety and abundance and freedom that I find wherever I turn ... it is the government's duty to put down any opposi-tion to this really free society with a firm hand, and I hope they will always do it, for I already regard myself at home here. This is home to me. I feel more kinship to the Russian people under their new society than I ever felt anywhere else. It is obvious that there is no terror there, that all the masses of every race are contented and support their government.[24]

Throughout the 1930s he was active in left-wing causes. In 1935, in the play

Stevedore he played a black worker falsely accused of raping a white woman but who rallies black and white workers to support him. He joined the left-wing Unity Theatre in 1938 to act in Ben Bengal's *Plant in the Sun*, a powerful plea for trade unionism. He toured the provinces singing to the workers at cheap admission prices. He visited Spain during the Civil War to lend support to the Republican cause and gave concerts in Britain to raise money for it.

He turned to the cinema as the most influential mass medium of the age to translate his views to wider audience. In a long interview in *Film Weekly* in 1936, he outlined his views on the depiction of blacks in films:

> Although negroes have made their mark in the world of music, in litera-ture, and in the theatre, they have never yet got anywhere in the cinema, because America has seen them persistently as Old Black Joes and Uncle Toms. They have never been allowed to be more than stage puppets, fig-ures in the coloured 'Mammy and pappy' legend created by sentimental authors … When you think of films instead of plays, you must be sur-prised how very, very few there have been about coloured people. In fact, I know of only two that have attempted seriously to reveal something of the negro mind and life. *Hallelujah* … was a splendid failure, largely because it was a film in advance of its time; and *The Emperor Jones*, which I made in 1933, was too unusual and imaginative to achieve the popular success necessary to change existing screen ideas about coloured people.[25]

One of the most important reasons for this state of affairs, he thought, was the fact that 'the Southern States of America might not patronize realistic films about coloured folk'. So he turned to Britain as the base for his filmmaking and there from the first not only did his name appear above the title of his films but he was invariably top-billed. This was in itself an achievement and something which accorded with his aim. He set out to play distinctively African black heroes in order to help his people overcome a deep-seated sense of inferiority and to demonstrate that blacks were equal to, but different from, whites. He wrote in 1934:

> The suffering he has undergone has left an indelible mark on the negro's soul and at the present stage he suffers from an inferiority complex which finds its compensation in a desire to imitate the white man and his ways; but I am convinced that in this direction there is neither fulfilment nor peace for the negro. He is too radically different from the white man in his mental and emotional structure ever to be more than a spurious and uneasy imitation of him, if he persists in following this direction. His soul contains riches which can come to fruition, only if he retains intact the

full spate of his emotional awareness, and uses unswervingly the artistic endowments which nature has given him[26]

Robeson could never have achieved the status he sought in the Hollywood of the 1930s. He did appear in the title role of Dudley Murphy's film version of *The Emperor Jones* (1933), the dramatic account of the rise and fall of a negro railway porter who becomes the ruler of a Caribbean island. But it was an independent production made in New York and, although praised by critics, received only limited distribution and failed to make money. Robeson's performance is a convincing study in swaggering bravado and equally compelling when charting the physical and mental collapse that follows Jones's overthrow. But some black critics complained that it implied that when given power a black becomes a vicious and grasping tyrant.

Robeson's only Hollywood performances were in supporting roles as the faithful bale-toting 'darkie' of the Deep South, part of Hollywood's generalized stereotyping of blacks as 'toms, coons, mulattoes, mammies and bucks'.[27] Robeson gave a powerful rendition of 'Ole Man River' in *Showboat* (1936) but had little else to do. Then he was part of an embarrassing shanty-town sequence in the all-star *Tales of Manhattan* (1942). In a world where Stepin Fetchit's slow-witted menial and Hattie McDaniel's beaming maid were the favoured archetypes, there was no room for Robeson to fulfil his ambitions least of all to be a film star.

But in Britain he made six films, all of which were built around him and his talent. His size, massive and compelling, his warming smile, his innate dignity, his magnificent bass-baritone voice equally at home in ballads, arias and spirituals, all proclaimed him a star, unquestionably the most important since the nineteenth-century black American tragedian, Ira Aldridge, who also sought in Britain and continental Europe the kind of recognition that he was denied in his own country.

But Robeson's first attempt to bring African culture to the screen misfired. In pursuit of a plan to make a film of the popular Edgar Wallace *Sanders of the River* stories, producer Alexander Korda sent his brother, director Zoltan Korda, to Africa to shoot location footage of tribal dances and customs, as well as jungle flora and fauna. Zoltan returned with many reels of documentary footage from East and West Africa, around which Korda and his writers constructed a narrative. Robeson saw this footage, felt it provided an opportunity to bring African culture to a mass audience and signed to play Sanders's faithful ally, Chief Bosambo. Robeson said: 'I wanted to show that while the Imperialists contend that the Africans are 'barbarians and uncivilized', that they have a culture all their own, and that they have as much intelligence as any other people.'[28] Robeson was given top-billing over Leslie Banks, who played Sanders, and sang four songs, based on authentic tribal chants recorded in Africa and Westernized by composer Mischa Spoliansky. But the finished film appalled Robeson. He walked out of the premiere and refused to work for Korda again. He also insisted in future on having approval of the final cut of his films written into his contract.

The tribal dances and music were there certainly but they were woven into a narrative in which Commissioner Sanders aided by Chief Bosambo puts down a tribal uprising in Nigeria, inspiring the trade paper *Kinematograph Weekly* to declare that it was 'a fine tribute to British rule in Africa'.[29] Bosambo was conceived in entirely Western terms, as an archetype well established in imperial fiction; a combination of courage, devotion, boastful sexuality and childish naughtiness. Similarly his relationship with his wife Lilongo is seen in strictly European terms. They love each other. She henpecks him. He risks his life to rescue her. Yet, as Boris Gussman has written: 'The main difference between African and European marriage is that the idea of romantic love does not occur among Africans.'[30] There is equally little appreciation of the African character judged in African terms. Gussman also writes:

> To these Europeans because they failed to understand the motives that prompted him or the bonds that held him in check, he was seen as super-stitious, irrational, lazy, immoral and of a childish or at least adolescent mentality.[31]

The father–child relationship between Sanders and the natives is repeatedly commented upon by characters in the film and the relationship between Sanders and Bosambo is established at the very start of the film when Bosambo, in reality a Liberian convict, passes himself off as the legitimate chief of the Ochori. Sanders confronts him with the truth; Bosambo shamefacedly admits it and is rewarded with the chieftainship. Appropriately enough, they meet over Sanders's desk, Sanders seated and Bosambo standing, establishing a headmaster–pupil relationship which is maintained throughout

The film was roundly attacked by left-wing and black organizations in both Britain and America. Robeson defended himself by saying that the imperialist slant had been introduced in the cutting and in scenes in which he did not appear. This is not, however, convincing, since Robeson himself in one of his songs hymns the praises of the Commissioner:

Sandi the strong, Sandi the wise
Righter of wrong, hater of lies
Laughed as he fought, worked as he played
As he has taught, let it be made.

Nor is there any sign of awkwardness or embarrassment in his virile, charismatic and engaging performance. His very presence in fact is a powerful boost to imperialism since his convincing and attractive performance as a loyal ally of the British serves to endorse the film's worldview. In 1938 he explained the reasons for his involvement:

> *Sanders of the River* ... attracted me because the material that London Films brought back from Africa seemed to me good honest pictures of African folk ways. The film has been criticized on the grounds that dressing up in a leopard skin I was letting down something or other. I looked at it from a different angle. Robeson dressed in a leopard skin along with half a dozen other guys from Africa, all looking more or less the same, seemed to me to prove something about my race that I thought worth proving. But in the completed version *Sanders of the River* resolved itself into a piece of flagwaving in which I wasn't interested. As far as I was concerned it was a total loss.[32]

By this point he had already made clear his views about imperialism in Africa in the prologue he recorded along with a theme song for Joseph Best's 1936 documentary *Africa Looks Up*, eventually released as *My Song Goes Forth*. Robeson explained:

> Every foot of Africa is now parcelled out among the white races. Why has this happened? What has prompted them to go there? If you listen to men like Mussolini, they will tell you it is to civilize – a divine task, entrusted to the enlightened peoples to carry the torch of light and learning, and to benefit the African people ... Africa was opened up by the white man for the benefit of himself – to obtain the wealth it contained.[33]

But before his view of *Sanders* firmed up, he does seem to have seen merit in it. In 1935 he was praising *Sanders* for the positive effect it was having on the perceptions and attitudes of American audiences:

> On many occasions people would come up to me in small towns, where formerly I could have walked unrecognized on the streets, congratulate me on my performance as Bosambo and tell me that the film had given them new ideas about the African Negro. Most of them confessed before seeing the picture they had regarded the negro as a violent savage, having gleaned their notions of him from such films as *Trader Horn* and the Tarzan adventures, in which the natives were depicted as paint-daubed,

7   The black man as ally of Empire: Paul Robeson in *Sanders of the River* (1935)

gibberish-mouthing, devil-worshipping creatures. But they had come to
see him as a man with lucid emotions and a code and language of his
own.[34]

The problem for Robeson was that black activists disliked it.

Robeson, however, did make some valuable contacts on *Sanders*. Major
Claude Wallace, the technical adviser, and Dorothy Holloway, Korda's casting
director, who together wrote for Robeson a new screen story, *Song of Freedom*
(1936), based on an old African legend recounted to Robeson by Wallace. *Song
of Freedom* (1936), directed by J. Elder Wills for a small independent company
(Hammer), was in many ways Robeson's answer both to critics of *Sanders* and
of *Emperor Jones* and the first systematic attempt to dramatize his own ideas.
He declared of it:

> I believe *The Song of Freedom* is the first picture to give a true picture of
> many aspects of the life of the coloured man in the west. Hitherto on the
> screen, he has been caricatured or presented only as a comedy character.
> This film shows him as a real man with problems to be solved, difficulties
> to be overcome.[35]

Robeson plays John Zinga, descendant of the ancient kings of Casanga, but born in London and now working as a London docker. After a prologue that uniquely in British films depicts the horrors of the eighteenth-century slave trade as well as its abolition in 1838, the opening scenes of the film show Zinga and his wife Ruth (Elizabeth Welch) totally integrated into the dockland community and accepted as equals by the white workers. Zinga is the 'life and soul' of the local pub, while his black friend Monty (Robert Adams) lodges happily with an amiable white couple Bert and Nell. But Zinga feels himself to be African and longs to return to his roots. The film movingly stresses, and Robeson feelingly portrays, Zinga's need to discover his true cultural identity. In a time-honoured Hollywood plot device, he is discovered singing in the pub by a voluble Italian impresario, Donozetti (Esme Percy), and transformed into an international opera star. His success enables him to fulfil his desire to return to Africa. He arrives at the island of Casanga to find it sunk in superstition, savagery and disease and run by witchdoctors. After various trials, he breaks the power of the witchdoctors and begins the introduction of Western technology and medicine, while assuring the natives that they will retain their own culture and identity.

The film demonstrates contrary to *Emperor Jones* that a black man ruling blacks can be wise, enlightened and dedicated to his duty. To point up the contrast, the opera in which Zinga sings is very obviously based on *The Emperor Jones*. Called *The Black Emperor*, it features Jones's final forest flight and death after his overthrow. The film also deliberately annexes the imagery of *Sanders*. White-suited and solar-topeed and accompanied by a comic black servant called Monty, Zinga and Ruth are held captive by witchdoctors at the end but they are rescued not by a white imperialist in his gunboat as in *Sanders* but by Zinga singing the King's Song which leads to his recognition by the natives as their rightful ruler. African culture triumphs over the need for Western military technology.

Song of Freedom was an honourable and well-intentioned film which stressed the central elements of the Robeson worldview (the validity of African culture, the return to African roots, the international solidarity of the workers). Noting that the film was 'a serious plea for the liberty and proper guidance of the negro race', *The Times* stressed the importance of Robeson to the whole venture:

> The whole story may be melodramatic and not well constructed but Mr. Robeson has an astonishing power of giving dignity and emotional significance to every event in which he appears, and that even when he only uses his voice in speech. When he sings, as he often does in the course of

the film, he at once raises the whole level of the production above that of popular entertainment or that of a simplified message and moral.[36]

Robeson's next two films may also be seen as a bid to exorcise the memory of *Sanders*. Robeson returned to a major studio, Gaumont British, for their screen version of Rider Haggard's classic *King Solomon's Mines* (1937). It is on one level a straightforward imperial adventure story, showing a group of white adventurers in search of the fabulous diamond mines and – despite Robeson's preface to *My Song Goes Forth* – celebrates European exploitation of Africa's resources. The Africans, characterized by singing, dancing, tyranny, slaughter and superstition, are cowed by a handful of whites who use firearms and a providential eclipse to persuade the Africans they are gods. The English are represented by canny pipe-smoking white hunter Allan Quatermain, aristocratic sportsman Sir Henry Curtis and monocled eccentric naval officer, Captain Good R. N., here joined, unlike in Haggard's original, by a brace of Irish fortune-hunters, Kathy O'Brien and her father Patrick.

But an alternative reading is possible. This version, unlike the book and the later Hollywood version of the film, centres squarely on the character of Umbopa, a part which Robeson accepted, seeing 'not just as a splendid savage but a man of real thoughts and ambitions'.[37] Robeson's Umbopa is indeed just that. Once again top-billed, and given three Spoliansky songs to sing, Robeson's Umbopa is not only mentor, protector, adviser and guide of the English explorers but he also uses them to further his own restoration to the throne of the Kukuana. Once he reaches Kukuanaland, Umbopa effectively takes charge of the expedition. He and the whites stand side-by-side in the battle to defeat the evil King Twala. It is Umbopa who rescues the whites when they are trapped in the mines by the witchdoctor Gagool. The film closes with Umbopa shaking hands with Allan Quatermain and seeing the whites off, singing *Mighty Mountain*. The final image, then, is not of the white explorers leaving but of Umbopa, now king of an independent black country.

The next film, for another independent company (Buckingham) was Thornton Freeland's *Jericho* (US title: *Dark Sands*; 1937), a vigorous and enjoyable melodrama, partly shot in superb North African locations. It provided Robeson with his first opportunity actually to visit Africa. He took the title role – the black American soldier Jericho Jackson – because the role of a black soldier 'is a new role for a negro. Then the idea of friendship between black and white is shown in the relationship between Jackson and the doughboy. Lastly, the background is going to be genuine.'[38] What is remarkable in the

The black man as independent ruler: Paul Robeson in *King Solomon's Mines* (1937)   **8**
with Cedric Hardwicke, Roland Young, Anna Lee and John Loder.

film, on the surface pure escapism, is the heroic central role of Jericho, college man, athlete, scholar, medical student. It might not have been remarked on if this super-hero had been white, but here he is black and is given a comic white sidekick (Wallace Ford) who dies saving Jericho's life. It is also remarkable in that it begins in 1917 with a black American regiment on a troop-ship bound for Europe and Jericho establishing his heroic credentials by saving a nervous private from bullying and later rescuing his trapped comrades when the ship is torpedoed. But when he accidentally kills the bullying sergeant, he is tried and sentenced to death. To escape death, he flees to North Africa.

Like *Song of Freedom*, *Jericho* contains a riposte to *Sanders* in the presence of a Sanders-type figure, Captain Mack, the white commander of the black regiment, who describes the blacks as 'children' and treats Jericho as his head prefect. Played by the British actor Henry Wilcoxon without a trace of an American accent, he conforms exactly to the stereotype of the white imperial hero. But the focus shifts from him after Jericho's escape, when Wilcoxon is imprisoned and cashiered for allowing Jericho to escape. Jericho, meanwhile, establishes himself as the ruler of an Arab tribe, to whom he brings unity, justice and Western medicine. When Mack, eventually released, tracks him down, he decides to leave Jericho in his Saharan kingdom rather than attempt to return him to America. So once again a Robeson hero had returned to Africa and shown himself capable of wise and majestic rulership. *Kinematograph Weekly* recorded: 'Paul Robeson, magnificently versatile in the main part, is the kingpin of the fantastic but interesting and popular entertainment. Very good general booking, one with novelty and star values, to consolidate its success.'[39]

Having played two chieftains, it was back to the docks for his next film, *Big Fella* (1937). Ostensibly based on the novel *Banjo* by the Jamaican writer Claude MacKay, it took only the setting (the Marseilles waterfront) and the leading character (a musical black vagabond) from its source. It was produced by the same team as *Song of Freedom*, with J. Elder Wills again directing and Elizabeth Welch co-starring. Robeson's wife Essie played a café proprietor. Robeson, singing five tuneful songs, played the title role, Joe, a shiftless dock-worker who enjoys loafing and singing. Like Jericho Jackson, he is given a loyal white sidekick (James Hayter) as well as a black one (Lawrence Brown), and he functions as an equal in the multi-racial, prejudice-free working-class community of the Marseilles waterfront.

The slender storyline hinges on Joe's relationship with a rich English boy, Gerald Oliphant (a very pukka Eldon Grant). Gerald, although believed kidnapped, has in fact run away from his parents in search of adventure. Joe befriends him and looking after him gives Joe a new sense of responsibility. Gerald is, however, snatched by another dockworker Spike and returned to his parents for a reward. The boy mopes but a visit from Joe cheers him up and his parents, with concern neither for colour nor class, offer Joe a position as Gerald's companion. But in the end Joe, with his newfound sense of responsibility, opts for a settled life with his girlfriend, café entertainer Manda (Elizabeth Welch).

Throughout the film Robeson appears as cheerful, generous and immensely likeable, and in his dealings with the boy wise, kind and loyal. One reviewer noted that, 'Robeson acts the part with such naturalness that you might think it was his own self.'[40] *Kinematograph Weekly*, summing up the general critical reaction, described the film as a

> colourful comedy drama … lifted to box-office heights by the intelligent acting and superb singing of Paul Robeson. He, partnered by Elizabeth Welch, … carries the slight but amusing story and converts it into entertainment of immense family and general appeal.[41]

The black man as working-class hero: Paul Robeson in *The Proud Valley* (1940).   **9**

Some commentators claimed he was demeaning his race by playing such a lazy, shiftless character, but Robeson pointed out that the story was about Joe's regeneration and he wanted his characters to be human rather than superhuman.[42]

Although *Big Fella* stressed the theme of black and white working-class solidarity, it was his final British film *The Proud Valley* (1940), the film of which he was later to declare himself proudest, that explored this theme in most detail. In 1938 he had told a reporter: 'I am tired of playing Stepin' Fetchit comics and savages with leopard skin and spear.'[43] *The Proud Valley*, produced by Michael Balcon's Ealing Studios, was specifically written for Robeson by left-wing theatre producer Herbert Marshall, who had produced *Plant in the Sun*, and his wife Alfredda Brilliant. Their screen story, inspired by a real character working in the Welsh mines, was turned into a screenplay by the social-realist novelist Louis Golding, Welsh miner turned writer Jack Jones and the film's young director, Pen Tennyson, whose previous film *There Ain't No Justice* had shown a concern for fidelity and dignity in its depiction of working-class life.

The Proud Valley sought to do justice both to the aspirations of the working class and of the black man in Britain, an equation not without foundation if Lorimer's thesis is correct. It is imbued with a respect for its subjects that is as moving as it was rare in British cinema of the 1930s. Robeson plays David Goliath, an unemployed stoker who gets a job at Blaendy Colliery with the help of Dick Parry (Edward Chapman), conductor of the local male voice choir, who needs a bass for a performance of *Elijah* at the Eisteddfod. Initial prejudice against him is overcome with the help of the Parrys with whom he lodges. But then Dick is killed in a mining accident and the colliery is closed down. Unemployment creates great hardship for the village – the miners are seen scrabbling for coal on the slagheap, queuing at the labour exchange, seeking credit at the corner shop, avoiding the rent collector. David joins a deputation of miners, led by Dick's son Emlyn, who walk to London to plead for the mine's reopening. In the original ending of the film, they were to take over the mine and run it as a cooperative. But the outbreak of World War Two overtook the film and a new ending was devised in which the mine is reopened to help the war effort. During operations to make the mine safe for the resumption of work, David is killed, sacrificing his life to save the new friends he has made. Despite the climactic tragedy, the film's mood is one of essential optimism as David is integrated into the community and the community itself is integrated into the nation with the onset of war. The last shots see the first coal being brought out of the pit through a pithed decorated with Union Jacks and crowds singing 'Land of my Fathers'.

The use of song in *Proud Valley* serves to underline the multiple identities embodied by Robeson's David Goliath and demonstrate the possibility of a black British identity. David is working class and sings with his mates 'They can't stop us singing', the 'them' and 'us' underlining the existence of a class society. He is Protestant, singing 'Lord God of Abraham' from Mendelssohn's *Elijah*, which, after Handel's *Messiah*, is the great Protestant oratorio in Britain. He is by adoption Welsh, singing over the final shots 'Land of my Fathers'. He is black, singing movingly in tribute to Dick Parry the negro spiritual 'Deep River'.

The film was a fitting climax to Robeson's British acting career. After the outbreak of war he returned to the USA. He opposed the war as an imperialist conflict until the Nazi invasion of Russia when he became an enthusiastic supporter of the Allied war effort, enjoying his greatest period of popularity with American audiences.

Two even more politically committed films remained unmade. Robeson was invited to Russia in 1934 to discuss *Black Majesty*, a film of the life of the Haitian revolutionary leader Toussaint L'Ouverture, for Sergei Eisenstein. Nothing came of it, though Robeson did appear in a play on the same subject by C. L. R. James in London in 1936. On his return from Spain, Robeson talked of making a film about the life of Oliver Laws, negro commander of the Lincoln Battalion of the International Brigade, who had been killed in battle. But nothing came of this either. Even if it had, it would very likely have been fatally compromised by censorship restrictions, like Walter Wanger's *Blockade*, Hollywood's only serious contribution to the Spanish Civil War debate and a film which conspicuously avoided naming the two sides in the conflict.

The total effect of Robeson's films is likely to have been greater in Britain than in his native America, for the simple reason that they were more widely shown in Britain than in the United States. Only *Sanders of the River* and *King Solomon's Mines* were widely shown there. *Jericho* and *The Proud Valley* had limited showings, while *Song of Freedom* and *Big Fella* were not shown at all. In Britain, on the other hand, *Sanders*, first released in 1935, was reissued in 1938, 1943 and 1947. *Song of Freedom*, first released in 1936, was reissued in 1940 and 1946. *The Proud Valley*, first shown in 1940, was reissued in 1943 and 1948. *Jericho*, first released in 1937, was reissued in 1947. *King Solomon's Mines*, also released in 1937, was reissued in 1942. Only *Big Fella* was not reissued. This meant that in Britain Robeson's starring vehicles had a lifespan that covered not only the 1930s but also the 1940s.

The precise effect of his films is difficult to gauge. The coloured population of Britain was small during these years. So he is likely to have achieved his greatest impact on white audiences. Since the prevailing stereotypes of blacks in films were variations on either subservience or villainy, it is likely that his greatest achievement was to create a distinctive, dominant and unquestionable black film hero. This hero was either a wise and just native ruler (*Sanders of the River, King Solomon's Mines, Jericho*) or a working-class stalwart (*Big Fella, Proud Valley*) or both (*Song of Freedom*). He offers to the mass audience two alternative images. Years before the popularity of *Roots*, his roles highlight the importance of the African origins of the negro and stress the value and integrity of African culture, particularly African music and song. Robeson projects the positive image of an African ruler ruling Africans and doing so beneficently, wisely and effectively. On the other hand, and in conformity with his Socialist beliefs, he offers the prescient vision of a multi-racial Britain in which black and white working-classes live side by side as equals in tolerance and mutual respect.

In addition, he neutralizes the perceived sexual threat from the black. The image he adopts is virile and commanding but dignified, friendly and non-threatening.[44] He is either given no love interest or a black wife/fiancée (black American singers Elizabeth Welch in *Big Fella* and *Song of Freedom* and Nina Mae McKinney in *Sanders of the River*, and Sudanese discovery Princess Kouka in *Jericho*) with whom he enjoys a relationship of tolerant and settled mutual affection.

For all Robeson's criticism of *Sanders*, for all his pessimism about his ability to get his ideas across in films and for all the inevitable limitations attached to putting a positive black image on the screen in a generally racist age, his British film career does constitute an important and honourable episode in the struggle to obtain racial equality and dignity for black citizens both in Britain and America.

Notes

1 Colin Holmes, *John Bull's Island: immigration and British society 1871–1971*, London, 1988; Colin Holmes, *A Tolerant Country? Immigrants, refugees and minorities in Britain*, London, 1991, Peter Fryer, *Staying Power: the history of black people in Britain*, London, 1984.

2 Jeffrey Richards, *Visions of Yesterday*, London, 1973, p. 11.

3 Christine Bolt, *Victorian Attitudes to Race*, London, 1971; Brian V. Street, *The Savage in Literature*, London,1974; V. G. Kiernan, *The Lords of Human Kind*, Harmondsworth, 1972.

4 Douglas Lorimer, *Colour, Class and the Victorians*, Leicester, 1978.

5 Lorimer, *Colour, Class and the Victorians*, p. 207.

6 Philip D. Curtin, *The Image of Africa: British ideas and action 1780–1850*, Madison, Wisconsin, 1964, p. 378.

7 Curtin, *Image of Africa*, p. xii.

8 Curtin, *Image of Africa*, p. 332.

9 G. A. Henty, *By Sheer Pluck*, London, 1884, p. 118.

10 Henty, *By Sheer Pluck*, p. 118.

11 Kiernan, *Lords of Human Kind*, p. 328.

12 Paul Robeson, *Here I Stand*, London, 1958, p. 60. For a full account of Robeson's life and career see Marie Seton, *Paul Robeson*, London, 1958, and Martin Bauml Duberman, *Paul Robeson*, London, 1989.

13 *Daily Express*, 5 July 1928.

14 Duberman, *Paul Robeson*, pp. 123–4.

15 Eslanda Goode Robeson, *Paul Robeson, Negro*, London, 1930, pp. 96–7.

16 Jim Pines, *Blacks in Films*, London, 1975, pp. 31–2; Donald Bogle, *Toms, Coons, Mulattoes, Mammies and Bucks*, New York, 1973, pp. 131–40.

17 Robeson, *Paul Robeson*, pp. 67–8.

18 Duberman, *Paul Robeson*, pp. 114–15, pp. 168–9; Peter Noble, *The Negro in*

Films, London, 1947, pp. 57–8.

19 *Daily Express*, 4 August 1933. On his choice of roles, see Duberman, *Paul Robeson*, pp. 166–9.

20 Duberman, *Paul Robeson*, pp. 172–3.

21 Philip Foner (ed.), *Paul Robeson Speaks: writings, speeches, interviews 1918–74*, London, 1978, pp. 351–2.

22 Foner (ed.), *Paul Robeson Speaks*, p. 91.

23 Robeson, *Here I Stand*, pp. 56–7.

24 Foner, *Paul Robeson Speaks*, p. 95.

25 *Film Weekly*, 23 May 1936.

26 *The Spectator*, 15 June 1934.

27 The classifications are those of the black writer Donald Bogle in his 1973 book of the same title. For a detailed and thoughtful account of Hollywood's depiction of blacks in this period see Thomas Cripps, *Slow Fade to Back: the negro in American film, 1900–1942*, London and New York, 1977. For blacks in British films see Peter Noble, *The Negro in Films*, London, 1947. Robeson also starred in the silent film *Body and Soul* (1924) one of a series of black 'underground' films for all-black audiences and the experimental film *Borderline* (1930), made in Switzerland and seen only by intellectual coteries.

28 Foner (ed.), *Paul Robeson Speaks*, p. 107.

29 *Kinematograph Weekly*, 4 April 1935.

30. Boris Gussman, *Out in the Midday Sun*, London, 1962, p. 82.

31 Gussman, *Out in the Midday Sun*, p. 64.

32 Foner (ed.), *Paul Robeson Speaks*, p. 203.

33 Duberman, *Paul Robeson*, p. 203.

34 *Film Weekly*, 23 May 1936.

35 *Film Weekly*, 23 May 1936.

36 *The Times*, 21 September 1936.

37 Seton, *Paul Robeson*, p. 108.

38 Seton, *Paul Robeson*, p. 109.

39 *Kinematograph Weekly*, 26 August 1937.

40 Unidentified cutting, BFI *Big Fella* microfiche.

41 *Kinematograph Weekly*, 24 June 1937.

42 Noble, *The Negro in Films*, pp. 120–1.

43 Duberman, *Paul Robeson*, p. 227.

44 The argument about Robeson's desexualisation in films is advanced at length in Richard Dyer, *Heavenly Bodies*, London, 1987, pp. 67–139.

Part II

Nation

4

World War Two

War always brings the concept of national identity into sharp focus for identity is at the heart of the national propaganda effort. At the centre of British propaganda in World War Two was the Ministry of Information, its task to present the national case to the public at home and abroad. To this end, it was responsible for the preparation and issue of national propaganda, the control of news and the maintenance of morale.

In a memorandum to the War Cabinet, Lord Macmillan, the first Minister of Information, laid down the principal themes for propaganda. These were: what Britain is fighting for, how Britain fights and the need for sacrifice if the war is to be won. The memorandum stressed that in all propaganda there was to be emphasis on British life and character, showing 'our independence, toughness of fibre, sympathy with the underdog, etc.' British ideas and institutions such as freedom and parliamentary democracy were to be contrasted with German ideas and institutions such as the Gestapo.[1] The memorandum even gave examples of pre-war films which fulfilled the task of depicting British character in the approved way. Fascinatingly, these included *Goodbye Mr. Chips* and *The Lady Vanishes* and histories of national heroes (Captain Scott, etc.). *Goodbye Mr. Chips*, made by Metro-Goldwyn-Mayer in Britain and a great success with audiences both in Britain and America, had traced the career of a young public school master from the beginning of his career to his death. Robert Donat had won an Oscar for his performance in the title role and Chips had clearly come to be seen as an epitome of British national character: stoicism, humour, dedication to duty.

The Lady Vanishes (1938), Alfred Hitchcock's superb thriller, was a light-hearted examination of the conduct of the British abroad. Most of the action takes place on a train crossing the fictional Central European country of Bandrika. Among its passengers are a couple of Englishmen, Charters and Caldicott, invented by scriptwriters Frank Launder and Sidney Gilliat and not in the original Ethel Lina White novel. Unforgettably played by Basil Radford and Naunton Wayne, they became national institutions. In *The Lady Vanishes* they are hastening back to England for the test match. They complain constantly about the food and the accommodation but cricket forms their principal topic of conversation. The other English travellers are equally eccentric. They include Miss Froy (Dame May Whitty), the tweedy governess with her personal supply of herbal tea, and Gilbert (Michael Redgrave), a feckless musicologist who is writing a book on Bandrikan folk music. But all reveal hidden strengths. Miss Froy is in fact a daring British secret agent being pursued by the Bandrikan secret police, who, from their uniform and accents, are clearly intended to be seen as the Gestapo. (When the film was remade – unsuccessfully – in 1979, it was set in Germany and the secret police were the Gestapo, Charters and Caldicott were played by Arthur Lowe and Ian Carmichael, but – sign of the times – the hero was a charmless American, Elliott Gould.) The restaurant car is uncoupled and besieged by the secret police who are after Miss Froy. The only passengers there are English – because it is teatime. Gilbert takes charge and organizes the defence. Charters and Caldicott acquit themselves courageously: Charters is shot in the arm, but carries on bravely, Caldicott turns out to be a crack shot. They embody the characteristics of stoicism, humour, decency, anti-intellectualism, determination, good sportsmanship. They became popular national characters, evidence of the British ability to laugh at themselves in a basically admiring way. They returned in the same characters in *Night Train to Munich* (1940), this time pitted against the Germans. They were featured in two radio serials, one of them filmed as *Crook's Tour* (1940). But fascinatingly, in a later Launder and Gilliat film they were used to emphasize the social transformation wrought by the war.

In *Millions Like Us* (1943) which charts the experiences of ordinary women drafted to work in an aircraft factory, Launder and Gilliat punctuate the film with three sharply funny sequences featuring the celebrated pair. In the first, newly commissioned and seated in a first-class train compartment, they are invaded by child evacuees; in the second, while aircraft watching on the coast, they discuss the plight of a wealthy man whose valet had retired to Weston-Super-Mare and who had had to follow him there because it was so difficult to get staff and he had not dressed himself for thirty years; and finally, they are observed standing in a third class carriage eating Spam sandwiches and saying they never thought it would come to this.

Perhaps surprisingly, Captain Scott, whose qualities have already been assessed, did not feature in a wartime film. Two national heroes, however, were featured, stressing parallels between the Second World War and the Napoleonic War, with Napoleon as an analogue of Hitler; Laurence Olivier played Nelson in *Lady Hamilton* (1940) and Robert Donat played William Pitt the Younger in *Young Mr. Pitt* (1942). Both Nelson and Pitt are constructed for the screen as embodiments of British character.

The national character remained in essence what it had been before the war. Two qualities in particular run through almost every wartime film. First – and most vital – is the sense of humour. This showed itself in the national penchant for comedy films, with George Formby the top British box-office attraction from 1938 to 1943, but it was also a strong component even in serious war films. In *Pimpernel Smith* (1941), General von Graum, the Gestapo chief, investigates the English secret weapon – their sense of humour. He ploughs through P. G. Wodehouse, Edward Lear, Lewis Carroll and *Punch*, reading extracts to his bemused assistants, without raising a laugh. He solemnly concludes that the English sense of humour is a myth. The point of this sequence is in a sense the justification of the entire film which successfully and consistently ridicules the Germans as uncultured, ungentlemanly and humourless. The film demonstrates unequivocally that a sense of humour is the English secret weapon: it is the essential quality which separates a civilized society from an uncivilized one. This is a point underlined in the final speech of *The Demi-Paradise* (1943), in which the Russian engineer Ivan Kouznetsoff, stressing the similarities between the British and Russian allies, sees their sense of humour as a key characteristic of the British and essential to their democracy.

The second quality is stoicism, or emotional restraint, the essence of the much parodied British fondness for understatement, reserve and the stiff upper lip. This is seen as a central and admirable national characteristic. *The Way to the Stars* (1945) was the last great film of the war and was voted by *Daily Mail* readers the best film of the entire war. There was a remarkable critical consensus about its qualities. The *Daily Mail* (24 April 1946) called it 'a masterpiece of understatement.' The *Daily Sketch* (8 June 1945) said: 'In all its admirable emotional restraint it is far more moving than any picture deliberately designed as a tearjerker.' C. A. Lejeune in *The Observer* noted: 'These people are real people, and like real people they do not make much of their private emotions.'[2]

10   Fighting for a better future: Michael Redgrave, Basil Radford and John Mills in *The Way to the Stars* (1945).

The *Sunday Times*'s Dilys Powell, surveying the films of the war years, wrote that director Anthony Asquith 'succeeded admirably in capturing the emotion trembling beneath the laconic phrase, the controlled emotion'.[3] The critics almost universally praised the film for its realism, Englishness and emotional restraint. In a sense, they were equating all three.

One of the central themes of the film is loss. During the course of the film, Squadron Leader Carter, Flight Lieutenant Archdale and Captain Johnny Hollis are all killed. These losses are invariably received with a pain that is doubly moving by its restraint. There is no flag waving, no soupy soundtrack music, no over-the-top emotionalism. Campbell Dixon, writing in the *Daily Telegraph* (8 June 1945), declared that 'few films have been more essentially English', and called upon his readers to 'imagine how Hollywood would have treated it – the tears from the women, the maudlin sentiment from the dead man's friends and at least one big bout of hysteria from somebody'. The Englishness is thus seen to lie in emotional restraint. It is most succinctly expressed in the two John Pudney poems, *Missing* and *Johnny-in-the-clouds*, which in the film are the work of David Archdale. Sparely and economically, the poems underline one of the principal morals of the film: do not make a fuss when people die but carry on working for a better world so that the sacrifice shall not have been in vain.

A third characteristic came to be stressed during the war and this was a direct outcome of the wartime situation. Heroic individualism had characterized pre-war depictions of the national character, whether it was in the comical adventures of working-class folk heroes like Gracie Fields and George Formby or the imperial adventures of upper-class officers and gentlemen like Leslie Banks and John Clements. But during the war individual heroes and heroines gradually took second place to collective heroes and heroines and tolerance became a vital characteristic. Ivan Kouznetsoff stresses it in his speech in *The Demi-Paradise*. The philosopher George Santayana had written of England that it is 'a paradise of individuality, eccentricity, heresy, anomalies, hobbies and humours'. The task of the authorities in wartime was to reconcile this paramount individualism with the need for corporate effort. As Professor F. C. Bartlett wrote, domestic propaganda must recognize

> that men act where their affections, sentiments and emotions are engaged, but that these must and can be led by intelligence without losing their strength. It knows that the stability of the social order does not depend upon everybody saying the same thing, holding the same opinions, feeling the same feelings, but upon a freely achieved unity which with many sectional and individual differences is nevertheless able to maintain an expanding and consistent pattern of life.[5]

It is this which inspired the making of those films which dealt with mixed groups of people from different class and regional backgrounds who are successfully welded together for the war effort while retaining their individuality. This was the key: individuality (characteristic difference) as opposed to individualism (a philosophy of the self), and individuality maintained within the collectivity of heroism, the people as hero, learning tolerance of each other and building cooperation, comradeship and community through it.

This is new, and it represents a significant change in the national image as projected by film. Initially, however, the cinema continued to reflect the class-bound tradition of the 1930s, resolutely middle-class in tone and values with little realistic depiction of the lives of working-class people. In films like *Night Train to Munich* (1940), the war was treated as a gentlemanly jape in which an upper-class hero (Rex Harrison) ran rings round the humourless, ranting, dunderhead Hun.

The period did produce one authentic British wartime gentleman hero:

Leslie Howard. When the plane carrying Howard back from a lecture tour of Spain and Portugal was shot down by German fighter planes over the Bay of Biscay on 1 June 1943, *The Observer*'s film critic C. A. Lejeune recalled: 'Perhaps no single war casualty gave the general public such an acute sense of personal loss. Leslie Howard was more than just a popular film actor ... He had become in an odd way a symbol of England, standing for all that is most deeply rooted in the British character.'[6] In a piece headed 'Lost Leader' she wrote:

> The public really loved him. I shall never forget the electric thrill that ran through the crowd outside St. Paul's Cathedral when he appeared as Nelson in the pageant of the *Cathedral Steps*. That brief moment stopped the show.[7]

She also wrote: 'he had a passion for England and the English idea that was almost Shakespearean.'[8] The *Manchester Guardian* talked of 'a frank intensely English quality in Howard's voice, face and bearing'.[9] Howard had returned to England from Hollywood as war loomed, burning with a desire to contribute to the war effort. His activities were prodigious. He broadcast regularly to the United States, his long residence in, and affection for, that country making him an ideal person to win over hearts and minds in a land where isolationism and Anglophobia were still strong. He joined the ideas committee of the Ministry of Information. He acted in the ministry's first full-length feature film *49th Parallel*, playing an English scholar and aesthete roused to action when fugitive Nazi submariners destroy his books and pictures, and in the documentary short *From the Four Corners*, in which he shows three Commonwealth soldiers round London and talks about the ideals they are fighting for. He spoke the final epilogue for Noel Coward's *In Which We Serve*. He produced a film about nurses, *The Lamp Still Burns*, and directed and narrated a memorable film tribute to the Auxiliary Territorial Service (ATS), *The Gentle Sex*. He made his final moving public appearance as Nelson on the steps of St Paul's reciting the last prayer before Trafalgar. But above all he directed, starred in and masterminded two of the finest British wartime films, *Pimpernel Smith* (1941) and *The First of the Few* (1942). Their humanity and humour, their sensitivity and idealism, and above all their quiet and abiding Englishness made them masterpieces of British cinema. Howard's pre-war career had seen him playing gentleman adventurers (*The Scarlet Pimpernel*, *British Agent*) but also romanticized and humanized intellectuals (*Pygmalion*, *The Petrified Forest*) and mystic visionaries (*Berkeley Square*, *Smilin' Through*). He brought all these elements together for his wartime British films, which are notable for their sense of spirituality but also for an Englishness characterized by a sense of humour – gentle, ironic, understated, witty – and a sense of proportion – emotional restraint, compassion, sensitivity. Howard's wartime Pimpernel is not an aristocrat but an apparently absent-minded Cambridge archaeologist who rescues artists and intellectuals from the Nazis in 1939. Although trapped by the Germans at the end, he delivers a denunciation of their philosophy of terror before vanishing almost before their eyes. The Swedish scholars Furhammar and Isaksson have seen an explicit religious allegory here, with Pimpernel Smith, a Christ figure, attended by a group of disciples, engaged upon the work of salvation, going knowingly into a trap but eluding his enemies by a miracle.[10] He followed *Pimpernel Smith* with *First of the Few*, a deeply felt and loving portrait of R. J. Mitchell, the inventor of the Spitfire, whom Howard played as a solitary visionary, battling against government indifference, commercial pressure and ill-health to realize his dream of the production of a plane that would be his country's salvation. He produces the plane but dies as a result of the effort involved. Noel Coward called his performance 'Acting that transcended acting'.[11]

The emergence of a new collective vision of England, in which Howard participated with his film *The Gentle Sex*, really developed after 1941. The turning-point was the release of Ealing Studios' *Ships with Wings* (1941), which was essentially a wartime reworking of *The Four Feathers*, with a disgraced Fleet Air Arm officer (John Clements) redeeming his honour by undertaking a suicide mission. Although an enormous box-office success, it received such a hostile reception from the quality press and several key commentators for being over-romanticized and out of touch that Michael Balcon took the decision to produce only realistic stories of Britain at war and turned to the documentarists nurtured in the 1930s by John Grierson to provide that realism.[12]

The image of a nation divided by class barriers and epitomized by the notorious slogan of the early war years '*Your* courage, *your* cheerfulness, *your* resolution will bring *us* victory' was replaced by the concept of 'The People's War', the idea of ordinary people pulling together to defeat the common foe. Ealing's war films exemplified this new image. In *The Foreman Went to France* (Charles Frend, 1942) a determined foreman (played by the Welsh actor Clifford Evans) retrieves a vital piece of machinery from France, aided by two soldiers (a cockney Tommy Trinder and a Scot Gordon Jackson) and an American secretary (Constance Cummings). *San Demetrio-London* (Charles Frend, 1943) is the true story of the salvaging of a merchant-navy tanker by part of its crew, a cross-section of various types of men. A similar cross-section make up an army patrol pinned down in a desert oasis, in *Nine Men* (Harry Watt, 1943). Significantly, none of these films had an officer as hero. Indeed, the personality and attitudes of the old-style officer and gentleman were searchingly examined and regretfully found wanting in wartime in Michael Powell and Emeric Pressburger's *The Life and Death of Colonel Blimp* (1943).

The purpose of Michael Powell and Emeric Pressburger in making *Colonel Blimp* was, as Powell recalled in 1971, to demonstrate cinematically that 'Colonel Blimp was a symbol of British procrastination and British regard for tradition and all the things which we knew and which were losing the war'.[13] But the film which emerged from this intention was very far from being an undiluted rejection of Blimp, the choleric, walrus-moustached, ultra-reactionary of David Low's cartoons who had become a byword for hidebound, class-ridden and outdated incompetence and complacency. Powell went on: 'The only change was instead of having a vicious, slashing, cruel, merciless Colonel Blimp, we had a dear old bumbler and of course everybody loved that. It blunted the message a good deal.'[14] But this crucial change did more than blunt the message, it subverted it. For Powell and Pressburger's Blimp emerged as something of a tragic hero, the embodiment of a chivalric ideal overtaken by the grim reality of modern war.

When Lieutenant 'Spud' Wilson is informed that in an exercise scheduled to start at midnight his unit's objective is Home Guard headquarters at the Royal Bathers Club, Piccadilly, he decides to launch the attack immediately, arguing that since Pearl Harbour Britain is involved in a 'total war' where the rules of the game do not apply. Wilson and his men capture General Clive Wynne-Candy (Roger Livesey) and his staff in the steam room of the Turkish bath. Candy attacks Wilson and they fall struggling into the water. Flashback to 1902, when young Lieutenant Clive Candy VC, on leave from the Boer War, responds to an appeal from English governess Edith Hunter (Deborah Kerr) to go to Berlin and refute false stories about British atrocities in South Africa. Contriving to insult the German officer corps, Candy is compelled to fight a duel with Lieutenant Theo Kretschmar-Schuldorf (Anton Walbrook). Both men are wounded but become firm friends while convalescing. Theo announces that he and Edith love each other. Candy congratulates them but only realizes en route for England that he loves Edith too. After the First World War, Candy, now a general, meets a nurse Barbara Wynne (Deborah Kerr) who strongly resembles Edith and marries her. He tracks Theo down to a German POW camp in Derbyshire but Theo refuses to talk to him. Later, on the eve of Theo's return to Germany, they are reconciled. In 1926 Barbara dies and

Candy adds her maiden name to his own surname. In 1939 Theo, now widowed and a refugee, is saved from internment by Candy, who vouches for him.
Candy, recalled from retirement, is back on the active list. In 1940, however,
when a post-Dunkirk radio talk he has prepared is banned as 'defeatist', he is
again retired and joins the Home Guard, becoming a national celebrity by promoting the new organization. Theo warns Candy that Britain can only beat
Germany by using German methods. End of flashback. Although hurt and
humiliated by the actions of Spud Wilson, Candy is reassured by Theo and by
Angela Cannon (Deborah Kerr), Spud's girlfriend and Candy's MTC driver,
and takes the salute at a march past of Spud's victorious unit.

The opening sequence of the film sets up the two opposing viewpoints with
stark clarity. The action of the sequence is fast and furious, thanks to bravura
cutting and almost continual camera movement, with motorcycles scorching
through the countryside, army lorries racing into London, troops pouring into
the Royal Bathers Club, orders given with urgent authority. This ferment of
action contrasts pointedly with the slumber of the supine, half-naked senior
officers in the steam room. Candy himself, shot in insistent close-up to establish his immediate identification with Low's Blimp, denounces the intruders as
'gangsters' and repeats uncomprehendingly 'War starts at midnight'. But Lieutenant 'Spud' Wilson, archetype of the new modern army officer, insists:
'When I joined the army the only agreement I entered into was to defend my
country by every means at my disposal ... by every means that have existed
since Cain slugged Abel.' The Secretary of War, James Grigg wrote disapprovingly of Wilson's philosophy: 'The suggestion is that if we were exactly like the
Germans we should be better soldiers.' This is indeed the suggestion but it creates a paradox at the heart of the film that is never completely resolved.

During the film German methods are quite clearly set out: fighting by foul
means, shelling hospitals, bombing open towns, sinking neutral ships and
using poison gas. This is what total war can lead to. But is Britain seriously
being urged to contemplate such enormities? The question is never directly
answered. But it is always there, and the film constantly returns to it, shimmering around it, sometimes sneaking up on it, always sizing it up. It may be
for this reason that it became, in Powell's words, 'Emeric's favourite picture and
his best.'[15] It is a unique film. Defying classification and almost impossible to
sum up, Blimp is a film of infinite subtlety, layers of irony and shades of meaning. Contemporary critics were perplexed as to what it was 'about'. In retrospect, it seems clear that it was an attempt to come to terms with Britain's
national ideology.

The ideology, as embodied by Clive Wynne-Candy, is chivalry, and chivalry operating in an imperial context, as Clive serves in Africa, India, and Canada between 1901 and 1939. The 1902 and 1918 sequences of *Blimp* clearly establish Candy as a chivalric archetype. An Old Harrovian, winner of a Victoria Cross in the Boer War, he rushes to the aid of a lady in distress, shows himself generous in victory, is devoted to his servant, truthful to a fault and steadfast in cherishing the ideal of the perfect woman whom he seeks throughout his life.

But Clive is not unique. His code is shared by the whole British ruling elite. There can be no other reason than this for the elaborate care which Powell and Pressburger take to set up the sequence in which Theo is brought from Victoria Station to join a dinner party at Clive's and is solemnly introduced to all the men around the table, each individually shown in close shot. The dinner guests constitute a cross-section of the Establishment: generals, admirals, colonial governors, Foreign Office diplomats, and so forth. They unite in stressing their absence of malice towards their defeated foe and their desire to get Germany back on her feet as soon as possible. It was just this attitude of decency, generosity and fair play which earned the admiration of such commentators as the philosopher George Santayana who referred to the Briton as 'the sweet, just, boyish master of the world' and which, according to Correlli Barnett, lay behind the pre-war policy of appeasement, a point which Theo hints at later in the film.[16]

The 1902 sequence is played for comedy, but comedy of a gentle and affectionate kind, the kind which sees the conduct it is depicting as outmoded and absurd but at the same time admirable. It is observed with a mixture of stately formality and jaunty charm, in marked contrast to the speed and snap of the preceding 1942 sequence. The ritual formalities of the arranging and staging of the duel are re-created with evident delight, and the movements of the duellists as they cross sabres and the camera cranes up away from them to the distant ceiling of the gymnasium have the same deliberate quality. Interestingly, the 1902 sequence with its marked comic tone is the only one in which Candy is played straight, suggesting that he is here in his natural milieu. He becomes more and more of a caricature in the succeeding episodes, as the action takes on a more serious and urgent tone, suggesting his increasing irrelevance to the age. Yet all the time the film is obliquely searching for ways of resolving the central paradox: how to reconcile total war and any concept of decent behaviour.

The film indicates differences in national character. Barbara, seeing the

German prisoners listening to a concert of Schubert and Mendelssohn in the POW camp, comments on the puzzle inherent in the German ability to compose beautiful poetry and music, and yet to start a war and commit atrocities. This comment should perhaps be taken in conjunction with Anton Walbrook's eloquent and moving soliloquy, done in a long single-take shot, as he is being questioned in 1939 about his reasons for coming to England. He speaks of conditions in Germany after the Great War, the rise of Hitler, the discovery of the loss of his sons to the Nazi party and then the death of his wife. Thoughts of his English wife, of his English best friend, of the British VIPs who had sought to comfort him in defeat and of the English countryside had filled him with a longing to go there. Implicit in all this is the idea that the Germans as a race are susceptible to bouts of madness and evil and that the British are just as inherently decent and good-natured. This would be bound to soften the pursuit of any total war engaged in by the British.

There is also an indication that World War One may not have been as noble as people like Candy liked to think. At the Armistice, he rejoices in the victory of 'clean fighting, honest soldiering', but this statement is given an ironic ring by the previous scene. Questioning captured German saboteurs, he had assured them that the British did not use German methods of interrogation. Naturally, they do not speak. But when Candy has gone, the South African Captain van Zijl takes over the questioning and sourly informs them that he is no 'simple English gentleman' and will use any method necessary to get them to talk. Candy is later supplied with reports of their confession. This suggests that chivalry may always have been to some extent a grand illusion and that all wars involve unpleasantness by both sides.

Perhaps the best way to make sense of the film is to see it as a dialogue between three different voices: Candy's as the voice of idealism, Theo's the voice of experience and the Composite Woman's, the voice of common sense. It is a dialogue rendered all the more meaningful and profound by the superlative performances of the three stars. Candy, whose code and character are fully formed by 1902, never changes. He remains throughout an officer, a sportsman and a gentleman, something acknowledged by the tapestry into which the credits are woven and which bears a picture of the elderly Blimp, clad in a battered suit of armour and riding a horse.

Theo, first seen as a German officer and gentleman, initially fails to comprehend the meaning of the English chivalric code and rejects Clive's hand of friendship at the camp. Later he seeks to take advantage of the code to benefit his defeated country, telling his fellow officers about his reception at the VIP dinner: 'They are children, boys playing cricket. They win the shirt off your back and want to give it back again. This childlike stupidity is a raft for us in a sea of despair.' But when Germany falls into the hands of the Nazis, Theo flees to England. Reading Candy's banned BBC talk in which he said he would rather be defeated than win by German methods, he speaks to Candy with the voice of experience:

> If you let yourself be defeated by them just because you are too fair to hit back the same way they hit at you, there won't be any methods but Nazi methods … You've been educated to be a gentleman and a sportsman in peace and in war. But this is not a gentleman's war. This time you're fighting for your existence against the most devilish idea ever created by the human brain – Nazism, and if you lose, there won't be a return match next year or perhaps for a hundred years.

Significantly, his statement is endorsed by Angela Cannon, Candy's MTC driver and the third incarnation of his ideal woman. She tells Candy he will have to change his ideas. In a very real sense, Edith, Barbara and Angela are the same woman, the eternal, sensible, forthright, independent-spirited British woman. Edith Hunter is an articulate and determined defender of women's rights, who took a job as a governess in Germany against her family's wishes, who summons Clive to assist her in refuting anti-British propaganda and in reply to his talk of good manners and decent behaviour, puts a common-sense perspective on the Boer War: 'Good manners cost us … 6,000 men killed and 20,000 wounded and 2 years of war when with a little common sense and bad manners there would have been no war at all.' In other words, the rules must be bent from time to time for the greater good. Angela Cannon, who prefers to be called 'Johnny', is an ex-photographic model who has trained as a driver since the outbreak of war. She is every bit the equal of the men, outwits 'Spud' in a bid to warn Candy of his attack but agrees with both Theo and 'Spud' on the need for total war. So common sense and experience are at one.

But what about idealism? Angela and Theo both love Candy for exactly the chivalrous gentleman that he is. So we are back with the paradox again. In the end, there is just a hint that if ever the paradox will be resolved, it will be by 'good old British' pragmatism and compromise. Candy decides not to punish 'Spud' for disobeying orders, but to invite him to dinner, just as his own superior officer had done with him when he disobeyed orders in 1902, that is, he chooses consultation rather than confrontation. More significantly, Barbara, who also loved Candy and shared his ideals, provides Powell and Pressburger with a sleight-of-hand means of concluding the dialogue after nearly three hours of screen time. Returning to his London house after their marriage, Barbara urges him always to remain the same and never change until there is a second Flood and a lake forms in the basement. During World War Two, Candy's house is destroyed by enemy bombs and a temporary water tank is installed upon its site. The cataclysm has come and now there is a lake in the basement. Perhaps the time has come to change after all. Candy recalls the prophecy and turns to take the salute of 'Spud''s unit, '*Sic transit gloria* Candy' says the motto woven into the opening tapestry, but even at the end of the film the glory has not yet departed.

The film *This England* (1941; tactfully retitled *Our Heritage* for its Scottish release) typifies the tendency of wartime propagandists to draw on the rural myth to define the nation. The celebration of the countryside as a source of national strength has been brilliantly expounded and indeed indicted by Martin Wiener.[17] Wiener sees the glorification of the countryside and all things rural as a deliberate rejection of the urban and industrial reality of Britain by a non-industrial, non-innovative and anti-materialist patrician culture. It was endorsed by a gentrified bourgeoisie which, having made its money, sought to turn itself into country gentlemen and distance itself from the 'dark satanic mills' where its 'brass' had been made. The rural myth, pumped out in novels, poems, paintings and advertisements from the 1880s onwards, had a direct effect on evocations of the national character. The Englishman was said to be at heart a countryman, and his character – thanks to his rural roots – to be based upon the principles of balance, peacefulness, traditionalism and spirituality.

The widespread dissemination of the rural myth is to be explained in part by its appeal both to the romantic right and to the romantic left. For the right, the country meant the country house and the country church, the squire and the parson, and a deferential, hierarchical society. For the left, it meant folk music, the village community, rural crafts and honest peasantry. Over the years the rural myth would count among its proponents such disparate figures as Rudyard Kipling and William Morris, Stanley Baldwin and F. R. Leavis. What united them was a distaste for modern industrial society which drove them to look back to some Arcadian golden age before the Industrial Revolution.

The attitude is typically embodied in a collection of essays, extracts and poems edited by J. B. Priestley under the title *Our Nation's Heritage*, first published in 1939 and reprinted in 1940. It concentrated exclusively on the countryside and contained a piece written in 1927 by H. V. Morton, the prolific travel writer and rural mythographer, who declared:

The village that symbolises England sleeps in the subconsciousness of many a townsman. A little London factory hand whom I met during the war confessed to me when pressed and after great mental difficulty that he visualised the England he was fighting for ... not as London, nor as his own street, but as Epping Forest, the green place where he had spent bank holidays. And I think most of us did. The village and the English countryside are the germs of all that we are and all that we have become: our manufacturing cities belong to the last century and a half; our villages stand with their roots in the Heptarchy.[18]

Morton was talking of World War One, but the same theme recurred regularly in World War Two.

Latterday commentators have had fun with such conceits. Angus Calder, not unjustly, noted:

Georgian poets and their associated cricket correspondents had dwelled nostalgically on the beauties of the English countryside and the virtues of the English yokel, while the former had decayed and the latter, if they had much enterprise, had fled to the towns. Even during the war, many writers who should have known better implied that the soldiers and airmen were dying to preserve an essentially rural Britain ... In fact, as evacuated schoolteachers found, the more picturesque parts of Britain were inhabited by increasingly demoralised, and often remarkably incestuous, communities of near paupers.[19]

Even during the war itself the real fallacy was exposed by Sir Denis Brogan in his book *The English People* (1943):

To believe that a people who have for generations lived in towns, of whom only a small proportion has any direct connection with the land, has in some mystical way evaded the consequences of this state of affairs, is to believe in miracles ... This illusion ... that England is full of workers anxious to return to the land which their great-grandfathers left ... is widely spread in England because two different things are confused, the love of flowers, gardens, open spaces and the holiday delights of rural life, with the less picturesque, less common, less literary passion for the utilisation of the land that marks the true farmer or the true peasant ... A nation of flower-growers like the English is a nation of shop-keepers, not a nation of farmers.[20]

Whereas Wiener regards the rural myth as a powerful factor in Britain's industrial decline, promoting hostility to progress, innovation, enterprise and industrialization, the myth nonetheless served an important role during the war. For while cities could be blitzed and bombed, the countryside remained, eternal, timeless, self-renewing and indestructible – a fitting symbol for Britain at bay. It is significant that in *The Way Ahead*, Carol Reed's 1944 film about a unit of conscripts, when the soldiers gather round a wireless in North Africa it is a talk about the countryside at harvest that plunges them into nostalgia for their homeland.

The complex of images and ideas embodied in the rural myth was dramatized in *This England*. It was prefaced by a poem:

The earth of England is an old, old earth,
Her autumn mists, her brambleberry flame,
Her tangled, rain-soaked grass, were still the same
Time out of mind before the Romans came,
Though from the skies men hurl their slaughter down
Still there will be the bracken turning brown.

The opening narration sets the tone for a film in which industrialization is seen as an aberration, and rural life and work on the land the ideal:

This England, among whose hills and valleys since the beginning of time have stood old farms and villages. The story of Rookeby's farm and the village of Clevely is the story of them all.

In view of this, it is perhaps not inappropriate that the film should have about it the air of a glorified village pageant. The action centres on four episodes from Britain's past, all designed to stress her heroic spirit in times of adversity: the Norman Conquest, the Spanish Armada, the Napoleonic Wars and World War One. The film stresses the timelessness and eternity of England and the English by having the same actors play the same symbolic roles in each episode: vicar, doctor, blacksmith, publican and – in particular – yeoman farmer Rookeby (John Clements) and farm labourer Appleyard (Emlyn Williams). It shows that they are prepared to fight and kill to defend the land, and it ends with the characters once more involved in a war and John Clements reciting the 'This England' speech from *Richard II*.

In locating the nation's source of strength against foreign aggression in an alliance of country gentry and rural working class, the film provides the necessary consensual message for a national effort in wartime. But in coupling this national resistance with local resistance in 1086, 1588 and 1804 against oppressive, corrupt or neglectful landlords, the film adds a distinctly radical element which mirrors the shift to the left in the national mood and the desire for a fairer, more just and humane post-war society which led to the election of the Labour government in 1945. It is significant that it is Appleyard – the working-class 'Hodge' figure – who is the perpetual conscience of gentleman farmer Rookeby, reminding him of his duty to the land in 1588 and 1804 when he is tempted to abandon the farm for a different way of life. It is perhaps equally significant that Appleyard remains the servant and Rookeby the master. Revolution, after all, must not be carried too far.

But *This England* was not a very good film and three later, and much better, films express the rural myth more convincingly. The enchanting *Tawny Pipit* (1944) was written and directed by Bernard Miles and Charles Saunders. Taking full advantage of the glorious rural location shooting, it tells how the local squire and the local vicar mobilize the village of Lipsbury Lea to protect the breeding ground of the rare tawny pipit birds. The defence of the pipits is the difference between the forces of democracy and the Hun. It is why we fight. As the squire Colonel Barton-Barrington (Bernard Miles) declares: 'Love of animals and nature is part and parcel of the British way of life.' The story, however, has an even wider symbolic significance. The village is Britain, electing to fight under its traditional leaders by democratic decision. They have to fight the forces of the military (the army wants to use the breeding area for tank manoeuvres), of bureaucracy (the Ministry of Agriculture wants to plough it up) and of fifth columnists (villainous egg-stealers infiltrate the village to appropriate the pipits' eggs). They also have a gallant ally in the person of a Russian sniper, Lieutenant Bokolova, who is saluted by the village children with a spirited rendition of The Internationale. The war brings to the countryside erstwhile nightclubbers as land girls and cockney kids as evacuees. They are all made better, both physically and spiritually, by their contact with the countryside and the pipits. A convalescing RAF pilot and his nurse play a prominent part in the struggle for the pipits, an equation of their work in the actual war effort with this symbolic struggle for Britain's national heritage. At the end, the pilot, now recovered, flies his plane, renamed *Anthus Campestris* (tawny pipit), over the village, dipping his wings in honour of the birds. The symbolism has become a fighting truth.

There is a radical tinge to another rural drama: Cavalcanti's *Went the Day Well?* (1942), a powerful and at times chilling account of the occupation of the English village of Bramley End by German paratroopers. 'There'll Always Be an England' is heard on the wireless at the manor house and the film lays the usual stress on the beauty and tranquillity of the Chiltern countryside, an idyllic setting which makes the intrusion of Nazi brutality and violence all the more horrific. But the village is also characterized by those elements of Englishness seen to be derived from the countryside: peacefulness, traditionalism and spirituality. The peacefulness is clear from the outset. Bramley End is a society that is warmly communal, devout and cheerfully deferential to its 'natural' leaders of the upper and upper-middle class. The chief focal points of village life are the pub (where the community celebrates its communality), the church (where it consummates its spirituality) and the manor house (home of the autocratic local chatelaine, Mrs Fraser).

Obedient to the concept of the 'people's war', a central theme of wartime propaganda, the whole village community unites: the publican and his sailor son, the land girl, the sexton, the postmistress, the policeman, all play their part, and some lose their lives, to regain their freedom from the Germans. But there is radicalism in the suggestion of the unsoundness of the old ruling class. The local squire, Oliver Wilsford (Leslie Banks), turns out to be a fifth columnist and the snobbish though likable Mrs Fraser complacently disregards evidence of German infiltration. The German officers, Ortler and Jung, posing as Englishmen, move easily among the ruling circles of the village because they 'speak the same language' (Jung, for example, had stroked the Jesus boat at Cambridge). This depiction accords well with the widespread feeling that elements of the upper class were pro-fascist. Sir Oswald Mosley, the British fascist leader, was after all a baronet and married to one of the Mitford girls. Admiral Sir Barry Domvile, Lord Tavistock and others actively sought to promote peace with Germany in 1940 because of their sympathy with Nazi Germany. There were rumours current in 1942 that five dukes were seeking a negotiated peace with Germany. It is also the case that two of the humblest and least considered figures in the village alert the outside world to the plight of Bramley End: poacher Bill Purves, who is killed, and cockney evacuee George Truscott, whom Bill has taught the country skills. Against this it should be noted that Mrs Fraser, who has filled her house with evacuees, dies heroically saving the children from a hand grenade, and it is the vicar's daughter who disposes of the treacherous Wilsford. Perhaps most telling of all is the fact that the manor house (symbol of England, history and tradition) is taken over by the people and defended by them as the last bastion of freedom against the Germans. It is a struggle of the whole people, of all classes: a united effort.

But perhaps the most notable rural paean is *A Canterbury Tale* (1944), a rich and complex fable by Michael Powell and Emeric Pressburger which perplexed critics and public alike at the time of its release. Powell subsequently described the film as his version of 'Why We Fight': 'a crusade against materialism', an exploration of the spiritual values that England embodies and the belief that the roots of the nation lie in the pastoral.[21] The film, ravishingly photographed in Powell's native Kent, rejoices in the sense of the living past, in country crafts, rural beauty, the intimacy of man and nature. The England evoked by *A Canterbury Tale* is the rural England of Chaucer and Shakespeare, and its spirit resides in Thomas Colpeper, gentleman farmer, magistrate, historian and archaeologist, a man who understands England's nature and seeks to communicate its values, a part played with chilling charismatic power by Eric Portman. The film re-creates the Canterbury pilgrimage for a trio of latterday visitors who discover spiritual peace and revitalization on the Pilgrims' Way.

The final sequence of the film, in which all the characters are gathered, uplifted and transfigured, in Canterbury Cathedral as bells ring, 'Onward Christian Soldiers' is sung and troops move off to war, prefigures the just and inevitable victory of those qualities for which Britain fights and which the countryside enshrines: freedom, stability, tradition, peacefulness and spirituality. The intention of the film was made clear by its press book, which declared:

> *A Canterbury Tale* is a new story about Britain, her unchanging beauty and traditions, and of the Old Pilgrims and the New. As the last scene of the picture fades away, to those who see it and are British, there will come a feeling – just for a moment – of wishing to be silent, as the thoughts flash through one's mind: 'These things I have just seen and heard are all my parents taught me. That is Britain, that is me.'

Alas, in general, the public seems not to have thought this. Instead, they seem to have thought, 'What on earth is this all about?' The film was not a box-office success.

The Demi-Paradise (1943) was directed by Anthony Asquith and written and produced by the Anglophile White Russian émigré Anatole de Grunwald. It was the British cinema's main contribution to Anglo-Russian friendship, with Laurence Olivier giving a brilliant performance as the bemused Russian engineer whose preconceptions about England are gradually dispelled and who comes to appreciate the secret of Britain's survival and success. In fact it emerges far more as a celebration of England and Englishness than of Russia. Ivan Kouznetsoff visits England first in 1939 to negotiate the building of an ice-breaker. He arrives believing that the English are humourless, arrogant, narrow-minded, hypocritical, warlike, the embodiment of capitalist and imperialist tyranny. He finds the country complacent, easy-going and old-fashioned, and goes to stay with the upper-class Tisdall family, who are both country gentry and industrial managers, in the composite market town and seaport with the resonant name of Barchester. Each of the members of the family has a distinct ideological role to play in enlightening Ivan over the falseness of the various myths about 'perfidious Albion'.

The father, Herbert Tisdall, a cricket-loving gentleman, tells Ivan that, far from being warlike, Britain will do all she can to avoid trouble. But when it comes to the crunch she will fight. When Ivan taxes Tisdall's wife with the English being narrow-minded, she disarmingly agrees. Daughter Ann gives a resounding defence of the British Empire when he talks of the English setting out to conquer the world. She claims that it was acquired by private adventure rather than state expansion, the work of explorers, romantics, individualists and that, since acquisition, it has been well governed. Most surprising of all for Ivan is his encounter with Ann's grandfather, Runalow, the acceptable face of Victorian values. Runalow is a gentle, wise and cultivated eccentric in wing collar and pince-nez, an engineering genius who has learned Bradshaw by heart (thus demonstrating the true Englishman's love of railways), a millionaire not interested in money but in playing the piano and reading poetry. He built up his firm from nothing by his own efforts, not for financial gain but so that he could afford the things he wanted: a piano, a garden and books. He did not stop work once he had got these things because he had responsibilities towards his employees. The motto of his firm is 'Duty and Service'. But Ivan is finally exasperated by the local pageant – a convincingly awful re-creation, complete with Women's Institute choir and doggerel verse on great moments from Britain's past such as the Armada and Waterloo. 'You are living in the past,' Ivan tells them accusingly, little realizing that tradition and the past are sources of Britain's strength.

When he returns, a year later, the war has started. England is galvanized into action; Ann has joined the WRNS; the Tisdalls are entertaining cockney evacuees, but still find time to listen to Miss Beatrice Harrison playing her cello to the nightingales on the terrace for a BBC broadcast (a re-creation of an actual wartime occurrence). Ivan tells Runalow that Britain is finished. Runalow says Britain will fight on. With what? The strength of her traditions and the belief in duty and service. With Hitler's invasion of Russia, Ivan suddenly finds himself an ally of the British. The annual pageant is held, exactly the same as last year except for a tableau for victory. It raises £1,000 for Ivan's home town and he finds himself applauding the pageant, at last having understood its meaning. The workers agree to overtime in order to complete the Russian icebreaker, which is duly launched amid a chorus of 'For he's a jolly good fellow' in honour of Ivan. The Russian then makes a speech explaining how he first arrived in England full of misconceptions but now realizes that the English are a 'grand, great people'. Much of the world thinks that they care only about money; in fact they care about cricket, nightingales and a good job well done. Much of the world thinks they are perfidious and hypocritical; in fact they are warm and kindly, but it amuses them to let the world think they are not because of their sense of humour. Their sense of humour is the key: if you can laugh, you can be tolerant and freedom-loving, for there is no laughter where there is no freedom. The Russians can laugh and the British can laugh and together they will win the battle against violence, selfishness and greed.

Ivan's final speech brings together the ideas that have run through the film defining the national identity: a sense of duty, a sense of tradition, a sense of tolerance, a sense of humour, a sense of service, a sense of community, but also a heroic individuality which at its most potent can invent, explore and conquer and at its most pronounced can blossom as a benign and lovable eccentricity, seen in *The Demi-Paradise* in the presence at the pageant of those most beloved of British eccentrics, Margaret Rutherford and Joyce Grenfell.

If in *This England* the downland village of Clevely is England and the countrymen are its heart, and if in *The Demi-Paradise* it is the seaport town of Barchester and the upper-middle class, in *This Happy Breed* (1944) England is No. 17 Sycamore Road, Clapham, and its heart is the lower-middle class. *This Happy Breed* was the play by Noel Coward filmed by the team he had assembled to make *In Which We Serve* in 1941: David Lean, Ronald Neame and Anthony Havelock-Allan. If *In Which We Serve* was a film about the present (fighting the war), *This Happy Breed* was its analogue and counterpart, a film about the past and future which avoided the war altogether, something which by 1944 filmgoers were anxious to do. It evokes the imminent end of the war, with narrator Laurence Olivier declaring that with the return of the troops, 'hundreds and hundreds of houses are becoming homes again'. But it also presents a selective view of the events of 1919-39 in such a way as to assuage any guilt feelings the lower-middle class may have entertained about their endorsement of the National Government and its appeasement policy. This Clapham Cavalcade intermingles the joys and sorrows of the Gibbonses, Frank and Ethel (Robert Newton and Celia Johnson) and their three children (marriages, births, deaths, quarrels and reconciliations), with the great events of the age (British Empire Exhibition, General Strike, the Abdication, Munich). It does so in such a way as to endorse the role of the lower-middle class as the backbone of the nation. For although, like the nation, the younger members of the Gibbons family can flirt with innovation, they settle in the end for the tried and the true. Son Reg and son-in-law Sam become involved in radical politics but both end up being tamed and neutralized by marriage. Daughter Queenie rejects her background as 'common' and runs away in search of the bright lights, but she too eventually settles down with faithful Bob from next door and shows every sign of becoming the archetypal supportive wife and mother than Ethel has been to Frank.

The film does, however, also make a resounding statement about the British political process which is essentially a plea for continuity and a return to 'normality' after the war. This involves Frank and/or Ethel during the course of the film rejecting Communism and Fascism, filing reverently past the coffin of King George V, visiting the Empire Exhibition at Wembley, breaking the General Strike and passionately rejecting appeasement. In discounting what Ethel calls 'that Bolshie business', Frank expounds his (and Coward's) evolutionary philosophy:

> Oh, there's something to be said for it; there's always something to be said for everything. Where they go wrong is trying to get things done too quickly. We don't like doing things quickly in this country. It's like gardening. Someone once said we was a nation of gardeners, and they weren't far out. We're used to planning things and watching them grow and looking out for changes in the weather … What works in other countries doesn't always work here. We've got our own way of settling things. It may be slow and it may be a bit dull, but it suits us alright and it always will.

In fact, only a year later, Labour took Clapham from the Conservatives at the general election and swept to power to initiate their peaceful revolution. But it *was* a peaceful revolution, and it was one which grew out of trends and developments initiated by the war. It called for no great change in the national character or self-image. Indeed, as Paul Addison has pointed out, reserved, terse, pipe-smoking, cricket-loving ex-army officer Clem Attlee was rather closer to the traditional English archetype than Winston Churchill, the flamboyant maverick, the romantic man-child with his puckish sense of humour, his unique command of the language and his highly developed sense of destiny. The strength of the nation was that it was able to produce, to accommodate and to profit from both of them.

In real life the 'happy breed' turned to the Labour Party for their 'brave new world'. But they recognized in the Gibbonses fellow souls. For the film provoked a remarkable reaction. It struck a chord of recognition and sympathy. It was perhaps the first time that the suburban middle class had been portrayed in the round; the sort of incarnation they were used to previously was in Ivor Novello's hilarious satire on Clapham manners and mores, *I Lived with You* (1933). In *This Happy Breed* they were being taken seriously and treated with respect. The *Manchester Guardian* (29 May 1944) called the film 'an essential photo for John Bull's family album'. William Whitebait of the *New Statesman* (27 May 1944), who had not liked *In Which We Serve* and admitted to being no fan of Coward, was completely overwhelmed by the film: 'It would be hard to overpraise the skill, the feeling and the enhanced fidelity of the film.' More important than the critics, the public liked it. C. A. Lejeune reported in *The Observer* that 'No film in my memory has brought in more letters of appreciation', and the film became the top money-maker of 1944.[22]

It touched people's hearts because Coward was writing from the heart, as he was when he broadcast to the Australian people in 1940 and said:

> There is one thing I do know, not only with my mind and experience but with my roots and my instincts and my heart, and that is the spirit of the ordinary people of England: steadfast humour in the face of continual strain and horror, courage, determination and a quality of endurance that is beyond praise and almost beyond belief.[23]

It is these qualities that are to be seen in the Gibbonses, albeit in a peacetime setting, and the Gibbonses can also be seen to possess what Coward in another broadcast called the assets of the British character: 'Our individual honesty, our horse-sense, our irrepressible humour and our strange power of adjustment to new circumstances.'[24] The picture, then, which emerges from all three films – *A Canterbury Tale*, *The Demi-Paradise* and *This Happy Breed* – is more or less consistent. It is applied equally to the countryman, to the upper-middle class and to the suburban lower-middle class.

Films about the People's War, whether they were devoted to the fighting services or to the home front, to men or to women, were characterized by the same qualities: comradeship and cooperation, dedication to duty and self-sacrifice, a self-deprecating good humour and unselfconscious modesty. For each of the services, the war produced a masterpiece: for the army, Carol Reed's *The Way Ahead* (1944), a semi-documentary account of how a group of conscripts from all walks of life are brought together and welded into a disciplined fighting unit, and for the RAF, Anthony Asquith's *The Way to the Stars* (1945), which recalled life on a single RAF station between 1940 and 1944, with its joys and losses, its tragedies and camaraderie. For the navy, it was *In Which We Serve* (1942), written, produced, co-directed (with David Lean) and scored by Noel Coward, who also played the leading role. It was based on the true story of *HMS Kelly*, which had been commanded by Coward's friend Lord Louis Mountbatten and which had been sunk off Crete. Coward loved Britain – he wrote in his autobiography, 'I loved British courage, British humour and

The class system mobilized for the war: Noel Coward in *In Which We Serve* (1942).

11

British understatement.'[25] He had already demonstrated this in his stage play *Cavalcade* (1931), his panoramic account of the first thirty years of the century which, *The Observer* (19 February 1933) noted, was 'so close to the emotional memories of every British man and woman that it must sweep British audiences off their feet wherever it is shown'. Asked by Filippo del Giudice of Two Cities Films to make a propaganda film, Coward came up with the story of the *Kelly*. It interweaves the story of a ship, HMS *Torrin*, and the great events of the war (Dunkirk, the Blitz, the Battle of Britain) but concentrates on three characters and their families, Captain Kinross, Chief Petty Officer Hardy and AB Blake, representing the upper-middle class, the lower-middle class and the working-class. These families share the same qualities: dedication to duty, stoicism, humour, decency. Coward believed in the class system. He had made his way from an impoverished lower-middle-class suburban background to fame and fortune by hard work, self-discipline and a stiff upper lip, and believed it was open to all to do the same. He was no egalitarian, believing that egalitarianism led to mediocrity, but thought that the class system should operate with greater sympathy, understanding and mutual respect between classes. This is what *In Which We Serve* showed and it achieved a remarkable reaction. It got rave reviews from the press, high brow and low brow, left-wing and right-wing alike.[26] The *Documentary News Letter*, scourge of the inauthentic, declared: 'This is an exceptionally sincere and deeply moving film … And it is one of the best war films ever made.'[27] Dilys Powell wrote of it:

> The emotional impact of *In Which We Serve* was immense. The experiences of civilian and fighting men were presented as essentially one, bound together by ties of human love and devotion … Noel Coward in *In Which We Serve* took a handful of *typically British* [my italics] men and women and made from their stories, ordinary enough in themselves a distillation of national character.[28]

This why it was the top British film at the British box office in 1943 and exceeded only by *Random Harvest* among the American hits. The box office never lies. It delighted the King and Churchill, and impressed the lower decks and the mass cinemagoing public. It won a special Hollywood Oscar.

The contribution of women to the war effort was vital and the cinema paid tribute to them, reflecting the dramatic change in their social roles and expectations. Leslie Howard's *The Gentle Sex* (1943) was a female version of *The Way Ahead*, a realistic account of the training of a group of women from all classes and backgrounds in the ATS. Frank Launder and Sidney Gilliat's moving and memorable *Millions Like Us* (1943) dramatized the experiences of a group of girls of different class and regional backgrounds drafted to work in an aircraft factory. Women, too, were shown to share in the national qualities.

In Frank Launder's superb *2,000 Women* (1944), a spa hotel accommodates interned British women in France. They are mainly southern English but include Renee Houston as a tough Scotswoman and Thora Hird as a good-hearted Lancastrian. The women collectively display stoicism, patriotism, humour, determination and love of home. Miss Manningford (Flora Robson) instructs her companion not to weep in front of the Germans. Together they later display a light to help RAF pilots overhead bomb their target. They are deported to a German punishment camp to the strains of 'For they are jolly good fellows' from their companions in the hotel. There are morale-raising jokes, Houston sings 'Too many women and not enough men' and there is black humour involving a dead German with whom escaping British flyers have to hide. Launder retrospectively thought there was too much humour but it is an essential part of the image and integrates into the drama well. Love of home is movingly demonstrated in the final concert when Lucy Wilson sings 'No place like home' as the camera pans along the faces of the listening internees, and then they all stand and belt out defiantly 'There'll always be an

England'. Their determination and resourcefulness is shown when they help three flyers – two British, one Canadian – to escape from the Germans.

Interestingly, the same national characteristics can be seen in documentaries as in feature films: *Target for Tonight, Coastal Command, Western Approaches.* There is one particularly instructive point of intersection. In 1943 the Crown Film Unit and Ealing Studios were making simultaneously filmed tributes to the Auxiliary Fire Service (AFS), Humphrey Jennings's *Fires Were Started* and Basil Dearden's *The Bells Go Down.* Both actually told, more or less, the same story. Covering the period 1939-40, each followed the training of a group of volunteers, showed the camaraderie of the company, tackled the firefighting during the Blitz and ended with the heroic death of a chirpy cockney 'character'. The difference was that *Fires* was performed by genuine firemen and *Bells* by actors, *Fires* was almost entirely location shot and *Bells* involved studio shooting. When they were released many critics unfavourably compared the two, though this demonstrated the dominance of the critical aesthetic of the 1940s involving the preference for pure documentary over fiction, respectable literature over popular melodrama and audience improvement over mere escapism. But the difference between *Fires* and *Bells* is more one of idiom than of anything else. The underlying ethics, values and characteristics are the same: the paramountcy of the group and the dominance of duty, service, decency, stoicism, humour and self sacrifice.

The cinema was careful to characterize its forces units as embracing all regions, countries and classes of the United Kingdom. Anthony Asquith's semi-documentary submarine drama, *We Dive at Dawn* (1943), peopled the *Sea Tiger* with a crew comprising a Scot (CPO Jock Duncan), an Irishman (PO Mike Corrigan), a Northerner (Leading Seaman Jim Hobson), a Cockney (CPO Dabbs) and for a Commonwealth dimension, a Canadian ('Canada'). Throughout the war there was often a representative Scotsman (Gordon Jackson, John Laurie) or Welshman (Mervyn Johns) in the multinational force. But the identity of Britain continued to be more or less interchangeable with England, as indicated by the use of the popular song 'There'll always be an England'. It is sung by the British POWs as they march into their prison camp in Ealing's *The Captive Heart* (1946), despite the presence of a Scot (Gordon Jackson) and a Welshman (Mervyn Johns) among the prisoners, and it is sung by the female POWs in Gainsborough's *2,000 Women*, again despite the presence of a Scotswoman.

The necessity for putting Great Britain and the struggle against Fascism at the forefront, ahead of a narrow Celtic nationalism, is one of the themes of

Basil Dearden's *The Halfway House* (1944) in which an Irish diplomat about to be posted to the Irish Embassy in Berlin and, as a result, estranged from his English fiancée, moves from defending Irish neutrality to rejecting it, and enlists in the forces to fight Fascism. He learns about commitment from Frenchwoman Françoise Rosay who insists that France is not beaten and will carry on fighting ('What is the use of living without freedom and dignity') and from the Welsh innkeeper (Mervyn Johns) that a nation keeps its soul with its language and its culture and he regards the English as friends and neighbours ('I wouldn't put the betterment of Wales before the betterment of humanity'). The film thus rejects a narrow disengaged Celtic nationalism in favour of a common cause – the struggle against Fascism – in which all good men should come to the aid of Great Britain.

Religion did not play as prominent a part in British films as it did in American films. There was a significant biopic, *The Great Mr. Handel* (1942, Norman Walker), shot in Technicolor, and devoted to the story of Handel's composition of *The Messiah*, nineteenth-century Protestant Britain's favourite oratorio, and the Boulting Brothers' powerful and grim *Pastor Hall* (1940) dramatized the experience of the real-life German Protestant minister Pastor Niemoller in resisting Nazi tyranny. But the use of religion was generally more incidental if nonetheless powerful. Churches served as symbols of Britain's indomitable spirit and resistance. St Paul's Cathedral looming above the smoke and flames of the Blitz became one of the most significant images of the war, featured in several documentaries (*Words for Battle, London Can Take It*). Similarly Canterbury Cathedral is the emotional focus of *A Canterbury Tale*, in which the modern pilgrims converge on the cathedral and where the film climaxes as soldiers and all the characters, renewed, purified and ennobled, gather to sing 'Onward Christian Soldiers', the bells ring and the last shot is of the cathedral as seen from the Pilgrims' Way. It prefigures the final victory for which the British people fight on behalf of their country, of freedom, beauty, tolerance and spirituality. Britain's favourite Hollywood England movie, *Mrs Miniver* ended in a bombed church with the vicar urging the congregation to strive for victory and the congregation singing 'Onward Christian Soldiers' as the camera pans up through a hole in the roof to the RAF planes overhead and the soundtrack bursts into 'Land of Hope and Glory'. The Ealing film *The Bells Go Down* ends similarly in a bombed church at the centre of the Blitz; a christening is taking place, indicating that life goes on.

But there are always alternatives to the dominant national identity and one was provided in wartime by the Gainsborough melodramas, *The Man in Grey*

(1943), *Madonna of the Seven Moons* (1944) and *The Wicked Lady* (1945). Critically excoriated as sensationalist, cliché-ridden, historically inaccurate and dramatically worthless, they not only outstripped Ealing's realistic war films at the box office, they created two new popular cinematic icons. In 1943 George Formby and Gracie Fields, who before and into the war, had been the top British box-office stars, were displaced by Margaret Lockwood and James Mason. There could not be a greater contrast in the nature of popular idols. But even greater than the contrast between flamboyant, sexy and extravagant Lockwood and Mason and sexless, cheerful, down-to-earth Fields and Formby is the fact that audiences were apparently identifying not with the ostensible hero and heroine of the Gainsboroughs, Stewart Granger and Phyllis Calvert, but with the anti-hero and anti-heroine, James Mason and Margaret Lockwood.

Despite the barrage of critical disapproval, the films themselves were great hits with the public and made large sums of money. This very dichotomy tells us as much about the critics as it does about the films. As John Ellis has demonstrated, the British critical establishment in the 1940s was rooted in certain traditions – of documentary realism, of literary quality and of a middle-class improvement ethic.[29] Gainsborough melodramas offended against all these criteria of excellence. They were not only not realistic; they were defiantly anti-realistic. They did not derive from respected literary sources, of the kind which earned plaudits for David Lean's beautifully crafted film versions of Dickens, or Carol Reed's atmospheric adaptations of Graham Greene. They were furthermore definitely neither improving nor uplifting. They were rooted in fact in that equally critically despised tradition of stage melodrama which had packed working-class audiences into the penny gaffs of the nineteenth century to thrill to tales of wicked squires, wronged innocents and virtue triumphant. The class basis of critics' distaste is confirmed by Richard Winnington's dismissal of *The Wicked Lady* as 'an ugly hodge podge of servant girls' lore'.[30]

Why were these films so popular with 1940s' audiences? The slick and easy answer is escapism, from the rigours of war and the deprivation of post-war austerity. There is, of course, an element of truth in this. Spectacular costumes, conspicuous consumption and extravagant goings-on *did* take people out of themselves and help them to forget for a little while flying bombs, clothing coupons and fuel shortages. But there is more to it than that.

First of all, Gainsborough created something which had not previously existed in Britain – 'the women's picture'. They did so in direct response to a perceived box-office need. The war had seen a great upsurge in female cinemagoing. Even in the 1930s women had been great filmgoers. But the huge army of women shift-workers and factory girls that the war had called into being, the legion of wives and sweethearts whose menfolk were away serving with the armed forces, created a defined and movie-hungry group who responded avidly to Gainsborough's new product. As C. A. Lejeune wrote in 1948 of the war years:

> With the curious reserve of pleasure that is characteristic of the British race, we settled down to enjoy ourselves seriously, even gravely, at the pictures. We were ready for a good cry over something that was far removed from war. We wallowed in the tragedy of *Fanny by Gaslight*, *Love Story* and *Madonna of the Seven Moons*.

Gainsborough deliberately designed pictures for, and geared them towards, women filmgoers. They were the British equivalent of the glossy, tear-jerking dramas that Hollywood was producing for American female audiences, built around the talents of Bette Davis, Joan Crawford, Ann Sheridan and Olivia de Havilland.

Stars were all important to these pictures, larger-than-life icons to undergo larger-than-life trials and tribulations. In providing them, Gainsborough created the first body of genuinely cinema-produced British film stars. In the 1930s stars came to the cinema ready-made from the West End stage, from the music-hall, from musical comedy. Only a handful of stars, notably Anna Neagle and Robert Donat, were actually *created* by the cinema. But in the 1940s Gainsborough films made stars of Margaret Lockwood and Phyllis Calvert, Jean Kent and Patricia Roc, James Mason and Stewart Granger, Michael Rennie and Maxwell Reed. There were women to identify with and take as role models; men to drool over and fantasize about. Stewart Granger, dashing, flamboyant, virile, was Britain's answer to Errol Flynn and Tyrone Power. James Mason, brooding, sneering, smouldering, raping Margaret Lockwood in *The Wicked Lady* and flogging her to death in *The Man in Grey*, provided the same powerful, sexual charge as those dark, cruel, fascinating outsiders of nineteenth-century Romantic fiction, Rochester and Heathcliff. The sexual allure of these stars, male and female, was emphasized by their costumes, tight trousers and shirts open to the waist for the men, and low-cut, figure-hugging dresses for the women.

But for all the surface appeal of handsome costumes, lavish sets, glamorous stars, highly coloured and highly spiced storytelling, the films also focused attention on two highly relevant subjects, sex and class, areas where established patterns and beliefs were being overturned under the impact of war. The films reflected the much greater importance placed on the role of women in society as a result of the war. As Winston Churchill acknowledged, 'This war effort could not have been achieved if the women had not marched forward in millions and undertaken all kinds of tasks and work.' By 1943, 90 per cent of all *single* women between eighteen and forty and 80 per cent of *married* women with children over fourteen were working. The proportion of women working in the traditionally male preserve of engineering and vehicle building rose from nine to thirty-four per cent, and the number of women working on the land in traditionally male jobs more than doubled. In consequence, the number of women on domestic service had fallen by two-thirds. This did not necessarily result in instant equality. Women were for the most part denied equal pay with men and they got less in compensation for industrial accidents than men. But there was an inevitable increase in their sense of responsibility and independence, in their mobility and their self-esteem. As Mass Observation noted of women in the services in 1944, they were 'being forced to think for themselves instead of falling back on some opinion taken ready made from husband or father'.[32] Women like this will have responded sympathetically to Margaret Lockwood's defiant cry in *The Wicked Lady*: 'I've got brains and looks and personality. I want to use them instead of rotting in this dull hole.'

The war also witnessed a change in sexual behaviour and attitudes. Dislocation, both social and psychological, caused by bombing, bereavement, conscription and separation put a considerable strain on pre-war behaviour patterns. There were more casual liaisons and a greater degree of sexual freedom as a result of a 'live for today' attitude. In consequence, there was by 1943 a 139 per cent higher incidence of venereal disease than in 1939. There was a doubling of the illegitimate birth rate between 1940 and 1945, with almost a third of all babies, a record 255,460, being born out of wedlock. In 1945, 25,000 divorce petitions were filed, compared to 10,000 in 1938. Concern was therefore widely expressed for the stability of the traditional institutions of monogamous marriage and the family unit.[33]

Gainsborough hit on a formula to accommodate both the changing aspirations of women and the traditional social values threatened by the war. So we get a succession of anti-heroines who are independent, aggressive and single-minded in their pursuit of wealth, status and sexual gratification, and whose exploits can be vicariously enjoyed by the audience. But they are always contrasted with the virginal and dutiful good girl, who suffers but in the end gets her man and her happiness, while the bad girl gets her comeuppance. Typically, Margaret Lockwood as Lady Barbara Skelton, the eponymous *Wicked Lady*, having schemed, cheated and murdered her way to the top, dies wretched and abandoned when the only man she ever really loved rejects her because of her record and her conduct.

Lady Barbara is the archetype of what Gershon Legman called 'the bitch-heroine'. He was writing in America in 1948 of a parallel development which produced The *Wicked Lady*'s notorious American counterpart, *Forever Amber*, but he could well have been describing Lady Barbara when he said:

> The bitch-heroine speaks in a loud tone, moves with a firm stride; one hand always on the reins, the other ever-ready with the whip. She wants what she wants when she wants it, yes and by God, she is going to get it … or she will whip, shoot, stab, scrounge, undermine, ruin, and drive to suicide, drink or drugs any damn' man that stands in her way … She is no accident neither of history nor pathology. She is a wishful dream – Venus Dominatrix – cunningly contrived out of the substance of women's longings. She is presented to the 'emancipated' but still enslaved wives – mothers and mistresses as a fantasy escape from their servitude to men, to fashion, traditional morality and the paralyzing uselessness of being nothing but the show-horses of their owners' success.[34]

The moral of the Gainsborough films may be impeccable but the effect of the films is rather more ambiguous. The sweet and virginal good girl is often colourless and insipid creating a greater degree of audience identification with the full-blooded bad girl. It was the bad girl, Margaret Lockwood, who was the top female star at the British box office in 1944, 1945 and 1946, suggesting a degree of identification by the fans that did not occur with say, Patricia Roc, the longsuffering good girl of *The Wicked Lady*.

Other Gainsborough films elaborated the debate over the role and nature of the new woman in even greater detail. *They Were Sisters*, made in 1944, featured the divergent careers and fortunes of three middle-class sisters, played by Phyllis Calvert, Anne Crawford and Dulcie Gray. Each provided a different role model. Dulcie Gray was the pathetic, tyrannized drudge, driven to her death by a sadistic and domineering husband, the inevitable James Mason. Anne Crawford was the flighty adulteress with a string of lovers and an adoring husband who eventually divorces her. These alternatives, what might be called the Victorian and the Bohemian, are rejected by the film in favour of the third incarnated by Phyllis Calvert, the sensible, balanced, decent and capable sister with an understanding husband who is partner and helpmate. They inherit the children of the other sisters' disastrous marriages and are clearly seen as an ideal embodiment of stable monogamous marriage, shared responsibility and enlightened parenthood.

In the splendid *Madonna of the Seven Moons* the two rejected role models from *They Were Sisters* are combined. For in this film Phyllis Calvert plays a beautiful Italian woman with a split personality. Part of the time she is a repressed, saintly, do-gooding banker's wife with no real life or mind of her own. But she also on occasion vanishes to take up another existence as a sensuous, wanton gangster's moll, the plaything of swarthy, virile, knife-wielding Stewart Granger. In the end, the conflict of personalities is resolved by her death, saving the life of her daughter, Patricia Roc, who represents a type of healthy, modern womanhood. She smokes, drinks and wears shorts, and has a natural, easy unpuritanical manner. But she also marries her boyfriend, a British diplomat, and settles for monogamy and stability.

But the Gainsborough melodramas not only highlighted sex, they also dealt with the thorny question of class. Margaret Lockwood's anti-heroines in, for instance, *The Wicked Lady* and *The Man in Grey* were usually penniless or low-born girls who turn to crime to rise in society. Even the pure heroines, like Phyllis Calvert in *Fanny by Gaslight* (1944), are sometimes from humble backgrounds which prevent them marrying the men they love because of class barriers. The villains in such films, men like Lord Rohan and Lord Manderstoke, both played by James Mason, are the worst kind of aristocratic cads and seducers. The clear implication of the films is that social change and a levelling of the barriers is needed. Indeed, one character in *Fanny by Gaslight* actually says, 'In a hundred years this kind of class distinction won't exist anymore.' *The Man in Grey* is told in flashback, framed by a modern-day sequence in which Phyllis Calvert and Stewart Granger, whose Regency ancestors were separated, in part for class reasons, appear to be on the point of consummating their romance.

This is the sort of idea that was coming to be expressed more and more during the war. How far class barriers actually fell is still debated. But there is no doubt that contemporary observers believed this to be happening, so that George Orwell could write in 1944:

> The obvious class differences still surviving in England astonish foreign observers. But they are far less marked, and far less real, than they were 30 years ago. People of different social origins, thrown together during the war in the armed forces, or the factories or offices, or as firewatchers and Home Guards were able to mingle more easily than they did in the 1914–18 war ...[35]

Any discussion of sex and class had always been treated with the utmost caution by the film censors. There was some relaxation during the war, a relaxation which at last allowed the filming of Walter Greenwood's Depression classic *Love on the Dole*, which had been kept off the screen during the 1930s. But one outlet for the treatment of controversial subjects had always been period settings. Costume seems to have had the effect of blinding the censors to social and political comment. Thus in 1934 when proposed films denouncing anti-Semitism in Nazi Germany were regularly vetoed by the censors as likely to cause offence to a friendly foreign country, Gaumont British were able to film *Jew Süss*, a costume drama attacking anti-Semitism in eighteenth-century Württemberg. Similarly, Gainsborough, by using stylized Regency and Restoration settings, were able to highlight current preoccupations without inviting censorial interference.

It is perhaps not too fanciful to suggest that one important reason why audiences liked Gainsborough melodramas was because they spoke to them about the changing nature of women's role in society and the inequities of a hidebound class system, albeit in highly coloured and highly charged surroundings. Once the war was over, the service men were demobilized and the great female workforce disbanded, there was a gradual return to a more traditional role for women as wives and mothers. This was matched by a gradual drift away from the mood of radicalism which had elected Attlee's post-war Labour government to the greater conservatism that heralded thirteen years of Tory rule. We can perhaps detect the beginning of this change in the national mood in the decline in popularity of the Gainsborough melodramas.

It is worth locating Gainsborough melodramas in the wider pattern of British culture. Gainsborough costume dramas were unashamedly directed towards female viewers. They were categorized as 'women's pictures'. The success of the first one, *The Man in Grey*, ensured follow-ups and commercial dictates prescribed a continuity of ingredients and personnel. This meant that when the originators of the principal Gainsborough star types became unavailable, direct imitations were sought: Jean Kent to replace Margaret Lockwood, Maxwell Reed to replace James Mason and Dermot Walsh to replace Stewart Granger. Gainsborough costume drama thus became a generic form so distinctive and so successful that it was imitated by other companies.

Women's costume drama has a direct male counterpart – the swashbuckler. Both forms developed generic conventions, situations and characters. Both genres operated within strict polarities of good and evil, revelled in plot and incident, utilized stylized historical settings and deployed strongly characterized archetypes of heroes and villains, heroines and villainesses. Swashbucklers

operated unambiguously from a male viewpoint and from an idealized aristocratic perspective. Masculinity was defined by the existence and operation of
the chivalric code: the code of the gentleman. Heroes and heroines abided by
it and endorsed it. Villains and villainesses departed from it, revelling in their
wickedness and got their comeuppance. Roles were strictly defined. Heroines
were objects to be fought for, adored, to look decorative and remain chaste.
Villainesses embodied sexual, and often social, independence, promiscuity,
and conspiracy against legitimately constituted authority. Villain and villainess
together embodied a threat to the social and moral order, a threat invariably
vanquished by the hero.

If one takes *The Three Musketeers* as a classic swashbuckler, the archetypal
chivalric hero is D'Artagnan, the villain Chevalier de Rochefort, the archetypal
pure heroine Constance Bonacieux and the villainess Milady de Winter. The
same types are to be found in the Gainsborough costume drama, but the classic Gainsborough, for instance *The Wicked Lady*, subverts them. Where the
swashbuckler is seen from the standpoint of the upper-class male, the Gainsborough costume drama is seen from the female point of view and often from
that of a disadvantaged woman (governess/companion/servant/poor relation).
The Gainsboroughs have a hero and heroine but they tend to be less domi-
nant/charismatic than the villain and villainess, who almost become anti-hero
and anti-heroine. Where the emphasis in the swashbuckler is on athletic action
(duels, chases, fights, escapes) centred on the hero, in the Gainsboroughs the
emphasis is on plots, secrets, stratagems, lies, generally initiated by the villainess. The climactic comeuppance of villain and villainess would seem to preserve the moral order, but they have provided identification figures to an extent
that their swashbuckling counterparts did not. It is no coincidence that it was
the Gainsborough villain and villainess (James Mason and Margaret Lockwood) who topped the box-office polls and not the nominal heroes and heroines of the Gainsboroughs. This suggests a greater degree of audience
identification with the desire for immediate sexual gratification and social success, however obtained, which villain and villainess epitomized, than with the
concepts of honour, duty, chastity and restraint embodied by hero and heroine
and shared by them with the leading figures of the swashbuckler. It may also
not be coincidence that the heyday of Gainsborough costume drama in Britain
(1943–48) was a period of relative dearth of Hollywood swashbucklers. The
swashbuckler was to pick up again dramatically in 1949. As is clear from these
comments, I am treating British and American films side by side, which, considering that both nations were experiencing similar socio-cultural effects from

the war, may not be deemed unreasonable.

Most of the Hollywood swashbucklers of the 1940s were based on works written by nineteenth-century male authors, pre-eminently Alexandre Dumas, Robert Louis Stevenson and Justin Huntly McCarthy. The Gainsborough costume dramas were on the whole based on books written by twentieth-century women authors: Magdalen King-Hall (*The Wicked Lady*), Lady Eleanor Smith (*Caravan, The Man in Grey*), Norah Lofts (*Jassy*) and Margery Lawrence (*Madonna of the Seven Moons*). But these women were writing in a nineteenth-century tradition, in a form which may give us a further insight into the genre. *The Wicked Lady* clearly owes a lot to Thackeray's *Vanity Fair*. *Fanny by Gaslight* uniquely among the Gainsboroughs was based on a novel by a male writer (Michael Sadleir) but one which was a deliberate pastiche of the Victorian 'sensation' novels of the 1860s.

The sensation novel appeared as a reaction against the trend to social realism and the cosy familiarity of the then pre-eminent domestic novel (compare Gainsborough's bursting in upon the regime of wartime social realism associated with Ealing). They were informed by the extravagant emotionalism and criminality of the Gothic novel and the florid romance, by the sensation scenes and stereotyped characters of the stage melodrama. They were very largely the work of professional women novelists such as Mrs Henry Wood, Mary Elizabeth Braddon, 'Ouida' and Florence Marryat, and were conceived with a particular market in mind and written increasingly to a recognizable formula. According to Elaine Showalter,

> These women novelists made a powerful appeal to the female audience by subverting the traditions of feminine fiction to suit their own imaginative impulses, by expressing a wide range of suppressed female emotions and by tapping and satisfying fantasies of protest and escape.[36]

The classic sensation novel was Miss Braddon's *Lady Audley's Secret* (1862), *The Wicked Lady* of its day, in which the eponymous heroine deserts her child, pushes her husband down a well and seeks to dispose of those who discover her secret. In the end she is declared insane and placed in a private asylum. But modern feminist critics have interpreted her insanity as a convenient way of labelling deviant female behaviour.

The classic elements of the sensation novel were doubles, secrets and accidents/coincidences. If we extend the idea of doubles to include double lives, these are also to be found in Gainsborough costume drama. Both sensation novels and Gainsboroughs were popular with audiences, particularly female audiences. But the general critical attitude to the sensation novel also uncannily prefigures that to the Gainsboroughs. Both genres were critically excoriated, because they were allegedly immoral, unrealistic and in bad taste. But Mrs Margaret Oliphant gave the game away when writing of the sensation novels in *Blackwood's Magazine*:

> What is held up to us as the story of the feminine soul as it really exists underneath its conventional coverings ... is a very fleshly and unlovely record ... Now it is no knight of romance riding down the forest glades, ready for the defence and succour of all the oppressed for whom the dreaming maiden waits. She waits now for flesh and muscles, for strong arms that seize her and warm breath that thrills her through, and a host of other physical attractions, which she indicates to the world with a charming frankness ... The peculiarity of it in England is ... that this intense appreciation of flesh and blood, this eagerness of physical sensation, is represented as the natural sentiment of English girls, and is offered to them not only as the portrait of their own state of mind, but as their amusement and mental food.[37]

The Gainsboroughs offered the same frank acknowledgement of female sexuality and the same displacement of chivalry by sensual gratification.

The sensation novel was popular, according to Winifred Hughes, for three reasons: reaction against an age of rational and scientific explanation, materialism and cosy domesticity by an appeal to the irrational and primeval emotions; escapist antidote to bourgeois convention, middle-class responsibility and the stultifying canons of taste and decorum; appeal to female fantasies and wish-fulfilment.[38] Some of these reasons can be applied to the appeal of the Gainsboroughs but always within the overall context of the massive disjuncture in politics, culture and society represented by the war.

Links with this mid-Victorian period during World War Two can be found in abundance. A group of films criticized the Victorian paterfamilias and his ruthless subjection of wife and household as part of a general reaction against 'Victorianism' initiated by the war (for example *Gaslight, Hatter's Castle, Pink String and Sealing Wax*). In such films, patriarchal despotism invariably leads to tragedy, madness and death. It should be noted that all these films were based on works by men (Patrick Hamilton, A. J. Cronin, Roland Pertwee), delivering straightforward critiques of the marital and social values of mid-Victorian bourgeois society. It should not, therefore, be thought that criticism of masculine tyranny was exclusively a female preserve. Gainsborough costume drama must be seen as part of a wider trend of social comment mirrored in films devoted to women's contribution to the war effort (for example *The*

Gentle Sex, Millions Like Us, The Lamp Still Burns) and the lowering of social barriers by the mixing of different classes in the services (*The Way Ahead, Journey Together, Fires Were Started*). The struggles of lower-class women or disadvantaged women in previous centuries can be seen as constituting something that post-war society aimed to eliminate.

However, the exploration of such issues in the costume picture became such an established part of the cinematic scene that it was taken up even by companies chiefly associated with social realism and prestige literary adaptations. Ealing's *Saraband for Dead Lovers* (1948; from Helen Simpson's novel), with its Technicolor passions, marital tyranny, Gainsborough icon Stewart Granger and even a 'wicked lady', albeit, middle-aged, frustrated and vindictive (Flora Robson), stands out like a sore thumb from the documentary-drama that surrounded it. Similarly, Cineguild, which produced David Lean's Noel Coward and Charles Dickens adaptations, turned out *Blanche Fury* (1947), directed by Marc Allegret, also in Technicolor, also starring Stewart Granger and with a story featuring those Gainsborough staples, gypsies, a family curse and a disputed aristocratic estate.

Blanche Fury was one of four novels by Joseph Shearing that were filmed in 1947–48, and provide an important link between the 1940s and the 1860s and between Britain and Hollywood. *Blanche Fury* was based on a novel published in 1939; *Moss Rose* on a 1934 novel; *So Evil My Love* on a 1947 novel; *Mark of Cain* on a 1945 novel, *Airing in a Close Carriage*. Joseph Shearing was one of several pseudonyms employed by the prolific Gabrielle Margaret Vere Long (1886–1952). Her 'Shearing novels' were all based on real-life Victorian murder cases; each centred on a female protagonist, featured the classic 'sensation' ingredients (secrets, double-lives, accidents, intricate plotting) and highlighted the disastrous consequences of repression and marital tyranny. But only *Blanche Fury* (1947) really fits four-square into the Gainsborough model. The others, however, along with their Gainsborough elements, suggest other linkages, as does the fact that four of her novels should have attracted film-makers in such a short space of time.

Blanche Fury (Valerie Hobson) is a classic Gainsborough girl, governess and poor relation, determined to rise in society. She marries a wealthy weakling cousin while loving illegitimate steward Philip Thorn (Stewart Granger), who is obsessed with proving his title to the Fury estate. Philip murders Blanche's husband and father-in-law with her knowledge but she denounces him to the law when he tries to dispose of her stepdaughter. He is hanged and she dies bearing his son, who will inherit the estate.

The Mark of Cain (1948), directed by Brian Desmond Hurst for Two Cities, relates back to Gainsborough and across to two other cycles: the critiques of Victorian familial tyranny (see above) and the charming psychopath cycle (see below). Here the central character is a French girl (Sally Gray) married to a boorish, domineering Manchester businessman (Patrick Holt). She asserts herself against his repression with low-cut dresses, French songs and an aristocratic lover (Dermot Walsh). But love of her child prevents her from leaving her husband. He is, however, murdered by his brother (Eric Portman), who implicates Sally Gray, in order to secure her acquittal and win her love. He fails but his plot is exposed by Dermot Walsh in time to save her.

Both *Blanche Fury* and *Mark of Cain* are British-made movies. *So Evil My Love* (1948), directed by Lewis Allen, was also British-made but by a Hollywood company (Paramount) and with full Hollywood panache. Repressed missionary's widow Ann Todd falls in love with dissolute artist Ray Milland and is drawn by him into a web of blackmail and murder, which culminates in her best friend (Geraldine Fitzgerald) being convicted of murdering her tyrannical husband (Raymond Huntley), a crime in fact committed by Todd. However, discovering that her lover has been two-timing her, Ann Todd kills him and gives herself up. In its corrosive intensity, this study in soul-destroying obsessive passion is in effect a Victorian *film noir*.

Moss Rose (1947), directed by Gregory Ratoff and made entirely in Hollywood, is set in a foggy Edwardian London and a palatial country house, and has socially ambitious cockney chorus girl Peggy Cummins investigating the murder of a friend, one of a series of murdered girlfriends of mother-dominated aristocrat Victor Mature. The culprit turns out to be the aristocrat's mother (Ethel Barrymore), who has been unbalanced since her husband deserted her years before, taking the boy with him. This is, of all the Shearing films, the most straightforward period thriller, but with ingredients familiar from other films of the time, both British and American (an apparent woman-killing psychopath, murderous madness in aristocratic family, an independent, lowborn, social-climbing female protagonist).

The four stories, which range in form from full-blooded 'Gainsborough' melodrama to Edwardian thriller, are clearly linked by themes which recur in various combinations: madness, obsession, social division, class-based ambition, sexual repression, patriarchal tyranny. The central characters in all four films are women, who to a greater or lesser degree, are both victims of, and at the same time rebels against, a system that denies them social and sexual equality and freedom of choice. These themes take us back to Gainsborough and beyond that, to the Victorian sensation novels.

Hollywood produced its own softened and sentimentalized 'Gainsborough' costume dramas (*Kitty, Forever Amber*). But a more potent point of comparison is provided by *film noir*. The production in England of *So Evil My Love* by Hal Wallis came in the midst of the string of deeply *noir* melodramas that he produced in Hollywood (*The Strange Love of Martha Ivers, Sorry, Wrong Number, I Walk Alone, The Accused, Dark City*). Indeed in some respects *So Evil My Love* directly resembles *Martha Ivers*. The height of the *noir* in Hollywood (1944–50) coincided with the heyday of Gainsborough costume drama in Britain. Like the Gainsboroughs, the typical *film noir* was bound together by themes of obsession and alienation. But like the swashbucklers, they were strongly male-centred. Unlike the swashbucklers, however, they were informed by a deep and pervasive misogynism, represented by a succession of hauntingly beautiful but greedy, ruthless, sexually voracious sirens who scheme, plot, betray and murder without compunction: Barbara Stanwyck (*Double Indemnity, Martha Ivers*), Ava Gardner (*The Killers*), Yvonne de Carlo (*Criss Cross*), Jane Greer (*Out of the Past*) among them. Historians of the *film noir* attribute this phenomenon to masculine fear and resentment of the financial, social and sexual independence that many American women were seen to enjoy as a result of the war.

These contemporary American *films noirs* were paralleled in Hollywood by a series of powerful period melodramas of Edwardian 'fatal women' who amid respectable upper-class British surroundings engage in lust and murder: *Ivy* (Joan Fontaine), *Temptation* (Merle Oberon), *The Paradine Case* (Alida Valli). They link directly with Ann Todd in *So Evil My Love*. It is interesting to contrast the total lack of sympathy accorded by these films to their female protagonists with the sympathy usually shown to female-murdering male psychopaths, driven to kill prostitutes or unfaithful wives (symbolic of the very sexual licence feared by the wartime male). The classic case of this is John Brahm's superb Jack the Ripper tale, *The Lodger* (1944), made in Hollywood with Laird Cregar. But in Britain, too, Eric Portman played with considerable charm a series of elegant psychopaths, obsessed by women and driven by them to kill (*Wanted for Murder, Corridor of Mirrors, Mark of Cain*).

There is then, and for the same reason, room in the Gainsborough melodramas for this male viewpoint. The wages of sin, particularly sexual sin, is still death, with Margaret Lockwood beaten to death by James Mason in *The Man in Grey*, and abandoned in death by the only man she has ever really loved in *The Wicked Lady*. Similarly, Valerie Hobson and Ann Todd are consumed by their illicit loves and destroyed by them in *Blanche Fury* and *So Evil My Love*. Film companies as commercial operations always sought to maximize the appeal of their product and Gainsborough costume drama was able to appeal both to women through the vicarious fantasy of identification with Margaret Lockwood and to men through identification with the brutal and misogynistic machismo of James Mason, ensuring that liberated women get their comeuppance.

Gainsborough costume drama was able to accommodate both the changing aspirations of women and the traditional social and sexual values threatened by the war, by deploying characters to embody both. In 1947 Anna Neagle overtook Margaret Lockwood as top British star and remained in that position until 1952. The popular series of films teaming Anna Neagle and Michael Wilding, while acknowledging the existence of, and setting themselves against, snobbery and class prejudice, were essentially fairytales in which love conquered all and the Prince claimed his Cinderella. The basic values of a class society and of monogamous marriage were validated. *The Courtneys of Curzon Street*, the top British box-office success of 1947, was little more than a cutprice *Cavalcade*, and *Spring in Park Lane* (1948) was a remake of Jack Buchanan's pre-war vehicle *Come Out of the Pantry* (1935). Anna Neagle's displacement of Margaret Lockwood mirrored the rapid post-war return to 'normalcy' as women vacated the jobs they had taken up for the duration of the war and resumed their pre-war roles of wives, mothers and sweethearts. This was pre-eminently the message of *Brief Encounter*.

The 1946 film version of Noel Coward's one-act play was directed by David Lean, who fashioned it into one of the classics of British cinema. The film tells the story of a tender but doomed love affair between two middle-aged, middle-class people, housewife Laura Jesson and local doctor Alec Harvey, who meet by accident and fall in love but eventually part for the sake of their families.

It was fashionable in the 'swinging sixties' to mock the well-bred anguish of the lovers and the film's exaltation of restraint over unbridled passion, duty over indulgence and concern for others over immediate self-gratification. I remember attending a showing of the film in Cambridge in 1967 when the student audience were convulsed with laughter throughout, incredulous that the lovers did not just leap into bed together and to hell with the consequences, responsibilities or beliefs. This was a measure of how far value systems had changed since the 1940s.

Irrespective of the whims of fashion, *Brief Encounter* remains both documentarily and emotionally true. Its documentary truth lies in the precise evo-

12   Emphasizing traditional values: Celia Johnson and Trevor Howard in *Brief Encounter* (1946).

cation of a middle-class woman's existence in the Home Counties in the 1930s and 1940s. Laura's life revolves around her family and her home. She is preoccupied with domestic arrangements, raising the children and her weekly Thursday trip to Milford to do the shopping, change her library book at Boots, have lunch at the Kardomah and go to the pictures. Her short-lived love affair is similarly conducted against the background of the bustling Kardomah with its comic female orchestra, the Grand Hotel with its respectable potted palms, the luxurious super cinema showing *Flames of Passion,* and the botanical gardens. But the lovers' chief meeting place remains the refreshment room at the station, the ultimate in prosaic settings but one which thereby points up the poignancy of their situation.

Not only did the station setting, which was actually filmed at Carnforth in Lancashire, enhance the atmosphere of the picture, it also fulfilled a symbolic role. The station itself, with its periodic announcements, prominent clock and punctual arrivals and departures stands for the regularity and routine which the lovers are defying. The express racing through signifies their passion. Laura plans to throw herself under it but changes her mind at the last moment. The local stopping trains taking them in opposite directions represent the hum-drum reality of their normal lives.

The emotional truth of the film shines through in the superlative playing of Celia Johnson and Trevor Howard. Celia Johnson's portrayal of an ordinary woman suddenly touched by a great love is subtle, sensitive and almost unbear-ably moving. Trevor Howard's honest, thoughtful and sympathetic Alec com-plements her perfectly. But the love does not bring them happiness. It cannot because of everything they believe in and stand for. 'We are neither of us free to love each other. There is too much in the way,' says Laura. In the end, duty and responsibility triumph over sex. There is a whole unspoken worldview in the pressure of Alec's hand on Laura's shoulder, which is his only parting ges-ture – a value system centred on decency, restraint and self-sacrifice which has characterized the lives of countless people in Britain over many generations.

The anguish of these very English and very middle-class lovers is cleverly contrasted with the cheerful, overt and uncomplicated sexuality of the buffet staff, the self-important manageress with her 'refained' accent, the robust, down-to-earth ticket collector who pays her court and the giggling assistant, preoccupied with closing time, feeding the cat and meeting her boyfriend. The genuine romantic passion lying beneath the gentle understatement of the lovers' meetings is pointed up by the use of Rachmaninov's Second Piano Con-certo on the soundtrack. *Brief Encounter* is in short a film that is both of its time and timeless.

It certainly touched a chord with reviewers at the time, particularly women reviewers. E. Arnot Robertson called it 'the most moving film ever made'.[39] C. A. Lejeune, calling it 'one of the most emotionally honest and deeply satisfy-ing films that have ever been made in this country', concluded that it was 'a film to be taken out and relished to one's heart's content; to be seen and savoured, in quietness, over and over again'.[40] Richard Winnington, too, praised it for its 'sincerity and its infallible evocation of High Suburbia' and called it 'uncomfortably true and fascinating'.[41] When I wrote about the film several years ago in the *Daily Telegraph* my article provoked a flood of letters from women readers of a certain age testifying to its enormous impact upon them and the extent to which they identified with Celia Johnson, her dilemma and the values that sustained her in making her final decision. The significance of the film as an expression of national identity is underlined by the fact that the French failed to comprehend why the two lovers did not go to bed together and while the film did very well in 'better class halls' in Britain, rough work-ing-class audiences greeted it with raucous scorn.[42]

Notes

1   P.R.O. INF 1/867, published in Ian Christie (ed.), *Powell, Pressburger and Others*, London, 1978, pp. 121–4.
2   C. A. Lejeune, *Chestnuts in Her Lap*, London, 1947, p. 151.
3   Dilys Powell, *Films since 1939*, London, 1947, p. 30.
4   George Santayana, *Soliloquies in England*, London, 1922, p. 30.
5   F. C. Bartlett, *Political Propaganda*, Cambridge,1940, p. 152.
6   C. A. Lejeune, *Thank You for Having Me*, London, 1971, pp. 188–9.
7   Lejeune, *Chestnuts in Her Lap*, p. 96.
8   *The Manchester Guardian*, 4 June 1948.
9   Lejeune, *Chestnuts in Her Lap*, p. 97.
10 Leif Furhammar and Folke Isaksson, *Politics and Film*, translated by Kersti French, London, 1971, p. 232.
11 Ronald Howard, *In Search of My Father*, London, 1981, p. 122.
12 On the significance of *Ships with Wings*, see Anthony Aldgate and Jeffrey Richards, *Britain Can Take It*, Edinburgh,1994, pp. 326–45.
13 Kevin Gough-Yates, *Michael Powell in Collaboration with Emeric Pressburger*, London, 1971, p. 8.
14 Gough-Yates, *Michael Powell*, p. 8.
15 Christie (ed.), *Powell, Pressburger and Others*, p. 32.
16 Correlli Barnett, *The Collapse of British Power*, London, 1972, pp. 62–3.
17 Martin Wiener, *English Culture and the Decline of the Industrial Spirit*, Cambridge, 1981.
18 J. B. Priestley, (ed.), *Our Nation's Heritage*,London, 1940, p. 158.
19 Angus Calder, *The People's War*, London, 1971, p. 483.
20 Sir Denis Brogan, *The English People*, London, 1943, pp. 235–6.
21 Interview with Michael Powell by Gavin Millar, *Arena*, BBC-2, October 17, 1981.
22 Lejeune, *Chestnuts in Her Lap*, p. 117.
23 Noel Coward, *Australia Revisited – 1940*, London, 1941, p. 7.
24 Coward, *Australia Revisited*, p. 23.
25 Noel Coward, *Future Indefinite*, London, 1954, p. 139.
26 Aldgate and Richards, *Britain Can Take It*, pp. 204. 6.
27 *Documentary News Letter*, 3 October 1942, pp. 143–4.
28 Powell, *Films Since 1939*, pp. 25–8.
29 John Ellis, 'Art, Culture and Quality', *Screen*, 19 (Autumn, 1978), pp. 9–49.
30 Richard Winnington, *Film Criticism and Caricatures 1943–53*, London, 1975, p. 167.
31 Guy Morgan, *Red Roses Every Night*, London, 1948, p. 72.
32 Raynes Minns, *Bombers and Mash*, London, 1980, pp. 31–41.
33 Minns, *Bombers and Mash*, pp. 175–85.
34 Gershon Legman, *Love and Death*, New York, 1949, p. 58.
35 George Orwell, *Collected Letters, Journalism and Essays*, volume 3, Harmondsworth, 1982, pp. 38–9.
36 Elaine Showalter, *A Literature of Their Own*, London, 1982, pp. 158–9.

37   Winifred Hughes, *The Maniac in the Cellar: sensation novels of the 1860s*, Princeton ,1982, pp. 29–30.
38   Hughes, *The Maniac in the Cellar*, pp. 34–7.
39   *Penguin Film Review* 3, (1947), p. 33.
40   Lejeune, *Chestnuts in Her Lap*, p. 162.
41   Winnington, *Film Criticism and Caricatures*, p. 48.
42   Kevin Brownlow, *David Lean*, London, 1996, pp. 203–5.

5

National identity
post-war

The nature of the change effected in Britain by World War Two is much debated. Some historians argue that it signalled substantial change; others that it changed little. The problem should perhaps be viewed on two levels which we can loosely call the political and the social. There certainly emerged a new political consensus based on plans for a welfare state; while the circle of power widened to include left-wing intellectuals and trade unions. Greater dignity was bestowed on ordinary folk and the end of the war saw a Labour victory at the polls. There was substantial political change: the radicalization of important sections of the working and middle classes who voted Labour for the first time in 1945, the introduction of the welfare state, independence for India and the nationalization of staple industries. But there was considerably less social and cultural change. The House of Lords, the public schools and the monarchy survived. Society continued to be to a large degree deferential. The class system remained intact. As James E. Cronin noted:

> The political triumph of Labour was ... accompanied by a consolidation of working class culture and ways of life. The war, such a powerful solvent of political allegiances, disturbed merely the surface of social relations and allowed the enduring structures of society to reassert themselves powerfully after the war.[1]

Perhaps what the war did was to create a greater degree of sympathy between the classes, more social mixing, the desire to recognize and fulfil the legitimate aspirations of ordinary people. This is what Orwell saw happening in 1944:

We are not justified in assuming that class distinctions are actually disappearing. The essential structure of England is still almost what it was in the nineteenth century. But real differences between man and man are obviously diminishing and this fact is grasped and even welcomed by people who only a few years ago were clinging desperately to their social prestige.[2]

But it is the distinction between political change and social conservatism that Anthony Howard evidently had in mind when he observed: '1945 saw the greatest restoration of traditional social values since 1660.'[3]

Nevertheless, one wartime condition continued for a while after the war – the cinematic celebration of the people as hero. Ealing, Gainsborough and other studios continued to present cross-sections of the population, groups of differing age, class, gender and region coming together, and with a variety of problems thrown up and resolved often by collective effort.

With the war over, these communal films often centred on leisure activities. Thus we see 'the people' as hero in films about holiday camps (*Holiday Camp*, 1947), the football pools (*Easy Money*, 1948), a cycling club (*A Boy, a Girl and a Bike*, 1948), a dance hall (*Dance Hall*, 1950), the races (*Derby Day*, 1952), and a pub darts team (*A Day to Remember*, 1954). Nothing could be more symbolic of the notion of the people as hero than *Emergency Call* (Lewis Gilbert, 1952) in which the police search for three blood donors to give a vital transfusion to a little girl with leukaemia. When the three donors are found (a boxer, a negro stoker, a fugitive murderer dying from a gunshot wound), all are ennobled by the act of giving blood: the stoker overcomes his fears of racial prejudice, the boxer refuses to throw a fight and the murderer helps to restore a life after taking one. Almost the last of these films was *John and Julie* (1955), the story of two six-year-olds who run away to see the coronation and are helped by a cross-section of the population. This last film suggests that what we are seeing in this cycle of productions is not so much the people as a proletariat but the people as the nation, which is something very different.

These films do not on the whole suggest radical revolution or classlessness. It was not in the nature of the film industry to promote such films. This is indicated by the fate of *Chance of a Lifetime* (1950). Bernard Miles's film, a mild and good-natured plea for industrial democracy, for mutual respect and cooperation between workers and management, shows the workers in a factory take over and run the business themselves, though when they encounter difficulties the former managing director (Basil Radford) returns to help them and stays on as joint managing director with one of the workers. It is far from being subversive and is very much in the spirit of the wartime consensus films. But all three cinema circuits, chary of anything smacking of politics or controversy, refused it a release until the Board of Trade intervened to insist it be shown. It was thereupon released without enthusiasm or promotion and made no money.

The era of the 'people as hero' peaked with the Festival of Britain in 1951 and the coronation of Queen Elizabeth II in 1953. Both were celebrated in the cinema. Humphrey Jennings, the poet of wartime documentary, offered an interpretation of the nation in the official festival film *Family Portrait* (1950). The film begins with a photograph album and narrator Michael Goodliffe talking of Britain as a family and the festival as a family reunion, a chance to bring old and young, past and future together. It is Jennings's equivalent of Orwell's *The Lion and the Unicorn* and echoed its findings. Jennings, like Orwell, observed that the British loved public pomp (pageantry, tradition) and private domesticity (the fireside, the garden). Both saw a country full of paradoxes and both sought for the pattern that would make sense of them. The word 'pattern' recurs throughout *Family Portrait*. Jennings stresses the variations in weather, landscape and race, the individuality and diversity, but he sees it integrated into a unity by the alliance of industry and art, science and agriculture, the mingling of poetry and prose. History, tradition and continuity provide the links: the Battle of Britain emulates the Armada; Shakespeare, the Royal Society and the Thames run through English history and culture. Britain is a small, varied and restrained country but has exported her men and ideas round the world: the skirl of the pipes in the Canadian forest, the crack of the bat in the outback, the idea of Parliament from the Thames to the Indus and the Ganges (music, sport and parliamentary democracy). Cook and Livingstone are mentioned, stressing the imperial dimension of the national identity. But Jennings concludes by looking also towards Europe:

> We have become both inside the family of Europe, and the pattern overseas. We are the link between them. For all that we have received from them, and from our native land, what can we return? Perhaps the very things that make the family, a pattern, possible – tolerance, courage, faith. A world to be different in – and free – together.

The spirit of the immediate post-war years was incarnated by the stars who in 1947 supplanted James Mason and Margaret Lockwood as the top British box-office draws: John Mills and Anna Neagle. When commentators like J. B. Priestley and George Orwell sought a word to describe the average Englishman, they settled on 'decent'. In a film career spanning more than fifty years

John Mills was to incarnate decent Englishness – restrained, good-humoured, determined, honourable, self-deprecating. Although few stars have donned service uniform as frequently as Mills, he has not confined his acting to the officer class. His great achievement has been to show the qualities of English decency operating at every level of society. His roles have ranged from the gallant doomed gentleman hero of *Scott of the Antarctic* (1948) through the would-be gentleman Pip of *Great Expectations* (1946) and the lower-middle-class draper's assistant in *The History of Mr. Polly* (1949) to the gentle, innocent Lancashire boot-maker Willie Mossop in *Hobson's Choice* (1953) and the gruff working-class paterfamilias in *The Family Way* (1966).

In thus spanning the classes, he has ended up becoming truly an English Everyman. His heroes have been on the whole not extraordinary but ordinary men whose heroism derives from their levelheadedness, generosity of spirit, emotional restraint and sense of what is right. For much of the 1930s the young John Mills was just another aspiring musical comedy juvenile lead, his vocal and acting style modelled on that of Bobby Howes. But he gave clear notice of his future development when he was cast in the leading role in Walter Forde's sober and convincing 1935 adaptation of C. S. Forester's *Brown on Resolution*, retitled *Forever England* for the screen. He played the ordinary seaman who armed only with a rifle single-handedly pinned down a World War One German battleship until the British fleet could arrive and gave his life in the process. It was one of the few 1930s films to feature an authentic working-class hero and Mills's Albert Brown became his first definitive expression of British decency.

It was the war which gave Mills the opportunity to build on the qualities he had shown in the role. Noel Coward, who had spotted his talent in a repertory production of R. C. Sherriff's classic stage exploration of British character under stress, *Journey's End*, in Singapore in 1930, subsequently cast him in his patriotic stage epic *Cavalcade* and the revue *Words and Music*. It was Coward too who gave him key roles in the films *In Which We Serve* (1943) and *This Happy Breed* (1944), the two biggest British box-office successes of those years. In both films he played cockney able seamen, blood brothers of Albert Brown.

Mills accomplished the difficult task of making the familiar figure of the 'boy next door' a creature of flesh and blood. But he proved equally adept at playing officers and endowing them with the quintessential British qualities (*We Dive at Dawn*, *The Way to the Stars*). *The Way to the Stars* (1945) gained universal critical approbation for its Englishness, its realism and its understatement, and these qualities could be seen at their purest in John Mills's performance as schoolmaster-turned-pilot Peter Penrose.

It is a mistake to see Mills's film image as unemotional. There is always emotion there, but it is controlled. He has been perfectly capable of showing what happens when that self-control is pushed to breaking-point and he has given truly remarkable performances as an amnesiac struggling to retain his sanity in *The October Man* (1947) and as the sensitive tormented English commander of a rumbustious Highland regiment in *Tunes of Glory* (1960), where conflict was rooted in a clash of national characteristics.

Mills's female counterpart in almost every sense and the top British female star at the box office from 1947 to 1952 was Anna Neagle, who in a career in which she was almost exclusively directed by her husband, Herbert Wilcox, succeeded in creating an image of British womanhood that was well-bred, patient and resolute, finding fulfilment in a life of service and sacrifice. She had already established this image before the war in her hugely popular biographical films *Victoria the Great* (1937) and *Sixty Glorious Years* (1938) in which she had incarnated an iconic Queen Victoria, who is simultaneously mother of a young family, of the nation and of the Empire. She continued to elaborate this image during and after the war. In 1942 a year after the death of pioneer aviatrix Amy Johnson in a flying accident, Neagle starred in a biographical tribute to her, *They Flew Alone.* It not only recounted her career but highlighted her role before the war in bringing the Empire closer together along the air routes and her role during the war as a symbol of the achievement of women pilots. The film that both she and Wilcox regarded as her best was *Odette*, a memorable account of the ordeals of the Special Operations Executive undercover agent Odette Sansom. Filmed in 1950 on the actual locations of the events themselves in a sober semi-documentary style, *Odette* confirmed Anna Neagle's ability as a dramatic actress. She played with conviction a real-life heroine who described herself as 'an ordinary woman' but who displayed 'courage, endurance and self-sacrifice of the highest order'. She followed this up with *The Lady with a Lamp* (1951), an effective and at times moving account of Florence Nightingale's campaign to establish the nursing profession in the teeth of opposition from her family, bureaucracy and unreconstructed male chauvinism. In between these later films she starred in a series of nostalgic, fairytale celebrations of the class system (*Spring in Park Lane, Maytime in Mayfair, The Courtneys of Curzon Street*), with Michael Wilding as her Prince Charming. It is significant in terms of mythmaking that, unlike Lockwood and Mason, Mills was eventually knighted (1977) and Neagle created a Dame of the British Empire (1969), in recognition of the role both had played in incarnating an acceptable and popular image of Englishness.

The heroic Englishwoman: Anna Neagle as Florence Nightingale in *The Lady with a Lamp* (1951).   **13**

Generically speaking, when Gainsborough melodramas petered out as a popular genre in the late 1940s, their place was taken in the affections of the cinemagoing public by a very different animal – the Ealing comedies. There is no doubt that Ealing Studios and their dynamic chief, Michael Balcon, saw their role as a helping to create British national identity. When Ealing Studios were sold to the BBC in 1955, a plaque was installed which declared: 'Here during a quarter of a century were made many films projecting Britain and the British character.' In 1945 Balcon outlined a programmatic schedule for post-war film-making which demonstrates a high level of civic responsibility and patriotic pride. Pointing out that German propaganda had throughout the war depicted the British as 'blood-soaked Imperialists, punch-drunk degenerates, betrayers of our allies, grovelling servants of fabulous Jewish plutocrats', he called for a positive picture in films, what he called a 'complete picture of Britain'. This he defined as:

> Britain as a leader in social reform in the defeat of social injustices and a champion of civil liberties; Britain as a patron and parent of great writing, painting and music; Britain as a questing explorer, adventurer and trader; Britain as the home of great industry and craftmanship; Britain as a mighty military power standing alone and undaunted against terrifying aggression.[4]

There is evidence of the partial implementation of this aim at Ealing in the series of films set in the Commonwealth (*The Overlanders, Bitter Springs, Where No Vultures Fly, West of Zanzibar*), in a Dickens adaptation (*Nicholas Nickleby*), in films dramatizing the work of the police (*The Blue Lamp*), hospitals (*The Feminine Touch*), the Church (*Lease of Life*) and the probation service (*I Believe in You*), in films dealing with problems posed by the post-war reintegration of returning prisoners of war (*The Captive Heart*) and reconciliation with Germany (*Frieda*).

But for most people Ealing's post-war output means the celebrated Ealing comedies. There is no doubt what view people have of the Ealing comedies and of the world they project. It is a world that is essentially quaint, cosy, whimsical and backward-looking, it venerates vintage steam trains (*The Titfield Thunderbolt*), old Clyde 'puffers' (*The Maggie*) and run-down seaside piers (*Barnacle Bill*). It is a world that enshrines what are seen as quintessentially English qualities: a stubborn individuality that is heroic to the point of eccentricity ('It's because we're English that we are sticking to our right to be Burgundians,' says a character in *Passport to Pimlico*); a hatred of authoritarianism and bureaucracy coupled with a belief in tolerance and consensus; a philosophy that can be summed up by the slogan 'Small is beautiful; old is good'.

Balcon recalled the attitudes of his team at Ealing (nicknamed 'Mr. Balcon's Academy for Young Gentlemen') in an interview he gave in 1974:

> We were middle-class people brought up with middle-class backgrounds and rather conventional educations. Though we were radical in our points of view, we did not want to tear down institutions ... We were people of the immediate post-war generation and we voted Labour for the first time after the war; this was our mild revolution. We had a great affection for British institutions: the comedies were done with affection

... Of course, we wanted to improve them, or, to use the cliché of today, to look for a more just society in the terms that we knew. The comedies were a mild protest, but not protests at anything more sinister than the regimentation of the time.[5]

He believed that 'the comedies reflected the country's mood, social conditions and aspirations'. The period spanned by the Ealing comedies, from *Hue and Cry* (1947) to *Barnacle Bill* (1957), covers the terms of office of both Labour and Conservative government. The Attlee government (1945–51) implemented Labour's plans to create a 'brave new post-war world'. But in 1951 the Conservatives won a general election and were to remain in power for the next thirteen years. In 1945 there was a desire for change. Labour duly met this desire through the introduction of much needed reforms, but rationing, shortages and restrictions persisted. The generation that had won the war wanted the welfare state, but it also wanted fun and spending money. The Conservatives stayed in office for thirteen years by maintaining the welfare state but dismantling restrictions, ending rationing and promoting affluence. So having veered leftwards and sanctioned major social changes, the country veered rightwards, settling down to enjoy the fruits of peace and turning its back on further change.

The first half of the 1950s was an era of peace, prosperity and order. The crime rate was falling. There was full employment and rising productivity. The greater availability of consumer durables blunted class antagonism. The coronation of Queen Elizabeth II in 1953 was seen as ushering in a new Elizabethan age, as the Empire was transmuted into the Commonwealth, a worldwide brotherhood of nations, and as Britain continued to notch up memorable achievements: the conquest of Everest in 1953, Roger Bannister's first four-minute mile in 1954 and, in 1956, Britain's tenure of all three speed records – air, land and sea.

Given Ealing film-makers' admitted allegiance to Labour, it is arguable that the early Ealing films (1947–51) constitute a programmatic attack on the evils that Labour wished to eradicate: entrenched aristocratic privilege (*Kind Hearts and Coronets*), the power of money (*The Lavender Hill Mob*), monopoly capitalism (*The Man in the White Suit*) and colonialism (*Whisky Galore*). *Passport to Pimlico* (1949) is perhaps the arch-Labour film, pointing to the evils of a blanket removal of restrictions and seeking to reconcile the public to its lot.

Dedicated to the memory of rationing, the film is informed by a desire to return to the wartime spirit of unity and cooperation as the best means of facing and overcoming the problems of the post-war world. The first part of

14   Community feeling: *Passport to Pimlico* (1949).

Passport to Pimlico shows greed and self-interest surfacing in society to sub-
merge the community interest when Pimlico Borough Council throws out
greengrocer Arthur Pemberton's scheme for turning a bomb site into a lido for
local children and decides to sell it for profit (the evils of the unrestrained free
market economy). When an unexploded bomb goes off, revealing a Burgun-
dian treasure and a charter of independence, all restrictions and regulations are
abolished, and black marketeers flood in. Naked self-interest rules. At this
point an enemy appears to unite the people. In 1939 it was Hitler. In 1949 it
is Whitehall, which seeks to bludgeon the inhabitants of Pimlico into surrender. Miramont Place, Pimlico, declares itself independent and fights the war
again in miniature. In the end the bureaucrats are beaten by communal effort
and self-sacrifice. A compromise is agreed by the two sides, and Pimlico re-
enters the United Kingdom, to everyone's relief ('You never know when you're
well off until you aren't'). The ration-books are redistributed, for, as the message clearly states, rationing and restriction are better than the unrestrained
growth of free enterprise. Cooperation is better than competition, communality than individualism.

But times change, and if the early Ealing comedies can be seen as an affirmation of Labour's programme, the later ones can be seen as a retreat from it. Interestingly, the early Ealing comedies were more or less remade in the Conservative era (1951–58) and show interesting and instructive changes. *Whisky Galore* (1949), in which a Scottish island community fools and frustrates an English laird in order to keep a cargo of illicit whisky, is reworked as *The Maggie* (1954), in which the crew of an old Scottish 'puffer' fools and frustrates an American laird to keep its ship. *Passport to Pimlico* (1949), in which a small urban community defies the attempts of Whitehall to suppress its independence, becomes *The Titfield Thunderbolt* (1953), in which a small rural community defies the attempts of British Railways to close its branch line. *Kind Hearts and Coronets* (1949), in which a shop assistant wipes out all those who stand between him and a ducal title, becomes *The Ladykillers* (1955), in which a group of criminals fail to wipe out a little old lady and polish off each other instead. The changes in emphasis, locale and personnel are significant. In *Whisky Galore* the entire community undermines the English colonial power; in *The Maggie* the community has shrunk to a crew defending a vintage boat, and the enemy is an *American* businessman. A full-scale revolt has become the small-scale defence of a relic of the past, a Scottish analogue of *The Titfield Thunderbolt*. In *Passport to Pimlico* a committee of shopkeepers under a democratically elected leader fight the monolithic power of Whitehall over an inner-city area; in *The Titfield Thunderbolt* a semi-feudal rural community, led by its traditional leaders, the vicar and the squire (shades of *Tawny Pipit*), defends a rural branch line against British Railways, one of the great nationalized industries. In *Kind Hearts and Coronets*, a lower-middle-class murderer successfully eliminates an aristocratic family; in *The Ladykillers* a little old middle-class lady successfully survives attempts by a criminal gang to eliminate her. So while the British character and identity remain the same, the shift of sympathies and values in every case is clear.

The Ladykillers in particular celebrates the victory of a quaint, backward-looking, morally secure Victorianism over the disruptive forces of crime and youth. *The Ladykillers* is marked by a total absence of sexuality and a relative absence of youth. It is, on the contrary, a paean to old age. The absence of sexuality is not in itself remarkable, in that it was usually suppressed in Ealing films, and indeed in British films in general until the late 1950s. Robert Hamer's films *It Always Rains on Sunday* and *Kind Hearts and Coronets* are notable exceptions within both Ealing and British cinema. The suppression of sexuality is a reflection of the underlying puritanism of British life, the continuing legacy of Victorian evangelical Protestantism. But its counterpart is the penchant which the British have for brisk, no-nonsense old ladies, of whom the archetype is 'The Old Queen' herself and other more recent examples are Dame Margaret Rutherford, Lady Violet Bonham-Carter and Mrs Barbara Woodhouse. The cult of the nanny and the concept of the nanny society is an extension of this. It is perfectly encapsulated in *The Ladykillers*, in which the little old lady rules supreme, evoking George Orwell's dictum on England: 'It resembles a family, a rather stuffy Victorian family … it is a family in which the young are generally thwarted and most of the power is in the hands of irresponsible uncles and bedridden aunts.'[6]

In *The Ladykillers* youth is represented by Peter Sellers's Harry, who is part of the gang. He, like contemporary youth itself, is emasculated and neutralized in one of the film's key scenes. The gangsters are forced to take part in an old ladies' tea party. They stand about helplessly, cups of tea and plates of cake in their hands, as they are swamped by old ladies, and Professor Marcus, the gang leader, glumly hammers out on the pianola 'Silver Threads among the Gold'. Similarly, at the start of the film, as Mrs Wilberforce heads for the police station, she pauses to smile at a baby in a pram. Instead of cooing, the baby screams with rage. It is the nascent revolt of extreme youth against a society dominated by extreme old age. Significantly, the cultural revolution of the late 1950s was characterized by those elements of sexuality and youth that are suppressed in *The Ladykillers*. Although there is evidence to suggest that director Alexander MacKendrick intended the film as a satire and critique on the state of mid-1950s England, parochial, complacent and backward-looking, it was taken by audiences and critics as a celebration of that England.[7]

The same view of England is celebrated on an international level in the post-Ealing but decidedly Ealingesque *The Mouse That Roared* (1959), with Peter Sellers playing, Alec Guinness-like, a trio of roles and a script co-written by Roger MacDougall, author of the Ealing films *The Bells Go Down, The Gentle Gunman* and *The Man in the White Suit*. The film recounts how the tiny duchy of Grand Fenwick in the French Alps declares war on the United States when Californian wine undercuts Grand Fenwick's wine and threatens to destroy its economy. The intention is to lose the war and gain US aid but Grand Fenwick accidentally wins the war when their invasion force arrives in New York during a practice nuclear alert and capture the latest superweapon, the Q-bomb. As a result, they are able to negotiate not only a US government loan and the withdrawal of the Californian wine but also world disarmament.

Grand Fenwick, allegedly the smallest country in the world and the only

English-speaking country in continental Europe, was founded by a wandering English knight in the Middle Ages who took a fancy to the area and settled down there. But it is in fact clearly intended to be an analogue of Britain, seen as Victorian/medieval, backward, quaint, antique and happily behind the times. It is ruled by a hereditary grand duchess, Gloriana XII, still mourning her lost consort, Count Leopold of Bosnia-Herzegovina, clearly intended to be Queen Victoria and played by Sellers as an impersonation of Margaret Rutherford. The hereditary prime minister, Count Rupert of Mountjoy (played by Sellers as an impersonation of George Sanders), and the working-class leader of the loyal opposition, Mr Benter (Leo McKern), are clearly intended to be seen as Tory and Labour leaders, cheerfully colluding to help lose the war. Monarchy, aristocracy and cosy deferential democracy are supplemented by an army which wears chain mail and carries bows and arrows. It is commanded by a hereditary marshal and constable, Tully Bascom (Sellers again), a holy fool who wins the war, the girl and the disarmament treaty. Critique of a backward Britain or celebration of a quaint and lovable backwater, it depends on your pre-existing point of view. Audiences, on the whole, seem to have taken it as a celebration and enjoyed identifying with the medieval underdog which takes on and humbles the new upstart superpower. But, fascinatingly, a New York theatre which the Fenwickians pass on their invasion displays a poster for *Look Back in Anger* reminding us that cultural revolution is already stirring.

Among Ealing's non-comic output perhaps the most significant film is *The Blue Lamp*, which was the top British moneymaker of 1950 and won the BFA British film award. *The Blue Lamp* established the dominant image of the police force for a generation, creating a long-lasting and still recognized myth figure, PC George Dixon, the ideal bobby. Dixon is the epitome of the respectable working class – solid, dependable, wise, decent, the ultimate bobby on the beat, who knows his patch and his people, and helps them solve their problems informally. He also tackles guntoting tearaways. Dixon smokes a pipe, plays darts, grows begonias, sings in the police choir. He is partnered by a young PC, played by Jimmy Hanley, who is a surrogate son but inheritor and successor of his role and ethos.

The Blue Lamp is in line with Ealing's collective ethos. For we see the police as a community – the police choir, the police darts team, the police as an epitome of British life, deeply rooted in the local community and committed to protecting it. The film re-creates the texture of day-to-day police life: the police dealing with lost children, drunks, dogs, dangerous drivers, domestic disputes. But the central thread of the narrative follows the criminal career of a violent

15   Public service: Jack Warner, Jimmy Hanley and Bruce Seton in *The Blue Lamp* (1950).

young thug, Tom Riley, played electrifyingly by Dirk Bogarde. He eventually guns down Dixon in a sequence which shocked contemporary audiences and the remainder of the film shows the process by which the police hunt down and capture Riley.

Dixon was played by Jack Warner, who, second only to John Mills, came to incarnate decent English values in films. A former music-hall and radio comedian and brother of Elsie and Doris Waters, whose Gert and Daisy are archetypal cockney wives, Warner graduated to films as a character actor after the war and was to incarnate two long-lasting and enormously popular figures,

George Dixon and Joe Huggett. After he played Dixon in the film, Warner did a stage version of *The Blue Lamp* in 1952, and in 1955 Ted Willis revived Dixon as the central character in the television series *Dixon of Dock Green.* Warner resumed the role and was to play it continuously until 1976, appearing in 434 episodes and becoming a British institution.

In his 1955 analysis of English public attitudes, sociologist Geoffrey Gorer found to his surprise that, although there were few attitudes subscribed to by two-thirds or more of the population, three-quarters expressed an 'enthusiastic appreciation of the English police'. He had expected many people to see them as the 'servants of the capitalist class'. Instead he found enthusiasm for them which he described as

> peculiarly English and a most important component of the contemporary English character. To a great extent, the police represent an ideal model of behaviour and character, an aspect about which many respondents are articulate.[8]

The qualities they embodied and which his respondents repeated over and over were reliability, courage and devotion to duty, decency, 'the best in the world'. They could have been describing George Dixon (Jack Warner became so associated with the image of the honest copper that he was cast as a policeman also in *It Always Rains on Sunday*, *The Ladykillers*, *The Quatermass Experiment*, *Emergency Call* and *Jigsaw*.)

But Warner also played an equally significant figure, Joe Huggett, who first appeared with his family in the film *Holiday Camp* (1947). The Huggetts, Joe and Ethel, their three children and their cantankerous Grandma were such a hit with the public that they came back in their own series, *Here Come the Huggetts* (1948), *Vote for Huggett* (1949) and *The Huggetts Abroad* (1949). Thereafter Jack Warner and Kathleen Harrison who played Joe and Ethel returned in *Meet the Huggetts*, a popular radio series than ran from 1953 to 1962. In terms of Jack Warner's role as the ideal working-class paterfamilias, it might also be noted that he did a summer season in Blackpool in a stage version of the long-running radio soap opera *The Archers*, playing Ambridge farmer Dan Archer. George Dixon, Joe Huggett, Dan Archer, if ever there was a roster of square, solid, decent Englishmen it is these and Jack Warner played them all.

The Huggetts are an all-purpose upper-working/lower-middle class family and above all else the epitome of respectability. They live in a suburban semi with a car and a phone (not typical working-class attributes). Joe is a factory foreman, honest, hardworking, decent. Ethel is his devoted, hardworking wife, who shops, cooks and cleans, calls everyone 'ducks', gossips over the garden wall and constantly makes 'the nice cup of tea' which Orwell saw as symbolic of working-class culture. In this she is the exact counterpart of Gladys Henson, who plays Jack Warner's wife in *The Blue Lamp* and *The Captive Heart*.

The three films endorse established male/female roles, family life and sexual respectability. *Here Come the Huggetts* runs several plotlines that reinforce these. It details the havoc caused by the arrival of a blonde floozie cousin (Diana Dors). Ethel worries that Joe may be seduced by her. But Joe reassuringly tells her: 'There are two things in the world I can't abide – a pretty woman and a clever woman. And you're neither.' Ethel is delighted. Daughter Jane Huggett has a dilemma. Attracted to a Bohemian intellectual who does not believe in marriage, she settles in the end for the boy next door, an ex-airman and steady dependable type played by Jimmy Hanley. She marries him and they plan to emigrate to South Africa.

In *Vote for Huggett* Joe stands for the Council. He is a Progressive and stands against the Moderates; code for Labour and Conservative. He has proposed creating a lido as a war memorial and community facility, just like Arthur Pemberton in *Passport to Pimlico*, and has to deal with the machinations of corrupt property speculators and the class snobberies of other councillors at their golf club. But he overcomes all this and wins the election. The film celebrates local democracy, public service and government by decent men.

Then, in *The Huggetts Abroad*, the couple decide to emigrate to South Africa, largely because of the weather. Ethel doesn't know the difference between South Africa and South America ('It's the same thing – natives and all that'). They go overland by lorry, passing through Algiers which Ethel thinks looks like Bournemouth, cross the Sahara making cups of tea whenever their spirits need raising. They survive sandstorms and sabotage and are rescued by French troops, but refuse the celebratory champagne ('It's not quite my cuppa tea,' says Joe). But Joe misses the pub, Ethel misses the queues and they decide to return home, leaving Jane and Jimmy to proceed to South Africa as the pioneers and settlers.

The film sees no contradiction between local communality (the pub, the youth club, family wedding, local election, form the background of the action), the nation (one important theme has the Huggetts sleeping in the street to await the royal wedding of Princess Elizabeth and Prince Philip, which they describe as 'a family affair of the nation') and the Empire (to part of which they propose to emigrate). Here the multiple identities – London suburbs,

British nation and British Empire – all interlock and are centred on permanent values: work, thrift, patriotism, family, loyalty, marriage. Moreover, the Huggett family structure and ethos is not an isolated phenomenon. It is part of a continuing cultural strand. The Huggetts are the direct successors of the Buggins family, a popular pre-war radio series, and the precursors of the first popular television soap opera family, the Groves, in the mid-1950s. They all endorsed the same basic values.

The Grove Family ran on BBC-TV from 1953 to 1956. The Groves were a hardworking, respectable, patriotic lower-middle-class family in a London suburb but had a national appeal because, while solid, decent, self-employed builder Bob Grove (Edward Evans) was a Londoner, his wife, sensible, motherly Gladys (Ruth Dunning), was a northerner. There was a grown-up son Jack, a posh-talking daughter Pat and two children, Lennie and Daphne, constantly getting into scrapes. But the nation's favourite was the cantankerous and opinionated Gran (Nancy Roberts), Gladys's Lancastrian grandmother who lived with them. She became a cult figure in the 1950s. The Grove family reached the cinema screen in a low-budget feature film, *It's a Great Day* (1955), in which Bob is falsely accused of stealing tiles to finish a building contract in time for the opening of a new estate by Princess Margaret. This drama is paralleled by Pat's boyfriend troubles and Lennie's getting trapped up some scaffolding and having to be rescued. But the highpoint of the film is the selection of the Groves as the family to receive an informal visit from the Princess on her tour of the estate. The film details the excitement, the arrangements, the comic mishaps and culminates with everyone bowing to camera as the Princess arrives for tea – the climax of the Great Day.

Despite an increased social realism in films in the late 1950s, influenced in part by the developments in television drama, gender roles and value systems continued to be those of *Brief Encounter*. There was even a *Brief Encounter* of the council flats, *Woman in a Dressing Gown* (1957), adapted by Ted Willis from his own highly praised television play. Upright and decent Jim Preston (Anthony Quayle) decides after much agonizing to leave his good-hearted but slatternly wife Amy (Yvonne Mitchell) after twenty years of marriage for an attractive and decent younger woman (Sylvia Syms). In the end, however, like Celia Johnson in *Brief Encounter*, he cannot go through with it and returns to be reunited with wife and son over the iconic 'nice cup of tea'. The commitment to marital fidelity and marital responsibilities is thus shown not to be just a prerogative of the middle classes. It is integral to all-round British decency.

However, what is striking about the 1950s, is the way in which for the most part, just as the nation drifted towards Conservatism from Labourism, so films returned to the themes and ethos of the 1930s. The 1930s had been characterized by Korda's imperial epics, Viennese and high-society musicals and the regional comedies of Fields and Formby. In the 1950s Ivor Novello musicals (*The Dancing Years*, 1950, *King's Rhapsody*, 1955) made a comeback; Norman Wisdom comedies occupied precisely the same niche as those of George Formby; while an unappealing cockney comic called Ronald Shiner appeared in direct reworkings of 1930s properties (*Top of the Form*, 1953, a remake of Will Hay's *Good Morning Boys*, 1937; *Up To His Neck*, 1954, a remake of Jack Hulbert's *Jack Ahoy*, 1934; *Girls at Sea* , 1958, a remake of *The Middle Watch* 1940;and *My Wife's Family*, 1956, a remake of *My Wife's Family*, 1931).

There was a revival of imperial films, dormant during the war. Some tackled the independence movements besetting the Empire, from a position of hostility (*The Planter's Wife*, 1952; *Simba*, 1955; and *Safari*, 1955). Others re-created the Empire in its heyday in celebratory mood: *Pacific Destiny* (1956), *Zarak* (1956), *North West Frontier* (1959). Korda even remade his 1939 *The Four Feathers* as *Storm over the Nile* (1955), but it was a sign of the cut-price times that all the action footage was lifted from the original version and stretched to fit cinemascope. Meanwhile, a real-life storm was bursting over the Nile, the Suez crisis, which was to signal the demise of Britain as a major imperial power.

Elsewhere other 1930s hits were being remade: *Hindle Wakes* (1952), *The Good Companions* (1957), *Hobson's Choice* (1957), *Orders Are Orders* (1954), *The Thirty Nine Steps* (1959), Ben Travers's *Cuckoo in the Nest* (remade as *Fast and Loose*, 1954). Anna Neagle revived her two great pre-war successes, Queen Victoria and Nell Gwynn, in *Lilacs in the Spring* (1954).

The major new generic development was the mid-1950s war film, re-creating Britain's finest hour, but now conspicuously not in terms of the People's War but as a celebration of the officer class, which had featured in the pre-war cinema: *Angels One Five* (1951), *The Cruel Sea* (1953), *The Dam Busters* (1955), *Reach for the Sky* (1956), *Appointment in London* (1953), *The Malta Story* (1953), *Above Us the Waves* (1955), *Ill Met by Moonlight* (1957), *Battle of the River Plate* (1956), *I Was Monty's Double* (1958), *Danger Within* (1959), *Albert RN* (1953) and *Sink the Bismarck* (1960).

But even as society seemed to be settling back into its groove, and Jack Warner and John Mills continued to epitomize old-fashioned British decency, an alternative vision of Englishness was stirring. It was precisely that form of English manhood epitomized by Dirk Bogarde in *The Blue Lamp*. Bogarde's

Tom Riley, at once neurotic and erotic, was both disturbing and exciting. In him, filmgoers found the sex and violence celebrated in the Gainsborough costume films but here located in the present and in the working class. The character related to growing concern in society about violent juvenile delinquents. The character audiences were expected to prefer was Jimmy Hanley's young PC Andy Mitchell, a junior version of Dixon, who now looks rather bland, conventional and, above all, sexless.

In *The Blue Lamp* Bogarde projected a brand of masculinity that the British cinema for the most part found uncomfortable and shied away from. This highlights a more general problem that bedevilled Bogarde's career during the years he was under contract to Rank, a period centred on the 1950s, a decade in which more sheerly tedious and uninspired films were produced in Britain than at any other time. Rank, like the British cinema in general, was always happier with the kind of rugged, clean-cut, unintellectual, conventionally masculine male epitomized by Anthony Steel, Michael Craig and George Baker, whose careers Rank was promoting in the 1950s and who, like Jimmy Hanley, came across as quintessentially bland and uninteresting. All three, incidentally, became considerably more interesting and watchable actors in middle age.

Instead of playing to Bogarde's strengths as an actor, Rank cast him in a series of conventional war stories, routine thrillers and facile romantic comedies, which drew on his undoubted elegance and charm but made few other demands on his talent. Such films, particularly the popular *Doctor* series, brought him a large female following but left him unsatisfied as he fought for roles with greater depth and subtlety. These were to come along in the 1960s when alternative forms of masculinity became possible.

The emergence of Tom Riley has to be seen in the context of the British low-life melodrama, which took a new turn after the war with the spiv films, which have been analysed by Robert Murphy.[9] The first screen spiv was played by – of all people – Stewart Granger in Sidney Gilliat's *Waterloo Road* (1944), in which John Mills, the epitome of dogged British decency, goes AWOL from the forces to rescue his wife from the attentions of the flashy pintable king and racketeer Granger. Thereafter 'ordinary people' were conspicuous by their absence from films which laid bare an alternative society with alternative values existing below the surface of the respectable world. It was a totally unregulated free-enterprise society where anyone can supply anything to anyone for a price, a society of human pirhanas swimming greedily through shoals of shady deals and sudden turbulent eddies of violence: *They Made Me a Fugitive* (1947), Noose (1948), *Night and the City* (1950).

After the spivs, the juvenile delinquent became the cinema's criminal alter-native to decent English humanity. The counterparts of Dirk Bogarde's Tom Riley were Richard Attenborough's Pinky in *Brighton Rock* (1947) and James Kenney's Roy Walsh in *Cosh Boy* (1952). Walsh, played by the goodlooking and sexy James Kenney, is a quickwitted, arrogant, unprincipled teenager, with a slow-witted older sidekick, evoking distinct echoes of Craig and Bentley. The film is explicitly constructed as a warning about juvenile delinquency, attribut-ing it to lack of parental discipline. Roy Walsh runs his own gang, organizes a series of robberies (including that of his own grandmother) and shoots a man-ager while stealing the takings of a wrestling match. His involvement in vio-lence is matched by his involvement in sex. He seduces his sidekick's sexy sister away from her respectable, sexless accountant boyfriend. She succumbs to his arrogance and glamour and becomes pregnant. He then ditches her and she attempts suicide but survives, providentially losing the baby. The populist out-come of all this, however, is that when the police arrive to arrest Walsh they take a walk for ten minutes to allow his new stepfather to give him a 'good thrashing' with his belt. This clearly expects audience applause, as familial authority is restored.

The dangerous attractiveness of Pinky, Tom Riley and Roy Walsh, all work-ing-class criminals, all young, all unmoved by codes of respectability, duty and authority, points to the development of an alternative national image, one that was to emerge in the late 1950s and the 1960s.

Notes

1 James E. Cronin, *Labour and Society in Britain 1918–1979*, London, 1984, p. 137.
2 George Orwell, *Collected Essays, Journalism and Letters*, Harmondsworth, 1971, volume 3, p. 39.
3 Michael Sissons and Philip French (eds.), *The Age of Austerity*, London, 1983, p. 31.
4 *Kinematography Weekly*, 11 January 1945, p. 163.
5 John Ellis, 'Made in Ealing', *Screen*, 16 (Spring 1975),,,p.,119.
6 Orwell, *Collected Essays*, volume 2, p. 88.
7 Jeffrey Richards and Anthony Aldgate, *Best of British*, Oxford, 1983, pp. 99–114.
8 Geoffrey Gorer, *Exploring English Character*, London, 1955, p. 213.
9 Robert Murphy, *Realism and Tinsel: cinema and society in Britain, 1939–48*, London, 1989, pp. 146–67.

6

The swinging
sixties and after

The 1960s witnessed a revitalization of British cinema and the emergence of a flourishing and diverse film culture after what was widely perceived to be the 'doldrums era' of the 1950s. In the 1950s the two great cinematic traditions of the 1940s – Ealing and Gainsborough – had gradually run out of steam and finally expired. Many of the great directors of the 1940s (Lean, Reed, Powell, Dickinson, Hamer, MacKendrick) had gone into decline, retired or removed to America. There was a sclerotic sense of old formulae being unimaginatively followed, of a failure of nerve and invention. The characteristic products of the decade reflected this: the war films that relived old glories, the Norman Wisdom comedies that trod in the footsteps of George Formby, the anaemic 'international' epics which aimed futilely to break into the American market and which misused the sensitive talents of such stars as Dirk Bogarde and Peter Finch. In ethos and outlook, in technique and approach, mainstream 1950s films were essentially conservative, middle-class and backward-looking.

The 1960s brought a small but influential body of films which captured the attention of critics by tackling the lifestyle and aspirations of the young and working class in a fresh, unpatronizing way. They adopted an approach that was to be seen and proclaimed as sexually liberated, politically radical and socially committed. They marked a definite advance on 1950s cinema but, seen from the perspective of the 1990s, seem more limited, particularly in their treatment of race, sex and gender, than critical orthodoxy has allowed. Over-concentration on these films at the expense of the many other cinematic products of the decade has also tended to distort the received picture of the age. This was perhaps inevitable given the fact that British film-makers now operated in the context of an expanding British film culture. Hitherto this had consisted largely of the British Film Institute, *Sight and Sound*, the Academy Cinema and a belief in the superiority of continental 'art' films. The 1960s witnessed a mushroom growth of film societies, film magazines and film books, creating a whole generation of film-literate young cineastes, willing to take an unprejudiced look at everything, notably the hitherto critically despised genre products of both Britain and Hollywood.

British 'New Wave' cinema was born out of the social and cultural upheaval of the late 1950s, which embraced the death of the Empire, the rise of working-class affluence, the emergence of a distinctive youth culture and the revival of the intellectual left. In form, it took its lead from French 'New Wave' cinema which preferred location-shooting to studio work, natural lighting to formal lighting and a fragmented, impressionist approach to traditional linear narrative. But, in content, British 'New Wave' cinema was deeply rooted in and strongly influenced by the social-realist novels of writers like Alan Sillitoe and John Braine, the theatre work of the 'Angry Young Men' like John Osborne and the 'kitchen sink' working-class dramas that were a feature of Sydney Newman's *Armchair Theatre* on ATV.

The principal mood of the 'New Wave' was one of discontent and dissatisfaction, a rejection of things as they were, a powerful sense that Britain was hopelessly mired in a hierarchical Victorian world of outdated values, disciplines and restrictions. The key year had been 1956– the year of Suez and Osborne's *Look Back in Anger*. It was also the year when a group of aspiring young film-makers, Tony Richardson, Karel Reisz and Lindsay Anderson, banded together, calling themselves 'Free Cinema' in a conscious act of reaction against the cosiness, complacency, consensus and class consciousness, which they saw as characterizing 1950s cinema. But, in fact, in personnel, approach and philosophy they resembled nothing so much as the 'documentary boys' of the 1930s grouped around John Grierson. There was the same middle-class romanticization of the working class, the same commitment to a realist aesthetic, the same belief in location-shooting, the same rejection of studio artifice.

The 'free cinema' group graduated from short documentaries to full-length feature films at a time of major change in cinema. The year 1946 had marked the peak of British cinema attendance, with a record 1,635 million attendances at 4,709 cinemas. Thereafter, there was a slow decline in the early 1950s which became precipitate after 1955 with the introduction of commercial television. Between 1955 and 1963 over two-thirds of the audience and over half the cinemas disappeared. The old family audience at whom the cinema had aimed its product transferred its allegiance to television, and there was consequently an increase in the proportion of young people in the audience. Although the industry continued for some time to produce family films, and with some success – the top British box-office hits of 1960 and 1961 were *Doctor in Love* and *Swiss Family Robinson* there was a greater emphasis on productions with an appeal to the young.

The British 'New Wave' films shared common characteristics: black-and-white photography, melancholy jazz scores, northern locations (Blackpool, Salford, Bolton, Bradford, Wakefield, Morecambe, Manchester). The recurrent images of steam trains, cobbled back streets, gasometers and railway viaducts gave the films the feeling of taking place at the fag-end of the nineteenth century. The bus ride around Manchester that opens *A Taste of Honey* (1961) captures perfectly this oppressive and decaying world of time-worn military statues, smoke-grimed buildings and weather-beaten Victorian iconography. Out-of-season seaside resorts and empty railway stations at night, recurrent locales in 'New Wave' films, visually encapsulate the mood of despair and desolation that suffuses many of them.

But most of all, perhaps, the 'New Wave' films were about sex and class. *Room at the Top* (1959) inaugurated the 'New Wave' and achieved sensational critical recognition. But the immediate popular reaction was to its sexual content. Film censor John Trevelyan put it in context:

> In retrospect one can see that Jack Clayton's *Room at the Top* was a milestone in the history of British·films … At the time its sex scenes were regarded as sensational and some of the critics who praised the film congratulated the Board on having had the courage to pass it. Ten years later these scenes seemed very mild and unsensational … There was no nudity or simulated copulation, but there was rather more frankness about sexual relationships in the dialogue than people had been used to.[1]

Honesty about sex was only one side of the picture. As John Braine, author of the original novel put it:

> The new dimension of the film was in presenting a boy from the working classes not as a downtrodden victim, but as he really was. It wasn't important that Joe Lampton was honest about sex, what was important was that Joe was honest about the whole business of class. Most ambitious

working-class boys want to get the hell out of the working class. That was a simple truth that had never been stated before.[2]

Room at the Top showed how under the existing system a working-class boy with the desire to succeed could only do so at the cost of his self-respect, peace of mind and personal happiness. The forces ranged against Joe are representatives of the patronizing upper class, the self-made middle class anxious to preserve the *status quo* and a conservative and conformist working class, pressing him not to rise above his station.

So in a sense *Room at the Top* could be construed as a 'state of England' film, paralleling the plethora of books and articles appearing in the late 1950s and early 1960s on the subject of 'what's wrong with Britain'. So, too, could the two films made from John Osborne's plays by Tony Richardson, *Look Back in Anger* (1959) and *The Entertainer* (1960), though neither enjoyed the box-office success of *Room at the Top*. Kenneth Tynan welcomed Osborne's play *Look Back In Anger* as a major breakthrough in a West End theatre world 'virtually dominated by a ruthless three power coalition consisting of drawing-room comedy and its two junior henchmen, murder melodrama and barrack room farce … united in their determination to prevent the forces of contemporary reality from muscling in.' Identifying what were to become key characteristics of the cinematic 'New Wave', he wrote:

> *Look Back in Anger* presents post-war youth as it really is … All the qualities are there … the drift towards anarchy, the instinctive leftishness, the automatic rejection of 'official attitudes', the surrealist sense of humour, the casual promiscuity, the sense of lacking a crusade worth fighting for … The Porters of our time deplore the tyranny of 'good taste' and refuse to accept 'emotional' as a term of abuse; they are classless and they are also leaderless.[3]

Look Back in Anger, the prototype 'Angry Young Man' film, has not worn well, partly because of Richard Burton's monumental self-pitying bombast in the role of Jimmy Porter, a working-class university graduate running a market stall. The play itself is also a problem, dominated by a disgruntled and deracinated intellectual delivering a wearying succession of tirades against the middle class, the system, things as they were, symbolized by his upper middle-class wife whom he cruelly ill-treats and abuses.

Intellectually, Jimmy is against the old value systems; he declares the age of chivalry dead and mocks the heroic imperialism of the 1939 film *Gunga Din* which he sees at the cinema. Emotionally, he is nostalgic both for the music-

hall which is seen as a symbol of working-class irreverence, vitality and solidarity, and for an idealized lost Edwardian golden age ('high summer, long
days in the sun, slim volumes of verse, bright ideas, bright uniforms'). But with
both gone he has nothing to put in their place. Despite a bleak reunion with
his wife at the end, the future seems to hold little prospect of change or
improvement. Jimmy has no constructive philosophy, no social vision. The
film, like the play, merely represents a cry of frustration against the system and
as such struck a chord with young middle-class left-wing intellectual theatre-
goers, though not with cinemagoers, who were alienated by its unrelenting bil-
iousness.

The ideas in *Look Back in Anger* were elaborated in *The Entertainer*. Britain's
greatest actor, Laurence Olivier, who as the wartime Henry V had become a
symbol of the nation, now took on another symbolic role. Third-rate variety
artist Archie Rice is England in the 1950s, seedy, bankrupt, run-down, at the
end of a great tradition. His father Billy (Roger Livesey), dignified, elegant,
patriotic, is a retired music-hall star who dies trying to make a comeback. His
world and his values are gone beyond recall. While Billy sings nostalgically
'Don't let then scrap the British navy', his grandson is killed at Suez in the last
imperial adventure.

But if Jimmy Porter and Archie Rice did not command the affection of cinemagoers, Arthur Seaton in Karel Reisz's *Saturday Night and Sunday Morning*
(1960) did, making the film a box-office success. Alexander Walker aptly
describes Arthur as

> unrepentantly sexy in a repressive community, sharper than his mates,
> tougher than the pub brawlers he worsts, anti-romantic in his view of
> women as providing a night's pleasure, reconciled to paying the penalty
> for his pleasure, but resistant to all life could do to him.[4]

Arthur has a philosophy: 'Don't let the bastards grind you down. What I'm out
for is a good time; all the rest is propaganda.' He is an authentic product of
working-class affluence. He denounces the system (the tax man, the bosses,
national service). He denounces the idea of the 'good old days' (the sentimen-
talization of the slums). But he is no radical or revolutionary. He is a totally
self-centred, wage-earning individualist with money to spend, who drinks
himself silly, seduces a workmate's wife and shows no concern for anyone but
himself. The film is a robust celebration of the 'rough' working-class ethic of
immediate gratification (through sex, drink, sport and fighting). Although the
film was set in Nottingham, this was the ethic and outlook that was to become

16   Sixties anti-hero: Albert Finney and Rachel Roberts in *Saturday Night and Sunday Morning* (1960).

known as that of 'Essex Man' and would dominate the 1980s. Arthur Seaton would unquestionably have voted for Mrs Thatcher in 1979.

Alan Sillitoe, who scripted *Saturday Night and Sunday Morning* from his own novel, also wrote the more ambitious 'state of England' film *The Loneliness of the Long Distance Runner* (1962), directed by Tony Richardson. Its central figure, Colin Smith (Tom Courtenay), shares Arthur Seaton's philosophy: 'I don't believe in slaving my guts out for the bosses to get all the profits' and turns to crime. He is sent to Borstal, the kind of total institution that classically functions as a symbol of the nation. It is repressive, socially controlled, run by a public school elite and headed by a paternalist governor. The film details Colin's rebellion against, and rejection of, the values they try to instil, winning his own battle by deliberately losing a cross-country race. Courtenay's Colin with his pinched 1930s features, grim and deprived home life and irrepressible bloody-mindedness looks back to the proletarian heroes of the past, social rebel rather than juvenile delinquent.

These and the other films of the 'New Wave' centred almost exclusively on the discontents of the young urban working-class male (Albert Finney, Tom Courtenay, Alan Bates). Often they were employed and not short of money. They were willing to engage in extra-marital sex but anxious to avoid marriage. But most of all they chafed against the weight of restriction and repression imposed by the combination of the class system, traditional Victorian morality and social convention.

But if the young male's pursuit of freedom was approvingly charted, there was no similar treatment of the young female. One of the continuing elements of the 'New Wave' cinema, seen in for instance *Look Back in Anger* and *Saturday Night and Sunday Morning*, is a pervasive misogyny: the idea of marriage as a trap and the end of freedom for the male, the maltreatment of women by violence or exploitation, abuse or neglect.

John Schlesinger's *A Kind of Loving* (1962), based on Stan Barstow's novel, explores the nature of a 'shotgun marriage' between Alan Bates, romantic, respectable working-class lad with an unsatisfied wanderlust, and his conventional unimaginative girlfriend (June Ritchie), tied to the apron-strings of her snobbish, reactionary, houseproud mother (Thora Hird), symbol of everything the 'New Wave' detested. Lindsay Anderson's *This Sporting Life* (1963), based on David Storey's novel, memorably examines the predicament of a brutalized, inarticulate working-class rugby player (Richard Harris), unable to express his affection and need for the widow he has a relationship with.

Sidney Furie's *The Leather Boys* (1963), based on Gillian Freeman's novel, is often described as a film about homosexuality. But it is more centrally about the problems of a working-class marriage. Reggie (Colin Campbell) is married to Dot (Rita Tushingham), but sex is the only link between them. They row continually and Reggie finds greater fulfilment in his mateship with Pete (Dudley Sutton), based on a shared love of motor bikes, the pub and having 'a good laff'. But the mateship is soured by the discovery by Reggie that blond, epicene Pete is gay. Reggie, having left Dot, now leaves Pete.

Dot is depicted as shallow and heartless; Reggie as decent and sensitive. He works; she idles. He looks after his widowed Gran; she neglects her. She has sex with other men; he does not. But the root of the problem is that she does not conform to his view of a wife as an obedient, demure, home-creating woman. She outrages his working-class puritanism by her tarty hair-style, telling dirty stories, neglecting her housework and devoting herself to a regime of 'the pictures', the hairdresser and *True Romance*. It is thus a film about the mismatch between the rough and the respectable working classes; but it is also about the joys of mateship, emotionally fulfilling but ultimately flawed by the need to avoid sexual expression. Rita Tushingham in *The Leather Boys* represents one of the two main female types in the 'New Wave', where women are either 'silly tarts' (June Ritchie, Shirley Ann Field, Tushingham) or 'selfish old bags' (Thora Hird, Dora Bryan, Avis Bunnage).

The only 'New Wave' film to centre on a woman is Tony Richardson's *A Taste of Honey* (1961), adapted by Shelagh Delaney from her stage play. It explores the uneasy relationship between a vulnerable gamine Jo (Rita Tushingham) and her tarty, self-centred mother (Dora Bryan). Jo becomes pregnant but rejects adulthood, womanhood and responsibility, retreating into a childhood signalled throughout the film by recurrent children's songs and chants, and becoming reconciled with her mother. It is perhaps significant that the woman-centred *Taste of Honey* also contains representatives of two other groups largely absent from the 'New Wave' and little seen in the cinema of the 1960s. Rita Tushingham has a black lover, a cheerful Liverpudlian sailor whom she idealizes as an African prince, and an effeminate homosexual friend and confidant, Geoff, whom she treats as a sister. But all three, the black, the gay and the single mother-to-be, are seen as marginal to mainstream society.

This is also true in Bryan Forbes's impressive *The L-Shaped Room* (1962), based on the novel by Lynn Reid Banks. A pregnant unmarried French girl (Leslie Caron) moves into a seedy London lodging house and is bracketed with its population of sympathetically observed but indisputably marginal inhabitants: a homosexual black trumpeter, an elderly lesbian music hall artist and two prostitutes. Her pregnancy alienates the struggling young writer (Tom Bell) with whom she has fallen in love. In the end, she rejects an abortion but also gives up a life as a potential single parent to return to her parents. Although this ending has been subsequently criticized, it is an authentic response for the period and made entirely believable by Leslie Caron's beautifully judged interpretation of love, loneliness, despair and resolution.

Both Murray Melvin's sexless Geoff and Brock Peters's Johnny, with his very understated affection for the young writer, are sympathetic and unthreatening gays. But they are peripheral. Despite the liberation of young men, British cinema was not yet ready to liberate gays, women or blacks. However, it was Britain which produced the first commercial feature films to plead for tolerance for homosexuals since the German film *Anders als die Anderen* in 1919. Two films in 1960, *Oscar Wilde* and *The Trials of Oscar Wilde*, showed Wilde as a noble, tragic hero, victim of personal infatuation and of social and judicial prejudice. But the events took place safely in the past and involved a Bohemian literary genius. It was Basil Dearden's *Victim* (1961) which finally showed homosexuals existing at every level of contemporary society and illustrated the prejudice against them. Dirk Bogarde gave a courageous and moving performance as a married barrister and non-practising homosexual, who lays his career on the line to expose the plight of homosexuals under the existing law, a blackmailers charter. The careful characterization of the barrister, as Vito Russo points out, meant that liberals could accept him as a non-threatening figure, and gays as a crusader.[5] It was not until *Sunday, Bloody Sunday* in 1971 that homosexuality could be presented as a valid alternative lifestyle. But then neither Gay Liberation nor Women's Liberation really got underway until the 1970s.

Racial minorities were largely absent from 'New Wave' films as they were from British cinema in general in the 1960s. Jimmy Porter defends an Asian stall-holder against racism and Rita Tushingham has her black lover in *A Taste of Honey*. But the classic anti-racist statement comes in Ted Willis's social-realist drama *Flame in the Streets* (1961), directed by Roy Baker. Highly schematic and didactic, it showed English society permeated with racism and highlighted the dilemma of a trade union shop steward with impeccably liberal views (John Mills), confronted by the prospect of his daughter marrying a black man. Hollywood's supreme exemplar of the noble black man, Sidney Poitier, came to Britain for the sentimental and predictable, but popular, *To Sir, With Love* (1965), directed and written by James Clavell from the novel by E. R. Braithwaite. Poitier plays a Guyanan teacher, who wins over a class of tough, unruly cockney kids – introducing them to good manners, culture and self-respect, and eliminating colour prejudice, mindless violence and scruffiness along the way. But no black British star emerged capable of emulating Poitier as charismatic standard-bearer of racial equality.

So 'New Wave' films had little positive to say about blacks, gays and woman. In fact the attitudes of the male characters of the 'New Wave' films were generally negative. They were against a good deal but not for very much except themselves. Colin Smith wants to line up the Establishment and shoot them. Arthur Seaton denounces the bosses and the system. But what did the 'New Wave' heroes want in its place? 'Everything … nothing,' says Jimmy Porter.

Along with hostility to the system in 'New Wave' films went hostility to the new materialism, affluence and the homogenizing effect of the mass media. This had been the keynote of Richard Hoggart's seminal book *The Uses of Literacy* (1957) and it haunted the mainly left-wing writers and directors of the 'New Wave'. Arthur Seaton claims that most people are content to conform as long as they can get 'their telly and their fags'. Jimmy Porter denounces the

Americanization of culture and celebrates the dying indigenous art of the music-hall. Thora Hird's obsession with tawdry TV quiz programmes in *A Kind of Loving* is part of her monstrousness. In *Loneliness of the Long Distance Runner*, Colin Smith's family splurge on consumer goods the compensation for their father's death, a sequence parodically shot as a TV advertizing magazine. But there is a major paradox here. One of the objects of the Labour movement's long struggle had been to ensure a share of the national prosperity for the working class. But now that the working class had achieved affluence, they had used it to endorse and participate in a consumerist world, a situation summed up and satirized in *Live Now, Pay Later* (1962).

The positive side of the films is sexual frankness, the willingness to acknowledge and depict sexuality in a way previously rare in British cinema, and respect for the traditional pattern and texture of working-class life as it was lived: the seaside holiday, the pub, the football match, the dance, the family party. These were integral to 'New Wave' cinema and part of the Hoggartian nostalgia for a warm old working-class culture of community. But it was a world that was vanishing even as it was being filmed. Society was becoming steadily more privatized, with television, individualist and home-centred, eclipsing the communal activities of the cinema, the football match and the pub; with private cars replacing public transport and Spanish package holidays superseding the domestic holiday camp. In a sense 'New Wave' films were part of this process, centring as they did on individual predicaments and particularly highlighting sex and self rather than work and class. As John Hill points out, this emphasis tends to make the films more conservative than radical, stressing individual fulfilment rather than social change.[6] Certainly, the individualism of the 'New Wave' films is in marked contrast to the communality and collectivity that was such a feature of wartime and post-war films, whether it be the service films about groups of men and women banding together to defend the nation or the Ealing comedies in which small communities join forces to defeat some outside power.

A dramatic change came over British films after 1964, a change that coincided with the victory of the Labour party in the general election of that year, with its emphasis on youth, progress and innovation, and with the birth of 'Swinging London'. The film which symbolized this change and caught the mood of the moment was *Tom Jones* (1963). Henry Fielding's picaresque eighteenth-century novel with its story of the rise of a poor boy to fame and fortune amid an uninhibited celebration of sex and conspicuous consumption was brought to the screen by John Osborne, Tony Richardson and Albert

Finney. The style they adopted was far from the reverent naturalism of previous classic novel adaptations. It was jokey and knowing and it employed slapstick comedy, speeded-up action, captions, asides to camera and an urbane narration. This irreverent eclecticism, inspired by the techniques and ethos of Pop art, set the tone and style for the rest of the decade. *Tom Jones*, bawdy and funny, celebrated a previous permissive age of gusto, gourmandizing and zestful free-living, appearing at a time when the Labour election victory promised '100 days of dynamic action' and a programme of social reform in an era of full employment and growing affluence. It signalled in its subject, its style and its attitude the end of the old order against which the 'New Wave' heroes had chafed.

Restraint and restriction, both personal and institutional, were in retreat and a new world was emerging, a consumerist world of colour supplements and pirate radio, glamorous television commercials, discos and boutiques, a cult of the new and the now. The accent was on youth. For the first time in history it became fashionable to be young and working class. Looks, style and attitude rather than birth and breeding became the keys to success. Rock musicians, fashion photographers and Pop artists were the role models of the moment. Sexy roistering Tom Jones was the symbol of this age. The cinema box offices confirmed the truth of the poster slogan: 'All the world loves Tom Jones.'

It was the involvement of 'New Wave' stalwarts Osborne, Richardson and Finney in *Tom Jones* that was the most significant development. It signalled almost overnight the end of the 'New Wave'. It was as if the unspoken agenda behind the discontent powering the 'New Wave' – the desire for a life of total and unrestrained freedom – had been met by the crumbling of the old order. Thus, in films, sober realism and earnest social comment gave way to fantasy, extravaganza, escapism; black-and-white photography to colour; the grim North to the glittering metropolis; puritanical self-discipline to hedonist self-indulgence; plain, truthful settings to flamboyant, unrealistic decorativeness. Where the emphasis had been on the dark side of the self, discontent, repression and deprivation, it now switched to the bright side, to self-assertion, personal fulfilment and the good life. John Schlesinger's *Billy Liar* (1963), based on the play by Keith Waterhouse and Willis Hall, was the transitional film for 'The New Wave'. Shot in black and white in Manchester, it highlighted the frustrations of early-1960s youth – a dull job, critical parents, a possessive, conventional girlfriend. But Manchester youth Billy Fisher (Tom Courtenay) finds escape from all this in fantasy daydreams. Julie Christie represents the icon of escape. Totally liberated, she is his soulmate, sexually free and secure. At the end, she leaves for London, though he cannot bring himself to go. But the stars and directors who had made their names in 'New Wave' films all forsook the pressures of working-class life in the North of England for the frenetic gaiety of the metropolitan maelstrom: Alan Bates in *Nothing but the Best* (1964), Rita Tushingham in *Smashing Time* (1967) and Tom Courtenay in *Otley* (1968). Julie Christie became the chief symbol of liberated womanhood in Swinging London, starring in *Darling* (1965), *Far from the Madding Crowd* (1967), *Petulia* (1968) and *The Go-Between* (1971). But there continued to be limits to and ambiguities about her liberation.

Tom Jones, meanwhile, inspired imitations: *The Amorous Adventures of Moll Flanders* (1965), *Lock Up Your Daughters* (1969), *Sinful Davy* (1969) and in more serious vein *Where's Jack?* (1969), confirming the view that the eighteenth century was the preferred model for the 1960s. Tony Richardson emphasized this by producing an historical counterpart to *Tom Jones* in *Charge of the Light Brigade* (1968), as unsparing an indictment of the nineteenth century as the earlier film had been an uninhibited celebration of the eighteenth. *Light Brigade* characterized Victorian society as squalid, repressive, brutal and irredeemably class-ridden, implying that it had survived into the twentieth century and was in need of a final sweeping away. But importantly the film was also anti-war and anti-military, a direct response to the Vietnam War which dominated the thinking of many of the creative and the young, who saw it as an affront to the new age of freedom, peace and love, as a reminder of great-power politics and of archaic imperialism. The nineteenth century was deemed useful only for providing the modish bric-a-brac for the new age, everything from hussars' jackets to Boer War biscuit tins. Victorian decor was utilized as high-camp and grand-kitsch backgrounds for the comic capers of *The Wrong Box* (1966), *The Assassination Bureau* (1968) and *The Best House in London* (1968).

Fantasy was never far from the surface of many 1960s films. It even featured in the work of the 'New Wave' veterans. Karel Reisz went on from *Saturday Night and Sunday Morning* to direct *Morgan – A Suitable Case for Treatment* (1966), based on David Mercer's play, which hinged on the fashionable Laingian idea that the mad were saner than the sane. Morgan (David Warner) dresses up in a gorilla suit and has fantasies of himself as Tarzan and King Kong. But he prefers his fantasies to reality and does nothing to bring about the Marxist revolution his father sought. Reisz next went for the fashionable historical parallelism, directing *Isadora* (1967), a lengthy and indulgent celebration of one of the 'bright young things' of the 1920s; Isadora Duncan, a pioneer of sexual liberation and defiance of convention. Both films were typical tracts for the times, highlighting individuals who either retreated into themselves or created their own world around them like a comforting cocoon rather than engaging with wider social issues.

Lindsay Anderson, always his own man, also turned to fantasy but used it in his devastating *If* (1968), combining the dream of youthful revolt and sexual liberation with a comprehensive assault on the public-school system and the hierarchical society of which it was a microcosm. Ominously for the new age, Anderson shows the forces of reaction massing at the end and fighting back. His hero Mick (Malcolm McDowell) turns his machine-gun on the audience, supinely watching the revolution from the stalls rather than participating.

If Richardson, Reisz and Schlesinger had been the characteristic directors of the 'New Wave', the celebrants of Swinging London were Dick Lester, Michael Winner and Clive Donner. Michael Winner's films encapsulated the most prized characteristics of the new era: coolness (*Play it Cool*, 1962; *The Cool Mikado*, 1963) and jokiness (*You Must Be Joking*, 1965; *The Jokers*, 1966; *I'll Never Forget Whatsisname*, 1967) – the decade's prime directive was that nothing was to be taken seriously.

Dick Lester's films were mercurial, modish mosaics, his style fragmented and breathlessly fast-moving, an amalgam of influences from silent comedy, television commercials, comic strips, Marx Brothers and Goon Show surrealism. His was the quintessential visual style of the second half of the decade, a daring and dynamic form of montage gleefully embracing parody, pastiche and Pop art. His career is emblematic of the way British cinema developed in the decade. In 1963 he directed the charming, whimsical *Mouse on the Moon*, a sequel to *The Mouse That Roared* and recounting Grand Fenwick's participation in the space race. With its antique monarchy, hereditary prime minister, medieval flummery and pretensions to great-power status, it looked back to the Ealingesque England of the 1950s. But in 1964 he directed *A Hard Day's Night*, followed by *The Knack* (1965) and *Help* (1965). All three films show provincial youth coming into their kingdom, conquering London and refashioning the world in their own image.

A Hard Day's Night is a celebration of the decade's greatest cult figures, the Beatles, and their music. The film is built around their image as cool, youthful, irreverent, quirky and quick-witted provincials. They were the first pop idols not to be processed into safe 'family entertainers' and in the process emasculated. Both Tommy Steele and Cliff Richard, initially viewed as threateningly sexy, had been carefully transformed into 'the boy next door', a Mickey Rooney *de nos jours*. Cliff in particular, who had starred in *Expresso Bongo* (1959) as a sexy working-class teen idol on the make, entered the 1960s as the distinctly unthreatening hero of a series of highly traditional screen musicals (*The Young Ones*, 1961; *Summer Holiday*, 1962; *Wonderful Life*, 1964). The Beatles, however, were securely anchored by Lester in the new Pop art and Pop culture.

The Knack, in which Michael Crawford, playing an inexperienced young schoolteacher, races round trying to find out how to make out with girls, was an affirmation of the new youthful sexuality. The film demystifies the archetypal male seducer Tolen (Ray Brooks), who in his dark glasses and leather gloves exercises a power over women that is initially unquestioned and irresistible. In his place it elevates the extension of sexual prowess to the young inexperienced provincials – male and female – as at the end Crawford pairs off with the newly arrived Rita Tushingham.

Help, the second Beatles film, is a brightly coloured Pop collage, a melange of Marx Brothers comedy, cod Oriental mayhem, inventive sight gags and imperial bric-à-brac. The film bubbles with Lester's feeling about the era:

> There was an enormous sense of optimism that I felt in England from 1962–3 until 1967, which is when it started to go wrong, it seems to me. During that time, the films had a sense of response to a feeling that anything could be achieved, that the class structure was breaking down, that there was a new opportunity for the structure of life in England.[7]

The year 1967 was also the time when Lester's films began to go wrong as he tried to tackle 'the big questions' (war and the nuclear threat), and to do so in the form of black comedy, in *How I Won the War* (1967) and *The Bed Sitting Room* (1969). *How I Won the War* aimed to illustrate the futility of war and to achieve something of the mood of Joseph Heller's cult novel *Catch 22*. But the abrupt changes of mood from way-out comedy to savage violence, the anger that was too close to the surface and the attempt to take on too much (the class system as well as the war) all flawed the film. It aimed at Brechtian alienation, but as Lester ruefully observed, 'One has learned over the years that Brechtian alienation is a euphemism for audience's backs seen disappearing down a street.'[8] *The Bed Sitting Room*, a surrealist all-star comedy about Britain after a nuclear holocaust, also failed. A hit-and-miss compendium of anti-Establishment squibs that never cohere, it ended up merely preaching to the converted. Much more effective as commentaries on war were Richard Attenborough's *Oh, What a Lovely War* (1968), which viewed World War One as absurdist but played off the music-hall traditions of the era, and Joseph Losey's *King and*

The Sixties swing: The Beatles in *Help* (1965).   17

Country (1964), an intimate, small-scale realist work dramatizing the court martial of an individual soldier for desertion.

Clive Donner's *Nothing but the Best* (1964) was the new era's black-comedy mirror-image of the 'New Waves's *Room at the Top*. This time Alan Bates played the working-class outsider who reaches the top. He does so by aping the lifestyle, speech patterns and value systems of the upper class, with the aid of coaching by a seedy Old Etonian renegade (Denholm Elliot). He jokily cons and murders his way to the top in stark contrast to the earnest and painful ascent of Joe Lampton, aided by a knowing, with-it and witty script by Frederic Raphael. The frantic knockabout of *What's New Pussycat?* (1965), Woody Allen's first script, highlighted the sex obsession of the Swinging Sixties, with Peter O'Toole as a magazine editor unable to cope with his irresistibility to women and neurotic Woody Allen driven to desperation by his inability to attract women.

Here We Go Round the Mulberry Bush (1967), based on Hunter Davies's engaging novel, was a suburban *Knack*, with an inexperienced teenager (Barry Evans) attempting to lose his virginity, this time amid the parks and shopping-precincts of Stevenage New Town. Fashionably including jaunty self-deprecating commentary direct to camera, fantasy daydreams (parodies of silent film, James Bond and Swedish sex film) and psychedelic titles, it dramatized the eternal questions in the fevered minds of questing young men: why do the ones you fancy never fancy you and the ones you don't fancy always fancy you; why do their dress zips always get stuck at the crucial moment; why do they always have hideous and unditchable 'best friends'.

The fashionableness of London proved a magnet for foreign directors who produced some distinctive work in British studios, generally in the fantasy mode: Antonioni (*Blow Up*, 1966), Truffaut (*Fahrenheit 451*, 1966) and Polanski (*Repulsion*, 1965; *Cul-de-Sac*, 1966). But it was Joseph Losey, expatriate American victim of the McCarthyite witch hunt, who engaged with Britain and British society rather than using it merely as a backdrop to work out personal obsessions. He directed a trilogy of scripts by Harold Pinter which laid bare the complexities of the British class system and exposed the web of deception and betrayal it enshrined, themes that have always fascinated both Pinter and Losey: *The Servant* (1963), *Accident* (1967) and *The Go-Between* (1971). They are shot and staged with a classical formality that underlines and reinforces their clinical examination of the social structure.

But even Losey succumbed to the prevailing mood of the age when he directed a brace of impenetrable baroque melodramas, *Boom* (1968) and *Secret Ceremony* (1968), both starring Elizabeth Taylor. Visually impressive and strikingly composed, they are slow-moving and portentous examinations of self-indulgent grotesques trapped in their own enclosed worlds, meditating on life, death and the cosmos. But Losey also made *Modesty Blaise* (1966), in many ways the archetypal late-1960s film. A nonsense espionage plot unfolded in chic, cool, cultish style with relaxed sexuality, voice-overs and even musical duets, it is a compendium of Op art and Pop art, kitsch and camp, an intellectual's homage to the comic strip, put together with artful zest. Losey saw it as 'a comment on a particularly empty and hideous era of our century' but it emerges as something of a celebration of that world of style and form over content and values.[9]

For all the emphasis on self-fulfilment, playfulness and youthful individualism, a few directors valiantly persevered with films about the excluded and the disadvantaged: the old (Bryan Forbes's *The Whisperers*, 1967), working-class boys (Ken Loach's *Kes*, 1969) and working-class wives (Ken Loach's *Poor Cow*, 1967; Peter Collinson's *Up The Junction*, 1968). There were some critiques of the prevailing atmosphere of selfishness and shallowness. John Schlesinger's

Darling (1965) was a moral tale of the self-centred rise and essentially empty success of a fashion model (Julie Christie), whose men are a succession of 1960s types – TV reporter, advertising executive and photographer. Frederic Raphael's screenplay was an unsparing indictment of the brittle, heartless world of metropolitan chic, its remorseless superficiality encapsulated in a whirligig of commercials, fashion photography, trendy art galleries, in-crowd parties and shop-lifting expeditions to Fortnum and Mason.

Lewis Gilbert's *Alfie* (1966), from Bill Naughton's play, focused on the adventures of a self-centred cockney Casanova who eventually comes to question his lifestyle. But Michael Caine's ingratiating charm as he addresses the audience directly, taking them into his confidence and engaging their complicity, made him a role model rather an object of condemnation. Contemporary commentators were beginning to observe the change in the national character betokened by the success of films like *Alfie*. Isabel Quigly wrote of *Alfie* in *The Spectator* (April 1, 1966):

> Vain, easy-going, autocratic, physically fastidious, cowardly, undomestic, irresistible, he is the sort of man once thought totally un-English but now being fished out of the proletarian pond where Englishness of the traditional sort never flourished. Like the new bright clothes on the new bright boys, he suggests a subterranean national character rising to surprise even the locals.

Naughton's other filmed plays, *The Family Way* (1966) and *Spring and Port Wine* (1969), looked back to the older, warmer, corporate values of community and family in the North and were among the rare productions to be set in the North after the 'New Wave' ebbed.

At about the same time as *Tom Jones*, the other great cult figure of the 1960s hit the screen – James Bond. *Doctor No* (1962) was the first of what became a series stretching to the present day. It starred Sean Connery as Bond and set the pattern for an unbeatable blend of conspicuous consumption, brand-name snobbery, technological gadgetry, colour supplement chic, exotic locations and comic-strip sex and violence. Although Bond was, in Raymond Durgnat's words, 'the last man in of the British Empire Superman's XI',[10] pitted against Fu-Manchu (*Doctor No*) or travelling on the Orient Express (*From Russia with Love*, 1963), there were crucial differences between Bond and Richard Hannay or Bulldog Drummond – both of whom experienced cinematic revivals around this time: Hannay in *The Thirty Nine Steps* (1959) and Drummond in *Deadlier than the Male* (1966) and *Some Girls Do* (1968). Bond was both a sexual adventurer and essentially classless, Connery's inextinguishable Edinburgh

18   New-style British hero: Sean Connery as James Bond in *Doctor No* (1962) with
Joseph Wiseman and Ursula Andress.

accent distancing him from the upper-class English gentlemen who customar-
ily played secret agents. This put him firmly in line with other 1960s icons.
The films were classically in the 1960s style – cool and knowing, sharing with
comic-strip adaptations like *Barbarella* (1968), *Batman* (1966) and *Modesty
Blaise* (1966) an ironic distancing from their source material. The combination
of form and content proved so appealing that the Bond films provided the top
box-office successes in Britain in 1963 (*From Russia with Love*), 1964 (*Goldfin-
ger*), 1966 (*Thunderball*) and 1967 (*You Only Live Twice*). Bond's success

sparked off a whole series of American imitations: Matt Helm, Derek Flint, Napoleon Solo, all informed by the same approach, though on rather lower budgets. There was also a series of caper movies made in Britain with titles like *Masquerade* (1965), *Kaleidoscope* (1966), *Arabesque* (1966) and *Fathom* (1967), in which form was all. They revelled in bright colours, flip dialogue, spectacular stunts, speed, style and sensation. Their complicated and irreverent plots, in which no-one is what they seem, everyone is engaged in elaborate role-playing, life is a game and both loyalties and relationships are flexible and shifting, effectively summarized that 1960s philosophy which saw immediate gratification, individualism and self-assertion as paramount.

It is arguable that such genre films were more subversive of the previous value-system than more overt, serious and intellectual 'state of the nation' films. In that event we should set alongside the espionage thrillers both the long-running 'Carry On' comedies and Hammer's horror films. The 'Carry On' series, which spanned the years from 1958 to 1980, allegedly included twenty-nine films, but in fact were the same film made twenty-nine times. The series deployed a talented cast of farceurs repeating in a variety of settings a familiar repertoire of sketches, jokes and characterizations derived from music-hall skits and routines and from the saucy seaside postcard world of Donald McGill, a world of fat ladies, and overflowing bosoms, nervous honeymoon couples and randy jack-the-lads, chamber pots and bedpans. They constitute a twenty-year act of defiance against every canon of taste, decency, decorum and responsibility but they operate in territory mapped out in the 1930s and 1940s by the likes of Frank Randle and Max Miller. Yet, in a real sense, appearing when they did, they functioned almost as comic counterparts both of the 'New Wave' and Swinging London. As Marion Jordan notes:

> Despite denying any place to women in their pantheon – portraying them, indeed, as goalers, sexual objects, or unnatural predators – they nonetheless asserted by their themes, and by the gusto with which they were presented, a lower-class, masculine resistance to 'refinement'; an insistence on sexuality, physicality, fun; on the need for drink in a kill-joy world, for shiftiness in an impossibly demanding industrial society, for cowardice amid the imposed heroism.[11]

Hammer, on the other hand, provided a symbolic and mythological counterpart to the 'New Wave' and Swinging London. Beginning in the key year of 1956 and continuing throughout the 1960s, Hammer remade and then provided sequels to the Universal horror classics of the 1930s. Hammer films consistently pointed up the contrast between the ordered, bourgeois normality of

Victorian England and the forces of unreason and excess lurking below the surface. In particular, they celebrated their anti-heroes' single-minded gratification of their desires. In film after film the conscienceless fanatical dandy Baron
Frankenstein (Peter Cushing) pursued his scientific experiments in defiance of
the laws of God and man, and the virile, arrogant, indestructible Count Drac-
ula (Christopher Lee) slaked his sexual desire on the bodies of a succession of
mainly female victims who, after the initial contact, became his willing con-
federates in pursuit of sensation. Initially symbols of a ruthless and exploitative
upper class, they soon became transformed into the heroes of an era of sex,
style and 'anything goes'.

Like other heroes of the 1960s, their concern was with self – 'What I want
is a good time; all the rest is propaganda'. It was a philosophy they shared with
the high priest of 1960s hedonism, Joe Orton. *Entertaining Mr. Sloane* (1969)
displayed Orton's wicked Wildean wit at its best, the stately formality of the
language brilliantly counterpointing the feverishly rococo nature of the sexual
shenanigans. Beryl Reid memorably incarnated a genteel suburbanite barely
able to contain her lust for Peter McEnery's amoral Brummie Adonis, his gleeful polymorphous perversity finding its counterpart in the exploits of Michael
York in *Something for Everyone* (1970) and Terence Stamp in *Theorem* (1968).

The almost simultaneous success of Connery as James Bond and Finney as
Tom Jones with both British and American audiences had convinced American film companies that a bonanza awaited them in the United Kingdom. Not
only was 'Britishness' 'in' but overhead costs were lower in Britain than in the
United States. So American companies began to announce big British production programmes. Paramount, Columbia, Warner Bros., Universal and the
other major studios poured money into their British operations. The independent British companies largely responsible for the 'New Wave' were simply
unable to compete. By 1966, 75 per cent of British first features were American financed; by 1968, 90 per cent. The attempt to maintain a viable programme of British film-making independent of American companies
foundered with the collapse of British Lion.

The apparently endless supply of American money prompted film-makers
to embark on more and more arcane and self-indulgent projects. Universal, for
instance, produced a dozen films in Britain between 1967 and 1969, few of
which made any profit and most of which were simply expensive fiascos: *A
Countess from Hong Kong* (1967), *Charlie Bubbles* (1968), *Work is a Four Letter
Word* (1968), *Three into Two Won't Go* (1969) and, to cap it all, the ludicrous
Can Hieronymus Merkin Ever Forget Mercy Humppe and Find True Happiness

(1969). Rarely can film-makers have so consistently set out to produce films just for themselves and without any regard whatever for their audiences. But more conventional film titles also failed at the box office in this period, including such hugely expensive British-made musicals as *Dr. Dolittle* (1967), *Star!* (1968) and *Goodbye Mr. Chips* (1969). By 1969 almost all the Hollywood film companies were heavily in debt, the taste for Britishness had passed and the films that were making money were such all-American works as *The Graduate* (1967) and *Butch Cassidy and the Sundance Kid* (1969). The American companies pulled out virtually all at once, leaving the British film industry flat on its back. At the same time the 1960s burned itself out and a Conservative government was elected in 1970 to face a future of economic recession, stagnation and unemployment. The 1960s generation awoke from their dream world to a cold dawn and a long hangover.

The Swinging London era of cinema had been London-centred, male-centred, style-centred and self-centred. The issues of class, race, region and gender had taken second place to the exaltation of a classless consumerist self. All this, reflected in cinema, tends to validate the interpretation of the 1960s advanced by Bernice Martin, who sees the decade as simply the latest manifestation of Romanticism, parallel to the late eighteenth and early nineteenth centuries.[12] Romanticism seeks to destroy boundaries, reject conventions, undermine structures and universalize the descent into the abyss and the ascent into the infinite. Its matrix is material prosperity, which releases people from the immediate disciplines of survival and concentrates their attention on their 'expressive' needs – self-discovery, self-fulfilment, experience and sensation. 1960s romantics reacted against a world that was highly structured, traditional and conventional, that was still in essence Victorian. In its place they advocated a culture of liminality, in which the outsider, the rebel and the deviant were heroes, the self was exalted, spontaneity was everything, and rules, restrictions, conventions and traditions, both in art and life, were ditched. In films this had the effect of highlighting fantasy and sexuality rather than serious political engagement. Eventually, however, there comes a reaction to Romantic excess, a return to order. It happened after the first Romantic period with the rise of Evangelicalism and the formation of 'Victorian values'. It happened, too, after the 1960s with a return to structure and eventually the rise of Thatcherism.

But it was not the same order and the same structure that had existed before the 1960s. The cultural revolution had long-term effects. Surrealism, particularly in comedy, became widely acceptable. The dominance of traditional linear narrative was broken and audiences were willing to accept much more fragmented narrative techniques. The cinema took the lead in extending the limits of what was permissible in the depiction of both sexuality and violence. Throughout the 1960s audiences became used to more nudity, simulated sex and profanity than they had known hitherto. Violence became more graphic and more frequent. Authority was no longer accepted as beneficent and paternalist. Most noticeably, the chivalric ethic, which had been central to British culture since the mid-nineteenth century, was rejected. Emblematic of this is the career of Jack Hawkins who had become a major star in the 1950s as the tough, dedicated, professional officer and gentleman both in wartime dramas (*Angels One Five*, *The Malta Story*, *The Cruel Sea*) and Scotland Yard thrillers (*The Long Arm*, *Gideon's Day*). In his key 1960s films he played a renegade officer using his professional skills for criminal ends (*The League of Gentlemen*, *Masquerade*) or the general as shrewd and unscrupulous politico (*Lawrence of Arabia*). The old-value systems were being turned on their head.

The twin processes of disillusionment with the *status quo* and liberation from restraint were reflected fully in the characteristic products of 1960s cinema: in the violence and cynicism of the spaghetti Westerns; in the disgruntlement of the working-class anti-heroes in social-realist dramas; and in the hedonism and self-indulgence of the Swinging London films. The ubiquitous spy films embodied the twin facets of the 1960s stance – in the anti-Establishment tone of the Le Carré brand in which suave, heartless upper-class spymasters manipulated and exploited proletarian agents and in the cool, classless, consumerist style of the Bond brand. What all these genres and forms and films have in common is the exaltation of the individual, the unrestrained self in pursuit of gratification. When there was affluence, that gratification took the form of sex, drink and drugs. During recession, this was replaced by the pursuit of money and the new direction taken by individualism was to plunge the nation into the abyss of Thatcherism.

While the cinema kept up a sustained and running critique of Thatcherism throughout the 1980s, with films such as *Looks and Smiles* (1981), *Britannia Hospital* (1982), *The Ploughman's Lunch* (1983), *My Beautiful Laundrette* (1985), *Sammy and Rosie Get Laid* (1987) and *The Last of England* (1987), these were art-house films with necessarily limited audiences and were largely preaching to the converted. The great British film success of the decade was *Chariots of Fire*, which won the Oscar for Best Picture of 1981. Although directed and written by Labour Party stalwarts (Hugh Hudson, Colin Welland), it played to an important strand in Thatcherite thinking. It celebrated the triumph of two outsiders (Scottish Christian Eric Liddell who refuses to run on a Sunday and English Jew Harold Abrahams who defies the amateur ethic by having a personal coach, the Italian-Arab Sam Mussabini) and damned the Old Establishment, headed by the Prince of Wales and Lord Birkenhead, as snobbish, racist and manipulative. Mrs Thatcher, the grocer's daughter from Grantham, was to become an outsider Prime Minister and declare war on the Old Establishment.[13]

If the critiques of Thatcherism achieved limited success, what were the successes of the 1980s and early 1990s? One of the most popular British genres has been the so-called 'heritage' films, such as *Room with a View, Howard's End, Maurice, Another Country, Remains of the Day, A Month in the Country, Where Angels Fear to Tread, A Handful of Dust, Shadowlands*. The period settings, elegant country-house locales, tasteful costumes, good manners and literate dialogue of such films have led short-sighted critics to dismiss them as nostalgic, backward-looking and reactionary.[14] In fact they are profoundly subversive. For together they provide a continuing and comprehensive critique of the ethic of restraint, repression and the stiff upper lip, of the surrender of personal happiness to higher notions of duty and self-sacrifice, hitherto key elements of the national character. Restraint is invariably depicted in these films as a recipe for personal unhappiness and something that should be rejected in favour of personal, usually sexual, fulfilment. They are the polar opposites of *Brief Encounter* and *Woman in a Dressing Gown*, which celebrate renunciation, duty and denial.

Similarly subversive is the spate of 'retro' movies, rewriting the history of the post-war decades so that figures formerly regarded as socially or culturally deviant and condemned by the legal system are revalued, revealed as hapless victims of an oppressive system or heroic rebels against repressive and outdated bourgeois values. There have thus been sympathetic cinematic depictions of real-life criminals of the late 1940s, 1950s and 1960s such as Craig and Bentley (*Let Him Have It*, 1991), Ruth Ellis (*Dance with a Stranger*, 1984), Stephen Ward (*Scandal*, 1989), Karl Hulten and Elizabeth Jones (*Chicago Joe and the Showgirl*, 1989). There has been a trend for casting pop idols as famous real-life criminals, thereby transforming these criminals into cultural heroes: Roger Daltrey in *MacVicar* (1980), Phil Collins in *Buster* (1988) and Martin and Gary Kemp as *The Krays* (1990). Even more notably, heroic homosexuals, the ultimate outsiders, have been celebrated, shown in a variety of historical eras defying the system, social prejudice and middle-class morality: *An Englishman Abroad* (1983), *Another Country* (1984), *My Beautiful Laundrette* (1985), *Maurice* (1987), *Prick Up Your Ears* (1987) and *We Think the World Of You*

(1988). Such a stance would have been unthinkable before 1960 when the subject was almost never mentioned in films.

Such films are complemented by the muscleman films starring the two actors who, according to popularity polls, are most favoured by young male British cinemagoers, Arnold Schwarzenegger and Sylvester Stallone, stars best described as inarticulate, Neanderthal killing machines. Series featuring Conan the Barbarian, Rambo, Rocky and Mad Max celebrate the rejection of civilization as decadent and corrupt, a return to primitive savagery (Conan's philosophy is 'Crush your enemies, see them driven before you and hear the lamentations of their women'), the glorification of violence, an emphasis on fighting as the definition of masculinity, the rejection of chivalry and the triumph of the individual will. In these films and many others like them boots crunch into groins, knives slice into flesh, arrows thud into chests, necks are snapped, machine-guns rip people and vehicles apart. It is worth noting in passing that the last era in which barbarism, musclemen and thuggery were so extensively promoted was the Third Reich, when pagan Germanic barbarians became race heroes and race warriors, exponents of the doctrine of 'Blut und Boden' – 'blood and soil'. Schwarzenegger and Stallone resemble nothing so much as the absurdly over-muscled, bulging thewed male statues produced by Arno Breker and Dr Josef Thorak, the favourite sculptors of the Reich.

As a definition of masculinity, it is the antithesis of the ethic of chivalry previously shared by both Britain and America and continuously promoted in the culture, with the result that, as John Fraser writes in his masterly study of the phenomenon, 'The family of chivalric heroes has been by far the largest and most popular one in twentieth century American culture and its members have entered into virtually everyone's consciousness.'[15] The figures Fraser cites, celebrated in books, plays, comic strips, radio, television and films up to the 1960s, include The Virginian, Prince Valiant, Robin Hood, The Scarlet Pimpernel, Captain Blood, Zorro, Dick Tracy, Philip Marlowe, Doctor Kildare, Superman, Tarzan, Buck Rogers, The Saint, Bulldog Drummond and the characters played by such actors as Fred Astaire, Ronald Colman, Gary Cooper, William Powell, Douglas Fairbanks Jr. and many more.

The last great age of cinematic chivalry was the 1950s when both in Britain and in Hollywood expensively mounted chivalric epics were made, virtually every Hollywood company producing one or more. The wheel came full circle as the works of Sir Walter Scott which had been the centrepiece of the nineteenth-century chivalric revival became the heart of the last age of chivalry in the 1950s, with such films as *Ivanhoe*, *Knights of the Round Table*, *The Adven-*

tures of Quentin Durward, The Warriors, The Black Shield of Falworth, The Black Knight, King Richard and the Crusaders and *Prince Valiant*. The heroes of all of them conformed to the same code – selflessness, duty, service and honour. The climax of this celluloid cycle was *El Cid* (1961), perhaps the greatest of all chivalric epics. The contrast in definitions of masculinity between such films as these and the muscleman films of the 1980s could not be more marked. In this as in so much else the 1960s was a crucial watershed.

Linked to the muscleman violence is the breed of films best described as 'violence chic' in which style is everything. The tone is cool, jokey and knowing; the violence is graphic and shocking; and the prevailing philosophy is that 'nothing matters very much and most things don't matter at all' other than the gratification of the sensation of the moment and the unrestrained desires of the individual. The high priest of 'violence chic' is Quentin Tarantino, whose sickening and pointless *Reservoir Dogs* (1991), in which a gang of foul-mouthed racist thugs shout and swear, shoot and torture people for an hour and a half, epitomizes the essential characteristics of the genre. In terms of plot (a carefully planned robbery that goes wrong and its aftermath), there is nothing here that has not been done much better a dozen times before (notably in *The Asphalt Jungle, Rififi* and *The Killing*). What is different is the application to the subject of a modish style and tone: the fashionable pounding rock score, the non-stop jokes, the streetwise attitude. Even this is not new but derives directly from Stanley Kubrick's *A Clockwork Orange* (1971), one of the three films which appearing simultaneously inaugurated the cinema's now longstanding celebration of violence for its own sake – the other two films were *Straw Dogs* and *The Devils*. *A Clockwork Orange* featured a teenage gang, the Droogs, led by Alex (Malcolm McDowell) who indulge in a reign of terror, revelling in what Alex calls 'ultra-violence' and which entails vividly and hideously depicted rapes, murders, beatings-up and disfigurements. The film denounces the police and the establishment who capture Alex and subject him to brainwashing to remove his violent tendencies. When Alex conquers the brainwashing and reverts to his true self at the end of the film, there is an exultant sense of triumph. The jokey tone of the film is set by the scene in which Alex cripples Patrick Magee, kicking him senseless to the strains of 'Singing in the Rain'. It is a sequence directly emulated by Tarantino when the psychotic robber Mr Blonde tortures a police officer while dancing to rock music. The ecstatic critical reception accorded to the film and the cult status that it and its successors have enjoyed with young cinemagoers testify powerfully to the coarsening of audience sensibilities and the brutalization of cinematic discourse. Tarantino's style and approach have been paralleled in other notable American films by leading directors, for instance Martin Scorsese's *Good Fellas* and Oliver Stone's *Natural Born Killers*. British films too have sought to emu- late the Tarantino formula in the areas of designer murder (*Shallow Grave*), football hooliganism (*I.D.*), and ramraiding (*Shopping*). Such films eschew any sociological analysis or contextualization of their subjects but simply re-create and celebrate the 'buzz' caused by the violence. They are celluloid anthems to adrenalin and testosterone.

Defenders of such films argue that they merely reflect society. So they do. But films also help to construct society by legitimizing systems, values and mindsets, by glamorizing lifestyles and setting standards of acceptability for behaviour. These films construct a society that is primarily self-centred and self-gratifying.

Notes

1   John Trevelyan, *What the Censor Saw*, London, 1973, p.106.
2   *The Movie* 57 (1981), p. 1134.
3   Kenneth Tynan, *A View of the English Stage 1944–63*, London, 1975, pp. 248–50 176–8.
4   Alexander Walker, *Hollywood England*, London, 1974, pp. 83–4.
5   Vito Russo, *The Celluloid Closet*, New York, 1981, p. 131.
6   John Hill, *Sex, Class and Realism: British Cinema 1956–1963*, London, 1986, p. 174.
7   Neil Sinyard, *The Films of Richard Lester*, London, 1985, p. 19.
8   Sinyard, *Films of Richard Lester*, p. 54.
9   James Leahy, *The Cinema of Joseph Losey*, London, 1967, p. 148.
10   Raymond Durgnat, *A Mirror for England*, London, 1970, p. 151.
11   Marion Jordan, 'Carry On – Follow that Stereotype' in James Curran and Vincent Porter (eds.), *British Cinema History*, London, 1983, pp. 312–327.
12   Bernice Martin, *A Sociology of Contemporary Cultural Change*, Oxford, 1981.
13   Lester D. Friedman (ed.), *British Cinema and Thatcherism*, London, 1993.
14   See, for instance, Cairns Craig, 'Poems Without a View', *Sight and Sound*, 1 (NS) (June, 1991), pp. 10–13.
15   John Fraser, *America and the Patterns of Chivalry*, Cambridge, 1981, pp. 12, 16.

Part III

Region

7

Scotland

The ways in which the outside world has seen Scotland, Wales and Ireland, and in which the countries themselves have connived, are in the terms crystallized by Hollywood and in particular by *The Quiet Man, How Green Was My Valley* and *Brigadoon*. John Brown has pointed out,

> What they are held to be guilty of is that they are attempts made from outside these countries and cultures, to embody some kind of definitive essence of them. They are not unsympathetic attempts but the way they represent the Scots, the Welsh and the Irish (and their success in being well received internationally) has long been the subject of bitter attack within these countries.[1]

He goes on to argue that they – and Ealing's Scottish films such as *Whisky Galore* – are disliked for portraying Scots as 'quaint and old-fashioned, comically innocent or comically cunning', living in a romanticized landscape that is superior to the real, modern, sophisticated and industrialized world.

The problem, as he concedes, is that the Scots as a whole have loved films like *Whisky Galore* – 'by a very large margin the most popular film ever screened in the islands' – and that 'the majority of Scots are eager consumers … of the very artifacts whose influence outside Scotland they would claim to deplore.' Why? Because the image is attractive and appealing. What commentators fail to recognize and acknowledge is the widespread and deep-rooted hatred of modernity – the dehumanization, the exploitation and pollution that it has entailed. The Arcadian image of the village and of the canny peasant is one that appeals across the national boundaries, as evidenced by the enduring popularity of *The Archers* radio serial, the bestselling *Country Diary of an Edwardian Lady* and the books, films and television series associated with Yorkshire vet James Herriot, notably *All Creatures Great and Small.* They also fail to understand the extent to which people are flattered when the mighty Hollywood and the great stars condescend to notice their country.

'Authentic' and 'truthful' are words much bandied about when considering desirable characteristics in films representing national identity. But whose truth and whose authenticity? They mean documentary authenticity. But authenticity, realism, documentary accuracy are much less important to the mass audience than myths, dreams and memories. Documentary films have been able to move audiences far more rarely than fictional film – much to the despair of intellectuals. Witness the litany of complaints directed against allegedly 'false' or 'inaccurate' or 'inauthentic' constructions of the nation or parts of it. But it is not just Scotland, Wales and Ireland that have 'suffered' from Hollywood's fictions, so has England. In 1942 *Mrs. Miniver*, a Hollywood film about the British at war, was filling British cinemas. *Documentary News Letter*, the standard bearer of documentary authenticity, reported with scarcely veiled disbelief: 'You can sit at the Empire and hear practically the whole house weeping – a British audience with 3 years of war behind it crying at one of the phoniest war films that has ever been made.'[2] But the combination of Greer Garson and Walter Pidgeon, an idealized middle-class England, an essentially noble picture of genteel suffering and patriotic endeavour was genuinely uplifting and a 'good cry' has always been therapeutic. In addition, the codes, conventions and character types of Hollywood were well known and accepted by audiences all round the world.

If you want to reduce a Welsh, Scottish or Irish intellectual to insensate fury, suggest that his/her country is most accurately represented by *How Green Was My Valley*, *The Quiet Man* and *Brigadoon*. But intellectuals are notoriously not 'real' people. It is real people who go to the cinema and as Arthur Marwick has sagely observed:

> There *is* a law of the market; the bigger its commercial success, the more a film is likely to tell us about the unvoiced assumptions of the people who watched it. It is the tedious documentary or the film financed by political subscription which tells us least.[3]

These three films were popular both inside and outside the countries they depicted, are endlessly revived and touch deep psychological and spiritual roots. They also demonstrate conclusively why Hollywood has conquered and colonized the imaginative inner life of the world.

One of the characteristics of the recent ferment in Scottish intellectual life triggered by increasing exasperation at the contemptuous attitude towards Scotland displayed by an apparently entrenched and immovable English Conservative government is the search for a Scottish cinematic identity. This has produced no fewer than three full-length studies of Scottish cinema.[4] They have lamented foreign distortions of Scotland's 'reality', excoriated 'outdated' myths of kailyard and tartanry, picked over the remains of long-forgotten documentaries produced by the Film Board of Scotland and searched the output of Channel Four for 'true' representations. But the harsh fact of the matter is, as David Hutchinson conceded, that in Scotland 'there has never been anything which could possibly be described as a film industry'.[5] Attempts to set up the Scottish National Film Studios in 1945–46 were a dismal failure. For the most part documentary shorts made no impact on the mass consciousness. Channel Four is a minority channel, and much – though not all – of its film output is art-house esoterica with little general audience appeal, shown once and rapidly consigned to the archive shelves. The workers film movement, in Scotland as in England, was a minuscule minority preaching to the converted, a worthy but comparatively insignificant fragment of the film culture. It is primarily Hollywood and secondarily England which have produced the definitive cinematic depictions of Scotland. It must be a cause of despair for Scottish intellectuals that the most enduring celluloid image of Scotland is represented by Robert Louis Stevenson's *Kidnapped*, which has inspired multiple film versions (in 1937, 1948, 1959 and 1971, with a new version in production in 1996). The same is true of Wales and Ireland. Apart from the early silent days when films were produced in Wales, there has been no Welsh film industry and attempts to create an Irish film industry have been sporadic and largely abortive.

There is a dichotomy between, on the one hand, rational cultural critics exposing and denouncing cultural colonization and, on the other, the largely non-intellectual audiences who respond emotionally and viscerally not to didactic documentaries or to Channel Four-funded minority-interest movies but to Hollywood productions, which mingle drama, spectacle and sentimentality. *How Green Was My Valley*, *The Quiet Man* and *Brigadoon* may not be documentarily true but they are poetically and imaginatively true and that is what counts for the mass audience.

Intellectuals joke about the fact that there is only one Welshman (Rhys

Williams) in the cast of *How Green Was My Valley* and that the rest are Irish, Scots and English, just as the villagers in *Brigadoon* are a mixed bag of Scottish, Welsh and Irish actors. But even this shameless Hollywood homogenization has some historical justification in that a pan-Celtic identity was invented in the eighteenth century, its mainspring being the need to be non- or anti-English.

Scotland, Wales and Ireland were all essentially 'invented' by Romanticism, all three countries characterized by wild landscape, music and song, and by the supernatural, the mainstream features of the Romantic movement. The Romantic movement began in the eighteenth century as a reaction against the Age of Reason, when order, symmetry and common sense prevailed, when compromise and equilibrium were the norms and science provided a rational explanation for everything. The dominance of reason and Enlightenment provoked a violent reaction – Romanticism, bold, individualistic, unconventional, exalting imagination, the emotions, dreams and fantasies, everything that was alien and abhorrent to the measured, passionless classicism that had prevailed. Romanticism had certain basic fascinations: the past (especially the medieval past), nature, the occult, individualism. It was in 1709 that the Third Lord Shaftesbury, the originator of the eighteenth-century cult of the sublime, of the belief in the beauty of terror, declared: 'The wildness pleases.'[6] Until then nature had been feared and hated as a source of danger. But during the eighteenth century there was a turn away from the artificiality of the formal gardens, which epitomized the qualities of the Age of Reason, to free, unspoiled, wild landscape, the natural world as the embodiment of the wonder and sublimity of God's creation. Simultaneously there developed a passion for the Gothic, for mediaeval castles, abbeys and towers, and particularly for picturesque ruins. There was also a vogue for 'Gothic' literature, tales of ghosts and monsters, murder and the supernatural, witches and demons. The celebration of nature in the wild led to the exaltation of the idea of 'natural man', the noble savage, the innocent primitive, the solitary hermit. The link between the wild landscape, primitive people, a stylized Gothic Middle ages and natural man was the bard, who in the eighteenth century became a cult figure. Thomas Gray's poem *The Bard*, which celebrated the last Welsh bard, who threw himself into a cataract in the face of Edward I's invading English army, inspired a raft of paintings (Fuseli, Blake, John Martin, de Loutherbourg, Thomas Jones). Homer was seen as the archetypal bard, a blind wandering poet, passionate, spontaneous and individualistic, drawing his inspiration from the people and from nature, and embodying the nation's soul. This led to a new interest in Druids and a fashion for contemporary primitive poets such as Stephen Duck, who was installed in a specially built cave in Richmond Park. Milton and Shakespeare were constructed as later versions of the Homeric ideal, and the idea of poetry and music came to be seen as expressions of the Romantic spirit.

Out of these elements of Romanticism, a Celtic identity was fabricated for the non-English parts of the Union. Three elements in particular were highlighted. The first was the wild landscape, attracting poets, painters and tourists. Life in the mountains was harsh and dreary until the Romantic movement celebrated it, and, thereafter, cascading waterfalls, glens and crags, mountain lakes and picturesque ruins became the prime elements in the identity of Wales, Ireland and Scotland, 'the land of the mountain and the flood'.

Secondly, music, poetry and bardic tradition became associated with all three countries. In Scotland, James MacPherson fabricated the Ossianic poems, inventing a poetic heritage that had an enormous impact all over Western Europe, inspiring music and song. In Ireland, the harp became a national symbol and Thomas Moore collected and provided words for Irish folk tunes. Wales was deliberately constructed as 'the land of song'. In the eighteenth century folk-song collectors found that most Welsh songs had English tunes, but in the late eighteenth and in the early nineteenth the Welsh fabricated a tradition of age-old musical heritage, based on the simultaneous appearance of a number of talented musicians. Blind John Parry, harpist to the Prince of Wales, collected and published *Ancient British Airs* (1742), a collection purporting to date back to the Druids. Penillion-singing developed in the early nineteenth century and was passed off as being archaic.

Thirdly, there is the supernatural element: the folktales of 'the little people', kelpies, banshees, pixies and so forth, associated with remote regions. All of these became enmeshed in the creation of a mythic Celtic past.

Wales, Scotland, Ireland and Cornwall are collectively known as the 'Celtic fringe' and are usually said to have been culturally, racially and linguistically distinct from those areas occupied by the Anglo-Saxons and to have inherited a continuous tradition dating back to pre-Roman times. But in fact as Malcolm Chapman provocatively but persuasively argues, the Celts probably never existed as a people at all but were essentially invented in the eighteenth and nineteenth centuries, when the Celts were defined as having a distinctive culture, language and racial origin and having a biological, cultural and linguistic continuity.[7] But the fact is that the term 'Celt' simply meant 'barbarian' or 'foreigner' and was applied to everyone who was not Greek by the Greeks (*Keltoi*) and not Roman by the Romans (*Celtae*). There is no evidence the so-called Celts ever called themselves Celts. After the fall of the Roman Empire and the Germanic invasions, other words came to be applied to non-Germans or foreigners, Walloon, Vlach and Welsh, all derived from the Germanic term Walxaz. The Welsh did not call themselves Welsh anymore than they called themselves Celts. They called themselves Romans or Britons or Trojans (because of the legend of the foundation of Britain by Brut, the great-grandson of Aeneas). Welsh was a derogatory term applied by the Anglo-Saxons to the inhabitants of Britain who remained outside their rule, hence the verb 'to welsh' which means to renege on a debt. So since there is no Celtic race, there is no Celtic racial continuity. The fact of the matter is that the population is a mongrel one, based not on folk movements but by the invasions of elites, often with racially mixed bands, who are usually absorbed into the dominant culture of the area they settle in, as was the case with the Britons who settled in Britanny, the Danes who settled in East Anglia and the East Midlands, and the Norse who settled in Normandy. Scotland was far from being racially united or distinct, with the Outer Isles settled by the Norse, the Highlands by Picts, the West by the Irish and the Borders by the Britons.

If there was no Celtic racial continuity, there was, as Chapman admits, linguistic continuity. Gaelic, Welsh and Breton all belong to one of the four branches of Indo-European, which has been dubbed Celtic; another branch, Germanic, includes English, Dutch and German.

What does remain constant, too, culturally speaking, is the relationship between the periphery and the centre, between the conqueror and the conquered. Cultural changes ripple out from the centre and are adopted by the periphery, sometimes imposed, but sometimes adopted voluntarily. The 'victim' theory of history in which the Welsh, Irish and Scottish are driven from their homes by oppressive English and their culture and language is stamped out is too simplistic. This sometimes happened, but there was also voluntary adoption of the language and culture of the alien power because it was seen as attractive and sophisticated. There was voluntary migration from the poverty and hardship of the countryside to the towns. The desire for individual social, cultural and economic improvement must not be underrated. Look at the way the English young have adopted American language, customs and culture. They do it because it seems to them glamorous, not because the Americans have invaded and forced it on them.

So there were no Celts after the fall of the Roman Empire until the eighteenth century when they were invented. The process began in the sixteenth century when the serious study of archaeology and linguistics started. It developed with particular intensity in the eighteenth century just at the time that nationalism was beginning to grow and Romanticism developed as a reaction against Classicism, with its cosmopolitan culture.

Nationalism led to the creation of a national identity – in England this took the form of Anglo-Saxonism – but the countries of the periphery needed a different identity to show themselves as distinct from the English. The context for this is the revaluation of the ideas of the noble savage and the wild landscape. Romanticism exalted rural as opposed to urban, wildness as opposed to civilization, solitude as opposed to the crowd, and this chimed with a hostility to growing industrialization. So in Wales and Scotland, nationalist scholars turned to pre-Classical cultures for their inspiration. James MacPherson forged his Ossianic poems to give Scotland an authentic Celtic culture and poetic tradition. Edward Llhuyd claimed a Celtic culture for the Welsh past and Iolo Morganwg fabricated it complete with Druidic lore and bardic inspiration.

The Celtic identity was then constructed and read back into the past. It was constructed out of three main processes. First there was the elaboration of a conscious opposition to the perceived character of the Anglo-Saxon. The Anglo-Saxon was seen as phlegmatic, stolid, practical, unimaginative, prosaic, individualist. Therefore the Celt was constructed as emotional, restless, poetic, imaginative, artistic, communal. This is completely unhistorical. For so-called Celtic kingdoms and Saxon kingdoms evolved in much the same way, from tribes to states. Saxons were no more individualist than the Celts and no less communal. It so happens that the characteristics ascribed to the mythical Celt were precisely the qualities most prized by the Romantic revival.

Secondly, there was the exaltation of old-fashioned cultural relics as a true culture. For instance, 'Welsh' costume which had once been worn by everyone became distinctively Welsh because everyone else had given it up. The bagpipe once played all over Europe survived only in the periphery because everyone else gave it up and so the bagpipe became distinctively Celtic.

Third, in the retrospective writing of history, Celticism is ascribed to those religions which had been overtaken by progress. So when Romano-British religion was overtaken by newer Christian forms at the Synod of Whitby, the old forms were dubbed Celtic. When Protestantism replaced Catholicism and Catholicism retreated to the periphery, this became identified with Celticism, and as Nonconformity began to lose its force, it soon came to be seen as Celtic.

Scotland's alternative to the Britain forged by the Act of Union was a composite Celtic/Jacobite Scotland. Jacobitism obviously stood for the alternative to the Hanoverians but it had the disadvantage for disaffected Scottish Protestants of being associated with Catholicism. So, as Murray Pittock has argued, a revamped Jacobitism emerged which became identified with a cluster of images: the image of the heroic Highlander as Scots patriot; the Stuart monarchy as the symbol of sacred kingship and tradition; history interpreted as a struggle for Scottish liberty in which the apostolic succession of heroes includes William Wallace, Robert the Bruce and Bonnie Prince Charlie; Scotland defined as an organic and Celtic culture with a pure pastoral tradition.[8] In this vision the Act of Union is the great betrayal and the urban, commercial, industrial, imperial world of Great Britain the opposite and the enemy of the Jacobite Celtic Scotland.

But as Hugh Trevor-Roper has pointed out, the whole concept of a distinct Highland culture and tradition, as epitomized by the kilt, the clan tartans and the bagpipes, is an eighteenth-century invention.[9] Until the mid-eighteenth century when it was 'opened up' after the Jacobite rebellions, the West of Scotland was 'racially and culturally … a colony of Ireland'. The inhabitants spoke Irish Gaelic; their instrument was the harp not the bagpipe; their literature and culture was a pale imitation of the Irish; their costume the long Irish shirt.

The creation of an independent Highland tradition and its imposition on the whole of Scotland as *the* national image was the product of the late eighteenth and nineteenth centuries. It had no ancient lineage. It represented a cultural revolt against Ireland, the creation of artificial new Highland traditions, masquerading as ancient ones and the adoption of these traditions by Lowland Scotland as the agreed national image.

As we have seen, an entirely fictitious history and culture of Celtic Scotland was created largely by James MacPherson. The entire cycle of Scottish ballads which he ascribed to an ancient bard Ossian were in fact Irish stories simply taken over and relocated in Scotland. Reverend John MacPherson then wrote a critical dissertation proving the existence of Celtic Highland history and culture based on this forgery. It had the effect of claiming that Celtic Scotland was the 'mother nation' and Ireland its cultural dependency whereas it was in truth the other way round. But the Ossianic poems, which inspired a whole generation of literati, became a central element in Romanticism and established the Celtic Highland Scots as a distinctive *Volk*. According to Murray Pittock, they were in addition a coded work of Jacobitism, providing an alternative history of an independent Scotland.

The second invention was the heroic Highlander and his dress. Before the eighteenth century the Highlander was seen as a wild and primitive savage. But in the later eighteenth century he was transformed into a heroic freedom fighter and the defender of a free Scotland, even though the armies of Prince Charles Edward Stuart comprised Highlanders, Lowlanders, English, French and Irish troops and several Scottish clans fought on the English side. The Highlander also benefited from the celebration of the noble savage and the picturesque by the Romantic movement. This heroic Highland warrior was now equipped with distinctive costume. The Highlander traditionally wore the long Irish shirt, a tunic and a cloak or plaid belted at the waist – the colour usually brown or saffron. Throughout the seventeenth century Highland soldiers wore belted plaids; their officers trews or trousers. The kilt was the invention of an eighteenth-century Lancashire Quaker, Thomas Rawlinson, who operated an iron-ore furnace near Inverness. Finding Highland dress inconvenient for his workers, he designed a short skirt – the philibeg (small kilt) – which was basically the bottom half of the old plaid.

After the 1745 rebellion, the English government banned Highland dress. By the time it was repealed thirty-five years later the peasants had got used to wearing trousers and did not return to the kilt. But the middle and upper classes took up trews, plaids and kilts. Again this was due to the influence of the Romantic movement, the desire to celebrate, and identify with, heroic primitive peoples. In 1829 the Celtic Society of Edinburgh was founded to promote the wearing of the 'ancient Highland dress' and when King George IV visited Edinburgh on the first state visit of a Hanoverian monarch to Scotland he also wore it, as did Queen Victoria's family while at Balmoral.

The next stage was the development of specific clan tartans. Originally there were none. They were devised as a marketing strategy by the kilt manufacturers to develop diversity and variety and were arbitrarily assigned to different clans off the peg. Clan tartans were encouraged by the expatriate Highland Society of London (founded in 1778), which after the repeal of the ban on Highland dress in 1782 encouraged the wearing of it. Two brothers, claiming to be sons of the Young Pretender, produced a lavishly illustrated book, *The Costume of the Clans*, creating a spurious history of the clan tartans, and although their royal pedigree was discredited, their work was taken up and promoted by others, since it claimed to recover the lost history of Celtic Scotland.

In addition to expatriates and upper-class romantics, the most powerful proponents of the kilt were the new Scottish regiments. They were specifically exempt from the ban on the kilt and they were systematically formed after 1745 by William Pitt the Elder to divert the martial spirit of the Scots into the service of the Empire. They became attached to the kilt as distinctive and convenient and the kilted Highland Devils became one of the notable images of both the Napoleonic Wars, where their charge at Waterloo became a mythic event, and throughout the British imperial wars. This was one way in which the new Scottish identity was accommodated by the Empire.

The other way was its romanticization once Jacobitism had become the romantic lost cause, a heroic past to be cherished but which did not interfere with the prosperous and progressive Whig future. Sir Walter Scott notably promoted this romantic myth while at the same time preaching harmony and reconciliation between Highlands and Lowlands, Protestant and Catholic, England and Scotland. Queen Victoria and Prince Albert were entranced by the romanticism of Scotland and Queen Victoria declared herself the successor of the Stuarts. This reinforces the idea of a Scottish identity as one of a multiple set of identities, including British. During the nineteenth century Scotland participated fully in the British Empire, but at the same time its intellectual and emotional energies were totally absorbed by the 'Great Disruption of 1843' when 456 ministers seceded from the Church of Scotland to form the Free Church, so that for the rest of the century internecine struggle raged within Scottish churches.

At the end of the nineteenth century, as a reaction against materialism, imperialism and industrialization, there was a revival of both Jacobitism and Celtic Scotland among the intelligentsia and romantic aristocrats. The Order of the White Rose was founded in 1886, the Legitimist Jacobite League in 1891 and the Society of King Charles the Martyr in 1894. The new movement had two strands: one was merely romantic antiquarianism but the other was political and separatist, calling for Home Rule or independence for Scotland, the restoration of the Stuarts, the teaching of Scottish history and the revival of Celtic culture, and opposition to empire and militarism. But this was all rather eclipsed by World War One, when the Stuart claimant to the throne, a Bavarian prince, recognized by the Jacobites as their rightful king, fought for the Kaiser, while Scottish regiments fought and died for the Empire and the Allies.

After the war, partly influenced by Irish independence in 1921 and by a Scottish cultural renaissance, the National Party of Scotland was formed in 1928, merging in 1934 with the Scottish Party to form the Scottish National Party (SNP), to fight for Scottish Independence. Although the modern SNP has sought to distance itself from the Jacobite myth, it remains a coherent and romantic alternative to the identity of Great Britain formed from Protestantism, empire and trade. Interestingly, the SNP has enthusiastically endorsed the Hollywood epic *Braveheart* (1995) as a cultural justification for its policy of independence for Scotland. The party might do well to reflect that the most notable regimes in the past to utilize such cinematic distortions of history for political purposes have been Nazi Germany, Fascist Italy and Stalinist Russia. Largely filmed in Ireland and directed by and starring the Australian/American actor Mel Gibson, *Braveheart* is a contrived, one-dimensional and schematic distortion of the known facts of the life of the thirteenth-century Scots patriot William Wallace, as established by such scholars as James Mackay in his *William Wallace: Braveheart* (Edinburgh, 1995).

In Gibson's film, the Scots wear woad a thousand years too late and clan tartans five hundred years too early. Wallace impregnates Princess Isabelle of Wales with the future Edward III whereas she did not in fact arrive in England until two years after his death. The Battle of Stirling Bridge takes place on a flat plain with nary a bridge to be seen. Robert the Bruce is inaccurately depicted fighting for the English at the Battle of Falkirk. And so on, and so on.

Far from being any kind of historical justification for Scottish independence, the film is carefully constructed to appeal to the 'politically correct' sentiments of 1990s Hollywood. It supports the struggle of a small and powerless country against a large, tyrannical and imperialist neighbour. Wallace talks constantly and anachronistically about freedom and democracy, with no hint of how such aims are to be achieved. The film shamelessly courts the Irish-American audience by foregrounding a 'lovable' mad Irishman who arrives from Ireland to join Wallace and to kill Englishmen. He is instrumental in persuading Edward I's Irish levies to desert at the Battle of Falkirk and join the Scots. Wallace himself insists that he is a commoner and not a gentleman and is contrasted with the greedy, self-serving Scottish aristocrats. Although highly educated and fluent in Latin and French, he proudly declares himself to be a 'savage' and the Scottish army he leads behave like a drunken rugby club on an outing, chanting, roaring and mooning at their opponents. This is calculated to appeal to the 'New Barbarians' who have already lapped up such epics as the Conan and Rambo films. In fact *Braveheart* is perhaps best judged not in relation to previous Scottish films at all but as a Scottish analogue of Gibson's *Mad Max* trilogy: *Mad Mac* perhaps. When he first appears Gibson's Wallace strongly resembles the hero of *Mad Max beyond the Thunderdome*. Both heroes seek to avenge murdered wives, and the depraved and psychotic English in *Braveheart* are best seen as the equivalent of the deranged army of nomad bikers that terrorize the outback in the *Mad Max* trilogy. The massive commercial success in Scotland and worldwide of what is essentially a simplistic,

Anglophobe, ahistorical farrago, demonstrates the continuing power of Holly-wood myth-making and the unaltered willingness of audiences to lap up 'the inauthentic' if it stirs the heart and wrenches the guts.

Scotland has received three principal depictions in cinema: which can be broadly grouped under the headings of tartanry, kailyard and faery. None of them are incompatible with Scotland's place in the Union but all serve to give her a distinctive Celtic identity. All three are closely related to the glories of the Scottish scenery that form the backdrops to the adventure stories of Sir Walter Scott and Robert Louis Stevenson whose popularity ensured the embedding of this image in the popular consciousness, not just of Britain but also of conti-nental Europe and America.

'Tartanry' – the deployment of clans, kilts, pipes and claymores – centres on the sacred 'lost cause' of Scottish independence. The cause, of course, involves war and rebellion but the war and rebellion are safely located in a romanticized past on which Scotland turned its back in the eighteenth century to become full and enthusiastic partners in the British Empire. But the cinema likes lost causes – the American Confederacy has surely inspired more celebratory films than the American Union, a case of the winners having won and being capa-ble of generosity to, and admiration for, the losers with whom they still have to coexist. The same could be said of Scotland. A similar cherishing of heroic defeat has been a long-established strain in British/English history: Battle of Hastings, Charge of the Light Brigade, Dunkirk.

The symbols of the lost cause and embodiments of Scottish romanticism are Bonnie Prince Charlie and Mary, Queen of Scots, and these have figured prominently in cinematic depictions of Scotland. The 1745 Jacobite Rebel-lion, the final throw of the exiled Stuarts to regain the throne, has all the ingre-dients of romance – the arrival, the raising of the standard, the gathering of the clans, initial success and then defeat, flight through the heather and escape to a life of exile over the water. It involves the dashing young prince and a glam-orous Scottish helper, Flora MacDonald. The story inspired a handsome British silent epic, *Bonnie Prince Charlie* (1923), starring the celebrated beau-ties Ivor Novello and Gladys Cooper.

Britain's premier producer in the 1930s, Alexander Korda, planned a Bonnie Prince Charlie epic as a tribute to Scotland and a counterpart to his own epics of English nationhood, *The Private Life of Henry VIII* and *Fire over England*. Leslie Howard was set to star and Forsyth Hardy recalled Howard telling him: 'I have always felt that the story of Charles Edward, with its lesson of unques-tioning loyalty to an ideal, should be the real expression of an undying Scottish national spirit.'[10] But the outbreak of war and Howard's death put paid to those plans. In 1945, on the 200th anniversary of the Rebellion, Michael Powell and Emeric Pressburger prepared and shot a sequence for a putative Jacobite saga, *The White Cockade*, with David Niven as Prince Charles Edward and Pamela Brown as Flora MacDonald. But Powell concluded 'the piece was dead … it never came to life' and abandoned the project.[11] But Korda persisted with the idea and in 1948 produced *Bonnie Prince Charlie* starring David Niven as Charles Edward and Margaret Leighton as Flora MacDonald, and which covered the familiar territory of the story. But the result was an almost total disaster. The production was dogged by misfortune. It went through four directors (Leslie Arliss, Robert Stevenson, Korda himself and Anthony Kimmins), constant script rewrites and enforced reshooting when Will Fyffe, playing one of the clansmen, died and had to be replaced by Morland Graham. The result was, at 138 minutes overlong, shapeless, disjointed and scrappy, an incoherent collection of bits and pieces, visually undistinguished, stodgy and one-dimensional, with precious little action and Niven hopelessly miscast. As the *Manchester Guardian* (30 October 1948) observed: 'To turn to dullness the most poignant and romantic episode in the last 250 years of British history was … a remarkable achievement.'

Rob Roy, the other Jacobite hero, who functions in the aftermath of the 1715 Jacobite Rebellion fared rather better. *Rob Roy* (1911) was the first British three-reel feature and the only version to be based on Scott's novel and was also shot in Scotland. Another version of his adventures appeared as *Rob Roy* in 1922 starring David Hawthorne in the title role. A Technicolor *Rob Roy* was announced by Gainsborough in 1938 and it was planned to star Michael Redgrave and Margaret Lockwood under Carol Reed's direction. But once again the war intervened and the project was abandoned.

The Rob Roy films that have been made since then testify to the influence of Hollywood history and mythology on depictions of Scotland. Walt Disney's *Rob Roy – the Highland Rogue* (1953), was openly described by its director Harold French as 'a Western in kilts'. It was not based on Scott but was an original screenplay by Lawrence Edward Watkin. It emerged as an exciting romp, interspersing impressive action scenes (staged by Alex Bryce, second-unit director, in spectacular locations) and joyous folk celebrations giving full vent to the skirl of the pipes, the singing of lilting Gaelic songs and the excitement of Highland dancing.

Set in 1715, the film dramatizes the resistance of Clan Macgregor to the excesses of the central government. Significantly however, the exploitation and tyranny is not the work of the English but of the Scottish Secretary of State, the Marquis of Montrose, lining his pockets by extortion and enforcing his will on the Highlands, backed up by vicious Scottish subordinates, notably Captain Killearn, who eventually comes to a well-deserved end at Rob Roy's hands. Ultimately these evils are reported to King George I by the Duke of Argyll and when Rob Roy presents himself in London, the King grants his clan amnesty and promises redress. Justice is done, the integrity of the British crown is maintained and the Union preserved. The Northern Irish born actor Richard Todd and the Welsh actress Glynis Johns played Rob Roy and his sweetheart.

The latest version of *Rob Roy* (1995), complete with stunning scenery, an Irish actor, Liam Neeson, as Rob Roy and an American actress, Jessica Lange, as his wife, merits the description as a 'Western in kilts' even more, concentrating as it does on cattle rustling, with small homesteader Rob confronting large landowner and the Scottish tribes hunted by the redcoat equivalent of the 7th cavalry. It is no coincidence that the script's Scottish author Alan Sharp had written some notable screen Westerns, among them *Ulzana's Raid*. This *Rob Roy* is set before the Rebellion, sidesteps the Jacobites but lays great stress on honour. Although there is a dandified English villain (a scene-stealing Tim Roth), he is the illegitimate son of Montrose, and the Scottish aristocrats are much more villainous than the English, making the film a classic tale of conflict between big landowners and small homesteaders rather than an anti-English tract.

The 1745 Jacobite Rebellion formed the background to Warner Bros.' *The Master of Ballantrae* (1953). Although shot in Scotland, it turned Stevenson's sombre and dark-toned adventure tale into a straightforward Hollywood swashbuckler with Errol Flynn as a dashing Jacobite Master and his dull, respectable pennypinching brother remaining loyal to the Hanoverians. Borrowing footage from the 1948 *Bonnie Prince Charlie* to recreate the 1745 Rebellion, it later transported the Master to the West Indies before a return to Scotland, reunion with his brother and escape from the redcoats.

The tragic saga of Mary, Queen of Scots, inspired a British silent film *The Loves of Mary, Queen of Scots* (1923), with Fay Compton as Mary, Gerald Ames as Bothwell and Ellen Compton as Elizabeth I, a Hollywood epic *Mary of Scotland* (1936) directed by John Ford, with Katharine Hepburn as Mary, Fredric March as Bothwell and Florence Eldridge as Elizabeth, and a British sound film, Charles Jarrott's *Mary, Queen of Scots* (1972), with Vanessa Redgrave as Mary, Glenda Jackson as Elizabeth and Nigel Davenport as Bothwell. They all feature the various romances and marriages, the plots and intrigues, the even-

Tartanry: *The Master of Ballantrae* (1953)

tual flight to England and execution with Mary as the emotional, doomed, romantic heroine governed by her heart, and Elizabeth the shrewd, calculating political animal, governed by her head. It is a metaphor for the differences between the Scots and the English with the two characters conforming to the stereotypes of Scottishness and Englishness, established by Malcolm Chapman. The 1972 version despite a good cast and authentic locations never takes fire and emerges as a respectable, workmanlike A-level version of the events with none of the visual distinction and bravura of Ford's expressionist, operatic version which was a box-office failure but a considerable artistic success. *Mary of Scotland* celebrates its heroine unashamedly as a 'Madonna of the Scottish

Moors', infinitely preferable to Elizabeth's calculating, loveless English Protestant shrew. A foreword reassures us that although the rivalry of the two queens
dominated the late sixteenth century, 'after three centuries they sleep at peace
side by side in Westminster Abbey'. Mary, performed by a radiant Hepburn, is
a staunch Catholic ('my religion is not a garment to be put on and off like
weather') but an advocate of religious tolerance. The people are devoted to her
('we'll fight for the queen, she's the fairest ever seen' they sing). Mary wants to
rule with justice and wisdom and is the innocent victim of an ambitious half-
brother, treacherous nobles, a dissolute husband, ranting, fanatical Protestants
and a jealous and vindictive Elizabeth. Katharine Hepburn, however, said of
Mary

> I did think I was terribly bad ... I can't stand Mary of Scotland. I think
> she was an absolute ass. I would love to have played Elizabeth: now she
> was a fascinating creature. But I had no patience with Mary. I thought
> Elizabeth was absolutely right to have her condemned to death. Mary was
> extremely silly; she fascinates some people, but not me.[12]

Alexander Mackendrick spent much of his career planning a Mary, Queen
of Scots film. Balcon rejected it when he was at Ealing. In 1968 Universal gave
the go-ahead but it was cancelled when Universal terminated its British production programme after a string of box-office failures. Mackendrick had
produced a script with James Kennaway which was a revisionist, deromanti-
cized version of the story. Mackendrick's biographer, Philip Kemp, recalls:

> The film they envisaged was to be tough, grimy and determinedly anti-
> romantic, a study in *realpolitik* in a dung-strewn Edinburgh ... Mary
> would figure as one of Mackendrick's self-destructive innocents, a fastid-
> ious, French-accented outsider as hopelessly outwitted as Captain
> Waggett by the ruthless Scots around her.[13]

There would be no grand-opera confrontations with Elizabeth, no noble death
on an English scaffold. The action was restricted to fourteen months, from the
murder of Rizzio, through her forced marriage to Bothwell to 'the moment
when – with the Edinburgh mob shouting "Burn the hoor" in the streets –
she's marched back a prisoner'.

It is interesting and characteristic that Korda should have envisaged an historical epic about Scotland, enshrining the myths and images of tartanry, the
clans, the national struggle, heroic defeat, but that his great rival Michael
Balcon should have turned to the rival 'kailyard' tradition, initiating a powerful tradition in film-making. 'Tartanry' and 'Kailyard', as disapprovingly

defined by Colin McArthur, emerged in the nineteenth century to give Scotland a distinctive identity that was not English. 'Tartanry' with its emphasis on the clans, the wild Highlands and Jacobitism, is tribal, neo-feudal and atavistic, defiantly pre- and anti-modern. 'Kailyard' is domesticated village Scotland, parochial, sentimental, backward-looking, small-scale, deeply religious. Each had its great celebrants: Walter Scott and J. M. Barrie.[14]

It would be impossible to overestimate the importance of *Whisky Galore* in its establishment of an image of Scotland which persists to this day. But it would be quite wrong to see these films as anti-British or hostile to the Union. The films very carefully avoid depicting the English as villains – the villains are bureaucrats, officials, Whitehall, something anyone in the British Isles can condemn. Also they are analogues of other similar films dealing with English communities.

Ealing, which produced *Whisky Galore*, was dedicated to making films celebrating Britain and the British way of life. It consciously made comedy films celebrating small communities in England (*Passport to Pimlico*), Scotland (*Whisky Galore*) and Wales (*A Run for Your Money*). But more significantly in its serious films it ensured a British dimension to the cast, with the prisoners of war in *The Captive Heart* including English (Jack Warner, Derek Bond), Scottish (Gordon Jackson) and Welsh (Mervyn Johns), and the police force in *The Blue Lamp* seen to include alongside the stalwart English Jack Warner and Jimmy Hanley, a Welshman (Meredith Edwards) and a Scot (Bruce Seton). Ealing were not setting out to give the film an anti-English flavour. Launder and Gilliat who regularly returned to Scotland and Ireland (*Geordie, The Bridal Path, Captain Boycott, I See a Dark Stranger*) for themes for their films had celebrated English communities (*Waterloo Road, London Belongs to Me*), English eccentricity (*The Happiest Days of Your Life*, the St. Trinian's films) and created the archetypal Englishmen abroad Charters and Caldicott, played by Basil Radford and Naunton Wayne. Group 3, nurtured under Balcon's aegis and run jointly by Scots documentarist John Grierson and English populist John Baxter, also produced films celebrating the virtues of small communities in England (*Time, Gentlemen, Please*), Ireland (*The Oracle*) and Scotland (*Laxdale Hall*).

Colin McArthur sternly denounces the 'regressive' and 'profoundly backward' nature of films in Scotland, their static timeless adherence to the conventions of tartanry and kailyard.[15] He wants films to confront the industrial reality of modern Scotland but when they do in *Floodtide* and *The Brave Don't Cry*, he denounces them as consensualist. What he appears to want are films constructed along class-conflict lines. He rightly perceives many of the kailyard films to celebrate a feudal set-up in which the laird presides benignly over a happy peasant people. But he fails to recognize that people have related very strongly to this image. The Scots have loved *Whisky Galore, Laxdale Hall* and *Geordie*. They have related to the stories, the communities, the sentiments, the background. The films have created an image of Scotland with which people identify, and which warms them. Class is now increasingly seen by historians as a one-dimensional way of analysing and defining individuals. It is only one, and maybe not the most important one, of the bundle of identities people carry around. For all people are not class-conscious; rather more are class-aware and for some people gender and ethnic identities are more important than class, while in the past, though decreasingly in the present, religious identities have also been important. These have crucially cut across class lines and rendered class less central.

John Grierson, in an essay on a 1959 television series of Neil Gunn's *Para Handy* stories (of which there have been at least three different television series since the 1950s), identifies why such films are liked: *Para Handy* concerns the crew of the *Vital Spark*, a Clyde puffer, and their adventures up and down the Clyde and along the coast. Grierson called it:

> a sort of Odyssey of the little men ... an Odyssey of the common man with all his prides and all his humours, wandering through the little places and getting a terrific bash out of life wherever he goes ... Where its appeal lies – and especially today – is that it is the epic of the non-metropolitan, and a reminder that life is life and the same life wherever it is, and that you don't have to go to London – no, nor even Edinburgh – to get the excitement. It's a tale that crops up a lot in the Scottish mind, and, of course, in Scottish writing. You get it with Linklater in *Laxdale Hall*. You get it with Compton MacKenzie in *Whisky Galore!* And one of the interesting things to me is that it is so basic in its appeal to our Scottish minds that we get to thinking that all the stories in the tradition belong to us personally.[16]

Reviewing *Rockets Galore*, he pointed out:

> it is yet again the old Scottish joke about how the little people of the Highlands bewitch and bewilder the Englishmen who come amongst them and try to control them for one reason or another. There was *Whisky Galore* to begin with ... *The Maggie* ... *Laxdale Hall* ... it's the same script in every case and the same joke. Be sure the islanders will be very cunning. Be sure the Englishman will be very sentimental. Be sure there will be a Highland school teacher or something, very beautiful,

Peasant Scotland: *Whisky Galore* (1949)   **20**

whom the English gent will fall for and give you your love interest ... It's
like a western to me. I know all the conventions. I know it is unreal and
out of this world. I know everyone will say it is outlandish and exagger-
ated and whatnot. But I loved the whole thing as ever – because of the
mad thought in it that the meek can inherit the earth.[17]

This is both wise and profound. It raises and covers a number of important
issues: the familiarity of the conventions, the underlying ethic, the basically
enjoyable joke.

Whisky Galore is the prototype. The island of Todday in the Outer Hebrides,
where the whisky has run out, is the ideal Ealing community, close-knit,
devout and canny. When a ship is wrecked carrying a cargo of whisky for
export only, they loot it and then follows a battle of wits as they seek to avoid
its seizure by the customs officers, who are aided by the local Home Guard
Commander, Captain Waggett. Waggett is the only Englishman on the island,
pompous and self-important but quite out of his depth. He admits to his platoon sergeant, Fred Odd, that he does not understand the islanders. He tried
to teach them football and when he called a foul, one of them kicked the ball

into the sea. He cannot comprehend such behaviour. He helps the customs officers out of a sense of duty ('Once you let people take the law into their own hands – it's anarchy'). But his concept of law is at odds with the islanders' view of natural justice (the wrecked cargo is a windfall). There is a precise parallel here with John Ford's powerful anti-colonialist drama *The Hurricane* (1937), in which a French administrator in the South Seas insists on the letter of the law against natural justice, tribal traditions and the community feeling of the natives of the island and is in consequence isolated and alienated. Waggett is in just this position, a gulf of incomprehension between him and the islanders. 'These people are impossible,' he remarks. But the film is not anti-English *per se*. Sergeant Odd is a cockney, but he marries one of the island girls, having learned words of Gaelic to propose, in other words he has 'gone native', and he cooperates in the islanders' deception. The customs officers are Scottish, so it is the community against bureaucracy as much as against the Englishman.

In 1958 Basil Dearden and Michael Relph reassembled the surviving cast, added several of the cast of *The Maggie*, brought in Roland Culver to replace Basil Radford, who had died, as Captain Waggett and made a sequel, *Rockets Galore*. This time the Ministry of Defence want to set up a rocket range on Todday and the locals mobilize to sabotage their attempts until the government sends in paratroopers, seizes the island and orders total evacuation. But local schoolteacher Janet McLeod (Jeannie Carson) and the islanders capture and paint the local seagulls pink, starting a national campaign for preservation of the island as a bird sanctuary and the Prime Minister capitulates.

The film is powerfully anti-nuclear, with Father McAllister, the Catholic priest, rejecting the prosperity offered by the rockets, denouncing the arms race and saying their wealth lies in their scenery, their little homes and their faith. A strong sense of community is expressed in recurrent gatherings of the islanders for religious processions, church services, community meetings, ceilidhs and celebrations, complete with singing, dancing and whisky galore. It is non-sectarian, with Catholic priest and Protestant minister friends and allies. Also, as the priest argues, 'a spirit of independence – or call it rebellion – still broods in these islands'. It manifests itself in a hostility to the English – Captain Waggett, the only Englishman on the island joins forces with the Ministry of Defence and at public meetings declares rockets necessary for the defence of England. 'Scotland is our country,' declares Duncan Macrae to cheers from the audience. This hostility is embodied in a shot of stonyfaced disapproving locals looking on in the pub as the English surveyors gather round the piano to sing 'Maybe it's because I'm a Londoner'. On the other hand, Squadron Leader Mander (Donald Sinden) falls for the island and for Janet; and Air Commodore Watchorn (Ian Hunter) is a dedicated birdwatcher. It is bureaucracy, outsiders, Whitehall that are the real enemy. In this is can be seen to appeal to broader British feelings, to that hatred of officialdom identified by Dr Stephen Taylor as a common characteristic of the British, and to the love of nature – the defence of the pink gulls' breeding ground parallels exactly the campaign by the English village to save the breeding ground of rare birds in *Tawny Pipit*, also against the Ministry of Defence. It is not anti-English but anti-bureaucracy, anti-authority, anti-outside interference, and, anyway, the English can take a few friendly sideswipes.

Laxdale Hall (1953), directed by Scotsman John Eldridge for Group 3, was originally intended as an Ealing script. Based on Eric Linklater's novel, it is *Whisky Galore 2*. The village of Laxdale opposite the Isle of Skye refuses to pay any road fund licence because there are only five cars in the village and the road is almost unusable. A parliamentary delegation is sent from London to investigate and eventually persuaded of the need for a new road, but only after the application of peasant cunning.

The film sets up the contrasts between England and Scotland, between city and country, but stresses the latter and softens the former. The mother of the chief English outsider, Samuel Pettigrew, came from Laxdale. One of the MPs, Hugh Marvell, is won over completely and falls for the laird's daughter and Scottish Office civil servant Andrew Flett decides to settle in Laxdale as schoolteacher. The country/city contrast is highlighted by poachers. Local poacher McLeod is tolerated by the laird, General Matheson, because he plays by the rules and uses his wits. But the organized Glasgow poachers, spivs who come in as a gang and use dynamite, are rejected and the village as a whole unite against them. Catriona Matheson tells Hugh that in the city people merely exist, in the country they live.

Laxdale is a cheerfully feudal society, run by the laird and the Protestant minister, Reverand Macauley. It is, by the laird's definition, a civilized society – tolerant and well-mannered. It is devoutly Protestant – the whole community turn out for services on the Sabbath. Samuel Pettigrew, MP, millionaire and industrialist whose crippled leg is a sign of a twisted soul, wants to move the inhabitants to a purposebuilt industrial new town, Drumliedubs, 'the new Jerusalem', he calls it. He tells them they are living in medieval hardship, with no running water, inside lavatories, gas stoves or cinemas, and they are a 'liability to Great Britain'. But the villagers declare they have freedom and scenery, they provide fish and foodstuffs to the cities and men for the fighting services:

'No doubt the 20th century could learn a thing or two from Laxdale.' Petti-grew, the dessicated Englishman ('I disapprove of scenery. It encourages people to be lazy'), is first softened up by whisky and later gently blackmailed into changing. Scottish peasant cunning triumphs over interfering English bureau-cracy.

Alexander Mackendrick virtually remade *Whisky Galore* by crossing it with *Para Handy* in *The Maggie* (1954) in which the community is the crew of the Clyde puffer, *The Maggie*, and they fight a battle of wits and wills with an American businessman who accidentally charts them to convey a cargo of bath-room fittings to his island bungalow. Airline tycoon Calvin B. Marshall starts out as a hustling, insensitive, self-centred, workaholic American businessman, a man who, the skipper says, is not 'at peace with himself', and who learns the value of life, loyalty, friendship and independence. After threatening several times to remove the cargo and after trying to buy the ship, he eventually joins in a ceilidh, helps repair engines and agrees to jettison the cargo when the boat runs aground. For him it is a voyage of discovery, while his officious, bowler-hatted, umbrella-wielding, stuffy English agent, Pusey (Hubert Gregg) who echoes Waggett ('I don't see anything amusing in breaking the law') in oppos-ing the crew's poaching, is continually humiliated, outwitted and put upon.

Launder and Gilliat excavated similar territory in *Geordie* (1955), a senti-mental and charming tale about an innocent Scots lad (Bill Travers) who becomes a champion hammer thrower and wins the gold medal at the Mel-bourne Olympics. The protégé of the local laird (Alastair Sim) whose game-keeper he is, and of the local minister (Jack Radcliffe), he represents the classic tale of the victim, an undersized bullied child who takes a bodybuilding course and becomes a champion. Significantly, it is Great Britain he represents at the Olympics. Almost a sequel, *The Bridal Path* (1956), has Travers as an innocent sheep farmer and islander who sets out to find a wife, escapes the predatory attentions of a succession of females, is mistaken for a gangster and pursued by police across the Highlands, eventually returning to his island and marrying his cousin. Both feature a Scottish innocent abroad, facing the dangers and trials of the wider world and retreating happily to rural home and rural sweet-heart. Stunning scenery, accomplished playing by the familiar repertory com-pany of Scottish players (Gordon Jackson, Duncan Macrae, Roddy MacMillan, Jameson Clark, and so on) and the idea of an innocent abroad appealed both locally and universally.

Monja Danischewsky, the Russian Jew who had produced *Whisky Galore* and scripted *Rockets Galore*, wrote and produced *Battle of the Sexes* in Scotland in 1960. Based on a James Thurber short story *The Catbird Seat*, it was relocated to Edinburgh. It was produced by another Balcon-led consortium, Bryanston, and directed by Ealing veteran Charles Crichton.

Scotland, says the narrator, is 'one of the last bastions of Man's supremacy', confirming a view that had emerged in film of a largely male world where women are 'bonnie lasses', romantically idealized Scottish 'colleens' or shrivelled, purse-lipped, matriarchal tyrants like Jean Cadell in *Whisky* and *Rockets*. Here a thoroughly modern American female, efficiency expert Angela Barrows (Constance Cummings), is imported into an old-established family-run tweed business, the House of MacPherson, with an accounts department 'like something out of Dickens'. Barrows, her piercing scornful laugh heard constantly, decides to update it – scrap the drinks cupboard, replace the Hebridean weavers by a factory and introduce synthetic fibre. The elderly chief accountant, Mr Martin (Peter Sellers), appalled by her proposals, first sabotages her improvements and then when she persuades MacPherson to sack the accountancy department, decides to kill her. But after a bungled attempt, he settles for convincing the boss that she is mad and she is dismissed.

The firm is staffed by Alex MacKenzie and Abe Barker from *The Maggie*, and Jameson Clark, Roddy MacMillan and Moultrie Kelsall from almost everything else. The idea that there is something twee and sentimental about cinematic Scots is refuted by this film where Martin is prepared to kill, like 'The Wee Boy' in *The Maggie*, to defend a way of life. Here modernity, Americanization and female liberation are all decisively rejected in favour of tradition, male dominance and quality of life.

There is more than a hint of Ealing in the work of Bill Forsyth, whose trio of films (*That Sinking Feeling, Gregory's Girl* and *Local Hero*) achieved a winning blend of innocence, charm and whimsicality, while rooting the stories in sharp observation of the contemporary scene. *That Sinking Feeling* (1979) was his *Lavender Hill Mob*, fresh, funny and inventive, with an eye to individual idiosyncrasy, about a group of unemployed Glasgow teenagers planning and executing a robbery. It shows an awareness of the realities of unemployment, poverty, depression, boredom and teenage angst but treats them with humanity, humour and observation. *Gregory's Girl* (1981), set in a Scottish new town, is a sheer delight in its account of the romantic misadventures of a group of teenagers (many of them played by actors from the previous film), notably gangling Gregory (John Gordon-Sinclair). It derived much humour from its depiction of the boys as gauche and incompetent and the girls as cool, knowing and in control.

Local Hero (1983) crossed *Brigadoon* and *Whisky Galore* to chart the victory of nature and the land over materialism and greed. The American oil men want to buy Ferness Bay and turn it into a gigantic oil refinery ('the petro-chemical capital of the Free World'). The Scots are only too happy to take the money and get out. But the oil men, corporate cosmopolitans Peter Riegert and Peter Capaldi, go native and succumb to the lure of the land, both falling in love with women symbolically named Stella and Marina (the stars and the sea). The situation threatens to turn ugly when old beachcomber Ben Knox (Fulton Mackay) refuses to sell and villagers advance menacingly on his hut, but oil company president Burt Lancaster descends from the sky literally as a *deus ex machina*, discovers a shared interest in the stars with the old man and settles for a research institute instead of a refinery. Lancaster urges early in the film 'Dream large' and the film, like other Forsyth works, is on the side of the dreamers. The Scots are not sentimentalized; they are ruthless, devious and greedy but they are saved from themselves by the eccentrics, romantics and lovers. It is full of inflections, ironies and nuances of the traditional images (for example the local minister Reverend Murdo MacPherson is black). Nevertheless, the underlying structure, ethic and narrative thrust is recognizably Ealingesque.

The Scottish world of faery, fantasy and magic has appealed to romantic outsiders, particularly to the Americans Lerner and Loewe (*Brigadoon*), the Frenchman René Clair (*The Ghost Goes West*) and the team of Englishman Michael Powell and Hungarian Emeric Pressburger (*I Know Where I'm Going*). In each case the Scotland of myth and legend is set in contradistinction to the materialism and spiritual emptiness of the present.

Brigadoon (1954), produced by Arthur Freed and directed by Vincente Minnelli from the Lerner and Loewe musical play, is the epitome of the ersatz Scottish story that Scots love to hate, the equivalent of the attitude of the Welsh intelligentsia to *How Green Was My Valley*. But it had an enormous influence worldwide in perpetuating a particular vision of Scotland. Entirely shot in the MGM Studios in California – producer Arthur Freed had rejected all possible real Scottish locations as inauthentic – it deploys painted backdrops, studio-constructed village and all the imagery of romantic tartanry – sheep, heather, mist, kilts, the pipes, Highland reels. It assembles the usual ragbag of Hollywood Celts, on the cavalier assumption that one Celt is pretty much like another: Irishman Albert Sharpe and Welshman Tudor Owen are pressed into service as Scots, just as Ford filled his Welsh village with Irish and Scots.

The basic idea is lifted from *Lost Horizon* with Brigadoon the Scottish equivalent of Shangri-La and a similar plot (two visitors, one of whom finds love and accepts the village while the other rejects it; also one of the villagers tries to leave and is killed). In an eighteenth-century Scotland plagued by witches, the minister Forsythe wants to protect his parishioners from evil and prays to God to swallow the village in mist. It emerges once every hundred years for a day. Anyone who falls in love with a villager can stay and live forever. The dominie Mr Lundie explains that many in the outside world seek a Brigadoon, a place of eternal life, love, faith and peace. The film posits a precise contrast between love, spirituality, community (Scotland) and materialism, individualism, the rat race (New York).

René Clair's elegant and whimsical *The Ghost Goes West* (1936) takes a more amused look at this contrast, constructing an eighteenth-century Scotland in terms of clan feuds, whisky drinking and tartanry, and setting aristocratic *noblesse oblige* and true love against the vulgarity and materialism of Americans who transport the castle, complete with resident ghost, to Florida.

In Powell and Pressburger's *I Know Where I'm Going* (1945), ambitious and determined secretary Joan Webster agrees to marry her employer, industrialist Sir Robert Bellenger. She travels north to Scotland so that the wedding can take place on the Hebridean island of Kiloran, which he is renting. Fogbound on Mull, Joan is given shelter by Catriona Potts at her manor house and there meets penniless naval officer Torquil McNeil, the laird of Kiloran, whose tenant Bellenger is. While they wait for the weather to change, Torquil shows Joan the island and tells her of its legends. She falls in love with him. Resisting her feelings, and determined to marry Bellenger, she insists against all advice on crossing to Kiloran. Torquil accompanies her. Their boat breaks down and is almost sucked into the whirlpool of Corryvrechan, but, thank to Torquil, they escape. She succumbs to her love and they are united.

The genesis of *I Know Where I'm Going* lies in the previous Powell-Pressburger collaboration, *A Canterbury Tale*. Powell said later: '*Canterbury Tale* was made as a crusade against materialism and Emeric said "Well, let's have another go at it"'. Pressburger wrote the script in four days ('It burst out – you couldn't hold it back ... I felt strongly about the idea').[18] *I Know Where I'm Going* and *A Canterbury Tale* thus stand together in the corpus of Powell and Pressburger's wartime work as their definitive statement of 'why we fight'. They had produced a programmatic account in *Forty-Ninth Parallel* of the evils of the Nazism against which Britain was fighting. But in *A Canterbury Tale* Powell and Pressburger had explored the spiritual values that they saw as the essence of the England for which the war was being waged and celebrated the beauties of Powell's native Kentish countryside, the source of these values. But with its discursive narrative structure, quirkily messianic hero and pervasive mysticism, *A Canterbury Tale* had bewildered and alienated critics and public alike.

For their second 'crusade against materialism', Pressburger provided a much simpler and more straightforward narrative line and they decided to set the film in the Scottish islands. In his first critical success *Edge of the World* (1937), Powell had already manifested a powerful attraction towards the Celtic fringe, with its mists, its legends and its un-reason. He responded joyously to the Hebridean setting of the new film. But the Gaelic flavour does not disguise the similarity to *A Canterbury Tale*. It was not just that Powell was using the same technical team, all working at the peak of their form, Erwin Hillier providing the glowing photography, Allan Gray the ravishing score and Alfred Junge the atmospheric sets. Both films hymn the rural beauties of Britain. Both chart the spiritual awakening of city-dwelling materialists. In both films, the travellers from the modern world are stranded at night in thick fog, emerging into a community rooted in older, deeper values. As the fog clears, so too do their misconceptions and muddles, as they move to a realization of the real meaning of life. Both invest in the local squire/laird an almost unearthly power, locating in him the source of ultimate wisdom. Ironically, when *I Know Where I'm Going* was released, the same critics who had damned *A Canterbury Tale* as a mystifying muddle, praised *I Know Where I'm Going* for its acting, photography, dialogue and landscape, but complained that the story was too simple.

The apparently simple love story, however, is worked out against a rich background of folklore, myth and mysticism, which embodies an entire worldview. The Australian Donald Horne, seeking to understand what made England tick, proposed two rival metaphors for Englishness: the 'northern', which was urban, pragmatic, empirical, calculating, Puritan, bourgeois, enterprising, adventurous, scientific, serious and struggle-orientated; and the 'southern', rural, romantic, illogical, lucky, Anglican, aristocratic, traditional and frivolous. *A Canterbury Tale* had been a defiant embodiment of Horne's southern metaphor. In *I Know Where I'm Going*, the southern metaphor is effectively transferred to the Celtic fringe, with the substitution of paganism for Anglicanism. Indeed, in the Powell-Pressburger cosmology, *I Know Where I'm Going* can be seen as a dramatization of a battle between the two metaphors with the southern/Celtic emerging victorious. It also emphasizes the necessity of seeing this battle as taking place in a British rather than an English context.

Joan Webster is a northern girl, urban, middle-class, a bank manager's daughter from Manchester. Modern, sensible, strong-willed, she is the secretary to the head of Consolidated Chemical Industries. The film opens with a succession of glimpses of her at various ages – as a baby, a twelve-year-old schoolgirl, an eighteen-year-old factory hand, all demonstrating that strong-mindedness and single-mindedness of purpose that gives the film its title. She is determined to marry her boss and enjoy the fruits of success. This determination is wrecked on the rock of her love for Torquil McNeil, the laird of Kiloran. Torquil stands for an unshakeable devotion to his Hebridean island home, a reverence for the past, and the tradition and responsibilities of the rural squirearchy. He declares his intention of spending his leave sea-bathing, grouse-shooting and salmon-fishing, in pointed contrast to Sir Robert Bellenger, who has installed a swimming pool in his castle and who buys rather than catches his salmon. Above all, Torquil epitomizes anti-materialism, a stance summarized succinctly in a dialogue exchange with Joan:

Joan: People around here are quite poor.
Torquil: Oh no, they haven't got any money.
Joan: That's the same thing.
Torquil: Oh no, it's quite different.

In this film, anti-materialism is specifically invested in the Scots, their traditions, their way of life, their beliefs, and not in the English, who have on the whole lost touch with it. Contact with the Scots, their land and their life gradually converts Joan. But significantly her education takes place against a background of a succession of mediaeval castles and baronial residences, the haunts of a proud if impoverished aristocratic tradition.

Torquil's stance is reinforced by that of Catriona Potts (née Maclean), owner of the manor house, steeped in history and stuffed with relics, whose first entry, preceded by great hunting-hounds, her hair wild and unkempt, proclaims her a knowing child of Celtic nature. She is the female seer figure that crops up in other Powell Celtic fringe fables (*Edge of the World*, *Gone to Earth*), who knows what is going on in the hearts of Joan and Torquil. Powell deliberately shot her appearance 'so that I would link her half-consciously and half-unconsciously with what was going on – not exactly spying on things but being drawn'. When Joan wonders why, if the Scots need money, Torquil doesn't sell Kiloran, Catriona the manor house, and Mrs Crozier Achnacroish, Catriona replies simply: 'Money isn't everything.'

Mrs Crozier of Achnacroish lends further support to Catriona's argument, rhapsodizing over the Highland Games, the costumes and the colour and hosting a traditional ceilidh, where the community joyfully celebrate the diamond wedding of her faithful old retainers, the Campbells. It is at the ceilidh that the magic of Highland life and traditions powerfully affects Joan, confirming that the feudal life of castles and retainers, hunting and fishing, community singing and tribal dancing is the 'real world'.

The English are seen to be on the whole impervious to this way of life. They are most typically represented by the Robinsons, who have rented the castle of Sorne – the English family Robinson, stranded on an alien isle. They have spaniels instead of hunting-hounds, prefer to play bridge instead of hearing about the Games and manifest an almost heroic shallowness. But there is a saving figure for the English in Colonel Barnstaple, the eccentric naturalist, who has an eagle called significantly Torquil. Whether re-enacting the eagle's 'kill' for his friends or preparing curry while wearing a turban, he demonstrates the redeeming ability of the pukka sahib to 'go native', succumbing, like Powell himself, to the life and legends of Scotland.

Powell's well-attested love of magic is to be seen here both visually and thematically. Myth and legend inform the story at every turn, and the essential and transforming truth of these legends and superstitions is underlined. Even the boat which carries Joan to Mull is called *Lochinvar*, prefiguring her carrying off by Torquil. Torquil tells her on her first night there to count the beams in her room and pray. She does so, praying for wind to drive away the fog, and summons up a gale. Thereafter the forces of nature play a vital part in dictating the action: the fog which strands her, the gale which confines her to Mull, the whirlpool which mirrors her contradictory passions and almost consumes her. The weather only settles down once she has succumbed to her love. When Torquil shows Joan Castle Moy he tells her that he may not enter it, because of a curse laid on the MacNeils of Kiloran. 'Aren't you curious?' she asks, to which he replies, 'No, it's always been like that', demonstrating a healthy acceptance of tradition. When in despair at losing her, he enters the castle he discovers that the curse in fact provides him with his heart's desire, reiterating the rightness of tradition. The legend of Corryvrechan, whose pull can only be resisted by the strength of true love, is similarly vindicated, even to the sweeping away of the wedding dress designed for her marriage to Bellenger. The triumph of nature over materialism is perhaps most pithily and amusingly represented by the only public telephone on Mull which is so close to a waterfall that the sound of rushing water drowns out all attempts to communicate with the outside world. The telephone box on the seashore in *Local Hero* links Bill Forsyth's film securely to this romantic ethic.

The peripheral nature of the Celtic fringe is highlighted in stories about the struggle of man against nature, the sea, the land and the elements, in order to survive. It is given graphic form in Michael Powell's *Edge of the World*, shot on the Scottish island of Foula, but inspired by the evacuation in 1930 of the Hebridean island of St Kilda. The evacuation of St Kilda, ending a thousand years of habitation and an unchanged and unchanging way of life, struck then, and has continued to strike, an extraordinary chord, symbolic as it is of the destruction of community, the violent uprooting of tradition, the victory of modernity about which society is deeply ambivalent. The film stressed community, centrality of church, faith and minister, and the perpetual struggle to survive. The story inspired a memorable television documentary and subsequently book by Tom Steel and later a film by Bill Bryden, *Ill Fares the Land* (1982).

The clear model in structure and ethos and even in incident for *Ill Fares the Land* is *How Green Was My Valley*. It is self-consciously Fordian. Shot on scenic St Kilda locations, it is narrated by the boy Neil after he has left the island. It opens with a huddle of shawled women watching a dead body brought ashore. There follows a series of sequences that stress community feeling. There is a funeral as the dead man is buried ('One family's death was the whole island's mourning'): posed, hieratic groups in the churchyard and Gaelic hymns. The island parliament meets, all the men in the community deciding democratically on the work and its division. The women sing as they make the tweeds. The sabbath sees everyone going three times to church. But change is on the way. The three MacKinnon boys leave after a Bible-reading from their father, exactly as in *How Green*. Willie MacDonald returns for a visit with tales of Glasgow and wages, and shows them moving pictures. They are amazed. But in winter many die from a flu epidemic. A nurse comes and tends them. Tourists visit and treat them as freaks. But still the old patterns persist. Neil Ferguson Jr goes courting, formally in his suit, and the ensuing wedding, wedding feast and dancing is pure Ford. They petition for evacuation, unable to sustain the hard life any longer, and are evacuated to Morvern on the mainland. They land there, bewildered, photographed curiosities. A narrator intones the list of those evacuated islanders who died from tuberculosis. The last shot is of a boy's face looking back out of the window of the car at his lost island. It is an intensely romantic and poetic Fordian vision of an Edenic community, democratic, Christian, familial, rooted in tradition and the land, succumbing to modernity.

But that the experience is not exclusively Scottish is borne out by similarities to Robert Flaherty's celebrated documentary *Man of Aran* (1934) about a similar struggle for survival on an Irish island, with its elemental images of crashing breakers, towering cliffs, wheeling sea birds and lonely crofts. On a broader level the perilous life of fishermen has been regularly featured (Grierson's *Drifters, The Silver Darlings*), though this too has parallels in Yorkshire fisherfolk films (*Turn of the Tide, The Last Adventurers*). The disappearance of this way of life was movingly charted in Ian Sellar's elegiac *Venus Peter* (1989) with its Fordian story of a boy (Gordon Strachan) growing up amid a changing world, learning about nature from the minister and about life, the community and the sea from his grandfather (Ray McAnally), whose fishing boat is sold and symbolically taken away by road, watched by the entire village.

Superficially, David MacDonald's *The Brothers* (1947) can be seen to cross-reference with other Scottish/Irish island movies (*Edge of the World, Man of Aran, The Silver Darlings, I Know Where I'm Going*). They all share basic thematic elements: man's struggle with the sea, the living power of myth, the rugged grandeur of the landscape, family feuds, the harsh existence of isolated communities. The contrast between the sheer natural beauty of the setting and the violence and tension that exist within that setting is mirrored by the visual style of the film, which alternates lyrical sequences of island scenery with almost Expressionist passages, using intense close-ups, looming shadows and enveloping mist. But more profoundly and more centrally *The Brothers* relates to the Gainsborough costume dramas. It has a setting in the past, actually 1900 but with its prophecies and 'second sight', primitive executions, formal pronouncement of curses and rigid Puritanism, seeming far more remote (the seventeenth century, perhaps). The action revolves around that Gainsborough mainstay, the disadvantaged orphan girl, usually a servant, governess or companion. It features a brooding anti-hero, who first flogs and then makes love to the heroine, with Maxwell Reed, clearly being groomed as the new James Mason, cast in the role.

Convent-bred Glasgow orphan Mary Lawson (Patricia Roc) arrives on the Isle of Skye to become the servant of Hector Macrae and his sons, John (Duncan Macrae) and Fergus (Maxwell Reed). The Macraes distil illicit whisky and sell it on the mainland. An informer who seeks to betray them to the excisemen is captured and put to death by drowning. Mary, who is attracted to Fergus, rejects the advances of John but encourages the attentions of Willie McFarish, a member of a rival family. When Willie tries to force himself on Mary, Fergus fights him in her defence and this leads to a confrontation between the two families which is settled in the traditional manner by a rowing contest. The Macraes win but Hector overstrains his heart and dies. On his deathbed he gets Fergus to promise to obey John in all matters concerning the family and urges John to marry Mary to Fergus. Fergus, however, is led to believe that his father disapproved of a possible marriage between him and Mary. He therefore represses his feelings for Mary and ignores her. She turns for solace to Willie McFarish. When Fergus finds out, he whips her but this leads them to making love on the beach. John marries Angusina MacDonald, a neighbour's daughter, but continues to make advances to Mary, which she continues to reject. Mary and Fergus are brought together again on a fishing trip but Fergus is forced to cut off his thumb when it is trapped by a conger-eel. John now persuades Fergus that Mary is the source of all the evil that has befallen their family and she must be destroyed. Fergus takes her out in a boat and kills her, but drowns himself in remorse. Dugald McLeod, the local seer, who has overheard the brothers discussing Mary's death, alerts the villagers who arrive at John's croft to exact retribution.

It is a film of profound and disturbing ambivalence, something which derives from the merging of rival genre elements and the intermingling of opposing viewpoints. Raymond Durgnat saw it as a British equivalent of the Hollywood Western.[19] It certainly sees masculinity as being defined by a series of tests: man against man (fist-fighting, drinking), man against nature (the rowing contest, the struggle with the conger-eel), Man against the Law (the whisky-smuggling). But it also relates to the deep-seated misogynism running through 1940s *film noir*, dark-hued dramas in which *belles dames sans merci* bring death, destruction and disaster to the hapless male protagonists. Seen from this standpoint, *The Brothers* could be interpreted as a misogynistic tract, a warning of the dangers of unrestrained female sexuality. For it is Mary's encouragement of Willie McFarish that leads to the rowing contest that kills Hector. Mary is sexually aroused by the beating and induces Fergus to take her on the beach, causing him the mental anguish of believing he has defied the dying wish of his father. Mary succumbs to Willie in the glen, and his boasting of this fact compromises the Macrae family honour. She drives John mad with desire, while refusing all his advances. The final attempt to exorcise the evil leads to the deaths of Mary, Fergus and John. Mary can thus be seen as a fatal sexual intrusion into a celibate male society. The visual iconography of the film tends to confirm this view. Mary's first appearance in the film, in little-girl pigtails but incongruously heavy make-up and lipstick is immediately disturbing: an acknowledgement of a sexual maturity, which the priest recognizes when he lectures her on the need for chastity and good behaviour. Once she gets to the Macrae croft, she literally lets her hair down. Later she goes bathing nude, the sight of her inflaming Willie and provoking his assault. It is when Fergus and Mary have been brought together by Captain McGrath that Fergus thrusts his hand into a hole in the rocks, traps his thumb and is forced to cut it off to avoid being drowned by the incoming tide. This is an obvious metaphor for castration, the loss of masculinity following on directly from his succumbing to the charms of the woman.

The Brothers, viewed as a Gainsborough melodrama, however, rather than a British 'Western' or *film noir* and seen from the female standpoint, is capable of a quite contrary, almost feminist interpretation. For as Pam Cook has pointed out, 'in order to appeal to a female spectator, melodrama must first posit the possibility of female desire and a female point of view, thus making problems for itself which it can scarcely contain'.[20] From the first Mary is attracted to Fergus and makes it clear that she wants him. But she is denied respect, affection or warmth by any of the family. Symbolic of this is the bold close-up of the heart-shaped box, a present from Willie, crushed beneath Hector's foot, when her dalliance with Willie is discovered. Mary, however, throughout the film makes a series of choices and expresses her free will sexually, by sleeping first with Fergus and then with Willie, but firmly and repeatedly rejecting John. She can fairly be seen as the victim of a repressive patriarchal system, tyrannized over, beaten and finally killed by the Macraes. The strict role differentiation and rigid subordination of women in this macho society is affirmed by the exclusively male presence at almost all the significant communal activities in the film: the trial and execution of the informer and Hector's funeral, for instance. It is also comedically endorsed in a scene of almost Fordian folk humour in which John visits his elderly neighbour Alistair MacDonald and they get drunk together as they haggle over a bride-price for his daughter Angusina, disposing of her effectively as a piece of property.

That the two viewpoints are never reconciled and the film remains ultimately open to either interpretation is a back-handed tribute to Patricia Roc. For she is badly miscast as Mary, being too old, too English and too staid. She fails to match up to the uniformly excellent standard of Scottish character acting by the rest of the cast. But paradoxically her blank inexpressiveness makes Patricia Roc a *tabula rasa* upon which either reading of the film may be inscribed, according to the inclinations of the spectator.

The industrial and urban reality of Scotland is something that has had only a minority impact on the cinema, Colin McArthur's principal source of com-

Working-class Scotland: *The Shipbuilders* (1944) with Morland Graham and Nell Ballantyne. **21**

plaint in his study *Scotch Reels*. Three films, however, stand out, *The Ship-builders*, *Floodtide* and *The Brave Don't Cry*.

The Shipbuilders (1943), John Baxter's wartime masterpiece, is a deeply felt and moving film which functions on several levels. Based on George Blake's novel, published in 1935, it is updated to include the war. It fulfils exactly the government's criteria for wartime propaganda: how we fight (dedication and hard work and skill of shipbuilders); why we fight (freedom, rights of the common man, the commonwealth); and the need for sacrifice (the sons of both Danny and Pagan are killed). There is no sign of 'Red Clydeside' here. In its depiction of industrial relations, it is consensualist, based on the dignity of and respect for workers, the dedication and concern of the managing director and everyone pulling together in mutual sympathy and understanding. It is a retrospective rewriting of the 1930s from the perspective of the war. It vigorously denounces the decision to allow shipbuilding to decline, charting the effects of unemployment both in general (demoralization, starving children) and on one family, the Shields (the son drifts into crime, the wife leaves home).

It castigates the folly of allowing Germany to rearm (Churchill, the lone voice of sanity); it is outspoken politically about the guilty (Chamberlain and Munich, the stasis of the 1930s and businessmen selling vital equipment to Axis powers).

It is also the first authentic Scottish film, full of genuine Scots with genuine Scottish accents, an effective blending of location shooting and studio-constructed streets and tenements, and a convincing evocation of the texture of everyday life (the pub, the football match, the pools coupon, the cinema). It highlights the communality and the camaraderie, but also the romanticism and puritanism of that world. The loyalty of Danny Shields to his boss is contrasted with the strong will and realism of his wife, her astringency convincingly complementing his soft-centred romanticism, in fine performances by Morland Graham and Nell Ballantyne.

The film is narrated by Harry Welchman who, at the beginning and end, stresses that Britain is an island and her story is a story of sea and ships, and ships have bound together 'the greatest commonwealth of nations the world has ever seen'. It opens with the launch of the *Milano* in 1931. But with no more orders there are fears of closure. Shipyard managing director Leslie Pagan (Clive Brook) promises to do his best to keep the workforce together. Riveter Danny Shields (Morland Graham), embodiment of the respectable working class, is loyal to Pagan, having been his batman in World War One, serving in Palestine, Gallipoli and France. The film stresses throughout the commonality of interest. War service is a shared bond. Leisure is another (Danny and his son go to a football match cheering from the terraces, Pagan and his son from the stand). When Danny is scorned as a boss's man, other workers defend both him and Pagan ('a shipbuilder first and a boss second'). The view is put forward that the recession in shipbuilding is not 'our fault or the government's fault but due to a slump in world trade'. The men loyal to family attend the funeral of old John Pagan. When Leslie Pagan has to pay off riveters because there is no more work, the men are philosophical knowing he has done his best. The characterization of Pagan is revealing. He is a classic chivalric figure, a pipe-smoking, courteous, public school-accented, paternalist gentleman. But his father John Pagan speaks with a Scots accent. His great-grandfather was a shipwright. His roots and loyalties are Scottish. He refuses to have any part in dismembering the industry. He scours London for jobs for his yard, appeals to government ('They've got to care. It's their job to care'), lobbies, mounts a national campaign for shipyards, making speeches, rallying MPs. Eventually the campaign pays off and the government commissions John Brown's Yard to complete the *Queen Mary*. Then rearmament begins and Pagan's yard builds a destroyer. Come the war, Danny and Pagan are ARP wardens; both their sons are killed serving together on the *Milano*. The work goes on.

The narrator urges that after the war shipbuilding must not be allowed to decline again, industry is part of the heritage of the nation and men like Danny with pride in their work, dedication and simple faith are needed now and will be needed again. Ships bind the people of the Commonwealth together to fight for freedom and the rights of the common man. This is all said over shots of the king, queen and Churchill launching ships.

It shows a patriotic alliance of workers and management engaged in a national effort presided over by the king and queen. The texture of Scottish working-class life and authentic accents were welcomed in the Scottish press. But it links exactly with *Shipyard Sally* in which Gracie Fields plays a Lancashire variety star running a Clydeside pub who intercedes with the government to get shipyards reopened, and the *Queen Mary* completed and launched. In both the Fields and Baxter films the British dimension and indeed the wider imperial dimension are stressed.

George Blake contributed to the screenplay of *Floodtide* (1949), the story of the progress of a serious-minded, dedicated country boy David Shields (Gordon Jackson) training as a shipbuilder. He gets on by merit and hard work, impressing the boss, Sir John Anstruther, a self-made man who educated himself at night school, and who also got to the top by merit. David Shields educates himself in emulation of Anstruther and pairs off with Anstruther's daughter. As with *The Shipbuilders* authentic Glasgow backgrounds, including Barrowland dance-hall and idiomatic Scots accents, were welcomed by Scots critics.

The Brave Don't Cry (1952), directed by Philip Leacock for Group 3 and scripted by the socialist Montague Slater, was a careful and sincere semi-documentary of mine disaster and rescue. With a stalwart cast of Scottish actors, the film highlights the dedication, stoicism and cooperation of the mining community, the courage of the men who work, the women who wait and the rescue services. It is characterized by community, cooperation and mutual effort, management and men sharing the same qualities and common purposes. Its tone and its stance are sober, unsentimental, decent and cooperative. McArthur denounces both this and *Floodtide* as consensualist tracts guilty of suppressing class and sectarian conflict.[21] But this did not affect their popularity with audiences.

In terms of Scotland's participation in the wider British identity, there is conformity to the key elements. In films produced in Hollywood and Britain, kilted regiments have marched and the skirl of the pipes has echoed over India, with Scottish regiments featured in *Black Watch*, *The Drum*, *Wee Willie Winkie* and *Gunga Din*. The role of the armed forces in representing the wider British identity in the face of war is as old as Shakespeare's *Henry V*, which has stereotypes of English, Scots, Welsh and Irish soldiers serving together during the invasion of France and fulfilling a more up-to-date propaganda purpose in 1945 when Olivier filmed the play as a clarion call to final victory after D-Day. Cast in the play were actors more familiar as modern-dress archetypes of nationality: Michael Shepley's Englishman, John Laurie's Scot and Niall MacGinnis's Irishman.

Protestantism has been much more pervasive in Scottish films than in English, with the Presbyterian minister regularly featured as a community leader and the observance of the sabbath and the devoutness of the community insisted on. In the film of *Whisky Galore* the sectarian divide between the Presbyterians of Great Todday and the Catholics of Little Todday was eliminated to the annoyance of Compton MacKenzie. The religious dimension was restored in *Rockets Galore* but priest and minister are made firm allies.

The darker side of Protestantism is present in the negative stereotype of the narrow, intolerant, puritanical fundamentalist Scot, who recurs both in serious and comic form and has been regularly incarnated by John Laurie, notably as the crofter in Hitchcock's *The Thirty Nine Steps*. The positive side was expressed in *Chariots of Fire* (1981), with divinity student and future missionary Eric Liddell (Ian Charleson), a real-life Scottish hero, refusing to run in the Olympics on a Sunday, believing that God acts through him when he is running, defying the Establishment and winning a gold medal on his own terms.

MacArthur denounces tartanry and kailyard as having had 'seriously stunting effects on the emergence of alternative discourses more adequate to the task of dealing with the reality of Scottish life'.[22] But this view takes no account of the popularity of the films. People evidently preferred myth to reality. No-one frogmarched them to the cinema. They went because they loved the films, because a repertory of Scottish character actors (Finlay Currie, John Laurie, Jameson Clark, Duncan Macrae, Roddy MacMillan) symbolized the nation for them and stars like Gordon Jackson, Will Fyffe and Alastair Sim represented the nation in British films.

Notes

1 John Brown, 'The Land Beyond Brigadoon', *Sight and Sound,* 53 (1984/4), pp. 40–6.

2 *Documentary News Letter* (August 1942), p. 112.

3 Arthur Marwick, *Class: image and reality,* London, 1980, p. 22.

4 Colin McArthur (ed.), *Scotch Reels: Scotland in cinema and television,* London, 1982; Forsyth Hardy, *Scotland in Film,* Edinburgh, 1990; Eddie Dick (ed.), *From Limelight to Satellite,* London, 1990.

5 Dick (ed.), *From Limelight to Satellite,* p. 31.

6 Christopher Thacker, *The Wildness Pleases: the origins of Romanticism,* Beckenham, 1983.

7 Malcolm Chapman, *The Celts: the construction of a myth,* Basingstoke and London, 1992.

8 Murray Pittock, *The Invention of Scotland: the Stuart myth and Scottish identity, 1638 to the present,* London, 1991.

9 Hugh Trevor-Roper, 'The Invention of Tradition: the Highland tradition of Scotland' in Eric Hobsbawm and Terence Ranger (eds), *The Invention of Tradition,* London, 1983, pp. 15–41. Trevor-Roper's view is modified in some respects but largely endorsed by Charles Withers, 'The Historical Creation of the Scottish Highlands' in Ian Donnachie and Christopher Whatley (eds), *The Manufacture of Scottish History,* Edinburgh, 1992 pp. 143–56.

10 Hardy, *Scotland in Film,* p. 72.

11 Michael Powell, *A Life in Movies,* London, 1986, pp. 540–1.

12 Sheridan Morley, *Katharine Hepburn,* London, 1984, p. 73.

13 Philip Kemp, *Lethal Innocence,* London, 1991, pp. 172, 233.

14 These ideas and concepts are developed in Colin McArthur (ed.), *Scotch Reels.*

15 McArthur (ed.), *Scotch Reels,* pp. 1–6.

16 Forsyth Hardy (ed.), *Grierson on the Movies,* London and Boston, 1981, p. 162.

17 Hardy (ed.), *Grierson on the Movies,* p. 164–5.

18 Ian Christie (ed.), *Powell, Pressburger and Others,* London, 1978, p. 34.

19 Raymond Durgnat, *A Mirror for England,* London, 1970, pp. 143, 216.

20 McArthur (ed.), *Scotch Reels,* pp. 51–7.

21 McArthur (ed.), *Scotch Reels,* p. 3.

22 McArthur (ed.), *Scotch Reels,* p. 3.

8

Wales
and Ireland

Wales

Wales in the Middle Ages had a distinctive national culture. This began dramatically to decay in the sixteenth century with the decline of Catholicism, the abolition of the Welsh legal system and the banning of the Welsh language from official use. By 1681 Welsh was being described as 'the gibberish of Taphydom' and being spoken only by the lower orders and Welsh folk song and dance had all but died out.

The Welsh ruling class enthusiastically opted into the Tudor empire. Wales became strongly Protestant, staunchly royalist during the Civil War, reluctantly Hanoverian (because of the Stuarts' Catholicism) but, in the nineteenth century, energetic junior partners in the expanding British Empire.

What was left of the old folk culture was suppressed by the Methodists who sought to eliminate drunken funeral wakes, violent football matches and secular singsongs as part of a programme for the 'improvement' of the Welsh people. When the Romantic movement focused attention on antique customs and medievalism, concern about the disappearance of the old ways began to be expressed, particularly by the London Welsh societies, who with the peculiar fervour of exiles celebrated St David's Day in great style and made a point of cultivating their 'Welshness'. It was these London societies that took the lead in reviving the old singing, music and reciting competitions, the *Eisteddfodai*, which became the focus for a Welsh cultural revival. A group of passionate and romantic men and women, intellectuals, aristocrats, clerics and writers consciously set out to recover, as they would have put it, but in fact to create a mythic Celtic identity for Wales, strongly influenced by the Romantic movement.[1]

The most significant of this group was a romantic antiquarian and laudanum addict Edward Williams who called himself Iolo Morganwg. He believed that the Welsh bards, revivified by the *Eisteddfodai*, were the heirs of the ancient Druids and so he invented a great tradition of Druidic lore and ritual, a full-blown Druid theology, backed up by forged documents and fake histories. He was thus the Welsh equivalent of James MacPherson with his Ossianic forgeries. In the new mythology the Druids, who were well known to have been at the heart of British resistance to the Romans and to have made their last stand on the island of Anglesey, were projected as heroic sages defending the faith and culture of the Welsh people. The revival of Druidism, writes Prys Morgan,

> was a movement of considerable significance, all in all, because it involved myths which showed the cultural tradition of Wales to be older than any other in Western Europe and it made the scholar/poet or teacher central to that culture.[2]

The Celtic identity of Wales was developed after the Welsh scholar Edward Lhuyd took up ideas originally promoted by the Breton *abbé* Paul-Yves Pezron, who in a book published in 1703, linked the Welsh and the Bretons and traced their common origin to the Celts whom, he argued, were the ruling race of Europe in ancient times. After Lhuyd, it became a 'given' that the Welsh were the ancient Britons and the ancient Britons were the Celts, a race of rulers, warriors, artists and poets. There was now a great revival of interest in Welsh language, and scholars like William Pughe sought to prove that Welsh was the oldest language of mankind and the root of all the others. Wales began to be projected as 'the land of song' and Welsh songbooks, choirs and competitions proliferated. The Welsh landscape was hymned. A Welsh national costume (red cloak, tall black hat) was devised by an industrialist's wife, Lady Llanover, in the 1830s and became the visual symbol of Wales, reproduced endlessly in postcards, cartoons and figurines. In fact, this national costume was only the typical lower-class country woman's dress of the seventeenth century which had survived in Wales until the nineteenth century because Wales was so backward.

A raft of Welsh heroes was launched: Owain Glyndwr, the last Prince of Wales, who was idealized as the man who foreshadowed the need for Welsh institutions such as a national church and a national university; Madoc, the medieval Welsh prince supposed to have discovered America centuries before Columbus; and the nameless last Welsh bard who, after the slaughter of the bards by Edward I, defied the English armies and hurled himself into a river from a clifftop in 1282.

While, as Dai Smith observes, what actually created the Welsh nation physically was 'mass literacy, schooling, banks, roads or railroads, and military conscription', to it were added the imaginative trappings of an archaically romantic cultural image that was distinctively different from Anglo-Saxon England.[3]

This dominant antique rural romanticism was overtaken by two major developments in the nineteenth century. First, the industrialization of South Wales brought about a rapid expansion of the population, from half a million in the eighteenth century to two and a half million in 1921. As Gwyn A. Williams writes: 'What is distinctive about 19th-century Wales is the peculiarly *imperial* character of the formation of its industrial society and of the Welsh working class.'[4] Imperial and industrial Wales, largely English-speaking and concentrated in the south-east, contained two-thirds of its entire population. Engels wrote: 'The English know how to reconcile people of the most diverse races with their rule; the Welsh who fought tenaciously for their language and culture, have become entirely reconciled with the British Empire.' Gwyn Williams adds: 'Engels understated it; they were not merely reconciled with the Empire, they were enthusiastic junior partners in it.' South Wales became what Sir Alfred Zimmern dubbed American Wales, taking to the commercialized leisure industries *en masse*, developing strong transatlantic links, rejecting the Welsh language culture as irrelevant, while at the same time affirming their Welshness. David Lloyd George, prime minister of Britain during World War One, was living proof that it was possible to be both Welsh nationalist and British imperialist, and many Welsh people were also.

But there was another Wales, Nonconformist, Welsh-speaking Wales, with its roots, thought and emotional life rooted in the increasingly marginalized rural areas. Its poetic and imaginative significance was great. The rise of Nonconformist Protestantism in eighteenth-century Wales was the other central fact of Welsh history. Nonconformity attracted three-quarters of the population. Gwyn Williams comments:

> From the middle of the 19th century onwards, most Welsh people lived their lives within the orbit of, or in reaction to, the chapel. Their literacy, their world outlook, increasingly their politics, were deeply affected by

the morality of the chapel, its often crabbed narrowness and its often sweeping spiritual vision, its populism, in both its warmth and its deacon-controlled and often mean-spirited tyranny, its social equality and its opening to talent, particularly in verse and music, its whole style and manner ... and a whole people did indeed form along this line ... they came to think of themselves as classless, a *gwerin* (a folk) ... Everything outside them came to seem only half-Welsh, they were the *real* Welsh. Henry Richard put it in so many words, 'The Nonconformists of Wales are the people of Wales.'[5]

Nonconformity made Wales Liberal for the whole of the second half of the nineteenth century.

The year 1847 was the turning-point in the defining of Welsh identity. It was the year of the so-called 'Treason of the Blue Books' when a group of English commissioners reported on the state of Welsh education, proclaiming it pitifully inadequate and claiming that Welsh immorality, backwardness and obscurantism were due to the country's language and Nonconformity. The Welsh reacted with fury. The antiquarians and scholars who had been on the whole hostile to Dissenters now joined forces with them to refute English charges and promote Welsh culture, language and education, taking over many of the romantic invented elements – leeks, bards, *Eisteddfodai*. 'The chapels of Wales were the colleges of the common people,' said Lloyd George.[6]

The Eisteddfod became from 1858 a formally organized national festival, facilitated by the railways; the Cambrian Archaeological Association was founded in 1846; the Welsh national anthem 'Land of My Fathers' was written in 1856; the Cymmrodorion was reorganized as a Welsh national cultural society from 1872. Methodist Hugh Owen embarked on a forty-year crusade to create primary schools, teacher training colleges and a Welsh university. The results of the campaign included Bangor Normal College (1858), the University College of Wales at Aberystwyth (1867) and the first state secondary schools in Britain. In 1907 Wales acquired a national library and a national museum. But, as Smith says,

Wales was seen by the Welsh as an integral part of the Empire of Nations. The Welsh could be thus Welsh by origins, language, territory and religion and British in politics, social aspirations and links. Except for a few nationalist patriots, there was no contradiction of this.[7]

But the Nonconformists weakened Welsh interest in the distant past, replacing it with interest in the Old Testament and emphasizing the new puritanical 'dry' Welsh Sunday, chapel, temperance assemblies, choirs, mutual improvement societies and so forth. The Welsh christened their villages and chapels Nazareth, Bethany, Zion, Sharon, seeing themselves as Protestant Israelites.

The Nonconformists and all the Welsh educational institutions – which existed within, and in response to, regions and ideologies remote from the majority of the Welsh in the south-east – perceived the Welsh nation, the *gwerin*, the folk as educated, responsible, respectable, self-disciplined, Welsh-speaking and Nonconformist. However, their style became the Welsh style, and it was eventually taken over by the Welsh working class, which was English-speaking, South Walian, but also populist and communal. Labour working-class Wales emerged out of imperial Liberal Wales. It was English-speaking (Welsh speakers declined from 40 per cent of the population in 1911 to 20 per cent by the 1960s) and American cultured, with cinema a particularly strong influence. American English was the language of popular culture, the wider world and political struggle. This Wales was strongly communal, centred on the Working Men's Clubs and miners' institutions, the colleries and the 'Fed' (South Wales Miners Federation), on rugby and boxing, choral societies. It generated its own legends every bit as potent as Madoc or the Druids. The 'Legend of Tonypandy' is the widely believed story that during the miners' strike in 1910 Winston Churchill, then Liberal Home Secretary, ordered in the troops who then shot down miners. It is totally untrue: Churchill, concerned over riots and looting, horrified at the prospect of troops firing on civilians, sent in unarmed Metropolitan Police and no-one was shot in Tonypandy. But the whole of South Wales believed and continues to believe the legend.[8]

Rugby became a vital expression of the community, despite the fact that it was a middle-class game originally organized and run by professional men – lawyers, doctors and businessmen. It remained amateur and created a 'sporting fraternity that cut across class divisions' Encouraged by the successes on the field of Welsh Rugby Union, particularly against the other home countries, it became the national game, and Wales's first triple crown in 1893 confirmed rugby as *the* forum for the expression of national feeling. A composite cultural image of Wales thus emerged, compounded of chapel, choir, pit and Rugby Union.

How Green Was My Valley (1941) is the defining Welsh film. It was based on the novel by Richard Llewellyn, first published in 1939 and continuously in print ever since. Dai Smith, one of the most shrewd and sensitive analysts of Welsh culture, has called *How Green* 'the most important "document" … ever written about South Wales'. It is, of course, a selective picture, and a deeply romantic one, and this is what upsets some. Smith says, 'as economics this is

Welsh working-class solidarity: *How Green Was My Valley* (1941).   **22**

infantile, as history a falsification, as literature ... it is feeble, but as Romance ... it is perfect.'[9] It contains most of the elements of Welsh myth – the pit and the heroic pitman, the choir, the chapel, the beauties of the countryside – but interwoven with the timeless elements of romance – growing up, falling in love, the joys and sorrows of family life, death. It was the realization of this blend on film that made it so successful. It was bought by 20th Century-Fox but an initial script by Ernest Pascal, which 'emphasized the labour strife and the industrial ruin of the valley, while virtually ignoring the warm human comedy and tragedy', was discarded in favour of Philip Dunne's masterly con-densation which captured the spirit and flavour of the original.[10] He worked on it with designated director William Wyler but Wyler (when he refused to make cuts in the script) was replaced by John Ford, who agreed to a limited budget and shooting schedule. Ford added his own touches, derived from his own family memories and from Irish tradition, observing, 'The Welsh are just another lot of micks and biddies, only Protestant.'[11] Plans to shoot on location in Wales were scotched by the war and a Welsh village was built in the Malibu hills. Crucially it was decided to abandon the idea of showing the grown-up

Huw (to be played by Tyrone Power) and to keep Huw as a boy throughout. This gave the film an emotional and perceptual unity as it becomes a child's-eye view of an idyllic world gradually destroyed. The film is narrated by an unseen adult, Huw Morgan, who is packing his belongings to leave his valley forever, an experience shared by many of the Welsh during the Depression. As he packs, he recalls his childhood there in the 1890s. Whether or not it is an accurate picture of the life of a mining family is irrelevant, for it is life as seen through the eyes of a small boy, and the family is classically Fordian: 'My father was the head of our house; my mother was its heart.'

With an affection born of personal experience, Ford re-creates the rituals of family life, with mother Beth Morgan (Sara Allgood) waiting in the yard for the men to drop their pay into her apron as they pass; the scrub-down at the day's end; dinner with the whole family silent around the table because father Gwilym (Donald Crisp) believed that 'no talk I ever heard was as good as good food'; the distribution of the family's spending money; the joys (marriages, births) and sorrows (deaths, illnesses, departures). The family is so important that Huw gives up his chance of a professional career outside the valley and insists on going down the pit to support his brother Ivor's widow, Bronwen, who no longer has anyone to provide for her. But with the passing of time, the family dissolves (Gwilym and Ivor are killed in mine accidents), the mine closes, slag heaps obscure the once green valley. Huw leaves but will always have his memories, his sense of having belonged, and still belonging to a family: 'Men like my father cannot die. They are with me still – real in memory as they were real in flesh – loving and beloved forever. How green was my valley then.'

Woven in and out of the story of the family are the threads of Welsh myth. There is song. 'Men of Harlech' is sung behind the credits and throughout there is music and singing, a stream of melody. The miners march home from the pit singing 'Bread of Heaven', and 'The Ash Grove' and 'Myfanwy' recur throughout, as every rite of passage is marked by song: marriages, departures, reconciliations. Ivor and the choir he conducts are summoned to a command performance at Windsor Castle and they sing 'God Save the Queen' on receipt of the news.

Then there is chapel and a simple devout Protestantism. 'Respect for chapel was the first thing my father taught us' says narrator Huw over a shot of the boy Huw pausing, in his headlong run to the sweetshop, respectfully before the building, which dominates the village spiritually as the mine workings domi-nate it physically. Father reads a chapter from the Bible or says a prayer to accompany every significant event. The true spirit of religion is represented by Mr Gruffyd, the minister who comes direct from university at Cardiff but who has spent ten years down the pit. He represents the open-hearted, generous-minded, strong-willed spirit of service and sacrifice. He supports the union as long as it seeks justice and does not itself resort to injustice. But there is a nasty side to chapel, mean-spirited, petty-minded, tyrannical, embodied with memorable malignancy by Arthur Shields as deacon Parry, who presides over the expulsion from chapel of an unmarried mother, thereby earning the denunciation of Angharad. Parry is also behind the removal of Gruffyd over unfounded gossip of an affair between him and Angharad, who is married to the mine-owner's son. Gruffyd, in a key passage, fiercely denounces the hypocrisy and malice of the gossip-mongers.

There is education too. Mr Gruffyd helps to coach Huw. Huw's father venerates education and supports his son going to the National School and is bitterly disappointed when Huw goes down the pit. There is the archetypal Welsh Mam: the indomitable, fiercely loyal Mam, who goes to the mountains in a snow storm to denounce the striking miners for speaking against her anti-union husband, and nearly dies on the way back.

But the film and the book also establish a trajectory of change for the worst. The united family is part of the community – a community whose unity is represented by common faith, common work, common leisure. There is an Edenic beginning, a white-painted village set in the majestic hills. But as time passes, the slag heaps encroach and the village becomes dirty and disfigured. The people change as the environment changes and they become spiteful, vicious and narrow-minded. But it also begins to change when Gwilym, a fiercely anti-Socialist figure, opposes the union which his sons support. He refuses to believe the owners are 'savages'. Some of the locals boycott Gwilym, stones are thrown through his windows. 'Something has gone from out of the valley that may never be replaced,' says Gruffyd: it is the sense of community. Industrialization and its attendant ills disfigure the landscape of the valley and the landscape of the soul; the union divides rather than unites; it polarizes and replaces reason and understanding with confrontation.

There are several reasons why *How Green Was My Valley* provokes so much hostility in certain quarters. One is the charge of inauthenticity. There was only one Welsh actor (Rhys Williams, excellent as Dai Bando the prizefighter); the rest were a mixture of Irish (Sara Allgood, Maureen O'Hara, Arthur Shields, Barry Fitzgerald), Scots (Donald Crisp, Mary Gordon), Canadians (Walter Pidgeon) and English (John Loder, Patric Knowles, Roddy McDowall,

Anna Lee). The accents are all over the place. Pidgeon does not even bother to do one. The sunshine is that of California rather than the Rhondda.

The second is political. There is an entrenched mythology of the Welsh coalfields; the villainy and exploitation of the owners, the heroism of the unions, the united struggle, a prevailing Socialism. This is bypassed completely. Not only is Gwilym fervently anti-Socialist and anti-union, but his is the value system of the film: 'I never found anything he taught me wrong or worthless,' says young Huw and this presumably means anti-Socialism. Furthermore, they are devout monarchists. 'You are our father but we look to the Queen as our mother,' says Gwilym in prayer as news is received of the command performance. Wales's deep involvement in the Empire is also woven in. As the family breaks up, it migrates to the Empire. Young Gwilym and Owen emigrate to the United States but Ianto goes to Canada, Davy to New Zealand and Angharad to South Africa. There is – and Ford would have enjoyed this – a residual element of anti-Englishry. Mr Jones, the sadistic schoolmaster who savagely beats Huw, and Iestyn Evans, the icily snobbish mine-owner's son who marries Angharad, are both Anglicized Welshmen.

But in fact none of this matters. It is a film that speaks from and to the heart. Only the most flint-hearted curmudgeon or diehard ideologue could fail to respond to its potent mixture of myth, romance, idyll, dream, memory, melody and emotion. Its centrality to Welsh culture is attested by the fact that BBC television subsequently produced two memorable serializations of the book, first with Eynon Evans and Rachel Thomas, and second with Stanley Baker and Sian Phillips, as the Morgans.

After *How Green Was My Valley*, perhaps the most famous cultural depiction of Wales comes in Dylan Thomas's celebrated radio play *Under Milk Wood*, produced for The Third Programme in 1954 by Douglas Cleverdon. It was narrated by Richard Burton in his dark-brown voice, with a distinguished Welsh cast. Intoxicated by the joy of language, and with its archetypal cast of poets and preachers, schoolmasters and shopkeepers, mams and boyos, it evoked the mythical Welsh fishing village of Llareggub '(Buggerall' backwards, typical of its sly humour). But beneath the regular routines of everyday life, it uncovers a seething sexual underworld of desire, the dark underside of the pious, chapel-going world, a rich texture of gossip, tension and disapproval, of forbidden relationships between classes and sexes. Its central mythic status prompted an all-star film version in 1972, which was by general agreement disastrous, and a new all-star recording in 1992, narrated by Anthony Hopkins. With symbolic appropriateness, that iconic Welsh presence, Rachel Thomas, played Mary Ann Sailors in the 1954 radio, 1972 film and 1992 record versions of the play. It is the earthy counterpart to *How Green Was My Valley*'s full-blooded romanticism, its mirror-image, just as the definitive Irish film *The Quiet Man* has its dark counterpart, *The Field*.

If *How Green Was My Valley* is how Hollywood has represented Wales, how has Wales sought to present itself? A film was commissioned by the Welsh Committee of the Festival of Britain in 1950 and it is possible to see it as a native Welsh riposte to *How Green*. It is Paul Dickson's small masterpiece, the moving and eloquent *David*, with its luminous black-and-white photography and plangent Grace Williams score. *How Green* begins with narrator Huw Morgan leaving his valley; *David* opens with Ivor Morgan returning to his Welsh home, the town of Ammanford, where the film is set and was actually shot. In a narrative voice-over, Ivor recalls his first day at school and his meeting with school caretaker Dafydd Rhys, 'a Welshman to remember'. Schoolboy Ivor is the son of a minister and of the archetypal Welsh Mam played by Rachel Thomas.

The film lays stress on those elements that go to make up Welshness: education, chapel, poetry, music, communality, the pit. Mr Rhys is devoted to his rugby-playing son Gwilym, who wins a scholarship to Cardiff University but develops TB and dies. After his death, Mr Rhys seems to lose interest in life, but he writes a poem in memory of his son and Ivor's father enters it for the National Eisteddfod. Walking in the hills above the town and looking much like Gwilym and Huw Morgan in the earlier film, Ivor hears from Dafydd Rhys the story of his life. He goes down the pit at twelve ('a real man's work'): ten-hour shifts and seven shillings a week. There is comradeship and education in the pit; young boys learn from older men, who are great readers and always carry books in their pockets. He recalls the town ('more a family than a town') and 'the centre of our social life – the chapel – where family pews passed from one generation to the next' (community, tradition, continuity, the faith). He courts his wife in the shadow of a ruined castle (heritage). The miners lead fulfilled lives outside the pit – one as a Sunday-school teacher, another a trombonist, a third a flower-grower. Dafydd's brother, another miner, wins a scholarship to the Labour College and becomes an MP.

Dafydd, however, is injured in a mine accident on the day his son is born – the birth and accident are intercut, but stress the separate spheres of men and women. Dafydd writes a book of poetry *From the Dust of the Pit*, the proceeds from which send miner Gomer Roberts to theological college. Dafydd retires from the pit and becomes a school caretaker, helping successive generations of boys who come to the school. At the Eisteddfod, Dafydd misses first prize but wins second. The film ends with the school prizegiving with Ivor winning a prize and the visitor, Reverend Gomer Roberts, paying tribute to Dafydd and urging pride in their country. They all stand and sing 'Land of My Fathers'.

It is a true story with D. R. Griffiths playing himself as Dafydd Rhys. His brother, Jim Griffiths, became the first Labour Party Secretary of State for Wales. He gives a performance of such nobility and dignity that it is impossible not to be moved by the potential in the human spirit he represents. But there is striking continuity with the elements of How Green. The chief difference is one of idiom. *How Green Was My Valley* is full-blown Hollywood romance with all the trimmings; *David* with its use of non-actors, genuine locations and sober realism is in the British documentary tradition – Dickson, indeed, had worked for the Crown Film Unit. But the mythic content is the same.

Different elements of the Welsh identity are highlighted in other British films. *Valley of Song* (1952), charming, fresh and funny, emphasizes the 'musical' identity of Wales, detailing the divisions and rancour caused when conductor Geraint Llewellyn (Clifford Evans), rehearsing Cwmpant Choir for Handel's *Messiah*, gives the contralto solo, traditionally sung by Mrs Mair Lloyd (Rachel Thomas), to Mrs Davies Shopkeeper. The two families are estranged, the village is split and fights break out at the Miners Welfare. Eventually Reverend Idris Griffiths (Mervyn Johns) proposes a compromise – the sharing of the solo, and honour is satisfied.

Music is also a central thread of *A Run for Your Money* (1949), Ealing's Welsh comedy which has been undeservedly overshadowed by the other products of that *annus mirabilis* of 1949 when English and Scottish communities were celebrated in *Passport to Pimlico* and *Whisky Galore*. Warm-hearted, endearing, likeable and delightfully funny, it is a Welsh variation on the 'Up for the Cup' tradition, the story of provincial innocents at large in London. Dai and Twm Jones win a newspaper competition for record coal output, bringing them £200 and two tickets for the rugby international at Twickenham. The film establishes the communality and comradeship of the pit and the village; on the Welsh Express to Paddington, there are long tracking shots past singing Welshmen. In London, Dai is fleeced by con girl Jo; while Twm rescues drunken derelict exiled Welsh harpist (Hugh Griffiths), whom he finds playing in the gutter.

In an key scene, Twm and Huw enter a talent contest held at a cinema, performing 'All through the Night'. The stiff, individualistic English audience

reacts at first with mocking incomprehension but end up joining in and redis-
covering their sense of community, just as Jo relents and restores the stolen
money, and Huw returns on the train with the others to Wales restored to the
brotherhood. The contrast is pointed up between the corrupt, unfeeling materialism of London and the decency, communality, good nature, spirituality and
courtesy of Wales.

The role of education, however, may be ambivalent for it can lead to dera-
cination, something which has preoccupied Emlyn Williams. He explored it in
his autobiographical play *The Corn Is Green*, about a dedicated English teacher,
Miss Moffat, who takes up a bright but uncouth Welsh lad and transforms him
into an Oxford scholar. With its superb central female role, it has always
attracted great actresses and there have been two film versions, both in their
ways memorable. Bette Davis played Miss Moffatt splendidly in the 1945 Hollywood version, shot entirely in the studio at Warner Bros., and handicapped
by an unconvincing, strident American performance from John Dall as the
boy, Morgan Evans. It was remade in colour on location in North Wales by
George Cukor in 1978, with Katharine Hepburn triumphant as Miss Moffatt
and a much more convincing Morgan from genuine Welsh actor Ian Saynor.
Both the villagers, who resent his loss of Welshness, and the local squire, who
does not approve of his being transformed into a gentleman, oppose Morgan's
transformation but he is finally seen off in triumph by the community to
Oxford: a victory for education. Another educated and deracinated Welshman,
Rob Davies, comes back in *Last Days of Dolwyn*, which Emlyn Williams
scripted and directed for Korda in 1949, giving a screen debut to Richard
Burton and a fine part to Edith Evans. Rob Davies (Emlyn Williams), who
describes himself as a 'cosmopolitan', is an agent of Lord Lancashire, and wants
to buy and flood the village of Dolwyn to form a reservoir for Liverpool,
moving the villagers to the city. Penniless Lady Dolwyn sells the valley but
chapel caretaker Merri (Edith Evans) refuses to sell the cottage she owns and
the move is stalled. Lord Lancashire agrees to route the water by a different way
and save the valley. Davies, who wants revenge on the village for expelling him
when, as a boy of twelve he was caught robbing the chapel, goes mad, sets fire
to the village and is killed in a fight with Merri's son (Richard Burton). To
cover up evidence of the crime, Merri herself floods the valley.

The film firmly establishes the communality, the centrality of chapel and the
importance of culture (in a nice poetic touch the shepherd-singer Huw
remains in the village and is drowned) but it does not develop either an English versus Welsh conflict (Lord Lancashire, after all does not want to flood the

valley) or an intra-village conflict about staying or leaving, but instead falls into unconvincing melodrama, flawing what could otherwise have been a major film.

Basil Dearden's *The Halfway House* (1944), based on a Priestleyesque time play by Denis Ogden, assembles a group of mixed-up people at a remote Welsh inn, which was in fact destroyed a year before by German bombing. There they learn wisdom and peace from the ghostly innkeeper (Mervyn Johns) and his daughter (Glynis Johns), all emerging better people at the end. Two sets of estranged couples, the Frenches and the Meadows, are reunited. Two crooks repent of their anti-social ways and are redeemed: black-marketeer Oakley will give himself up and serve a prison term, and newly released embezzling army officer Fortescue will rejoin his old regiment as a private. An exhausted, over-worked and terminally ill Welsh conductor, David Davies, learns to face his impending death with dignity and serenity. A neutral Irish diplomat decides to abandon his neutrality and join the fight against Fascism.

The film from the outset constructs a particular image of Welshness, link-ing music (the opening sequence of David Davies conducting in Cardiff) and communality (a group of Welsh women take over a train compartment and begin handing out Welsh cakes and singing). Later the influence of chapel is established: both Davies's grandfather and the grandfather of Rhys the innkeeper were chapel ministers. But central to the film is the supernatural, the bombed inn that reappears and the Welsh sage, wise and serene (a wonderful performance from Mervyn Johns), who helps his visitors come to terms with themselves.

Initially the Welsh image in cinema was, like that of Ireland and Scotland, rural. David Berry, in his monumental history of cinema in Wales, has uncov-ered twenty-six fictional films made in Wales between 1912 and 1927 by major British and American companies, most of them now lost. He describes them thus:

> Filming forays into Wales sprang from a recognition of the country's pho-togenic locations … It would be possible to conclude from the films that industrial Wales did not exist at all and that rural Wales was composed entirely of mentally fragile shepherdesses, gypsies and potential suicides pursued by worried, usually rather rich and apparently myopic young men who needed rather more than earthly powers to effect the obligatory last-ditch rescue. The real world, as most Welsh people understood it, rarely appeared in this material.[12]

It was not until the late 1930s that industrial Wales featured in films. Thirties documentaries such as *Today We Live* and *Eastern Valley* established the now familiar images of slag heaps, pit villages, unemployed miners and smog. But they received emotional permanence by translation into feature films, notably *The Citadel* and *The Proud Valley*, of which the latter, though British and smaller scale, is the more significant. *The Citadel* (1938), based on the bestselling novel by A. J. Cronin, who had worked as a doctor in Tredegar and Treherbert, is the moving story of an idealistic Scottish doctor (Robert Donat) who abandons his practice in a Welsh mining village for life as a society doctor in the West End, but realizes the emptiness of the life and returns to the fight for humanity. The Welsh section involves him tending the victims of a pit disaster, blowing up sewers that are causing typhoid and seeking the cause of silicosis by experiments. But although the miners' agent (Emlyn Williams) is sympathetic, the superstitious and suspicious miners wreck his experiments, unite to end them and cause him to leave in despair. The miners appear completely backward and unregenerate.

The Proud Valley, of which a Welsh mining village was also the setting, is more upbeat. Begun in 1939 but completed and released in 1940, the film faced head-on the subjects of conditions in the mining industry, racial prejudice, unemployment and hunger marches. Seen today, and in spite of some obvious studio exteriors and the West End accents of the juvenile leads, it remains a sympathetic and committed work, warmed and enlarged by the personality and the glorious singing voice of Paul Robeson (see Chapter 3). Despite the climactic tragedy of the death of the Robeson character, David Goliath, the film's mood is one of essential optimism as David is integrated into the village community and as the community itself is integrated back into the nation with the onset of war. Nevertheless, the problems which it depicted would still need to be solved when that war was over.

The presence in the cast of Clifford Evans, Rachel Thomas and Jack Jones give the film an authentic Welsh flavour, and the film convincingly conveys both the communal spirit (in choir rehearsals and in the reactions to pit disasters) and the incidental details of everyday life (in the unwelcome visit of the rent collector, the seeking of credit at the post office and the management of large and hungry families). One person who was deeply impressed by the film was 'the Welsh wizard', David Lloyd George, who wrote to the producer Michael Balcon in 1940: 'It is one of the most moving and dramatic films I have ever seen … I must congratulate you upon producing such a work which, apart from its artistic merits, has a real educational value.'[13] (Interestingly, another Cronin adaptation, *The Stars Look Down*, though set in the north-east of England, has many similar elements, even to the presence of Emlyn Williams as villain, and Nancy Price gives one of British cinema's finest performances as the Mam. The same elements (communality, the importance of education, comradeship, pit work), all the imagery and ethic of a Welsh film, are there, indicating the broad appeal of 'Welsh' myths to the working class in general.

The image of community solidarity represented by Wales was drawn upon by Humphrey Jennings for his moving *The Silent Village* (1943), shot on location in Cwmgiedd. It was a transposition to South Wales of the massacre of the mining village of Lidice in Czechoslovakia after the assassination of Heydrich. Jennings established the texture of Welsh life with familiar images that although shot with real people in real places resonate with Ford's imagery: hymns sung in chapel; miners marching home from the pit to the strains of 'Men of Harlech'; family meals. The Nazis arrive and occupy the village; the teacher produces an underground Welsh newspaper; the miners resist (strikes, sabotage), meeting secretly in castle ruins (Welsh heritage). Finally after the assassination of the *Reichsprotektor*, the men are all shot, singing 'Land of My Fathers' and the village burned. Throughout there is Welsh singing on the soundtrack.

Jennings greatly admired the people he met in Cwmgiedd, writing: 'I never thought to live to see the honest Christian and Communist principles daily acted on as a matter of course by a large number of British – I won't say English – people living together.'[14] But he clearly saw the Welsh as part of the wider British nation, as he confirmed in *Diary for Timothy* where the four representative figures whose lives intermesh in the last years of the war are Bill the engine driver, Alan the farmer, Peter the fighter pilot and Goronwy the miner. Yet there is a radical tinge to *The Silent Village*, perhaps unintended, when the Nazis ban the Welsh language and the teacher urges the children never to forget their native tongue and reminds them of the history of Welsh resistance to outside conquerors, from the English on. The reasoning here in wartime must be that Welsh and English enmity is so far in the past it can be referred to, now that Wales is an integral part of Britain.

The only film to deal with the consequences of nationalization of the coal-mines is Jill Craigie's *Blue Scar* (1949), which, like *A Run for Your Money*, contrasted the 'real' world of Wales with the false world of London, in this case 'Bohemian London'. It conveyed the texture of Welsh life but also suggested that not much had changed after nationalization and saw its hero transformed from idealistic pitman to rather more ambivalent manager.

Kingsley Amis has had a very jaundiced view of Wales and the Welsh since his early days as an English lecturer at University College, Swansea, and has drawn on that experience for his novels *Lucky Jim,* T*hat Uncertain Feeling* and *The Old Devils,* all of them filmed, the latter for television. In *Only Two Can Play* (1962), based on *That Uncertain Feeling,* Wales's commitment to culture and education was mercilessly caricatured as bogus, pretentious and chauvinistic.

The social and cultural transformation of Britain affected Wales in one respect. Although Richard Burton is perhaps the most famous ever Welsh actor, there clung to him the patina of Olivier and of international stardom, but it was the Welshman Stanley Baker, whom Richard Burton called 'the authentic dark voice of the Rhondda valley',[15] who epitomized the major cultural change that brought working-class actors from the North, the East End of London and the Celtic fringe to the fore, playing working-class heroes as the gentleman went into eclipse. Baker, who had spent his early career playing out-and-out villains, now made a career of playing the newly fashionable anti-hero, tough policemen (*Blind Date, Hell Is a City*) or tough criminals (*The Criminal, A Prize of Arms*) with the same combination of sexual and class aggression, what Losey called 'machismo and puritanism'.[16] But he always retained that Welshness which allowed him to play movingly, in what was almost his last screen appearance, Gwilym Morgan in a television version of *How Green Was My Valley* (1976). It was Baker who as producer and star contributed the major dramatization of imperial Wales in *Zulu. Zulu* (1963) is an awe-inspiring re-creation of the defence of the mission station of Rorke's Drift by 105 men of the South Wales Borderers against 4,000 Zulus in 1879 following the defeat of Lord Chelmsford's army at the Battle of Isandlwana, which was itself subsequently re-created in the film *Zulu Dawn* (1979). The Welshness of the troops is well-established and, in one memorable scene, the Zulu war chant is met by a rousing chorus of 'Men of Harlech'. The officers, Chard the tough professional engineer (Stanley Baker), and Bromhead, the effete aristocrat (Michael Caine, cast against type in his first major role) begin with class antagonism but are bonded by their experience. It ends with Richard Burton reading the list of the record number of Victoria Crosses awarded for that single engagement.

The British Army had always been, and not just in wartime, the vehicle by which the men of the Celtic fringe and indeed of the English provinces had served the wider United Kingdom. The Empire is their battleground and the recurrence of Scots and Irish in imperial films is regular, though neither country has achieved its own imperial epic to match Wales's *Zulu.* The tradition goes back to Shakespeare's *Henry V* and was re-created by Olivier for his memorable 1945 film, with soldier stereotypes from the four home countries: Captain MacMorris from Ireland, Captain Fluellen from Wales, Captain Jamy from Scotland and Captain Gower from England, all played by representative actors of those nations, respectively Niall MacGinnis, Esmond Knight, John Laurie and Michael Shepley. But it should also be noted that the English provinces are also carefully characterized in the Olivier film, with the English troops represented by a West country man, a Northerner and a Cockney, paralleling the contemporary pattern for war films, and Olivier's film was dedicated to the commandos, commissioned by the Ministry of Information and intended as a final clarion call to victory.

Welshman as rugby player/fan; Welshman as boxer and as boozer; Welshman in all-male pits and all-male choirs are familiar images of Welshman. What of Welshwomen? Deirdre Beddoe, in a scathing and pithily accurate essay on images of Welshwomen, declares:

> Welsh women are culturally invisible. Wales, land of my fathers, is the land of coalminers, rugby players and male voice choirs. Welsh cultural identity is based almost entirely on the existence of these three male groups. Not only are these groups exclusively male but they are *mass* groups. Think of Wales and you think of Welshmen in *large numbers*: at the rugby match, in the mines and in the concert hall. Besides their corporate ranks, the tiny, usually solitary figure of the Welsh woman in national costume pales further into insignificance. She was only a bit of trimming on the male image of Wales anyway. Not only is the dominant image of Wales male and mass, it is also macho. Coalminers and rugby players evoke visions of strong male bodies caked with grime and of rippling muscles glistening with sweat: this hard image is brought into somewhat softer focus around the edges by the sweet harmony of tenor, bass and baritone voices. The picture of Welshness is complete. The amazing point about this picture, is that it is constructed on an extremely narrow base. It has been constructed with reference to only one sex, to only one class and to only one sector of the Welsh economic base; the industrial sector.[17]

Beddoe goes on to give reasons for this: patriarchy (Welsh patriarchal society), capitalism (coal-mining as the basis of Welsh industry), history (history of Wales written by men). What are the Welsh images of women? Beddoe isolates five: the Mam – pious, clean, hardworking, small, a nineteenth-century invention; the Welsh lady in national costume of black hat and red cloak; the pious lady – a chapel regular; the sexy Welshwoman (Ruth Madoc as Gladys Pugh in

Hi-de-Hi); funny Welshwomen (Gladys Morgan and Maudie Edwards). But the Welsh lady is a postcard image not a real person, the pious lady is an extension of the Mam. The funny and sexy Welsh women are minority figures. They all pale into insignificance beside the indomitable, all embracing Mam, the bulwark of the Welsh industrial working-class home, who is neither funny nor sexy, but is devout, hardworking, loyal, indomitable – Beth Morgan in fiction, Rachel Thomas on the screen.

The Welsh image, then, is industrial, communal, masculine but family based. Cinematically, it has been consensual rather than conflictual. This would have been inevitable, given the strict censorship of the cinema's heyday. However, when that censorship relaxed and the cinema became much more oppositional, conflict between the Welsh and the English figured in *Rebecca's Daughters* (1991). Karl Francis, an eminent Welsh film-maker revamped an unproduced Dylan Thomas screenplay and turned it into a broad and farcical 'Carry On up the Valleys' romp, missing a golden opportunity to film a key episode in the history and mythology of Wales.

Ireland

In cinematic terms, the image of Ireland has been largely in the hands of the British and American film industries. For Ireland experienced on an even greater scale the problems Britain faced in seeking to establish a native film industry: chronic under-investment, technical backwardness and the overwhelming dominance worldwide of Hollywood.[18] Nevertheless, in America, Britain and Ireland alike the same images of Ireland and Irishness have been purveyed. They are based on a cultural construction of Irishness in which the Irish themselves have happily collaborated. The figure of 'Paddy', the Irish stereotype, goes back at least to the sixteenth century.

L .P. Curtis Jr has argued that 'Paddy' was defined in the nineteenth century specifically as the mirror-image of John Bull. So the ideal Englishman was defined as a sober, law-abiding, mature, straightforward, phlegmatic, clean, rational gentleman, individualistic and private. By contrast, the Irishman was depicted as a drunken, lawless, unstable, emotional, dirty, devious, childlike, superstitious, lazy, vengeful and irrational peasant, clannish and tribal. In particular the Irish were violent: so a 'paddy' became a colloquial term for a rage; 'hooliganism' a description of mindless violence after a legendary family of brawling London Irish; and a 'donnybrook' became a generic term for a free-for-all fight after the notoriously combative encounters at the eponymous fair.[19]

Prejudice against the Irish spread right across society. It was a prejudice that was partly racial, reinforced by the new 'science' of racialism which graded human beings according to a scale of race and civilization; partly religious (Protestant prejudice against Catholics); partly class (urban industrial progress against peasant backwardness); partly imperial (as a subject people, the Irish were automatically inferior and in need of good government).

All of this is true up to a point, particularly in the nineteenth century. But Curtis's view has been modified and nuanced by Sheridan Gilley, who argues that 'Paddy' was the creation of both Englishmen and Irishmen and popular with both, particularly in the eighteenth century when the Irish were better liked in England than the Scots. 'Paddy' before the nineteenth century was a feckless, reckless, devil-may-care, hard-drinking, hard-fighting peasant, generous, hospitable and immensely brave, and as such celebrated in popular ballads in both England and Ireland. Gilley admits that a more hostile view emerged in the eighteenth century as a consequence of the increasing resort to violence to achieve independence. But he concludes that rather than the one-dimensional view adumbrated by Curtis:

> It would be truer to say that Englishmen had drawn from their long experience of the Irish a national stereotype which had both its good points and its bad: as good and bad points were defined by the Irish themselves. So the English invoked the good points or the bad according to their temperament, moment or mood. Thus an Irish riot or rebellion typified Celtic lawlessness, though Irish military valour always came in for English praise; the remittances which poured into Ireland from overseas were in English eyes the hallmark of Celtic family loyalty, as the railways were monuments to Irish industry, although a single drunken Irishman proved all Irishmen drunkards, as the idleness of unemployed Irishmen in a slum established Irish indolence. The one observer might consider both industry and indolence equally Irish and happily hold either opinion on different occasions without resolving the contradiction, for it is the very nature of an idea of 'national character' that as often as it aspires to consistency it leaves contradictions of this kind unresolved.[20]

Gilley argues that the principal opposition to the Irish was due to a view of their nationalism as narrow and parochial against the supranationalism of the British Empire. It is this comment which gives us the imperial context; the idea of Ireland judged in relation to its attitude to the Empire. The imperial dimension is a vital element in the construction and evaluation of the Irish character.

The English occupation of Ireland was the context from which the cultural images of Irishness sprang. The stage Irishman was developed in the sixteenth and seventeenth centuries. In English plays set in England the Irishman appeared usually as a servant or a soldier, accurately reflecting the reality of the Irish presence in England. These two characters evolved during the eighteenth century, often in the hands of Irish playwrights, into familiar but attractive archetypes: the whimsical but faithful and resourceful servant frequently and generically called 'Teague' and the penniless, high-living, amorous, roistering soldier of fortune. Both were held in affection, for as J. O. Bartley writes of the 18th century: 'There is no doubt that the Irish had come to be generally quite well liked in England. In 1760 they had long ceased to be a threat and were no longer even a nuisance.'[21]

These character archetypes survived into the nineteenth century when the era of mass-produced culture took them deeper into the popular consciousness. The nineteenth-century novels of Charles Lever and Samuel Lover embodied both the soldier and the servant. The principal difference from the eighteenth century is that these characters were now observed in an Irish setting. The same was true of the stage. There was greater individualization of the archetypes within a given range of Irish characteristics, which now included eloquence, pugnacity, superstition, blarney, resourcefulness and a fondness for women and whiskey, song and dance. In this vein, plays combined romantic Irish landscape, sentimental plots and humanized character types.

The new literary and dramatic interest in Ireland was a product of the Romantic movement. Ireland, like Scotland, had become a prime location and preoccupation for the creative imagination of artists, poets and balladeers, who saw in the Emerald Isle the elemental wildness and primitive picturesqueness that so appealed to the Romantics and which in Ireland took the form of caves and cliffs, ruined castles, rugged landscape, ghosts, moonlight and fair colleens. This image was reproduced on stage in the work of scene-painters who provided an evocative background to Irish melodramas, directly reflecting the interest embodied in the rash of books of engravings of Irish scenes in the 1830s and 1840s. A celebration of the romantic Irish landscape was to become one of the enduring features of Irish films.

The Romantic spirit also permeated the work of the Irish Catholic poet Thomas Moore, whose ten volumes of *Irish Melodies* made a major contribution to the construction of a romantic Irish identity. The songs, in which Moore provided words for traditional airs, were enduringly popular, and were continuously and enthusiastically sung in Britain, Ireland and America. The songs which stress loss, tears, sorrows, battle and death became an integral part of the nationalist sensibility and run through the plays and the films of Ireland, binding them together. A snatch of one of them is sufficient to evoke a picturesque and troubled past, whose legacy is still being lived through.

The tradition of the lyrical Irish ballad survived well into the twentieth century, notably in the career of John McCormack. One early Hollywood sound film, *Song o' My Heart* (1930), partly filmed on location in Ireland, was virtually a filmed McCormack concert, with him singing eleven ballads. He also sang in the first British Technicolor feature *Wings of the Morning* (1937), perpetuating the image of a romantic and Arcadian Ireland.

A standard Irish play emerged in the nineteenth century, popular in England, Ireland and America, which usually involved a romantic triangle with a villain seeking to discredit the hero and take over his land and his sweetheart, and a comic subplot usually involving the violent humiliation of some minor English functionary. But Richard Allen Cave has argued persuasively that the standard Irish play format was consistently and successfully subverted in the nineteenth century to create sympathy for, rather than mockery of, the Irish stereotype, against a new favourable background created by the Catholic Emancipation Act (1829), the extending of parliamentary representation in the Irish Reform Bill (1832) and a more liberal attitude to Ireland.[22] So plays written by and for Tyrone Power and later Dion Boucicault created much more rounded and sympathetic characterization, in which the leading character assumes the guise of the stage Irishman (with his blarney, his blather and his booze) to fool opponents and the English confronted with their preconceived notions of the Irish are thus sent up.

The most celebrated exponent of the strategy was Dion Boucicault, whose Irish plays *The Colleen Bawn* (1860), *The Shaughraun* (1875) and *Arrah-na-Pogue* (1865) were continuously popular and played with success in England, Ireland and the United States from their first appearances. They had romantic settings, exciting incident and engaging heroes (Myles-na-Coppaleen, Shaun the Post, Conn the Shaughraun) who were daring, loyal, quickwitted and able to use the stage Irish persona to fool the English. His Irish melodramas appealed to the universal sentiments of the age, linked Irish and English by common adherence to gentlemanliness and dramatized the Irish problem in such a way as to awaken sympathy for the Irish without alienating the English audience.

Yet this same writer penned the classic imperial melodrama, *Jessie Brown* (1858), dramatizing the siege of Lucknow, drawing on the widespread horror in Britain and America at the massacres of English people, particularly women and children, and ending with a patriotic tableau of the relief of Lucknow by

General Havelock. There is little evidence of sympathy here with the sepoys. There is no equating of the Irish and Indian struggles for independence but an endorsing of the role of the Irish soldier in defence of the British Empire. This highlights an ambivalence inevitably created by the existence of Empire; a desire for emancipation from it at home but a willingness to participate in it abroad. What is common to both is a love of fighting, which brings us back to the stereotype of 'Paddy'.

Throughout all the cultural manifestations, three continuing images have attached themselves to Ireland – violence, humour and communality. An Irish association with violence is as old as England's association with the island. As early as the twelth century the chronicler Giraldus Cambrensis described Ireland as 'barren of good things, replenished with actions of blood, murder and loathsome outrage.'[23] Fighting mercenaries have long been a prime Irish export. It was Shaw who said – not without some justice – that the best comedies in the English language had been written by Irishmen (Congreve, Farquhar, Goldsmith, Sheridan, Wilde and himself). They are all marked by a love of language, quick wits and high spirits, which in a negative sense, as loquacity, blarney and fecklessness, have also been attached to Irishness. The communality, product of a peasant society, is the mirror-image of the bourgeois individualism and imperial supranationalism of England. The informer, the perennial Irish hate figure, is the quintessential individualist in the Irish context.

In this context, there can be no disputing the fact that the defining Irish film is *The Quiet Man* (1952), which in the cinema and on television and latterly on video, is far and away the most popular representation of Ireland and Irishness in America, Britain and Ireland itself. It was the ultimate evocation of the idealized Ireland cherished by Irish-American director John Ford and it marked the first time he actually went to Ireland to shoot a film, his previous 'Irish' films all having been shot in Hollywood (*Hangman's House, The Informer, The Plough and the Stars*). Significantly, Ford commissioned Richard Llewellyn, author of *How Green Was My Valley*, to turn Maurice Walsh's short story into a novella, which was then turned into a screenplay by regular Ford scenarist Frank Nugent.

The film is an expression of Ford's deep love for the land of his fathers and this love informs every frame from the opening credits, which unfold to the strains of a lilting Irish air, against the scene of a mellow sun setting over a grey stone castle and gilding the waters of the lake before it. The cool and fresh Technicolor photography which won an Academy Award for Winton Hoch

23   Pastoral Ireland: *The Quiet Man* (1952) with Maureen O'Hara and John Wayne.

perfectly captures the greens and browns and greys and whites that are the basic colour motifs and the symbols of an unchanging rural Ireland: the white-painted cottages, the little country station, the sandy beach lapped by a grey sea, the rolling hills and verdant meadows studded with reminders of the past like the venerable Celtic cross. Over all pours a cascade of Irish folk melody.

The eponymous hero Sean Thornton (John Wayne) is an American who seeks to make the transition from the free and easy democratic society of the United States to the strongly ritualized and traditionalist society of his fore-bears. His reluctance and incomprehension when faced with the customs of the country are ended by a ritual acceptance: fighting for one of them. It is clear from the first that Sean, like Ford, has idealized Ireland and that for him it is a magic world. When he first sees the old family cottage, White O'Morn, we hear the voice of his mother on the soundtrack telling him how it used to be there ('When I was young, Innisfree was another name for heaven'). He seeks to re-create this imagined world, purchasing and renovating the old family home to the point where Reverend Playfair remarks: 'It looks like all Irish cottages should – and so rarely do.' Finally, he marries a storybook colleen, first glimpsed barefoot and wildly beautiful, tending sheep in the woods. 'Hey, is that real?', he asks, entranced by yet another faery vision.

But Sean finds the traditions of this country restricting and infuriating. He has to ask her brother's permission to court the lovely Mary Kate Danaher (Maureen O'Hara) and this is at first refused. He has to conduct a ritual courtship under the eyes of the village matchmaker but breaks away from it to court her in his own way. But the matter of Mary Kate's dowry (family furniture and cash money) provokes a conflict which almost destroys the marriage. Her brother Red Will (Victor McLaglen) refuses to pay it and although Sean wants to carry on without it, Mary Kate cannot. She is totally immersed in the tradition: 'There is 300 years of happy dreaming in those things. I want my dream.' She refuses to consummate the marriage and becomes estranged from the angry and uncomprehending Sean. When eventually he looks like losing her, he faces the question head-on and fights Red Will for the dowry. The money is paid over and ritually burned: for it was never the money that was at stake. It was the tradition. Sean, Mary and Red Will are reconciled and the marriage can commence properly.

The society that Sean enters is agrarian and traditionalist. It is also strongly communal. There are no real leaders. In so far as guidance is needed, it is provided by the Catholic priest Father Lonergan (Ward Bond). It is also a decidedly male-dominated world. The women invariably stand apart in shawled groups: one of them hands Sean a stick 'to beat the lovely lady with' when Mary Kate tries to leave him. Mary Kate herself is defined by her role as homemaker and when the big fight starts, sets off home to prepare the supper – a fight is no place for the womenfolk.

Drinking and fighting become ritual elements affirming rather than destroying community spirit. Drinking is used to seal bargains, to cement friendships, to welcome visitors and friends. When Sean first arrives in Innisfree, he goes into the pub and says 'Good day'; no-one answers. He offers to buy drinks: no-one answers. He announces that he is Sean Thornton come home again; and the regulars surround him, drinks all round are poured and they launch into 'The Wild Colonial Boy'. The community is welcoming one of its own.

Sean's position in this male-dominated society is, however, threatened by his initial refusal to fight. His reason is that he killed a man in America in a prize-fight but he does not explain his reluctance and it is interpreted as cowardice. Ford is quite clear on this matter. There can be no absolute pacifism. There are occasions when a man must fight – here it is to preserve his home and family. Unyielding pacifism is the same as cowardice. So Sean fights. But he does not fight vindictively. He fights in defence of a tradition and in accordance with the Marquis of Queensberry rules. Ford handles the fight as a comic marathon donnybrook, in which the protagonists gleefully knock seven bells out of each other to the strains of an Irish jig, and as a community ritual, participated in by the village and presided over by the priest.

The community nature of the occasion is emphasized by the sly dig at the English which Ford cannot resist. A stuffy old English gentleman is sitting in the pub, reading a newspaper. He is the only person in the entire village who takes no notice whatever of the fight, remaining where he is while the others surge into the street to watch the fun. For the Englishman in Ford's view is naturally anti-social and unfeeling by contrast with the gregarious and outgoing Irish. The fight is the film's triumphant high point, a rousing and irresistible justification of community, tradition and strict gender role differentiation. It signals Sean's final integration into the community. *The Quiet Man* is thus the apotheosis of the definition of Irishness by violence, humour and communality. Its mythic significance is underlined by the recent opening of a *Quiet Man* heritage centre at the village of Cong, County Mayo, where the film was shot.

In the British imperial context it is in particular struggle and violence that have characterized Ireland in cinema. The crimson thread running through the long and tangled story of Anglo-Irish relations is the Irish fight for independence, which has been imbued with a romantic aura as the classic struggle of a simple, united, rural people against imperial military might. Even in melodrama, plays were often set at the time of rebellion: *Arragh-na-Pogue* in 1798, *The Shaughraun* in the context of the Fenian troubles in the 1860s; other Victorian melodramas featured pre-Fenian groups, the Peep O'Day boys, the White Boys, the Ribbonmen. The recurrent tropes are the use of violence, the role of the hated informer and communal solidarity. These myths, as Kevin Rockett has pointed out, mean that the cinema has consistently ignored interclass rivalries and internal Irish conflict in favour of the communal solidarity necessary for sustaining the hallowed myth of united struggle.[24]

But the desire to dramatize the Irish struggle for freedom brought filmmakers into conflict with the censors. The cinema in both Britain and America operated under the tight control of the censors, whose aim was to maintain moral rectitude and eliminate political controversy.[25] While Ireland remained in the Empire, there was anxiety to avoid films stirring up ill-feeling. Irish-Canadian Sidney Olcott, who had directed Hollywood film versions of the Boucicault plays, *The Colleen Bawn*, *Arragh-na-Pogue* and *The Shaughraun*, in 1910–12, returned to Ireland in 1914 to film *Bold Emmet, Ireland's Martyr*, which was banned in 1915 by the authorities on the grounds that it interfered with the British wartime recruiting drive in Ireland.

Even after independence, the British censors were for some years chary of allowing films about the Irish Rebellion. The film *Irish Destiny* (1926), released to coincide with the tenth anniversary of the Easter Rising, told a love story set against the struggle between the IRA and the Black and Tans, reconstructing the events of 1920-21 with many of the actual participants re-creating their roles. It was banned in Britain by the British Board of Film Censors (BBFC). But time healed the old wounds and when in 1936 Irish cinema produced *The Dawn*, it was passed by the BBFC for showing in Britain. Directed and co-written by Thomas Cooper, who also played IRA Commandant O'Donovan, *The Dawn* is a truly dreadful propaganda feature, technically crude, badly acted and appallingly heavy-handed. It is a celebration of the IRA ('the boys'), highlighting the brutality of the Black and Tans and featuring the taint of informing, described as the one sin an Irishman can never forgive.

Although after several years of rebellion, Ireland had been partitioned in 1921 with Ulster remaining part of the United Kingdom and the South becoming a self-governing dominion, the Irish Free State, there had been civil war in the Free State in 1923–24 and outbreaks of IRA activity in England during the 1930s. Under these circumstances, J. C. Robertson, historian of the BBFC, observes that 'potentially the greatest source of friction between the BBFC and American and British studios from 1919 to 1939 was Ireland'.[26] Several proposed films dealing with the 'Troubles' were rejected by the British censors, including a proposal from Universal Studios for a biopic of Sir Roger Casement, executed by the British for treason in 1916.

The general attitude of the Board seems to have been a grudging willingness to accept the Irish 'Troubles' as a background as long as a personal story, usu-ally a love story, was foregrounded. This remained the approach most favoured by Hollywood. An excellent example of this approach is H. C. Potter's *Beloved Enemy* (1936), a highly romanticized and fictionalized version of the career of Michael Collins. Brian Aherne played the dashing Irish rebel leader Dennis Riordan who meets and falls in love with Lady Helen Drummond (Merle Oberon), daughter of the British peace negotiator. Their secret love affair runs parallel with the end of the rebellion and when, in 1921, Riordan is instru-mental in securing a treaty which partitions Ireland and sets up the Free State, he is accused by hardline colleagues of selling out the republican cause. Cam-paigning for peace in Dublin, he is shot by his closest friend, and dies in the arms of Lady Helen. Concern at audience dissatisfaction led the studio to shoot an alternative happy ending, in which Dennis is wounded but survives. Although the original release print featured the unhappy ending, it is the happy ending which has been used in TV prints of the film. Basically, it is the age-old 'Romeo and Juliet' theme, set against a recent political problem and arguing for peace and reconciliation.

The formula of love story against tangled political background remained a popular approach as late as David Lean's *Ryan's Daughter* (1970), a kind of *Brief Encounter* with sex set against the background of 'The Troubles'. Ryan's daughter (Sarah Miles) is the unsatisfied wife of a local Irish schoolmaster (Robert Mitchum). She has a passionate affair with a shell-shocked British officer (Christopher Jones), which ends when he is killed. The film shows communal support for the IRA in a spectacular scene in which a whole village turns out to help bring smuggled arms ashore, but it depicts the darker side of communality in the revenge of the villagers against Rosie Ryan who is stripped and cropped by them for her sins before leaving the village with her forgiving husband.

The cinema recurrently presented two visions of Ireland: the Ireland of the 'Troubles', of oppression, darkness, suffering, tyranny and death, the Ireland of the struggle against the English, 'the sacred just cause'; and the Ireland of exiles' memories and poets' dreams, a peaceful, happy, pastoral, communal, tradition-steeped, sun-lit Erin. In the films of the Irish-American John Ford, who returned persistently to the subject of Ireland, the two images uneasily co-exist, epitomized in *The Informer* and *The Quiet Man*.

The Informer (1935) is at once a tale of the 'Troubles', an Expressionist drama of fog and shadow whose basic story is timeless and universal, and a Catholic parable of redemption and forgiveness. The story, based on a novel by Liam O'Flaherty, was substantially altered in a way that clearly demonstrates Ford's priorities in depicting the Irish Rebellion and constructing a particular image of Ireland. As George Bluestone comments: 'What do these deletions, additions and alterations amount to? In general, they endow the characters with a nobility, honesty and reasonableness which the originals do not possess.'[27] IRA Commandant Dan Gallagher, who in the book is a pitiless, sadistic despot, feared and mistrusted by his own organization, becomes in the film a handsome, upright, fair-minded, pipe-smoking and respected leader, who seeks justice and not vengeance. The Katie Madden of the book is a drug addict and degenerate revelling in her degradation and wilfully betraying the informer Gypo to his pursuers; in the film she is a prostitute sympathetically treated in the tradition of Ford's fallen women, driven to the streets by poverty,

Violent Ireland: *The Informer* (1935) with Victor McLaglen and J. M. Kerrigan.   **24**

genuinely loving Gypo and betraying him unwittingly. The Frankie McPhillip of the film, a likeable, clean-cut, fugitive patriot, who returns to Dublin to see his mother, is in distinct contrast to the brutalized murderer of the book who returns seeking money to finance his escape.

Even more interesting than the character changes are the two major structural changes, which are quintessential Ford. He moved the period of the film back in time from the 1922 Civil War to 1920 and the last years of the British occupation. The Communist organization of the novel became the IRA and Ford was at pains to stress the regular military nature of this secret army. Men are addressed by their ranks, a full dress court martial is held for Gypo, the IRA headquarters with its row of rifles has the appearance of a genuine field post, military discipline is enforced. Ford could have it no other way. Undisciplined revolt or sheer anarchy were no part of his worldview. If he was a rebel, as he claimed, Ford was a conservative one. For him the Irish Rebellion was a war of independence and he depicted it accordingly.

The killers of Frankie in Ford's version are the hated 'Black and Tans'. For it is easier for Ford to tell a story in which the Irish fight the British rather than one in which the Irish fight the Irish. Although the story of Gypo Nolan, who betrays his friend to the British and is then tracked down and executed by the IRA, holds the foreground, the alien British presence remains threateningly in the background. One little scene early on contrives eloquently to convey the tragedy of occupied Ireland. On a street corner, a shabbily dressed tenor sings 'The Rose of Tralee', watched by a crowd of his countrymen. A British patrol passes, stops to frisk the singer and as they march off a soldier flips a coin into his hand. Continuing his song, the singer twirls round and contemptuously flings the coin away. The melancholy lyricism of the song and the simple reflex act of defiance set against the search, the presence of the armed men and the poorly clad crowd of onlookers combine to symbolize the poetic soul of Ireland, oppressed but not crushed by foreign occupation. Thereafter the shadowy presence of British patrols remains a permanent, but never intrusive, reminder of this occupation, emerging into the foreground only once, when on information received they break into the McPhillip house and shoot the escaping Frankie. But even then a touch of humanity is permitted in the obvious distaste with which the British officer hands over the blood money to the treacherous Gypo.

The opening statement of the film makes it clear that the story also has a definite religious dimension: 'Then Judas repented himself and cast down the thirty pieces of silver and departed.' The story that follows charts the torment and confusion and eventual repentance of 'Judas' Gypo. The other characters take on analogous New Testament roles: Katie as Mary Magdalene, Frankie as Christ and Mrs McPhillip as the Mother of Christ.

While the film's themes are quintessential Ford, the style is broodingly Expressionist, giving it the dimensions of a universal predicament. Low-angle shots, low-key lighting, many close-ups and the ubiquity of shadows and fog give the story a moody fatalism and Teutonic intensity. But the menacing presence of the British troops throughout, the lyrical, melancholy thread of Irish melodies and the heroization of the IRA never let the audience forget the Irish dimension.

It is interesting to compare Ford's film with the unjustly neglected silent British version of O'Flaherty's novel, directed in 1929 by the German filmmaker Arthur Robison. Ironically, Ford's version is far more Expressionist than that of Robison, himself the arch-Expressionist creator of *Shadows*. But, like Ford's film, it is a work of pure cinema, making little use of dialogue titles. Robison employs a vividly fluid camera style and crisp, authoritative editing, but there is no fog and little shadow.

Robison duly sets his film during the 1922 Civil War and although he includes many of the same episodes as Ford (the betrayal and shooting of Frankie, the visit to the wake, the betrayal of Katie and Gypo's death in the church while seeking forgiveness), the motivations of the characters are different and the whole ambiance of the film is at variance with Ford's. It is not a film about the 'Troubles'. It is not a Catholic parable. It is not even an exploration of the informer's psyche. It is a characteristically Germanic drama of Fate, sexual passion and revenge. Concerned as he is with human emotions, Robison has no need to justify the legality of IRA activities and the 'execution' of Gypo. So he conspicuously omits the trial, which is the high point of Ford's film and legitimizes the IRA's activities. Robison's protagonists are simply members of a faction in the Irish Civil War, carrying out vengeance on one of their number who has turned traitor.

Lars Hanson's Gypo is a very different figure from Victor McLaglen's pathetic, half-comprehending, brute-man. Hanson's Gypo is a flashing-eyed Byronic figure, a Romantic anti-hero dogged by Fate and doomed to an unhappy end. In the memorable finale, he emerges from Katie's room and descends the stairs to face his pursuers, pointing dramatically at his heart. They fall back in awe until Gallagher arrives to shoot him. This is in marked contrast to Ford's Gallagher who not only does not kill Gypo himself but comforts Katie as the sound of shooting is heard.

Throughout the film the motivations of the characters are different from those of Ford. Gypo and Frankie are rivals for Katie's affections in Robison's version. Gypo betrays Frankie when he believes Kate intends to go away with him. Kate betrays Gypo when she in turn believes that he plans to leave her for another prostitute. Robison uses an almost identical church and forgiveness finale as Ford but with none of the religious build-up and Christian analogy leading up to it.

The style and emphasis of Robison's film only serve to point up the distinctively Fordian characteristics of the American *Informer*, and the different national and cultural contexts from which the two films spring. Ford followed up the Oscar-winning *Informer* with a film version of *The Plough and the Stars* which was a resounding failure. *The Plough and the Stars* certainly employed many of the same technical crew and actors as the earlier film. The censors demanded a toning down of the language and the box office demanded the softening of criticism of the British role in the Easter Rising. But the film's real failure lies in the way Ford has subverted the play for his own nationalist purposes. Sean O'Casey's play has humanity, warmth and humour, backed by a raw tenement realism, the feel of life in the backstreets as the rebellion rages.

But Ford and his scenarist Dudley Nichols, in cutting the text and opening out the action, disastrously shift the play's emphasis. The 1916 Easter Rising, which is the background to O'Casey's play, is in the foreground of Ford's film and this cannot but express his personal preoccupation with the 'Troubles'. He could not resist the opportunity to dramatize the central myth of the Irish struggle, and so grafted it on to a play which could not accommodate it within its own terms of reference. The Easter Rising is depicted unequivocally in terms of heroism, sacrifice and the homeland. Events which are simply reported in the play are shown in the film: the proclamation of the republic by Padraic Pearse, the siege of the General Post Office, the execution of James Connolly.

Yet, as in *The Informer*, Ford shows himself to be a conservative rebel, concerned to legitimize the rising as a war of liberation. In a stirring and characteristic sequence, Ford depicts the gathering of the rebel army. It is done with all the pageantry usually associated in Ford's world with the US cavalry. Soldiers march in, bearing flags; boy pipers play 'The Wearing of the Green'; the troops, drawn up in ranks, give the republican salute. Even the women and children who watch are arranged in ranks, conveying the impression of the entire population under arms, fighting for freedom. They listen to a rousing speech from 'General' Connolly. Connolly, in fact a union leader, is depicted throughout in exclusively military terms. Never seen without his uniform, always addressed as 'general', he is played as a soldierly archetype and photographed from the apotheosizing low-angle which Ford always reserved for his great men and leaders. Catholic imagery and symbols are deployed to sanctify the struggle: the priest with his cross in the Post Office, the Madonna-like shawled women in their posed attitudes of mourning and, most vividly, the death of a boy sniper, shot from the roof by British troops and sliding down from it, arms outstretched like a suffering Christ.

The box office dictated that in some way the British must be exculpated. But Ford could not forgive. So he undercuts each conciliatory gesture towards the British. Connolly is courteously treated by the British as he is led out to be shot, forgives his enemies as they fire but is taken to his death in a wheelchair, an image which transcends all the mutual soldierly courtesies. When the Socialist Covey denounces the British troops searching the tenement, a British corporal replies: 'I'm a socialist myself. But I have to do my duty. A man's a man and he must fight for his country.' But this is offset by Fluther's passionate defence of sniping as the only recourse of a handful of unarmed patriots against the armed might of an Empire.

The uncompromising tragic ending of the play, with both Jack Clitheroe and Mrs Burgess killed, is transformed by Ford into an optimistic finale. Jack and Mrs Burgess survive. The film instead ends with the funeral of the young girl Mollser, which comes to symbolize the dead hopes of the rising. But as Jack and Nora follow the coffin, they see the Tricolour being torn down from the roof of the Post Office and flung into the streets. Nora asks: 'When will it all end?', and Jack returns: 'This is only the beginning. We'll live to see Ireland free.' It is a defiant and noble ending, totally at odds with the tenor of the play but in keeping with Ford's heroic view of the Irish struggle for independence.

The other side of the image, the positive side, is the Old Ireland first evoked in *The Shamrock Handicap* (1926). Its plot is a familiar one: impoverished Irish nobleman and daughter travel to America, enter their horse in the eponymous race, win a fortune and return to Ireland. The opening section is a loving, sentimentalized evocation of Old Ireland, a land drenched in tradition and *noblesse oblige*. It is an idealized land of penurious but goodhearted aristocratic landlords, innocent young lovers, faithful retainers and loyal tenants. Community feeling is encapsulated in the bustling details of marketday in the little country town. The picture is one of a peaceful, traditional, agrarian society, slightly run down and sometimes in debt (a condition common to lord and tenants) but happy in shared traditional values, the beauties of the landscape and the feeling of belonging. There is no sign of any alien English presence to mar the Arcadian idyll.

It was this image to which Ford returned in *The Quiet Man* (1952), the ultimate celebration of an Arcadian Ireland. The dissatisfaction some Irish intellectuals feel with the mythified Ireland of *The Quiet Man* found powerful expression in Jim Sheridan's *The Field* (1990), based on John B. Keane's play. It is almost the dark mirror-image of *The Quiet Man*. The visiting American (Tom Berenger), known as 'The Yank', is not integrated into the community. He remains an outsider, seeking to acquire the land long rented by 'Bull' McCabe (Richard Harris), who puts him in the same category as previous exploitative outsiders – the English – whom 'Bull' helped to drive out. In the big fight, played by Ford for laughs, Bull kills 'the Yank'. Bull is the equivalent of Red Will Danaher, here obsessed to the point of madness with the land – and despising the rootless tinkers who lost their land, the invading English who sought to take over the land and 'the Yank' who wishes to acquire Bull's field. The priest, who in Ford's community is a leader and a full participant in community rituals, is here an outsider – 'just passing through' says the Bull. He sides with the Yank and locks the congregation out of the church after the murder. The widow, who in Ford married Red Will, is here hounded out of the village by a campaign of persecution by Bull's son Tadgh. Tadgh is eventually killed too – and Bull now has no family to whom to hand over the land for which he has fought and killed. This is a grim, tragic, relentless story, without humour, of a land cursed by its past (famine, emigration, English occupation, poverty).

Ford's final Irish film, also made in Ireland, was *The Rising of the Moon* (1957). It was narrated by Tyrone Power, film-star great-grandson of the eponymous actor who helped to transform the Irish stereotype. It was a minor and unsuccessful work, which in addition to Lady Gregory's short play, also included adaptations of Frank O'Connor's story *The Majesty of the Law* and Michael McHugh's *A Minute's Wait*. Like *The Quiet Man* these stories stress the importance of tradition, ritual, communality, drink and reverence for the church. It is interesting and significant then that in March 1957 Limerick County Council unanimously approved the suggestion of one of its members Mr D. P. Quish that the Irish government should 'contact all countries with which Ireland has diplomatic relations and have *The Rising of the Moon* withdrawn from exhibition'. The reason for this motion was that 'the film is a vile production and a travesty of the Irish people'.[28]

By one of those ironies with which the history of Hollywood is replete, Ford, while making his celebrations of Irish freedom-fighting for RKO Radio Pictures, was contractually obliged by 20th Century-Fox to make a trilogy of films celebrating the British Empire in India: *Black Watch* (1929), *Wee Willie Winkie* (1937) and *Four Men and a Prayer* (1938). Ford's involvement with the Empire goes back to the earliest days of his film career. He assisted his elder brother Francis Ford, director and star of two now-lost films with intriguing imperial settings. In 1915 Francis Ford directed *The Doorway of Destiny*, in which he played Colonel Patrick Feeney, with John Ford as his brother Edward. It told the story of an Irish regiment sent on a suicide mission by the British in India and assaulting a sepoy citadel waving an Irish flag, made by Feeney's mother. In the same year, *The Campbells Are Coming* appropriated the plot of Boucicault's *Jessie Brown*, with Francis Ford playing Nana Sahib and the heroic Scots regiments relieving Lucknow.

The British cinema's equivalent of Ford as a director returning regularly to Irish themes is Brian Desmond Hurst. Hurst was a Belfast-born Protestant who worked with Ford in Hollywood in the silent days before returning to Britain to launch his own directorial career in 1932. Despite working in a wide variety of genres which include adaptations of Dickens (*Scrooge*) and Ivor Novello (*Glamorous Night*), he managed a number of Irish subjects, including adaptations of Synge (*Riders to the Sea*, 1935; and *Playboy of the Western World*, 1962), and *Irish Hearts* (1934), a drama about a small-town Irish doctor fighting a typhus epidemic.

In 1936 he was asked by the head of production at British International to take over at short notice *Ourselves Alone*, a production which had run into difficulties under director Walter Summers. Hurst brought in Irish playwright Denis Johnston to rework the script, and took over and completed the film. It emerges as a Fordian drama of the 'Troubles', garnished with Irish songs performed by popular balladeer Cavan O'Connor. It conforms to the preferred BBFC model of foregrounding a love affair: RIC inspector John Hannay (John Lodge) and army intelligence officer Captain Guy Wiltshire (John Loder) are both in love with Maureen Elliott of Castle Elliott. In the end Hannay resigns her to Guy, taking on responsibility for shooting her brother (actually shot by Guy) and earning the admiration of his sergeant who says he's done a wonderful thing: 'You've seen a miracle in Ireland – two people out of three who are going to be happy.'

The film seeks to strike a balance between the sides. On the British side, the gentle, pipe-smoking gentleman Wiltshire who is reluctant to be in Ireland is contrasted with Inspector Hannay, keen to pursue the IRA ruthlessly and played in such a bad-tempered and brusque manner by John Lodge as to evoke no audience sympathy. On the IRA side, hardline Commandant Connolly (Clifford Evans), who favours total war against the English is contrasted with Maureen's brother, Terence Elliott, who is legendary IRA commander 'Mick O'Day', preferring to tie up rather than shoot captured British soldiers and wishing to spare civilians from the consequences of IRA violence. The title itself becomes an ironic commentary on the Irish situation as Wiltshire tells another officer: 'Sinn Fein – "Ourselves Alone". It ought to be our motto – we're the ones who are alone.' But sympathy tilts towards the Irish, emphasized by the successful hunt for the obligatory informer, and the characterization of dedicated patriot Mick O'Day, charming and likeable, fighting for love of Ireland and freedom and seeking to avoid unnecessary bloodshed but killed by the English.

After the war, Hurst directed an adaptation of Daphne du Maurier's nineteenth-century Irish family saga, *Hungry Hill* (1946). Constructed within the conventions of the three-generations family saga and including romances, marriages, deaths and separations, it is almost an allegory of Ireland intertwining the fortunes of the wealthy Protestant Ascendancy family the Brodricks and the dispossessed Catholic Irish peasant family the Donovans. The tension between them and their mutual dependency run through the film.

The Brodricks of Clonmore Castle take over and exploit the copper deposits on Hungry Hill, claimed by the Donovans as their own. 'Copper John' Brodrick (Cecil Parker) denounces the Donovans for failing to exploit the resources and highlights the difference of outlook: Protestantism, work, wealth, progress, exploitation of natural resources against Catholicism, tradition, contentment, ecology. It leads to violent confrontation when Old Donovan stirs up the people against the mine and a gunpowder explosion at the mine kills both him and Copper John's younger son. Eventually 'Wild John', Copper John's grandson (Dermot Walsh), wants to close down the mine when it begins to fail. But the locals, who now depend on it for a livelihood, want to keep it open and a Donovan leads the opposition to closure. In the ensuing violence, Wild John is killed. But the faithful family retainer 'Old Tim' persuades his mother Fanny in the interests of reconciliation not to demand Sam Donovan's hanging. She expresses hope for peaceful reconciliation and co-existence of the Donovans and Brodricks in future, and by extension of Catholics and Protestants in Ireland.

There is one particularly memorable scene at a wedding at which the English are waltzing sedately with the locals looking on from the door. A fiddler arrives, strikes up a jig and suddenly everyone lets rip, spilling out onto the lawn and dancing wildly until they drop – conventions, differences forgotten, English and Irish, Catholic and Protestant carried away by the native music of Ireland. It is an exhilarating moment.

The centrality of violence to the identity of Ireland is emphasized by its presence even in comic films. The entire action of *The Quiet Man* is based on the idea that 'a real man' fights and it ends in a marathon donnybrook. Old Mother Riley in fifteen popular English slapstick comedies (1936-52) celebrated the combative Irish washerwoman as comic anti-heroine. The persona was developed from a classic stage sketch 'Bridget's Night Out' in which a violent row between mother and daughter results in the smashing of all the crockery in the kitchen. Arthur Lucan who played Old Mother Riley, though English-born, took his name from a Dublin dairy, was popular in Ireland and formed a team with his Dublin-born wife Kitty McShane, who played his daughter in the act.

Mario Zampi's comedy *Happy Ever After* (1954) links communality and violence. It centres largely on the attempts (bungled and unsuccessful) of the villagers of Rathbarney to kill off the caddish new squire (David Niven) who has stopped poaching, called in debts, ejected tenants and disbanded the hunt. The Irish villagers are seen as cheerful, boozing, quarrelsome 'characters', sentimental (gathering in the pub to sing 'My Heart Is Irish') and with a propensity for violence. It is a comic exploitation of the clash of cultures: the incoming English landlord seeking maximum financial exploitation of resources and ignoring tradition, and the villagers seeking to retain their cheerful, feckless, age-old, easy-going ways. The community unite to dispose of the incomer.

Violence inevitably figures in historical films too. Both *Captain Lightfoot* (1955), set in the eighteenth century, and *The Fighting Prince of Donegal* (1966), set in the sixteenth, uncompromisingly endorse armed resistance against the occupying English force. But an historical setting has always been seen – quite erroneously – as a way of distancing a film from contemporary problems by implying that it is all in the past. Myths are fed by history, and history is often rewritten to conform with myths. In British films since independence, Ireland has come to be almost synonymous with the IRA which has figured as a locus of violence. The IRA has tried intermittently since 1921 and continuously since 1969 to seek to reunite the two parts of Ireland by violence and this has coloured almost all depictions of Ireland. The message, however, has been consistently the liberal-democratic one of rejection of violence with *Odd Man Out* (1947) and *The Gentle Gunman* (1952) tracing the destructive effects of violence, and *Shake Hands with the Devil* (1959) and *A Terrible Beauty* (1960) showing the IRA leaders as psychopaths and centring on individual IRA members redeemed by love and renouncing violence. Recent British films set in the 1920s have been strongly informed by post-colonial guilt and have stressed the violent consequences of the English presence in Ireland: thus, for instance, *Ascendancy, The Dawning* and *Fools of Fortune*. Launder and Gilliat's excellent *Captain Boycott* (1947) celebrated the constructive alternative to violence. It tells the story of Captain Boycott (Cecil Parker), highlighting the evils of landlordism in such a way as to endorse the non-violent alternative that succeeds in defeating and routing him. It pointedly contrasts the self-centred individualism of Boycott with the strong sense of communality embodied by the Irish: the hero Hugh Davin declaring: 'We're all part of a community. Either you're for it or against it.' The Land League of Parnell, which sought change in Ireland by peaceful means, is represented in the village by the publican and the priest, the potent alliance of pub and church, the twin centres of the community. The hero, farmer Hugh Davin (Stewart Granger), who is first seen training men for violence, is converted to peaceful methods by a powerful speech from Parnell (Robert Donat), urging ostracism of those who take over cottages of evicted tenants. The film seeks to be fair to everyone. The commander of the British troops indignantly tells Boycott: 'You cannot make British soldiers fight for what any fool can see is an unjust cause.' Even Boycott in the end helps Davin save threatened tenants. But the message is clear – non-violence is the way and communality the best way of life.

It is fighting which provides the link between Ireland and the Empire. For the Irish soldier was ubiquitous in the armies of Empire at every level from the celebrated generals (Wellington, Roberts and Wolseley to Montgomery, Alanbrooke and Alexander) to private soldiers. The Irish soldier has been a figure of popular myth from Shakespeare's MacMorris in *Henry V*, to Mulvaney, one of Kipling's 'soldiers three'. Niall MacGinnis played MacMorris in Olivier's *Henry V* (1945) and Cyril Cusack the Mulvaney figure in MGM's *Soldiers Three* (1951).

A third element invariably linked to the Arcadian vision in depictions of Ireland is the supernatural – ghosts, leprechauns and 'the second sight'. *The Luck of the Irish* (1947) has hard-bitten American journalist Tyrone Power humanized and taught decent values and responsibility by a lovable leprechaun (Cecil Kellaway). In *The Oracle* (1953), a visiting English journalist discovers an oracle at the bottom of a well in a romantic Irish village. The villagers, wise and sensible in the ways of rural folk, consult him only for local domestic matters (the weather, location of good fishing grounds) but the journalist (Michael Medwin) gets him to supply accurate horse-racing predictions (threatening the horse-racing industry with bankruptcy) and then matters of national significance which cause mounting unhappiness until the sensible colleen Shelagh persuades the oracle to migrate. *Darby O'Gill and the Little People* (1959), Disney's charming piece of Irish whimsy, deeply rooted in an Irish image of faery, whiskey and storytelling, has Darby pitting his wits against the King of the Little People, gaining his four wishes, saving his daughter's life and escaping the Banshee and the Death Coach. The chief occupations of the Little People are shown to be hunting, dancing and drinking. *High Spirits* (1988), a frantic farce which is the Irish equivalent of *The Ghost Goes West*, has American tourists confronted by a variety of ghosts in a crumbling Irish castle, presided over by Peter O'Toole as the impoverished lord.

There has been cultural continuity between the Ireland projected in the stage melodramas, popular ballads and novels, and the Ireland of the cinema. There have been two prevailing, complementary images: a peaceful, pastoral, rural, traditional and communal Ireland, an Arcadian image idealized because it is untainted by the English presence; and a darker, more violent and often urban Ireland, struggling against English occupation. Of Irishness, there have been several predominating characteristics, but often seen, as Gilley suggested, from different perspectives. Pre-eminent is violence, which can be viewed positively as freedom-fighting, negatively as terrorism, or comically as a manifestation of masculinity. Then there is humour, to be deployed against the Irish in the form of the booze and blarney 'thick paddy' stereotype or by the Irish against the English as a quick-witted, high-spirited subversion of stereotype. Finally, there is communality, usually seen positively, whether as supportive of traditional social structures or as resistance to the British, but sometimes negatively as hostility to outsiders. However they are interpreted, the characteristics remain constant. That is the power of popular culture.

There have been occasional attempts to challenge the dominant views. One was *The Field* with its dark mirror-image of *The Quiet Man*. Another is a thoughtful and provocative film made in Ireland called *This Other Eden* (1959), directed by Muriel Box, which centres on the mysterious blowing-up of the newly unveiled statue of an Irish nationalist leader in the village of Ballymorgan. The film contrives to debunk both the romantic Englishman in love with Ireland, insisting on speaking Irish (which no-one in Ballymorgan can understand) and endorsing unquestioningly all the nationalist myths about the English treatment of the Irish, and the humourless hardline nationalist with his uncritical hagiographical view of the 'patriot martyrs'. The way in which both sides in the conflict have distorted history is neatly demonstrated in a scene in which the visiting Englishman (Leslie Phillips) deflects a lynch mob who believe he has blown up the statue by giving an impassioned rendering of John of Gaunt's deathbed speech from Shakespeare's *Richard II* ('This earth, this realm, this England') and adapting it to eulogize Ireland. But such films are mere drops in the ocean. It is *The Quiet Man* in its mythic power and enduring popular appeal which carries the day.

There are common features about the majority of the mainstream films about Wales, Scotland and Ireland, for all that Wales's imagery tends to be industrial and the other two rural: the romanticization of the past, a sentiment of resistance to the English, a celebration of traditional leadership and communal solidarity, a greater emotionality and spontaneity, the much greater presence of religion. Very often these aspects are highlighted by the presence of an Englishman, individualistic to a degree, phlegmatic, stubborn, unromantic, an outsider. It is conditioned by the equation of England with modernity, individualism and secularism, all the things not approved of by the Celts, and seen as alien to decent, warm-hearted Celticism.

Notes

1   On the construction of the Welsh identity see in particular Prys Morgan, 'From a Death to a View: the hunt for the Welsh past in the Romantic period' in Eric Hobsbawm and Terence Ranger (eds), *The Invention of Tradition*, Cambridge, 1983, pp. 43–100; Dai Smith, *Wales! Wales?*, London, 1984; Gwyn A. Williams, *When was Wales?*, Harmondsworth, 1984; Tony Curtis (ed.), *Wales: the imagined nation*, Bridgend, 1986; Dai Smith, *Aneurin Bevan and the World of South Wales*, Cardiff, 1993.

2   Morgan, 'From a Death to a View', p. 66.

3   Smith, *Wales! Wales?*, p. 44.

4   Gwyn A. Williams, *When Was Wales?*, pp. 176, 202. Cf. Smith, *Wales! Wales?*, p. 30.

5   Williams, *When Was Wales?*, p. 206.

6   Smith, *Wales! Wales?*, p. 48.

7   Smith, *Wales! Wales?*, p. 45.

8   On the truth behind the legend, see Smith, *Wales! Wales?*, pp. 55–64.

9   Dai Smith, 'Myth and Meaning in the Literature of the South Wales Coalfield – the 1930's', *The Anglo-Welsh Review* (Spring, 1976), p. 40.

10 Philip Dunne, *How Green Was My Valley: the screenplay*, Santa Barbara,1990, p. 18.

11 Dunne, *How Green Was My Valley: the screenplay*, p. 26.

12 David Berry, *Wales and Cinema: the first hundred years*, Cardiff, 1994, pp. 66–74.

13 Jeffrey Richards, *The Age of the Dream Palace*, London,1984, p. 309.

14 Mary Lou Jennings (ed.), *Humphrey Jennings: film-maker, painter, poet*, London, 1982, p. 33.

15 Peter Stead, *Richard Burton: so much, so little*, Bridgend, 1991, p. 93.

16 Berry, *Wales and Cinema*, p. 261.

17 Deidre Beddoe, 'Images of Welsh Women' in Tony Curtis (ed.), *Wales: the imagined nation*, p. 227.

18 On Ireland and the cinema, see in particular Kevin Rockett, Luke Gibbons and John Hill, *Cinema and Ireland*, London, 1987; Anthony Slide, *The Cinema and Ireland*, Jefferson, North Carolina and London, 1984; and Jeffrey Richards, 'Ireland, the Empire and Film', in Keith Jeffery (ed.), *An Irish Empire?*, Manchester, 1996, pp. 25–56.

19 L. P. Curtis Jr, *Anglo-Saxons and Celts*, Bridgeport, CT, 1968.

20 Sheridan Gilley, 'English Attitudes to the Irish in England, 1780–1900' in Colin Holmes (ed.), *Immigrants and Minorities in British Society*, London, 1978, pp. 81–110.

21 J. O. Bartley, *Teague, Shenkin and Sawney*, Cork, 1954, p. 167.

22 Richard Allen Cave, 'Staging the Irishman' in J. S. Bratton *et al.*, *Acts of Supremacy:*

the British Empire and the stage 1790–1930, Manchester, 1991, pp. 62–128.

23 Charles Townshend, *Political Violence in Ireland,* Oxford, 1983, p. 1.

24 Rockett, Gibbons and Hill, *Cinema and Ireland,* p. 23.

25 On the British Board of Film Censors and Irish subjects, see Jeffrey Richards, 'Ireland, the Empire and Film', pp. 33–37, and J. C. Robertson, *The British Board of Film Censors: film censorship in Britain, 1896–1950,* London, 1985, pp. 86–89.

26 Robertson, *The British Board of Film Censors,* p. 86.

27 George Bluestone, *Novels into Films,* Berkeley and Los Angeles, California, 1968, p. 77.

28 Slide, *The Cinema and Ireland,* p. 83.

9

Lancashire

Within England and outside London, the county with the most sustained and influential cinematic image is Lancashire. There has been a continuous tradition of representations of Lancashire and Lancashire folk, particularly in comic form, throughout the era of mass entertainment media. It was developed in the music-halls and has been transferred intact to films, radio, records and television. This Lancashire identity grew out of the experience and the effects of the Industrial Revolution.

Before the nineteenth century Lancashire as a whole was a sparsely populated, remote, forested and backward region, the poorest in Britain. The Industrial Revolution changed all that. The North, and especially Lancashire, decisively came into its own in the nineteenth century. It became 'the workshop of the world', the source of Britain's global pre-eminence. Industrial England was to a great extent Northern England. The government may still have sat in Whitehall and the Queen in Windsor but much of the nation's wealth was being created in Manchester, Sheffield, Newcastle and Leeds.

The nineteenth-century North became a monument to the Victorian values so prominent in recent political rhetoric – hard work, thrift, self-respect and patriotism. The great nineteenth-century Northern cities, many of them in Lancashire – Manchester, Bolton, Blackburn, Burnley, Preston, Oldham, Rochdale, for example – were animated by a fierce civic pride. This led them to provide, by a mixture of private benefaction and the levying of special rates, a whole range of libraries, museums, art galleries, orchestras, schools and colleges, to improve the mental, spiritual and cultural welfare of their citizens, at the same time as municipal provision of gas, light, water and public transport was enhancing the quality of life. The great Victorian statesman John Bright, Rochdale's most celebrated citizen until the advent of Gracie Fields, encapsulated the Civic Gospel philosophy lying behind such programmes:

> I only hope that the corporations generally will become very much more expensive than they have been – not expensive in the sense of wasting money, but that there will be such nobleness and liberality amongst the people of our towns and cities as will lead them to give their corporations power to expend more on those things which, as public opinion advances, are found to be essential to the health and comfort and improvement of our people.[1]

A strong Northern culture developed, both in Lancashire and Yorkshire, with a flourishing local press, vigorous party political organizations, a rich dialect literature, a distinct musical tradition centred on brass bands and choirs, and a growing interest in regional history and archaeology.

Given the inevitable existence of sub-groups and sub-cultures in Lancashire – immigration produced a substantial Irish Catholic minority which was never entirely integrated – and given the fact that there was always strong loyalty to individual towns, the county was nevertheless remarkably cohesive. Its heart was Cotton Lancashire, a society characterized by John K. Walton as a stable, tightly knit, conservative society, which, despite a significant minority of badly-off people and the problems of pollution, disease and overcrowding, generated a uniquely prosperous high-income working-class culture.[2] It was bound together by shared employment experience, traditions of good neighbourliness and mutual assistance. Its communality was enhanced by participation in the commercialized leisure industries that emerged in Victorian Britain and centred on the music-hall, seaside holidays, football and the pub. All of these contributed to the creation of a cultural identity and enduring images of Lancashire and Lancashireness.

Culturally and geographically, this was an urban, industrial working-class world, which came into existence in the early nineteenth century and remained in place until the 1960s. J. B. Priestley observed it when he toured England for his classic 1933 work, *English Journey*. He discovered three Englands co-existing. There was Old England, 'the country of the cathedrals and minsters, and manor houses and inns, of Parson and Squire; guide book and quaint highways and byways England' and there was post-war England,

> the England of arterial and by-pass roads, of filling stations and factories that look like exhibition buildings, of giant cinemas and dance halls and

cafés, bungalows with tiny garages, cocktail bars, Woolworths, motor-coaches, wireless, hiking, factory girls looking like actresses, greyhound racing and dirt-tracks, swimming pools and everything given away with cigarette coupons.

It was a democratic, accessible, cheap, mass-produced England.

In between came the second England 'the nineteenth-century England, the industrial England of coal, iron, steel, cotton, wool, railways':

> Thousands of rows of little houses all alike, sham Gothic churches, square-faced chapels, Town Halls, Mechanics' Institutes, mills, foundries, warehouses, refined watering places, Pier Pavilions, Family and Commercial Hotels, Literary and Philosophical Societies, back-to-back houses, detached villas with monkey-trees, Grill Rooms, railway stations, slag-heaps and 'tips', dock roads, Refreshment Rooms, doss-houses, Unionist or Liberal Clubs, cindery waste grounds, mill chimneys, slums, fried-fish shops, public houses with red blinds, bethels in corrugated iron, good class drapers' and confectioners' shops, a cynically devastated countryside, sooty dismal little towns, and still sootier grim fortress-like cities.[3]

This was the familiar landscape from which Lancashire comedians sprang and which formed the background to their humour.

Life in this world has been described in detail by many who experienced it.[4] It is a life which, as Richard Hoggart (brought up in Hunslet) says, was 'dense and concrete', a life where the main stress was on the intimate, the sensory, the detailed, the personal, where conversations centred on people, relationships, sex, work and sport, and not on theories or ideas.[5] It was a world of hierarchies, traditions, rituals and routines, bound together by shared beliefs in patriotism, luck, fate and clear definitions of manliness and womanliness. All of this was to provide the raw material for Lancashire comedians.

But within this working-class world, there was a crucial distinction between what the Victorians called 'the rough' and 'the respectable' working classes. 'Respectability' involved a belief in education, self-advancement, domesticity, thrift, restraint and good manners; 'roughness' was living for the moment, rejecting authority, education and thrift, drinking to excess, fighting, swearing and fornicating without restraint. Some people embraced 'respectability' wholly, others 'roughness'. For some, these concepts represented twin facets of their experience or different phases in their lives.

Historians have long seen class consciousness as crucial in understanding the history of modern industrial society. But recently greater attention has been paid to other ideas transcending class differences. One is the idea of gender roles, the nature and significance of being a man or a woman. Another is the concept of a shared regional identity.

Patrick Joyce has argued for the importance of regional identity, which he sees as embodied in a dialect culture that cut across class lines. Examining broadside ballads, dialect writing and local humour, Joyce notes the absence of class vocabulary and the presence of a moral vocabulary which lays stress on honesty, decency, dignity, hard work, stoicism and good humour, values shared by both rich and poor. The keynote for Joyce is fraternity and social justice rather than egalitarianism and class conflict. He sees dialect literature and humour as preserving and maintaining a collective social identity, celebrating the people as folk rather than class. Because this cultural populism was essentially consensual rather than conflictual, Joyce argued that there was no inherent conflict between loyalty to street, to town, to region, to nation or ultimately to Empire, each integrated into the other. Lancashire pride derived partly from the fact that it felt itself to be the industrial heart of Britain and thus of the Empire.[6]

Joyce's argument highlights the important fact that people define themselves in different ways at different times. Being proud of being Lancastrian, therefore, did not preclude being proud of being British. Equally, some people view the world from a class perspective, others from a moral one and still more from a gender standpoint. What is interesting to observe is how the Lancashire stars embody, comment on and interpret these multiple identities.

Whether the North was defined in terms of class or people or gender, there was something that was recognized as a Northern personality. Frank Ormerod, writing in 1915, identified its characteristics as natural independence, candour, a sense of humour and a democratic spirit. The Lancastrian was, he thought, plain-speaking, sentimental, forthright and stoical.[7] Sir Henry Miers in a 1929 essay on 'Some Characteristics of Manchester Men' singled out strenuousness and determination, directness and independence of judgement, intense civic pride and a belief in 'that fundamental and cheering principle: namely that every man is as good as his neighbour'. 'The characteristics of which I am speaking,' he concluded, 'are those that strike one as belonging to the whole population, whether well educated or not.'[8]

The industrial landscape of Lancashire and the plain-speaking, independent-spirited, good-hearted Northerner were continuously promoted by popular culture from the earliest days of the commercialized leisure industries. It was in comedy in particular that these images or myths of the Lancastrian were preserved, burnished and transmitted to audiences who affectionately recognized and identified with their essential truths. Lancashire humour was honed and nurtured in the music-halls, where the Lancashire comedian became so familiar a part of the turns that J. B. Priestley, visiting the county on his 'English Journey', observed that being there was like landing among a million music-hall comedians. The Lancashire accent, flat and broad vowelled, lent itself to ironic understatement and was 'admirable for comic effect, being able to suggest either shrewdness or simplicity, or … more likely a humorous mixture of both'.[9]

The music-hall was the dominant popular cultural form of the second half of the nineteenth century. Music-hall grew out of pub entertainment. 'The free and easies,' the informal sing-songs in eighteenth century taverns, led to separate song saloons, and song and supper rooms were built on to pubs. From the 1860s onwards there were purpose-built music-halls where food and drink were served, and a chairman kept order. The music-hall became the prototype of the modern entertainment industry, rapidly commercialized as capital was invested, advertising techniques were developed to promote stars, and a hierarchy of stars and supporting acts was evolved. By the 1870s many music-halls were mounting shows twice nightly to maximize returns on investment.

Initially, music-halls were independent operations normally set up locally by enterprising publicans. But the railway system made touring possible and circuits developed with artists touring regularly. By the 1880s and 1890s there were several nationwide circuits, represented by the Empires, Hippodromes and Palaces which appeared in the high streets of many towns and cities. There were also specific Northern and Southern chains and many independent houses survived. Audiences included old and young, middle-class and working-class, male and female patrons, but the predominant element in the audience was the young employed unmarried adult.

The music-hall programme mainly consisted of songs, with occasional sketches, which became more common in the twentieth century as music-hall evolved into the aptly named 'variety'. Songs and choruses provided a shared experience, a chance for the audience to express solidarity, to recognize and affirm their values, attitudes and aspirations. The writers of songs had to take into account the mixed nature of audiences, the need for escapism, a catchy tune and sentiment. For it was the audience who 'made' both songs and stars. So songwriters sought to dramatize general attitudes, and songs strongly reflected the aspects and characteristics of working-class life noted by Hoggart: love (treated as romantic), marriage (treated as a trap and a disaster), work (and how to avoid it), city life, food and drink, clothes and holidays. The values were patriotism, fatalism, comradeship, a mild anti-authoritarianism, defined gender roles and the idea of an immutable social order.

Despite the trend towards a national culture in the music-halls, some stars remained local stars and never ventured beyond the boundaries of their region, mainly because dialect humour and songs, whether in Scouse, Geordie or broad Lancashire, did not travel. This underlined and reinforced local patriotism.

There were regional differences in humour. Cotton Lancashire's humour tended to be slow-building, anecdotal, character-based humour; London humour was much faster, patter, joke and dialogue based. This is encapsulated in the difference, for instance, between Lancashire-based Frank Randle and London-based Max Miller. In this regard, Liverpool is much closer to London and not to be identified with Lancashire proper. For Liverpool is not a Lancashire city at all. It is a Celtic city that happens to be situated on the Lancashire coast; the Irish and Welsh influences are much stronger than the English. It is also a seaport and like all seaports, London and Newcastle for instance, it generates a different kind of humour from the hinterland. Liverpool-born comedians like Tommy Handley, Arthur Askey and Ken Dodd have been much more verbal, surreal and faster than the slower, more realistic character comedians of Cotton Lancashire.

It was the music-hall which fed the new media of the twentieth century – radio, records, films. It provided the stars, the sketches, the songs and prolonged the life of the music-hall tradition on celluloid. Cinemagoing was indisputably the most popular form of entertainment in Britain in the interwar years. By 1938 there were nearly 5,000 cinemas in operation in Britain. Lancashire and Scotland boasted the greatest number of cinema seats per head of the population: one cinema seat for every nine people. The cinema had now eclipsed both the music-hall and the theatre to become '*par excellence* the people's entertainment'.[10]

In his evocative autobiographical account of his Bolton childhood, *Seats in All Parts*, Leslie Halliwell vividly re-creates the life of a youthful film fan in 1930s Lancashire. 'For a film fanatic,' he writes, 'Bolton was almost like Mecca. At one time there lay within easy reach no fewer than forty-seven cinemas of varying size, quality and character. None was more than five miles from Bolton's Town Hall, and twenty-eight were within the boundaries of the borough.'[11]

In their local cinemas, Lancashire filmgoers would often see the stars they had previously watched in the music-halls. The greatest Lancashire stars were undoubtedly George Formby and Gracie Fields, who succeeded in appealing both to Lancashire in particular and the working classes in general. Mass-Observation, investigating the preferences of working-class holidaymakers in Blackpool in 1937–38, concluded unambiguously, 'The biggest heroes of the working classes are their 'own' Gracie Fields and George Formby.'[12]

The sampling of opinion at Blackpool is significant, for Blackpool was the Mecca of the North. All of Lancashire went there regularly for its annual holiday, creating a massive audience for entertainment. The Lancashire stars recognized this. Gracie Fields (*Sing as We Go*) and Frank Randle (*Holidays with Pay*) made films there. George Formby sang about 'My Little Stick of Blackpool Rock'. Formby, Randle, Harry Korris, Jimmy Clitheroe, Al Read and the rest regularly appeared there, often for summer seasons.

But Fields and Formby were more than simply Lancashire stars. They became national stars: Fields was the top British female star at the cinema box office from 1936 to 1940 and Formby the top male star from 1937 to 1943. Both were rooted in the music-hall tradition. Both remained inextinguishably Lancashire. Both became symbols of the people. Both indicate the truth of Patrick Joyce's contention that it was possible for people to be simultaneously loyal to family, street, county, nation and Empire: Formby and Fields embodied such multiple loyalties.

There was never any doubt but that George and Gracie were Lancashire and proud of it. Their accents remained as thick and strong as hotpot. George proclaimed his origin in a string of songs ('The Emperor of Lancashire', 'A Lancashire Romeo', 'The Lancashire Toreador', 'A Lad fra Lancasheer'). Gracie herself wrote and performed 'Lancashire Blues', an exile's lament for a region represented in the song by clogs and hotpot. She also celebrated life and work in the cotton mills in *The Clatter of the Clogs* and *Clogs and Shawl*, sang songs built around dialect expressions like 'Ee By Gum' and 'Nowt about Owt' and recalled the county's passion for football, complete with terrace banter, in *Pass, Shoot, Goal*. Of Gracie, J. B. Priestley wrote:

> Listen to her for a quarter of an hour and you will learn more about Lancashire women and Lancashire than you would from a dozen books on the subjects. All the qualities are there, shrewdness, homely simplicity, irony, fierce independence, an impish delight in mocking whatever is thought to be affected and pretentious.[13]

But there is something more revealing about them too. When Formby died in 1961, the *Manchester Guardian* (7 March 1961) compared his popularity to Fields's writing: 'The two Lancashire comedians in fact had much in common:

the characters they created might have been man and wife, the one springing from Wigan, the other from Rochdale, with such pride in their roots that they never let us forget them.' This creates an intriguing conjunction: the dominant, no-nonsense Gracie and George, whom W. J. Ingoe described perfectly as 'a platoon simpleton, a mother's boy, the beloved henpeck, the father who cannot hang a picture. Underlying his everyday follies there is the sublime wisdom of the ordinary fool who loves and trusts the world.'[14] This conjunction accurately reflects the North-West as matriarchy. The sociologist Geoffrey Gorer found in his researches for *Exploring English Character* (1955) that this was a particular characteristic of the region. 'Put briefly, in the North-Western region, women have greater authority in their family and greater independence' than in any other part of England. In the North-East and the North, he found that paternal authority was highest and there was the greatest number of all-male associations.[15] One reason for matriarchy is almost certainly the high level of female employment in the North-West by contrast with the North-East.

It is interesting to reflect that those three typical Lancashire men, who did so much to record the cultural image of the North-West, the writer Walter Greenwood, the historian Robert Roberts and the painter L. S. Lowry came from just such families with dominant, strong-willed mothers and easy-going, good-natured fathers. Leslie Halliwell records another such family in *Seats in All Parts*. They would all have recognized the essential truth of the characters of George and Gracie, both of whom, it should be noted, also had dominant mothers. Culturally, the strong-minded, independent-spirited Lancashire lass is also celebrated in the forthright, honest mill-girl heroine of Stanley Houghton's 1912 play *Hindle Wakes* (filmed in 1927, 1931 and 1952) and the shrewd, characterful bootmaker's daughter in Harold Brighouse's 1916 play *Hobson's Choice* (filmed in 1920, 1931 and 1954). Their lineal successors are the matriarchs of *Coronation Street*: Ena Sharples, Elsie Tanner, Annie Walker, Hilda Ogden and Bet Lynch.

If Lancashire recognized in George and Gracie qualities specific to the region, the nation also identified characteristics to admire. For Gracie and George shared certain qualities that were at a premium during the Depression and subsequently the war – optimism, cheerfulness and indomitability. These were encapsulated in George's catchphrase 'Turned out nice again, hasn't it' and in Gracie's repertoire of spirit-lifting songs ('Sing as We Go', 'Looking on the Bright Side', 'Look Up and Laugh').

Formby was second-generation music-hall, and his original stage act was

25   English Everyman: George Formby in *It's in the Air* (1938).

copied completely from his father, George Formby Sr, whom he strongly resembled vocally. Formby Sr, billed as 'The Wigan Nightingale', had been born illegitimate in great poverty in Ashton-under-Lyne in 1875. He learned his trade as a singing beggar and suffered all his life from a permanent cough and a weak chest which he wove into his act with the catchphrase 'Coughing better tonight'. But he developed TB which killed him at the age of forty-four in 1921. Formby Sr had created the character of John Willie, the gormless Lancashire lad in baggy trousers, tight jacket and bowler hat, slow-talking, henpecked, accident-prone, fond of his beer but able to muddle through in the end.

Although George Jr had been training as a jockey, his mother launched him on a stage career as soon as his father died, coaching him in George Sr's songs and routines and putting him into the John Willie costume. It was in this character that George made his first two adult films – he had made one screen appearance as a boy in a film now lost. *Boots! Boots!* and *Off the Dole* were produced by John E. Blakeley's Mancunian Films in 1934. Made on tiny budgets in a one-room London studio, they were effectively filmed revues. *Off the Dole*, made for a mere £8,000, netted £30,000, and the success of both films attracted the attention of Basil Dean, the Liverpool-born head of Ealing Studios. Dean had already signed Gracie Fields and saw Formby as another likely success. Formby was to make eleven highly successful films for Ealing, before moving to Columbia British where he made seven more films in similar vein. There was never any attempt to play down the Lancashireness of either star. Basil Dean deliberately sought writers for their films 'able to appreciate to the full the special qualities of Lancashire folk, their particular brand of humour and above all their uninhibited approach to life'.[16] So he signed Yorkshire novelist and playwright J. B. Priestley to provide screen stories for Fields, and Walter Greenwood, author of *Love on the Dole*, to provide the script for Formby's first Ealing film, *No Limit* (1935).

Formby's first two Ealing films, *No Limit* and *Keep Your Seats Please* were directed by Gracie Fields's husband, the accomplished Italian comedy director Monty Banks. Thereafter a special Formby unit was set up at Ealing, headed by writer-director Anthony Kimmins, to produce his films. The films usually conformed to a set pattern. At their centre is George, a shy, innocent, gauche, accident-prone Lancashire lad. Frequently he is in a skilled trade (photographer, typesetter, gramophone engineer) and lives in the South, either the suburbs or the countryside, thus nationalizing his appeal. He has a bashful courtship with a brisk, sensible heroine with an upper-class accent. He is put through a succession of comic humiliations but he eventually wins the girl and achieves success in his job or in sport or later in war. The point of universal identification was that if George could win through against adversity then anyone could. Class barriers thus prove no restriction.

It was partly by becoming a universal symbol that Formby achieved his success. He was Northern and working-class, but more important, he was the little man who wins through against all the odds, as Chaplin had been on the silent screen and as Norman Wisdom was to be in the 1950s. He was, as Colin MacInnes observed, Everyman, 'the urban little man defeated – but refusing to admit it'.[17] Mass-Observation recorded that the fantasy sequence in his 1940 film *Let George Do It* in which Formby landed at Nuremberg and knocked out Hitler was one of the biggest cultural morale boosters of the early war years.[18] It was the visual encapsulation of the People's War with the English Everyman flooring the Nazi Superman.

There was also an innocence about George that was essentially childlike, which explains why he was as popular with children as with adults. The cry 'Ooh, Mother' which he emitted whenever in danger and the gleeful 'Aha, never touched me' when he escaped his pursuers were the reactions of a child. He even put his tongue out at pursuers on occasions.

It was this innocence and the sunny outlook that neutralized the potential offensiveness of some of his songs. His songs – he recorded 189 in all – were a vital part of his appeal. Many of them dealt with sex but in a way which stressed shyness, voyeurism, caricature and saucy innuendo: 'Me Auntie Maggie's Remedy', 'My Grand-dad's flannelette nightshirt', 'My Little Stick of Blackpool Rock', 'When I'm Cleaning Windows', 'In My Little Snapshot Album'. In their approach and their themes – honeymooners, nudists, fat ladies, underwear – they recall the comic seaside postcards of Donald McGill and they served the same function – the harmless defusion of a major area of tension in a deeply repressed and conventional society. As Orwell wrote of McGill's postcards, so he might also have said of Formby's films:

> These things are a sort of diary upon which the English have unconsciously recorded themselves. Their old-fashioned outlook, their graded snobberies, their mixture of bawdiness and hypocrisy, their extreme gentleness, their deeply moral attitude to life, are all mirrored there.[19]

During the war he maintained his popularity both in films and on the Entertainments National Service Association (ENSA) tours he undertook, entertaining the troops frequently in close proximity to the front line. He received an OBE after the war for his morale-boosting activities in this area. His final film *George in Civvy Street* (1946) was a box-office failure but it had a symbolic significance. It is the story of the rivalry between two country pubs, the Lion and the Unicorn. George inherits the run-down and semi-derelict Unicorn and with the aid of a group of ex-army friends turns it into a going concern and wins the hand and heart of the female owner of the Lion. The Lion and the Unicorn were the heraldic symbols standing for the two sides of the British national persona – character and imagination, each reinforcing and enriching the other. So George bowed out of films unifying the nation mythically, communally and matrimonially, just as on a larger scale World War Two had done, demonstrating, as Orwell argued, that when it came to the crunch, 'national solidarity is stronger than class antagonism'. Although his film career ended with the war, Formby continued to appear on stage, achieving a notable West End success in the musical *Zip Goes a Million*. In his projecting of a spirit of good nature, good humour and goodwill George was able simultaneously to embody Lancashire, the working classes, the people and the nation. When he died in 1961 at the age of fifty-six, the nation mourned his passing.

Gracie Fields was an even more significant national figure than George Formby. She was more than just a film and stage star. She was a phenomenon.

Lancashire Britannia: Gracie Fields in *Sing as We Go* (1934). **26**

She was a music-hall star who by being herself became a national symbol. To the British as a whole in the 1930s she was simply 'Our Gracie'. What was it that made her so universally beloved? First there was her talent. She was neither beautiful nor in her cinema heyday youthful, and paradoxically this endeared her even more to audiences. But she combined an extraordinary singing voice, a natural comic talent and an inexhaustible vitality. One critic analyzed her appeal to the urban proletariat in these terms: 'She is the apotheosis of all the pleasure of their annual week's holiday from the mills; the clown member of any family who can be relied on to chase away the blues. She was a mill girl and now she has made good.' Gracie represented the English 'ideal of high spirits and "the good sort", a favourite character in England with which hordes of English identify themselves'.[20]

Everyone knew Gracie's story. Born over a chip shop in Rochdale, she had been launched on her singing career by her mother Jenny, and as a child sang for coppers and pies around the Rochdale pubs. After touring with various troupes of child performers, she got work in touring revues and learned her craft the hard way round the provinces. It paid off when *Mr. Tower of London*, the show in which she had starred on tour, was booked into the West End in 1922. It established her as a major stage star. The move into films in 1931 was a logical development.

The cinema completed Gracie's rise to superstardom. She was signed to a contract by Ealing Studios head, Basil Dean, and in 1931 he produced her first film *Sally in Our Alley*, named after her hit song. The film featured an unglamorized Gracie – the working girl as heroine, complete with broad Lancashire accent, homely cheerful appearance and breezily good-natured manner. A fundamental decency, forthrightness and commonsense shines through everything she does. In a recognizably working-class slum setting, the film combines a sentimental romance between Gracie and her soldier sweetheart and a powerful account of the rehabilitation by Gracie of a teenage delinquent who is both a liar and a thief.

But over the years the nature and content of Gracie's films changed. Back-street stories give way to back-stage stories. The fact that her producer Basil Dean records no West End success for Gracie's films until *The Show Goes On* in 1937 suggests a conscious desire to win approval in that quarter and hence a shift of emphasis in subject matter.

First, Gracie was given a succession of theatrical stories, in which her own rise to stardom was re-created (*Queen of Hearts, The Show Goes On*) and she was deliberately transformed from a raw, unrefined mill girl into a glamorized theatrical *grande dame*, the very fact of her stardom removing her form the exclusive possession of any one class and making her the property of all. But the 'rags to riches' theatrical story also had the ideological significance of demonstrating the continuing validity of the doctrine of self-help, the idea that if you had talent and were prepared to work hard, you would achieve success without any need to alter the existing structure of society. This was something that middle-class audiences could endorse without qualification. Also, an increasingly patriotic element was injected into her films through the singing of patriotic songs and by the recurrence of the Union Jack, which increasingly enshrined her in the nation's consciousness as a Lancashire Britannia.

In her first two films, *Sally in Our Alley* and *Looking on the Bright Side* (1932), working-class Gracie briefly enters an upper-class world, only to be patronized and slighted, and to return in disgust to her own people, leaving the class barriers intact. But in her third film *This Week of Grace* (1933), she enters the upper-class world permanently, marrying an impoverished viscount and bridging the gulf between the classes. In her best films, *Sing as We Go* (1934) and *Look Up and Laugh* (1935), both written by Priestley, she acts as intermediary between, and reconciler of, the opposed forces of capitalist big business and labour/small business. She returned to this theme in her last British film,

Shipyard Sally (1939). In this film she played an unemployed variety artiste running a Clydeside pub. When the shipyards close, Gracie is chosen to deliver a petition to the government, requesting government aid to reopen the yards. Her appeal is successful and the shipyards reopen. The film ends with Gracie singing 'Land of Hope and Glory' over a montage of the *Queen Mary* being launched and Union Jacks being waved. As Graham Greene, then a film critic, wrote:

> All Miss Fields' films seem designed to show sympathy for the working class and an ability to appeal to the best circles: unemployment can always be wiped out with a sentimental song, industrial unrest is calmed by a Victorian ballad and dividends are made safe for democracy.[21]

This is true as far as it goes. But it must also be recognized that it was the talent and personality of Gracie that made this message palatable. Her personality remained true to her Lancashire roots and the public repaid her with a devotion that hardly faltered until the war. Significantly, it was intellectuals who criticized her films for not being realistic enough and not advocating radical solutions. But it is evident that audiences did not want to see people sinking into depression, apathy and torpor. The value of Gracie was that she was one of them but could rise above it. The titles of her films constitute a set of injunctions to avoid despair or apathy, anger or revolution: *Looking on the Bright Side, Sing as We Go, Look Up and Laugh, Keep Smiling, The Show Goes On*. It was a message of courage and cheerfulness, delivered to the people not by a politician but by one of their own, one who knew what they were enduring and whose advice could be trusted. If they had felt that she was betraying them, they would have shunned her. That they took her to their hearts suggests that she really did represent something that the nation wanted and that, as demonstrated by the election in 1931 and re-election in 1935 of a National government and the genuinely joyous Silver Jubilee celebration for King George V, was consensus.

So during the 1930s Gracie was able to embody simultaneously Rochdale, Lancashire, Britain, the Empire, the working class, women and the people at large. But 1939 was a watershed year for Gracie as it was for the nation at large. She underwent two major operations and was still recuperating when war broke out. She was one of the first to offer her services to ENSA, newly formed by her old boss Basil Dean. Then in 1940 Italy entered the war and Gracie's Italian-born husband Monty Banks was faced with internment. So to get him out of the country, she accepted an engagement to tour Canada to raise money for the Navy League. Monty hastened to the USA, where he had been brought up, to take out American citizenship, and Gracie raised £300,000 on her Canadian tour. But she had not anticipated the furore that her departure would cause. She was denounced in the press, accused of fleeing with a fortune in jewels and planning to sit out the war in comfort. Although she subsequently toured the world with ENSA, singing for the troops in North Africa, Italy, India and the Far East, and received tributes to her war work in the House of Commons, she never regained the position of national symbol she had held in the 1930s. After the war and the death of Monty Banks, she retired to Capri with her third husband, Bessarabian engineer Boris Alperovici, emerging from time to time for stage and television appearances. She was made a Dame of the British Empire shortly before her death in 1979.

Gracie's centrality to British culture is evidenced by the appearance of imitators. After Gracie signed for 20th Century-Fox in 1938, Ealing Studios immediately replaced her with another Northern performer, who looked and sounded very like Gracie. Betty Driver, born in Leicester but raised in Manchester, starred for Ealing in two Fieldsesque vehicles, *Penny Paradise* (1938) and *Let's Be Famous* (1939). Interestingly, she later became a stalwart of *Coronation Street* as barmaid Betty Turpin, a milieu into which Gracie herself could have fitted without difficulty. Gracie's sister Betty Fields also made a Gracie-type screen appearance for a minor company in *On Top of the World* (1936), which was modelled closely on the pattern of her sister's films. But neither Betty Driver nor Betty Fields established themselves as major film stars.

Fields and Formby represent the 'acceptable face' of popular culture, the upbeat, optimistic, essentially decent face. But there is another face. As George Orwell writes in his account of the British people, *The Lion and the Unicorn*:

> In all societies, the common people must live to some extent against the existing order. The genuinely popular culture of England is something that goes on beneath the surface unofficially and more or less frowned on by the authorities. One thing one notices if one looks directly at the common people, especially in the big towns, is that they are not puritanical. They are inveterate gamblers, drink as much beer as their wages will permit, are devoted to bawdy jokes, and use probably the foulest language in the world.[22]

This is at once too sweeping and too one-dimensional. It takes no account of the complex interplay within the working classes between 'rough' and 'respectable'. But there are elements of truth here and this aspect of popular culture was catered to by a submerged and subversive culture, rooted in the music-hall and preserved on celluloid by Mancunian Films.

The only film company and film studio operating outside the South-East of England was Mancunian Films, based in Manchester. It was the brainchild of John E. Blakeley (1889–1958) who was from a family of cinema owners and film renters in the North-West. Blakeley saw a market for Northern humour on film and put together a consortium of film and theatre owners from the region to form Mancunian Films. Blakeley was to produce twenty-five films for the company over the next twenty years, distributing them through Butchers Films. Initially, he rented sound-stages at minor London studios, like Riverside at Hammersmith, and took his company down to film his comedies. But in 1947 he fulfilled his long-held dream of creating his own Manchester film studio, in a converted Methodist chapel in Dickenson Road, Rusholme. There were two sound-stages and Mancunian was run very much as a family business, with John E. Blakeley ('John E.' as he was always known) as producer-director, his sons Tom as production manager and John Jr as cameraman and son-in-law Bernard Kelly as head of the props department. Arthur Mertz was the regular scriptwriter and his sons Arthur Jr and John worked as casting director and boom operator respectively. The studio was opened with great ceremony attended by George Formby, Frank Randle, Norman Evans, Dan Young and Sandy Powell, all Mancunian stars. Formby, who had made his first two adult films for Mancunian, and Powell, who was starring in their current production *Cup-Tie Honeymoon*, made speeches wishing the studio well. But as television began to make inroads into the faithful cinema audience, John E. decided to retire, and in 1953 Dickenson Road Studio was sold to the BBC, to become the first regional television studio, thus exactly emulating the fate of Mancunian's grand London rivals, Lime Grove Studios, home of Gainsborough Films, sold to the BBC in 1949 and Ealing Studios, sold to the BBC in 1955. It was symptomatic of the replacement of one mass medium by another, though many of the performers switched from films to television as easily as they had previously switched from music-hall to films, maintaining the continuity of the comic tradition.

Historically, the great value of Mancunian Films is that they are almost totally uncinematic. Although John E. was billed as director, the films were not so much directed as staged. The acts do their 'turns' in front of the camera. The films were in reality photographed variety shows, a series of sketches by music-hall stars who knew their trade, with musical interludes. The musical interludes employed as guest stars popular singers of romantic ballads Anne Ziegler and Webster Booth (*Demobbed*), Cavan O'Connor (*Under New Management*) and Josef Locke (*Holidays with Pay*) – reflecting that deep strain of sentimentality running through working-class culture alongside the delight in subversive knockabout.

A Mancunian script, such as it was, often contained blank pages with the word 'bus' at the top, which was the sign that the comics should insert their own comic 'business'. Although Blakeley had Arthur Mertz and Bert Tracy, who had been a gag-writer for Laurel and Hardy, on hand to provide the scripts, the names of the non-existent Roney Parsons and Anthony Toner on the credits always meant there had been a good deal of improvisation. Since the performers worked regularly together, they developed a creative rapport, and ad libbing and improvisation came naturally. The films were cheaply made but audiences loved them because they reflected their own attitudes, lifestyles and mores.

The prototype Mancunian Films production was *The Penny Pool* (1937), which set the pattern followed by virtually all subsequent films. There would be a series of virtually self-contained sketches, strung upon two tenuous plot-threads: a romantic tale performed by two appallingly untalented juveniles and a criminal tale in which some embezzlement/robbery/swindle by the villain is foiled by the comic heroes. The film would usually centre on an activity common to working-class culture and culminate in a factory concert, celebrating simultaneously communality and the spirit of the music-hall.

In *The Penny Pool*, the familiar activity is the football pools and the film has the boss's son (played by Gracie Fields's brother Tommy) falling for and winning the hand of a working-class employee (the hopelessly unconvincing Luanne Shaw), while a crooked foreman seeks to cheat her of her pools winnings. The film proposes a familiar fantasy solution to life's problems (marriage to the boss's son and a pools win).

But the plot is more or less irrelevant. What counts is the succession of speciality acts: Jack Lewis's Singing Scholars, top-hatted and Eton-collared juveniles with pronounced regional accents, Macari and his Dutch Serenaders, and, in one grotesque sequence, an epicene boy singer and a Gracie Fields soundalike Elsie Brown, performing a duet: 'How Sorry I Am for Old People'. The highlight of the film is Duggie Wakefield and his Gang, knockabout zanies who display superb timing, rubber-limbed contortionism, and a rich sense of fun in some expert slapstick. There is a garage sketch in which they demolish a car, an incompetent singing waiter sketch, a Home Defence sketch with the Gang sending up the captain and the medical inspection, a comic brass-band sequence in which the Gang accompany Elsie singing 'Lancashire' and, in the final works concert, Duggie and the diminutive Billy Nelson doing

Rough working class: Frank Randle in *Somewhere in Politics* (1949).   **27**

a drag double act as Julie and Myrtle which anticipates the Two Ronnies by four decades. Duggie Wakefield (1899-1951), the lanky, melancholy, long-toothed clown who was Gracie Fields's brother-in-law, did another Mancunian Film, *Calling All Crooks* (1938) and also appeared with distinction supporting his sister-in-law in *This Week of Grace* (1933) and *Look Up and Laugh* (1935).

Mancunian's leading star was Frank Randle, who was also an investor in the company. Randle, born Arthur McEvoy in Wigan in 1902, had been a boy-hood friend of George Formby and later became his principal rival in North-ern cinemas. He made ten films, eight of them for Mancunian. A former circus acrobat, he became a fixture of Northern music-halls and variety theatres, eventually touring with his own show, 'Randle's Scandals'.

Randle, rather like his cockney counterpart Max Miller, never became a national success as a film star. But he was a great regional success in the North. He was not taken up and transformed into a national star as both Gracie Fields and George Formby had been, almost certainly because he was too disrep-utable and subversive. Gracie, the big sister figure, and George, the overgrown urchin, were essentially safe; indeed Gracie was the embodiment of 'the respectable' working class. Randle, toothless, lecherous, combative and insub-ordinate, embodied the 'rough' working-class ethic. One of his regular characters was a scrofulous old man, frothing with ale and senile lust.

Randle's films consist of a series of sketches highlighting the various aspects of his anarchic persona. He is totally disrespectful, showing contempt for authority, giving two-fingered salutes to officers and being generally bloody-minded, scrimshanking and obstructive. In his earliest films, *Somewhere in England* (1940), *Somewhere in Camp* (1942) and *Somewhere on Leave* (1942), which put him in a service context, he can be found disrupting pay parades, medical parades and drills, and permanently baiting and defying the sergeant-major. He returned to this service setting for his final film, *It's a Grand Life* (1953).

He is also violent, lecherous and drunken, as indicated by his catchphrases which included 'I'll fight anyone' and 'I'll spifflicate the lot of you', 'Bah, I've supped some ale toneet' and 'I bet you're a hot 'un'. So there are regular sketches showing him wrecking rooms such as the sergeant's mess, trying to get up stairs while drunk and taking a bath fully clothed in the same state, and amorously pursuing pretty girls.

The comedy is physical, destructive, sometimes surreal, often funny and expertly choreographed. Much of the character and the activity reflect the real Randle, who was given to punishing drinking bouts, outbursts of violence, wrecking dressing-rooms and once setting fire to a hotel where the service had displeased him. He died bankrupt in 1957 at the age of fifty-five from tuberculosis and cirrhosis of the liver.

In contrast to the individualism of Fields and Formby, which reflects the self-help ethic of the 'respectable' working class, Randle was always part of a gang, a frequent characteristic of the 'rough' working class. A fixture in almost all Mancunian Films, with or without Randle, was Dan Young, billed as 'the dude comedian'. He played an ersatz monocled toff, who indulged in verbal nonsense routines and gleefully participated in the collective mayhem. He would never have been taken as a genuine toff but was a working-class send-up of the upper classes by one of their own. There would also usually be a gormless Lancashire lad stooge: either diminutive Robbie Vincent or lanky Gus Aubrey.

Randle's appeal in the North is encapsulated in the recently discovered attendance figures for one cinema, the Majestic, Macclesfield. They reveal that in 1940 the top attraction had been George Formby's *Come On, George* and *Let George Do It* with Randle's debut film *Somewhere in England* the fifth most popular. But in 1942 Randle's *Somewhere in Camp* attracted a bigger audience than any film, British or American, other than *Mrs. Miniver*, and in 1943

Somewhere on Leave was the top British attraction and second only to *Holiday Inn*. Randle was now outdrawing Formby.[23] For some, he was a comic anti-hero, a celebration of the 'rough' working class; for others, a safety valve, a mocking of authority at a time of restriction and regulation. But he worked in the idiom and accent of Lancashire.

Mancunian Films also directly reflected people's lives: the football pools (*The Penny Pool*), seaside holidays (*Holidays with Pay*), the factory (*Demobbed*), the football match and the chip shop (*Cup-Tie Honeymoon*), the pub and the concert (both regular features). *Holidays with Pay* (1948), filmed partly on location in Blackpool and Douglas, Isle of Man, recreated the rituals and communality of the mass working-class holiday. Frank Randle and Tessie O'Shea as Jack and Pansy Rogers take their two daughters and their brother-in-law (Dan Young) to Blackpool; the film re-creates the chaos of departure, the routines of boarding-house life and hi-jinks on the pier, at the open-air swimming-pool and on the beach.

Sandy Powell (1898–1982), the genial, bespectacled, Rotherham-born comedian, whose catchphrase was 'Can you hear me mother?' and who was best known for his incompetent ventriloquist and lost policeman routines, heads the usual Mancunian team for *Cup-Tie Honeymoon* (1948). It celebrates the working-class obsession with football, with a notable sequence in which Sandy and his chums, unable to get into a vital cup tie, listen to it on the wireless and begin an increasingly frenetic re-enactment of the match in the living-room. The sketch is intercut with authentic football footage representing the victory of third division Townend United over first-division Townend Rovers.

Exactly the same format as the Randle films was adopted in the films starring Norman Evans (1901–62), a Rochdale-born comedian who was an altogether gentler and more genial figure than Randle. He was best known for his impersonation of an ample-bosomed Lancashire housewife, in the sketch 'Over the Garden Wall'. Toothless, aproned, half-shocked and half-gleeful, she leans on the wall retelling local gossip and confidentially discussing family scandals and people's ailments. It is the comic evocation of the Lancashire matriarch, a characterization taken over and faithfully reproduced by Les Dawson and Roy Barraclough in their double act as Cissie and Ada.

Evans made three films for Mancunian. *Demobbed* (1944) has Evans and his ex-soldier comrades seeking work. His gang consist of the inevitable Dan Young, Tony Dalton as the gormless idiot and rubber-necked, loose-limbed, cheekily grinning Nat Jackley, who although born in Sunderland in 1909 had made his stage debut with 'The Lancashire Lads' at Chesterfield Hippodrome in 1920. They get jobs at a scientific instrument factory, where they join forces with a diminutive feisty office cleaner Betty Jumel, and amid a repertoire of funny walks, slapstick and nonsense chat, are seen defying, sending up and bamboozling senior officers, foreman, managers, and wrecking the managing director's office. At the end, having foiled a robbery, the gang are appointed directors. They arrive in full morning dress in the boardroom and are drenched when Betty Jumel pours a bucket of water over them, bringing them back to earth with a bang. *Under New Management* (1946) has the same comic team trying to run a hotel. But *Over the Garden Wall* (1950), taking its title from Evans's well-loved sketch, is Norman Evans' celluloid apotheosis. In the concert sequence of *Demobbed*, Evans had done a self-contained 'Over the Garden Wall' sketch. Now, he spends the whole film in drag as Fanny Lawton. It is a prototype sitcom, with Fanny's husband played by chain-smoking Jimmy James and two lodgers (Dan Young and Alec Pleon). The plot has Fanny preventing the break-up of her daughter's marriage but there is the usual succession of sketches: using the bathroom, having breakfast, washing up, going to bed, gossiping with the neighbours. Jimmy James (1892–1965) also gets to do his celebrated drunk act, one of the three sketches which formed the basis of his stage act for years.

A sharper and feistier version of the Lancashire matron of Evans and Dawson was provided by Hylda Baker (1905–86). Hylda Baker was born in Farnworth, near Bolton, the daughter of a comedian, and made her stage debut at the age of ten. She developed a persona accurately characterized by John Fisher:

> With her well-rounded malapropisms, and air of cocky defiance, the archetype of the ever-so-slightly snobbish gossip, always hopeful of moving to a better class of neighbourhood and yet whose accent, clothes, demeanour, sadly no more than caricature her aim.[24]

Her stage act was based on her observation during the war of two girls, one short and one tall, of whom the short one did all the talking, while the tall one just nodded agreement. Hylda as the voluble short one employed a tall man in drag as her stooge, 'Cynthia', and bounced her monologue off this silent foil, with liberal use of her catchphrases, 'Be Soon, I said, Be Soon', 'You big girl's blouse' and 'She knows, y'know', and malapropisms, referring, for instance, to juvenile delinquents as juvenile detergents. She epitomized that combination of shrewdness and simplicity that Priestley saw as key Lancashire characteristics. Hylda had huge energy, indomitability and knowingness. Her act took her audience into her confidence as she shared with them the details of the lives of herself and her friends. Hylda Baker starred in a low-budget British comedy film *She Knows Y'Know* (1961) and later successfully transferred her stage persona to a Granada TV series, *Nearest and Dearest*, which ran from 1968 to 1972. She co-starred with Jimmy Jewel and they played a brother and sister, Nellie and Eli Pledge, running a Northern pickle factory. It inspired in turn a cinematic spin-off, also called *Nearest and Dearest*, in 1973. She also became a successful character actress in British 'New Wave' films (*Saturday Night and Sunday Morning, Up the Junction*). She could play straight roles as well as comic because, like all the great Lancashire comics, her act was essentially truthful and rooted in observation of reality.

Norman Evans's comic monologue and proto-sitcom routines perfectly epitomize a mainstream tradition in Northern humour, the slowly developed character piece, building up detail and drawing on familiar situations, dialogue and reactions. It is the comedic manifestation of Richard Hoggart's definition of working-class culture, noted earlier, as rooted in 'the intimate, the sensory, the detailed and the personal'. The important features are the slow build-up, the ladling-on of detail and the shared sense of recognition of familiar situations between performer and audience.

Radio was the perfect medium for this kind of monologue and a master of the form was Al Read (1909–87), who made his name on radio in the 1950s and 1960s. Read had complete mastery of the patterns, preoccupations and situations of the Northern audience. Listening to recordings of his programmes, you continuously hear the laughter of recognition from the audience. The nagging wife 'from the kitchen', the embarrassingly forthright and questioning child ('Dad, dad, what's that man doing, dad'), the know-all from next door ('You'll be lucky, I say you'll be lucky'), a gormless phone-user ('Just a minute – just, just, just a minute'), the gossiping neighbour dropping in uninvited, were all regular features, as were send-ups of institutions: the police force, the post office, hospitals, garages.

Al (short for Alfred) Read was born in Salford, the second of six children, and spent the first six years of his life in 'a two up, two down, in Kipling St., Salford'. In his autobiography he recalled a classical working-class background:

> Poverty – though we never called it that – was a way of life, something to be coped with. Everybody was in the same boat. It was a close-knit place full of sights and sounds which have disappeared today: travelling knife-grinders; the knockers-up … ; the coalmen … , the corner shop, sawdust on the floor … Outside our house lay an exciting world, the life of the

street … Even as a lad my built-in scanner was busily working away, absorbing the warm, cluttered life around me – housewives gossiping over the garden fence, their husbands yarning away on the street corner as they waited for the pub to open – and storing it away for future use.[25]

Al Read's family had been in the meat-processing business but went bankrupt during World War One, hence the 'two up, two down' in Salford. Later the family fortunes recovered, the business was relaunched and Al became a salesman for it, incorporating anecdotes, jokes and accents into his sales patter. Eventually he took over the family business but continued to tell stories and what he called 'pictures from life' in after-dinner speeches. A BBC producer spotted him doing one of these speeches and signed him up for radio. Working with the experienced scriptwriter Ronnie Taylor, he produced the scripts for his radio-shows, a succession of comic monologues in which he did all the voices, even the dog. His signature tune, 'Such is Life' ('Such is life – life is what you make it, Show 'em you can take it on the chin'), was in the tradition of Fields and Formby optimism. The stories were drawn from life:

> The comedy had grown up with me and reflected my own personal experience … I never tried to make people laugh, and there were never any 'gags' as such in my routines … All the story lines were culled from the small embarrassments and frustrations of everyday life.[26]

Radio made him an instant star, his catchphrases 'Right, monkey' and 'You'll be lucky' sweeping the nation. From radio he moved onto the variety stage, topping the bill in Blackpool and at the London Palladium. He turned down a role in Frank Randle's film *It's a Grand Life* but replaced Randle at the Adelphi Theatre, London, after his show failed. Why did Read succeed where Randle failed? First, there was nothing 'blue' or suggestive in his material, and second, radio had given him universal appeal. His career faded, however, when television eclipsed radio. He tried television but never liked it and his whole style and format were quintessential radio.

Victoria Wood, on the contrary, is wholly at home on television. She shares with Gracie Fields a naturalness, a down-to-earth common sense and a sharp eye for absurdity. In her songs, sketches and full-length plays such as *Pat and Margaret* she persistently contrasts the snobbery, artificiality and inhumanity of media folk, Southerners and the middle classes with the essential decency and candour of working-class Northerners. But she is fully aware of the dangers in portraying the North, one of her funniest songs, 'Northern Song' tells how as a singer she was a failure until an agent advised her to write Northern songs compounded of clichés. She lists them: tripe, clogs, brassbands, whippets, cloth caps, mushy peas, shawls, hotpot, braces, head scarves, games in the street, privy at the back, gaslight, nutty slack, Gracie Fields, fog, cobbles in the morning mist, fish and chips, next door's mam, Blackpool trams. She concludes by explaining that she derived her clichés from *Coronation Street* and Lowry and her success enables her to spend six months of the year in Crete. The song encapsulates the problems now faced by those seeking to depict life in the North.

The incompetence of institutions and authority were a familiar element in comedy. They were the stock in trade in particular of Robb Wilton (1882–1957), Liverpool-born but Lancastrian in delivery, pace and characterization. His classic sketches, done on radio, records and short films, saw him as a fire chief, a police sergeant, a prison governor and an ARP warden, constantly failing to do his duty by reason of a comic but good-hearted incompetence. He was most popular on radio as a justice of the peace, Mr Muddlecombe, a character he repeated on film, with Gracie Fields (*Love, Life and Laughter*, 1934) and Arthur Askey (*The Love Match*, 1955). The deliberate delivery and the repertoire of mannerisms (tooth-sucking, brow-wiping, finger-chewing) created a character so well-rounded and much-loved that Ken Dodd took it into his gallery of characterizations under the name of Andy Mann.

Several of Frank Randle's film stooges had notable radio careers of their own. The figure of authority in his early films, the perennial sergeant-major, was Harry Korris (1888–1971), who was large, harassed and good-natured. Born in Douglas, Isle of Man, he had appeared throughout the 1930s on Blackpool South Pier in the Arcadia Follies. He enjoyed his greatest success on the radio during the war as the star of *Happidrome*, of which a film version was made in 1943. He played the large, grandiloquent and magnificently seedy old-style actor-manager J. Sheridan Lovejoy, impresario of Happidrome, his North-Country accent periodically breaking through the theatrical lah-de-dah. He was teamed with suave stage manager Ramsbottom (Cecil Fredericks) and gormless assistant Enoch (Robbie Vincent), whose catchphrase was 'Let me tell you'. Their comic misadventures in running their theatre were in the tradition of muddling through also espoused by Will Hay and his team. Their signature tune, 'We three in Happidrome, working for the BBC, Ramsbottom and Enoch and me' was much imitated. Both Cecil Fredericks and Robbie Vincent appeared in supporting roles in Randle films.

Jimmy Clitheroe (1922–73), born in the eponymous town and brought up near Burnley, was a midget who spent his life playing a cheeky schoolboy. He stooged in this guise in films for both George Formby (*Much Too Shy*, 1943) and Frank Randle (*School for Randle*, 1949). But he achieved his greatest success on radio in a Northern domestic sitcom *The Clitheroe Kid*, produced and co-written by James Casey, son of Northern comic Jimmy James, in Manchester. It ran on the BBC from 1958 to 1972. It featured Jimmy in a family with a characteristically Lancastrian matriarchal structure: a long-suffering widowed mother (Patricia Burke), her Scottish pensioner father (Peter Sinclair), a snooty daughter (Diana Day) and her gormless boyfriend, played by George Formby soundalike Danny Ross. Clitheroe was another of the Northern performers who had in real life a dominant mother to whom he was devoted. His death, a suspected suicide, followed shortly after hers.

The North's nineteenth-century pre-eminence was undermined by the massive structural changes in industry and the economy that Britain underwent in the years after World War One. The Depression of the 1920s and 1930s initiated a long process of decline in the staple heavy industries of the North that has continued until the present. Industrial, commercial and financial hegemony in Britain passed irrevocably to the South-East. The great Victorian towns and cities of the North had their hearts ripped out in the redevelopment schemes of the 1960s and the tightly-knit communities were broken up and scattered. Cultural and technological change, centred on the growth of television, motor cars and private housing, promoted a more privatized society in place of the bustling communality of the nineteenth century. All of this had a profound impact on projections of Lancashire and Lancashireness.

The mass media in general, television and the commercialized youth culture in particular, have had a universalizing and, up to a point, Americanizing effect in all areas, including humour. Although there remains a tradition of raucous, scatalogical Northern humour in the Randle vein, it has retreated to the clubs because it is too 'blue' and politically incorrect (in its sexism and racism) for television. It is unrepentantly practised by the likes of Bernard Manning.

There remains a rich tradition of character-based comedy on television, particularly in the work of David Croft and his collaborators (*Dad's Army*, *Hi-de-Hi*, *Are You Being Served?*, '*Allo 'Allo*, *You Rang, M'Lord?*), but few of these are set in the North. The long-running *Last of the Summer Wine* by Roy Clarke, set and filmed in Holmfirth, is a notable exception. But much of the richest and most popular comedy is rooted in the idioms and life patterns of the South, either cockney (*Only Fools and Horses*, *Birds of a Feather*) or suburban (*Keeping Up Appearances*). A Southerner, David Jason, is currently Britain's best-loved comic character actor.

In terms of performers, many post-war comedians have chosen not to emphasize their Northerness, but to draw instead on transatlantic models. Ted Ray (1906–77) was born in Wigan but adopted a mid-Atlantic style of perfectly timed gag-cracking in the manner of George Burns, Fred Allen, Bob Hope and Jack Benny, whom he emulated by using a violin as prop and adjunct to his act. Eric Morecambe (1926–84), born in Morecambe, and Ernie Wise (born in Leeds in 1926), started out in variety but went on to become Britain's best-loved double act on television in the 1960s and 1970s. Their act was rooted in the world of show business in all its aspects and showed little sign of Northerness. Rather the inspiration for the double act, with an overgrown, hyperactive, surreal, adult-child (Eric) and a long-suffering, rather pompous parent-substitute (Ernie), is again America, where Laurel and Hardy, Abbott and Costello and Martin and Lewis had perfected the model.

There have been two notable exceptions to the decline in Northern comedy. One is Liverpool, which, as has already been argued, has always had a distinctive culture and a humour different from that of Cotton Lancashire. It has survived and flourished in the long-running sitcoms of Carla Lane, *The Liver Birds*, *Bread* and *Luv* and in a succession of stand-up comics who exploit the same vein of verbal surrealism as Ken Dodd. The other great standard-bearer of Northern humour was Les Dawson (1935–93), probably the last great representative of the cultural milieu that produced Norman Evans, George Formby and Frank Randle. Les Dawson was born, the son of a bricklayer, in Collyhurst, Manchester, and his humour was rooted in that working-class world that inspired Al Read and in the tradition of using deadpan humour to overcome misery and deprivation. But along with the elaborated anecdotes of Northern misery – their content, style and delivery inspired by Robb Wilton – went an exuberant linguistic grandiloquence, based on his idol W. C. Fields, which often prompted him to claim that his latest story is one he learned 'from the gin-sodden lips of a pock-marked Lascar in the arms of a frump from a Huddersfield bordello'. He also wrote several comic novels, allowing his rich imagination and linguistic inventiveness to take flight on the printed page.

But for the most part today Cotton Lancashire serves as the butt for parodic humour, as in the ITV series *Brass*, starring Timothy West as ruthless Northern mill-owner Bradley Hardacre, a series which hilariously and systematically sent up all the conventions of the North Country 'trouble at t'mill' drama. Liverpudlian Peter Tinniswood more gently and nostalgically but nonetheless thoroughly celebrated all the clichés of Northern life in his novels, the TV series *I Didn't Know You Cared* based on them and in the monologues of his unrepentant Northern chauvinist Uncle Mort, created by Robin Bailey but since played by other actors. Mort is the self-conscious elegist of a lost world:

> All gone now, all of them back to back terraced houses with the women sandstoning the doorsteps and black-leading the tram lines. All of them street corner grocers' shops with sweating bacon joints and tubs of pickled walnuts and bare floorboards stained with mouse droppings. All them pawnshops and black pudding factories and pubs with cast iron spittoons. All swept off the face of the earth. And do you know what they've put in its place? A bloody sports centre ... A sports centre full of silly buggers playing squash in plimsolls and showing the nicks in their arses playing indoor badminton. What's wrong with kicking a tin can about in a cobbled street? ... They were the good old days of the North, them were ... You didn't have dogs on leads in them days. And they bloody well bit you regardless.[27]

But the cultural identity forged in the nineteenth century has two lasting legacies, in the enduring popularity of the paintings of L. S. Lowry and the Granada soap opera *Coronation Street*, which has run continuously since 1960 and which might itself have stepped from the canvases of Lowry. Lowry was a melancholy man who declared: 'I'm attracted to sadness. Everywhere you see suffering and it gets worse. I've a one-track mind. I only deal with poverty, always with gloom. You'll never see a joyous picture of mine. I never do a jolly picture. The thing about painting is that there should be no sentiment.' But it was not the recurrent images of cripples, accidents and funerals that people responded to in Lowry's work. It was the fairgrounds and football matches, the railway stations and factory gates, the VE Day celebrations and Whit Walks processions, the texture of a vanishing world, a nineteenth-century industrial landscape teeming with life. Faced with the destruction of these surroundings, their inhabitants retrospectively imbued Lowry's canvases with their own sentiment and warmth, a longing not for the dirt and noise and poverty of the past but for the communality, comradeship and ordinary decencies that they associated with a world they were rapidly losing. It is for this reason that Lowry inspired a sentimental pop song *Matchstalk Men and Matchstalk Cats and Dogs* and was offered a knighthood by that shrewd populist, Prime Minister Harold Wilson. It also explains the continued affection for *Coronation Street*, which combined the richly comic music-hall tradition with the genre of Northern working-class realism embodied in the work of Harold Brighouse, Stanley Houghton and Walter Greenwood in a celebration of a way of life that for many Northerners, imprisoned in tower blocks or marooned on bleak estates, has ceased to exist.

Notes

1   Jeffrey Richards, *Stars in Our Eyes*, Preston, 1994, p. 2.
2   John K. Walton, *Lancashire*, Manchester, 1987, pp. 283–324.
3   J. B. Priestley, *English Journey*, London, 1968, pp. 397–402.
4   See for instance, Robert Roberts, *The Classic Slum*, Harmondsworth,1973 (on Salford); Bill Naughton, *On the Pig's Back*, Oxford,1987 and *Saintly Billy*, Oxford,1988 (on Bolton); Don Haworth, *Figures in a Bygone Landscape*, London, 1986 and *Bright Morning*, London,1990 (on Bacup); William Woodruff, *Billy Boy*, Halifax,1993 (on Blackburn); Elizabeth Roberts, *A Woman's Place*, Oxford, 1984 (on Lancaster,Preston and Barrow).
5   Richard Hoggart, *The Use of Literacy*, Harmondsworth, 1958, pp. 102–12.
6   Patrick Joyce, *Visions of the People*, Cambridge, 1991.
7   Frank Ormerod, *Lancashire Life and Character*, Manchester, 1915.
8   Sir Henry Miers, 'Some Characteristics of Manchester Man' in W. H. Brindley (ed.), *The Soul of Manchester*, Manchester, 1929, p. 36.
9   Priestley, *English Journey*, p. 253.
10 D. C. Jones, *The Social Survey of Merseyside*, Liverpool, 1934, p. 281.
11 Leslie Halliwell, *Seats in all Parts*, London, 1985, p. 12.
12 Gary Cross (ed.), *Worktowners in Blackpool*, London, 1990, pp. 132–5.
13 Priestley, *English Journey*, p. 253.
14 Alan Randall and Ray Seaton, *George Formby*, London, 1974, p. 15.
15 Geoffrey Gorer, *Exoploring English Character*, London, 1955, pp. 302–3.
16 Basil Dean, *Mind's Eye*, London, 1973, p. 212.
17 *The Sunday Times*, 13 January 1963.
18 Nicholas Pronay and D. W. Spring (eds), *Propaganda, Politics and Films, 1918–1945*, London, 1982, p. 238.
19 George Orwell, *Collected Essays, Journalism and Letters*, volume 2, Harmondsworth, 1971, p. 79.
20 *World Film News* 1 (June 1936), p. 5.
21 *The Spectator* 18 August 11939.
22 Orwell, *Collected Essays*, volume 2, p. 78.
23 Julian Poole, 'British Cinema Attendance in Wartime: audience preference at the Majestic Macclesfield, 1939–1948', *Historical Journal of Film, Radio and Television*, 7 (1987), pp. 15–34.
24 John Fisher, *Funny Way to Be a Hero*, St. Albans, 1976, p. 177.
25 Al Read, *It's All in the Book*, London, 1985, pp. 17–20.
26 Read, *It's All in the Book*, pp. 68–71.
27 Peter Tinniswood, *Uncle Mort's North Country*, London, 1987, p. 37.

Part IV

Culture

10

Vaughan Williams, the cinema and England

In his 1912 article entitled 'Who Wants the English composer?', Vaughan Williams set out his understanding of the role of the composer in society. The composer 'must live with his fellows and make his art the expression of the whole life of the community', cultivating 'a sense of musical citizenship'; he should as a servant of the state 'build national monuments'; and he could 'take and purify and raise to the level of great art' the popular forms of musical expression.[1] These remained central strands of his philosophy and in the supreme national crisis of wartime, he put his beliefs into practice by entering the sphere of film music, which had hitherto gone largely unnoticed critically but was an integral part of people's lives and entertainment, and was precisely one of those forms of national expression to be taken and purified and raised to the level of great art.

Just as British films attained 'a golden age' in the 1940s, so too did British film music. The war transformed the standing of film music in Britain. As John Huntley noted in his classic study, *British Film Music* (1947): 'Almost every modern British composer has nowadays made some contribution to the film.'[2] It was the war that made the difference. Personal commitments to the struggle against Fascism led artists and intellectuals in unprecedented numbers to put their talents to the service of the national effort, to celebrate the united struggle of a free people against a monstrous tyranny. The composers who did so included Sir Arnold Bax, Constant Lambert, Lord Berners, Lennox Berkeley, Noel Mewton-Wood and William Walton. Many of their film scores were arranged as concert suites and performed both in live concerts and on BBC radio which regularly featured film music throughout the war. Some of them were also issued on gramophone records.

It is not surprising that Vaughan Williams, generally acknowledged as the doyen of Britain's serious music composers, should have thrown himself enthusiastically into the wartime film effort. In a 1940 broadcast talk on the role of the composer in wartime, he called for the composer to 'serve the community directly through his craft'. He suggested that the composer without derogating from his art, without being untrue to himself, could 'use his skill, his knowledge, his sense of beauty in the service of his fellow men'. He concluded: 'Art is a compromise between what we want to achieve and what circumstances allow us to achieve. It is out of these very compromises that the supreme art often springs: the highest comes when you least expect it.'[3] Here was the rationale for his entry into film music.

His introduction to films came through Muir Mathieson, long established as the leading musical director in films. During the war he was Director of Music for the Ministry of Information and responsible for commissioning the scores for their film productions. Mathieson had clear views about the role of music in the documentary. He saw it compensating in part for the absence of star names, Technicolor and large-scale publicity campaigns from which feature films benefited.

> Music plays a doubly important part, providing, as it must, a larger than usual share of the entertainment. Music can help to humanize the subject and widen its appeal. Music can make a film less intellectual and more emotional. It can influence the reaction of the audience to any given sequence.[4]

His first wartime encounter with Vaughan Williams, however, was in connection with the Ministry of Information's only major feature film production, *49th Parallel.* Mathieson recalled visiting Vaughan Williams at his Dorking home to sound him out about composing the score for the film.

> When I went to see Vaughan Williams at his country home in the spring of 1940, I found him strangely depressed at his inability to play a fuller part in the war. He felt that the musicians had done little to express the spirit and resolve of the British people. At this time he was 'doing his bit' by driving a cart round the village and countryside, collecting scrap metal and salvage ... I told him the story of *49th Parallel* and tried to show how the cinema could help to achieve those very objects for which he was striving. He got to work right away – and remember this was the first time he had ever consented to write for the screen5.

Vaughan Williams set down his ideas about composing for films in an essay he contributed to the *R.C.M. Magazine* in 1945. Given the time constraints placed upon the production of the music, the necessity to write to existing action, dialogue and structure; the requirement to cut, to extend, to compress on demand, he asks if any art is possible, and answers: 'Yes, if we go the right way to work.'

There were two ways of writing film music, 'one is that in which every action, word, gesture or incident is punctuated by sound.' That approach he felt was too scrappy. He preferred 'to ignore the details and intensify the spirit of the whole situation by a continuous stream of music', which could be modified where appropriate 'by points of colour superimposed on the flow'. He believed 'the film contains the potentialities for the combination of all the arts such as Wagner never dreamt of'. So he outlined his ideal position in which music would be central to the whole conception of film making.

Author, director, photographer and composer should agree in advance on the emphasis and direction of the music, and it should be composed ahead of shooting for the actors to hear as they rehearsed. The result would be 'a great film' which 'will be built up on the basis of music'. Vaughan Williams concluded:

> I have often talked over these difficulties with authors, directors and conductors; they have been inclined in theory to agree with me. I acknowledge with gratitude that when I have worked with them they have, within their scheme, stretched every possible point to give my ignorantly composed music its chance, but they have not yet been able to break down the essentially wrong system by which the various arts are segregated and only reassembled at the last moment, instead of coming together from the beginning. It is only when this is achieved that the film will come into its own as one of the finest of the fine arts,[6]

As it happens, apparently unbeknownst to Vaughan Williams, this had already occurred. In 1936 the German Friedrich Feher had composed the score for a film called *The Robber Symphony* and had then directed the film to fit the score. It was a very strange film. With Expressionist sets and surrealistic story, lifted from the classic children's story *Emil and the Detectives*, the film was described by Graham Greene, then a film critic, as 'restless, scatter-brained, amusing, boring, cheap, lyrical, farcical'.[7] But the trade paper *Kine Weekly* described it as 'too artistic and whimsical for any but the most high class districts' and it was not a success with audiences.[8] The same procedure was later followed by Michael Powell and Emeric Pressburger in their film *The Tales of*

Hoffman (1951), designed and shot to Offenbach's pre-recorded score. But both films were way beyond the taste and expectations of the mass film audience. The role of film music continued to be to underline and punctuate the action, to focus and heighten emotion. It was a subordinate though important role.

Vaughan Williams's method of work was different from that of the Hollywood composers. In Hollywood the composer would normally run the rough-cut of the picture first in its entirety, then reel by reel, and, in consultation with the director, producer, film editor and music editor, would agree a set of cues and timings for the score, and the composer would write the required music rapidly. Owing to the speed required of the composer, it would often be orchestrated by someone else, as he continued the task of preparing the main themes. The music would then be recorded with the film being run on a screen behind the orchestra, timings were made and the recorded music was finally dubbed on to the soundtrack and mixed with the dialogue and sound effects.[9]

Vaughan Williams worked in a much more detached manner. He would receive a script and a set of cues and often composed his score before the film was even finished. He then left it to the musical director to fit it to the finished film, remaining ever-ready to make whatever adjustments and alterations the director required. This procedure enabled him to pursue his philosophy of providing a score consisting of a continuous stream of music paralleling the action rather than, as in Hollywood, underlining the action and often the dialogue. The scores of *The Loves of Joanna Godden*, *Scott of the Antarctic* and *Coastal Command* were all delivered this way. His method of writing had a beneficial by-product. Because he was writing continuous passages of music, coherent and self-contained in their own right, it was easier to arrange it into concert suites, as happened with several of his scores.

He was very fortunate in the musical directors with whom he worked because they held his music in the highest regard. Muir Mathieson was musical director on *49th Parallel* (1941), *Coastal Command* (1942), *The Flemish Farm* (1943), *The People's Land* (1943) and *Stricken Peninsula* (1945). *Coastal Command* was Vaughan Williams's first pure documentary assignment and his music fulfilled exactly the role that Mathieson envisaged for documentary scores. Mathieson recalled that for *Coastal Command* Vaughan Williams 'composed a delightful score which met with the unqualified approval of everyone both inside and outside the unit'.[10] The respect with which the music was treated was recalled by sound recordist Ken Cameron:

When we heard the music, we knew that here was something great, something indeed finer and more alive than any music we have ever had before. Nor did we waste. On the rare occasions when the music was slightly too long or too short to match the existing picture, then it was the visual material which suffered the mutilation. The music for *Coastal Command* is as Vaughan Williams composed it.[11]

Mathieson subsequently created a concert suite from the *Coastal Command* score, as he did later from the music for T*he England of Elizabeth*. Vaughan Williams's other musical director was Ernest Irving of Ealing Studios, who commissioned, conducted and supervised the scoring of *The Loves of Joanna Godden* (1946), *Scott of the Antarctic* (1948) and *Bitter Springs* (1950). Like Mathieson, Irving believed in recruiting the best of contemporary composers to score Ealing's films. He wrote in 1943:

Recently there has been a welcome tendency on the part of film 'magnates' to commission musicians of repute to provide scores for the films. There is no reason why a master *should* write more effective film music than a hack, for artistic merit and authenticity of style have no 'film value' per se, but it is pleasing to record that in point of fact they do.[12]

During the war Irving drew on the services of William Walton, Lord Berners, John Ireland, Alan Rawsthorne, Gordon Jacob and Frederic Austin to provide scores for Ealing films. It was Irving who thought Vaughan Williams the ideal composer for *The Loves of Joanna Godden*, even though in his 1943 article he was critical of the score for *Coastal Command*, thinking it 'perhaps not quite up to his best standard; neither was it particularly good film music. Solid, musicianly and melodious, of course.'[13] He also disagreed with Vaughan Williams's idea of the role of film music, writing:

Dr. Vaughan Williams has an idea that the film should be shot to the accompaniment of the music, but here I think he is over-valuing the composer's work. Millions of people who go to films know nothing about music at all, and there are quite a number of film fans who positively dislike music.

He believed that the composer's score:

must not be allowed to be a stumbling block or to prevent the enjoyment of the pictorial side by people who are not in sympathy with him. That implies that the music must always be subsidiary and ancillary and cannot be allowed to develop on formal lines for musical reasons only; it is not being played at a concert, its principal effect should be upon the subconscious mind, and if the film is a good film the music will be felt rather than listened to.[14]

But he was delighted with the score for *The Loves of Joanna Godden* ('it is the best music we have ever had here'), was instrumental in securing Vaughan Williams's services for *Scott of the Antarctic* and played an important role in ensuring that the music emerged as Vaughan Williams wanted it.[15] Michael Kennedy records: 'How much was owed to Ernest Irving's tactful and understanding mediation can never be overstated.'[16] Vaughan Williams acknowledged this by dedicating the score of the *Sinfonia Antarctica* to Irving.

Both his wartime and post-war film scores involved Vaughan Williams defining Englishness in musical terms. Vaughan Williams was profoundly convinced that music must be national in its origin, endorsing Parry's view that 'style is ultimately national', and rejecting the idea that the 'artist invents for himself alone'. Anyone who set out to be cosmopolitan, he thought, must fail:

> The greatest monuments of music ... have worldwide appeal, but first they must appeal to the people and in the circumstances where they were created ... Every composer may reasonably expect to have a special message for his own people ... Many young composers make the mistake of imagining they can be universal without at first having been local. What a composer has to do is to find out the real message he has to convey to the community and say it directly and without equivocation ... If the roots of your art are firmly planted in your soul, and that soul has anything individual to give you, you may still gain the whole world and not lose your soul.[17]

This view parallels almost word for word that of Sir Michael Balcon, the head of Ealing Studios. His studio was committed to making films 'projecting Britain and the British character'. He wrote in his autobiography: 'My ruling passion has always been the building up of a native (film) industry in the soil of this country.' He rejected in retrospect the 1930s policy of importing American stars and trying to make cosmopolitan films, testifying to his 'growing conviction that films, to be international, must be thoroughly national in the first instance, and that there is nothing wrong with a degree of cultural chauvinism'.[18]

In 1945 Balcon outlined a programmatic schedule for post-war film-making that demonstrated a high level of civic responsibility and patriotic pride:

> The world must be presented with a complete picture of Britain ... Britain as a leader in Social Reform in the defeat of social injustice and a champion of civil liberties; Britain as a patron and parent of great writ-

ing, painting and music; Britain as a questing explorer, adventurer and trader; Britain as the home of great industry and craftsmanship; Britain as a mighty military power standing alone and undaunted against terrifying aggression.[19]

It is no coincidence that Vaughan Williams worked for Ealing on three films (*The Loves of Joanna Godden, Scott of the Antarctic, Bitter Springs*) or that his film *oeuvre* embraced many of the same themes: the resistance to tyranny and the championship of civil liberties figured strongly in *49th Parallel, Stricken Peninsula* and *Flemish Farm*; exploring and adventuring in *Scott of the Antarctic* and *Bitter Springs*; industry and craftsmanship in *Dim Little Island*; and virtually all the themes were recapitulated in *The England of Elizabeth*.

Vaughan Williams's principal definition of Englishness in his films as elsewhere in his work lay deeper still, in the pastoral and in the visionary. His great achievement was to unite the two. The rural myth, pumped out in poems, novels, paintings and music since the 1880s, had a direct effect on evocations of the national character. The Englishman was said to be at heart a countryman and his character thanks to his rural roots – to be based upon the principles of balance, peacefulness, traditionalism and spirituality.[20] In wartime, the countryside was a peculiarly potent image. For while cities could be blitzed and bombed, the countryside remained – eternal, timeless, self-renewing and indestructible, a fitting symbol for Britain at bay. The musical symbol of all this was folk song. Vaughan Williams believed that song was the basis of all music and that purely instrumental music was a later development. Folksong was 'the spiritual lifeblood of the people' – intuitive, oral, applied, purely melodic, 'an art which grows straight out of the needs of a people'. Church music derived from folk music and Vaughan Williams saw in church music a continuous tradition of organized response to the need for spiritual expression. By applying folk tunes to the words of well-loved hymns in *The English Hymnal* he effectively fused the two great expressions of the people's music, implementing his own stated belief: 'The composer must love the tunes of his own country and they must become an integral part of himself.'[21] The pastoral image and the centrality of folk song received full expression in *The People's Land* (1943), *Dim Little Island* (1949), *The Loves of Joanna Godden* (1946) and *The England of Elizabeth* (1957), while the visionary aspects of Englishness were expressed in *Scott of the Antarctic* (1948) and the *The Vision of William Blake* (1958).[22]

But how did Vaughan Williams reconcile his intense English nationalism with his socialism? Easily – as he outlined in 1942:

We all want peace, we all want international friendship, we all want to give up hateful rivalries of nations; we must learn to plan the world internationally, we must unite or we shall perish. This is a very different thing from that emasculated standardization of life, which will add cultural to political internationalism.

Vaughan Williams believed that political internationalism could coexist perfectly comfortably with cultural nationalism:

> I believe that love of one's country, one's language, one's religion, are essential to our spiritual health. We may laugh at these things but we love them nonetheless. Indeed it is one of our national characteristics and one which I should be sorry to see disappear, that we laugh at what we love. This is something that a foreigner can never fathom, but it is out of such characteristics, these hard knots in our timber, that we can help to build up a united Europe and a world federation … I agree that loyalty to one's country can only come to full flowering when it is merged in a wider loyalty to the whole human race. But without that local loyalty there can be nothing for the wider issues to build on. I believe that all that is of value on our spiritual and cultural life springs from our own soil; but this life cannot develop and fructify except in the atmosphere of friendship and sympathy with other nations.[23]

It is not, therefore, surprising to find this 'quintessential English composer' providing the music for films about other countries, both in Europe (Belgium for *The Flemish Farm*, Italy for *Stricken Peninsula*) and in the Commonwealth (Canada for *49th Parallel* and Australia for *Bitter Springs*).

His film music cannot be isolated from his other music. It is all part of an organic whole in which there is both continuity and development. This can be seen most obviously in the history of his involvement with Bunyan's *Pilgrim's Progress* from the twelve episodes of incidental music provided in 1909 for the Reigate Priory production through the pastoral episode *Shepherds of the Delectable Mountains* (1921–2), the score of the 1942 radio dramatization, the Fifth Symphony (1943) and eventually the long-cherished opera in 1951–52. In the same way, the film scores relate to the main body of his work, on several occasions inspiring and generating new work, most notably of course *Sinfonia Antartica* developing out of the score for *Scott of the Antarctic*. Vaughan Williams very much enjoyed writing film music, as both Ursula Vaughan Williams and Michael Kennedy testify.[24] He relished the challenges it threw up, for instance to provide music to illustrate an outbreak of foot and mouth disease in *Joanna Godden* or penguins on the ice in *Scott*, subjects that would have been unlikely to come his way in the normal run of things. But the experience

Democracy versus Fascism: *49th Parallel* (1941) with John Chandos, Leslie Howard   **28**
and Eric Portman.

of writing for films also enriched his musical language, his flexibility, his use of
orchestral colour and his freedom in writing. Since film music is the ultimate
in programme music, a close examination of the films Vaughan Williams chose
to score and how he went about it may tell us more about the meaning of his
'serious music', for which he was notoriously reluctant to accept the programmatic interpretations offered by critics.

Powell and Pressburger's *49th Parallel* was the only full-length feature film
to be financed by the MoI. It aimed to fulfil the Ministry's propaganda objectives: to show what Britain was fighting for, how Britain fights and the need for
sacrifice if the war is to be won.[25] After it, the Ministry concentrated on financ-
ing a programme of short documentary films, leaving the commercial industry to provide the features. But the Ministry retained control of the allocation
of film stock, suggested themes and subjects through its ideas committee and
provided technical assistance rather than finance. But initially it invested heavily in *49th Parallel*, which emerged as one of the great films of the war and one
of the best works of Britain's premier film-making team, Michael Powell and

Emeric Pressburger. On *49th Parallel*, Powell directed and Pressburger provided the original story and then wrote the script with Rodney Ackland. The aim of the film, which was shot partly on location in Canada, was, according to Powell, 'to scare the pants off the Americans, and bring them into the war sooner'.[26] It sought to pay tribute to Canada, to stress Canadian-American friendship and outline programmatically the evils of Nazism. Powell and Pressburger lined up a distinguished roster of stars.

The film told the gripping story of a stranded crew of Nazi submariners making their way across Canada towards the neutral United States and encountering *en route* various representatives of democracy. An uncommitted French-Canadian trapper (Laurence Olivier) turns against the Nazis when they maltreat the 'racially inferior' Eskimos. An immigrant community of German Hutterites, led by Anton Walbrook, demonstrate the workability of a system of democratic equality, cooperation and Christian love. A donnish aesthete (Leslie Howard), who is writing a book on Red Indian customs and culture, beats one of the Nazis to a pulp when the Nazis burn his 'decadent' books and pictures. Finally, an ordinary Canadian soldier (Raymond Massey), the grumbling individualistic democratic 'Everyman', takes on and defeats the ruthless Nazi superman commanding the fugitives (Eric Portman). The Nazis are thus effectively depicted as standing for cruelty, tyranny, racism, arrogance and philistinism. The action of the film encompasses the whole of Canada from the icy wastes of Hudson Bay to the grain-filled prairies, from the deep dark forests and lonely limpid lakes to the frontier where at one end the mighty crashing Niagara Falls marks the undefended boundary with the United States.[27]

Vaughan Williams's score was clearly regarded as a major prestige coup and he was billed as one of the stars of the film, the credits reading: Leslie Howard, Laurence Olivier, Raymond Massey, Anton Walbrook, Eric Portman and the music of Ralph Vaughan Williams in *49th Parallel*. Given Vaughan Williams's preferred method of work, his score inevitably functions very much more as a series of musical interludes rather than the sort of cohesive and integrated musical texture that Korngold and Steiner achieved in Hollywood films.

The prelude is a broad, stately theme which musically encapsulates the breadth and majesty of Canada. It is followed by a visual evocation of the landscape of Canada, of mountains, wheatfield, rivers and cities, with a sweeping grandiose passage of music, featuring 'O Canada', the Canadian national anthem. As the scene changes to the Gulf of St Lawrence, a submarine rises, to a dark-toned version of 'Ein feste Burg', the Lutheran hymn, which develops into sinister agitated variations; an ironic comment, surely, on the perversion of German faith by the Nazis. This theme recurs in the urgent pursuit music that accompanies the submarine's escape northwards to elude pursuing Canadian planes. As the submarine passes icebergs, we hear eerie, sombre music which contains the first seeds of the *Scott of the Antarctic* score. Then a menacing falling staccato figure punctuates the texture, a phrase that recurs throughout the Nazis' flight across Canada. At Hudson's Bay trading post, cheerful flowing watery music accompanies scenes of Eskimos in their kayaks and a jaunty version of *Alouette*, the first appearance of the French Canadian trapper (Laurence Olivier). A folk song figures, too, in the encounter with the Hutterite girl (Glynis Johns), who is first discovered singing a German song, 'Lasst uns das Kindlein Wiegen'. The Hutterite harvest is accompanied by English harvesting music with vigorous dance patterns. The Nazis walk across Canada to rhythmic walking music. From Banff on Indian Day, evoked by a snatch of Red Indian-type music, the Nazis flee to agitato pursuit music, with the menacing phrase from the Nazi submarine recurring. When the Nazis encounter Leslie Howard at the Lake, their conversation takes place against a piece of piano music, impressionistic, light and delicate. The film ends with a reprise of the prelude as the beaten Nazi is shunted back across the border from the United States to Canada. Throughout the music is either functional or atmospheric, heightening emotion or scene-setting. It is mostly competent rather than outstanding.

But Vaughan Williams was well aware of what elements within the score could be retrieved. A suite was prepared from the music and played at a festival of British film music in Prague in 1946 but this was subsequently suppressed by the composer.[28] The prelude survived, however, to be recorded by Bernard Herrmann for an LP of British film music in 1976 and by Andrew Penny for a 1993 CD of Vaughan Williams's film music. It was also arranged for organ by Christopher Morris in 1960 and was set to words as an anthem *The New Commonwealth* by Harold Child, librettist of his opera *Hugh the Drover*, for unison voices with piano or orchestral accompaniment. Its optimistic and uplifting sentiments stress international brotherhood, the triumph of faith, hope and love over hate and fear, and emphasizes the tune's hymnlike properties, underlining the vision of the war as a struggle for Christian civilization. *The Lake in the Mountains* music appeared as a solo piano piece under that title and dedicated to Phyllis Sellick in 1947.[29] The music had largely been lost in the film, heavily damped down under dialogue between Leslie Howard and Eric Portman. It emerged as a tranquil, impressionistic piece, opening with an English pastoral melody, sounding like gentle running water with a sudden threatening change from B-flat to F-sharp minor. After the pastoral melody is elaborated, it returns to F-sharp minor, developing the air of menace and ending with a bleak D minor. There is no musical reason for the change but in the context of the film it signals the arrival of the Nazis in the hitherto peaceful location.

The Nazi theme recurred in the scherzo of the Second String Quartet, composed in 1943–44. The Sixth Symphony has often been seen as Vaughan Williams's response to the war. Sir Malcolm Sargent for instance called it

> A frightening symphony … here we have a complete testament of a man who, in his seventies, looks back on the human sufferings of his time. I never conduct the Sixth without feeling that I am walking across bomb sites … Chaos, despair, desolation and the peace that flows from desolation.[30]

Vaughan Williams always denied the validity of such interpretations. But his film music gives us an important interpretative clue to the inspiration to such works. The Second String Quartet is a product of the same period of musical development as the Sixth Symphony and can be seen to share the same mood. The first three movements are bleak, anguished and jagged, and the scherzo repeats over and over again the stabbing motif that accompanied the Nazis in *49th Parallel*, the title of which Vaughan Williams marked in his score against this movement. The final movement is also a product of his involvement in the cinema. The movement is marked 'Greetings from Joan to Jean'. The Jean is Jean Stewart, violinist of the Menges Quartet and the dedicatee of the piece. The Joan is St Joan and the main theme of the movement comes from his sketches for a score for a film on St Joan which never materialized.

Although details about the film are lacking, it can only be the long-mooted film version of Shaw's play. In 1943 film tycoon J. Arthur Rank formed a partnership with Hungarian producer Gabriel Pascal to make three Shaw films. Pascal had already produced film versions of *Pygmalion* (1938) and *Major Barbara* (1940). Shaw had entrusted him with exclusive rights for filming his plays, and films of *St Joan, Caesar and Cleopatra* and *The Doctor's Dilemma* were planned. Shaw was working on the scenario and, given Pascal and Shaw's commitment to employing leading composers (Arthur Honegger scored *Pygmalion* and William Walton *Major Barbara*), it seems highly likely that Vaughan William was approached to do the music, and in keeping with his usual working methods had started sketching the score. Shaw had originally intended that the score for any film version of *St Joan* would be written by John Foulds, who had composed the highly praised score for the stage play in 1924.

But Foulds had died of cholera in India in 1939.[31] What Foulds and Vaughan Williams shared was a deep sense of spirituality in their music, which was what was required for this subject.

But the project was abandoned. This was due in part to the difficulty in finding a suitable actress to play Joan – Greta Garbo, Katharine Hepburn, Wendy Hiller, Deborah Kerr and Ingrid Bergman were all considered at various times and rejected for various reasons. But more seriously, the Ministry of Information, who had the final say on film projects, objected that 'it would be the most injudicious time to make a film about St. Joan and remind their French allies of England's little mistake in burning their saint.'[32] Shaw and Pascal switched their attention to *Caesar and Cleopatra* which became notorious as one of the most expensive films in British history. The final movement of the String Quartet preserves what would have been Joan's theme, a serene and spiritual theme which concludes the turbulence and agony of the first three movements on a note of uplift. Is there not a key here to Vaughan Williams's thinking? The bleakness and cruelty of war (embodied in the Nazi theme from *49th Parallel*) is transcended ultimately by the faith and spirituality of St Joan, who died in the service of her country against cruel invaders. 'Nowhere,' writes Hubert Foss of this movement, 'has Vaughan Williams written music so philosophical, so resigned, so restful in simplicity.'[33]

If *49th Parallel* was Vaughan Williams's contribution to 'Why We Fight', his next film *Coastal Command* showed 'How We Fight'. Produced by the Crown Film Unit and directed by J. B. Holmes, this film like other notable wartime documentaries (*Target for Tonight, Fires Were Started, Merchant Seamen, Western Approaches*) – utilized men and women of the armed forces playing themselves. Seventy-one minutes long, tightly constructed and impressively shot, the film does for Coastal Command what the more celebrated *Target for Tonight* did for Bomber Command. A narrator introduces the film explaining that behind the drama of attacks, lies the 'ceaseless, patient, humdrum vigil of patrol' and the film takes us to Portferry Bay in Scotland where Ralph Reader is appearing with his RAF Gang Show entertaining the crews when the show is interrupted by a call for the crew of Sunderland Flying Boat T for Tommy. The Sunderland is sent off to protect a convoy. Their patrol is uneventful but they sight and report a German sub, which is sunk by their relief, a Catalina flying boat. The German raider *Düsseldorf* is reported to be leaving Norway. T for Tommy is sent to shadow it. They lose her but eventually spot her after a search. Hudson bombers and Beaufighters take off from Ireland to sink the ship. She is duly crippled. The Sunderland is sent in to report on damage, get information back but is hit by flak and loses its port engine. Attacked by a Junkers 88, the Sunderland is rescued by an Australian-crewed flying boat and limps back to Portferry. As the skipper, Lieutenant Campbell visits his injured men, he tells them that they are to be transferred to West Africa.

The film is a highly effective dramatized re-creation of the work of Coastal Command. But what it remarkable is the tone throughout. Like so many wartime films, it is a study in British character. Both on the flying boat T for Tommy and back in the control room, the prevailing mood is one of quiet dedication, unselfconscious professionalism, self-deprecating good humour. The skipper has a dog and there is much smoking of pipes and drinking of cups of tea. Continuing strands of the film are the calm methodical routine of the Ops room, the warm camaraderie, good-natured banter and efficiency of the crew. It is impossible not to notice the class difference between the strangulated upper-class drawl of the skipper, Lieutenant Campbell, and the unaffected regional accents of the crew – Hughie, Roy, Sean, Pam, Joe, Jammy, Henry, Izzy, Lew – who are Welsh, Irish, Northern, Southern, Jewish – but the film emphasizes the cross-class cooperation and genuine sympathy and affection between the crew and the shared qualities of dedication and good humour. The imperial angle is unobtrusively stressed, as Canadians participate in the attack on the *Düsseldorf* and Australians crew the relief flying boat. The overall unity and comradeship is stressed by their participation in the audience of the Gang Show, a common device in wartime films, showing all ranks, both sexes, many different Allied nations' personnel, sharing enjoyment of and participation in an entertainment. It fulfils the MoI criteria of showing how we fight, British character and the need for sacrifice (Hughie is shot in the arm; Pam is burned by escaping petrol).

Vaughan Williams's score for *Coastal Command* is consciously heroic, celebrating the deeds of the RAF but also seeking to evoke British character. It opens with a vigorous prelude which encapsulates the main musical themes of the score, including a folklike theme which recurs throughout. A piece of mood music evokes Portferry in the Hebrides and T for Tommy floating at anchor – a delicate, wistful evocation of sea, wind and mystery, which again looks forward to *Scott*. The attack on the U-boat is urgent and arresting with a hint of Satan's dance from *Job*, a sea-shanty rhythm but orchestral and agitated. Three percussive chords signal the crash of the bombs on the U-boat. But Ken Cameron's observation that the music took precedence over the visuals is borne out by the fact that the three chords occur in the music after the bombs have fallen and the submarine has been sunk.

A majestic, broad, expansive theme, recalling the end of the Fifth Symphony, covers the return of the Sunderland and a stately, solemn tune as it takes off again. As the Hudsons take off in Iceland, the main theme of the score is reworked. The music revs up along with the planes and then soars gracefully into the sky with the strings, across the rugged landscape of Iceland and into the clouds, tailing off gently with a clarinet recapitulation of the main theme. As the Sunderland searches, strings are plucked to indicate the ticking of a clock; the tempo increases as the search goes on with the basic motif repeated with variations. Then as the Beauforts attack, the broad heroic theme becomes aggressive. As the Sunderland goes in close, there comes the passage marked by Vaughan Williams 'quiet determination', the musical encapsulation of 'how we fight', the heroic theme taken up on clarinet and oboe. The tone gradually darkens as the plane emerges from the clouds and then full-blooded brass chords signal the flak hitting home. The attack music is repeated, as Beaufighters come to the rescue and, after a final triumphant surge of the heroic theme, there is the serene landing music and the expansive optimistic ending as they take off for West Africa.

In 1943 Muir Mathieson constructed a seven-movement suite from the music for Coastal Command, which was dedicated to the RAF. It included the title music; the island station in the Hebrides; taking off at night; Hudsons taking off from Iceland; the battle of the Beauforts; the Sunderland goes in close ('quiet determination'); the J88 attack and finale. In 1992 Christopher Palmer constructed an eight-movement suite from the score, adding the U-boat attack to the music Muir Mathieson had used. Both scores reversed the order of the Beaufort attack and the 'quiet determination' movements from that in the actual film. Two new CD recordings of this suite reveal it as a richly textured, deeply felt score, well worth retrieving and a marked advance on the score for *49th Parallel.*

The Flemish Farm (1943) was made with the cooperation of the Belgian government in exile and the Air Ministry and was based on a true story. Directed by Jeffrey Dell and written by Dell and his then wife, Jill Craigie, the film opens in 1940 with the last five planes of the Belgian Air Force fighter squadrons stationed on a Flemish farm near the coast. When news of the Belgian surrender comes through, the commandant, Major Lessart (Clive Brook), orders the regimental standard to be destroyed to prevent it falling into enemy hands. It is formally buried at sea. When the Germans bomb the farm, the surviving planes take off, with two friends, Matagne (Philip Friend) and Duclos (Clifford Evans), sharing the cockpit of one aircraft. A year later in Britain where both are now serving with the RAF, Matagne reveals to Duclos that he had secretly buried the real flag on the farm, at Lessart's orders, and the sea burial had been staged to fool the Germans. He also reveals he had secretly married the farmer's daughter, Tresha (Jane Baxter), and she had helped him bury it. He plans to return and retrieve the flag. But Matagne is killed in the Battle of Britain and Duclos gets permission to go instead. Parachuting into Belgium, Duclos makes contact with Lessart, now leading the local resistance, reaches the farm and with Tresha's help retrieves the flag. The remainder of the film concerns his adventures as he escapes across Belgium and France to safety. Before he leaves Belgium, however, he learns that Lessart has given himself up to the Germans who have taken hostages for the murder of one of their agents. Lessart confesses to the murder and is shot but the hostages are released. Duclos, however, succeeds in getting the flag back to Britain where it is presented to the Belgian squadron of the RAF.

The film fulfils completely the MoI's stress on the need for sacrifice if the war is to be won. The film is constructed of a series of heroic sacrifices. The lovers Tresha and Matagne sacrifice their happiness together so that he can serve in the air force in England; Matagne sacrifices his life in the Battle of Britain; Lessart sacrifices his life to save the hostages. But all this is worthwhile because the struggle against tyranny and Fascism will go on. The Air Force standard becomes a holy relic, a symbol of resistance, faith and struggle, the guarantee that Belgium will continue to fight, whatever the cost, until the war is won and freedom restored. Several characters in the film comment on the symbolism of the flag and the Germans' desperation to lay hands on it show that they appreciate this equally.

The film is richly scored, illustrating a variety of moods and episodes, with the emphasis on heroism, sacrifice and spiritual uplift. The title music, full of fanfares, contains what sounds like a Flemish hymn or folk song, which recurs throughout the film, as when the flag is located on the farm. The music that accompanies the burial of the flag is noble and elegiac, with a stirring fanfare to indicate continuing defiance. By contrast, there is a wistful, lyrical love theme surging up as the lovers kiss in the barn at dawn before parting forever. There is a jaunty little tune, likened not inaptly by A. E. F. Dickinson to a calypso, as Duclos walks through the town and meets Lessart at a café. There is menace in the music that accompanies the Germans' search of the cart conveying Duclos and the flag from the farm.[34] A slow, solemn, sombre passage building up to a crescendo accompanies Lessart's last walk towards German headquarters. Then there is quite a lengthy passage of escape music, similar to the exciting and agitated passages accompanying such episodes in previous films, but also including a heroic march theme which is repeated and reworked. There is a final recapitulation of the main theme as the flag is re-presented to the squadron.

Vaughan Williams thought well enough of this music to retrieve much of it for a 26-minute concert suite, *The Story of a Flemish Farm.* It consisted of seven movements: 1) The Flag flutters in the wind; 2) Night by the sea. Farewell to the Flag; 3) Dawn in the barn. The parting of the lovers; 4) In the Belgian café; 5) The Major goes to meet his fate; 6) The dead man's kit; 7) The wanderings of the Flag. This enabled the music to assume a more permanent form and to get a proper hearing. In the film itself, for instance, the music accompanying Duclos's examination of the dead Matagne's kit is the merest snatch, and the lovers' music was considerably banked down behind the dialogue. The suite was premiered at the Proms on 31 July 1945 with Vaughan Williams conducting the London Symphony Orchestra at the Royal Albert Hall. The *Musical Times* considered it the best of that season's novelties. Their review confirms the coherence and musicality of Vaughan Williams's film scores:

> One feared that film music separated from the action it is meant to describe and emphasize might lose some of its vividness, or perhaps that the duties imposed by the brisk doings on the screen had robbed the composer of the liberty of developing his ideas freely. The event proved such fears to be completely unfounded. Not only has each period full development, but each episode contrasts with the rest as effectively as the main sections in any well-built symphony. Between the war-like tunes that rightly begin and close the suite Vaughan Williams has provided chapters cast in very different moods. One describes the parting of two lovers with extraordinary tenderness; the other is concerned with the search amongst the effects of the dead airman who has given his life to save his comrades. This is an eerie affair with perfectly simple but most striking orchestral effects. This suite has come to stay, and is sure of being as popular with the sophisticated as with the unsophisticated.[35]

Regrettably the suite has rarely been heard since but a recently issued CD recording (Marco Polo 8.223665) provides an excellent opportunity to reappraise this fine score. Apart from the suite itself, Vaughan Williams recalled that two of the themes written for the film, but not included in the final score, were the germs of the opening themes of the second and fourth movements of the Sixth Symphony.[36] Given the subject, mood and context of the film, this further suggests that we should see Vaughan Williams's Sixth Symphony as his war symphony.

In 1943 Vaughan Williams provided the score for a ten-minute Technicolor documentary, *The People's Land*, produced for the National Trust by Strand Films. It was clearly conceived in the spirit of 'The People's War' propaganda thrust endorsed by the MoI. The only overt mention of the war came at the end when narrator Freddie Grisewood declared that the land had been defended against every foe by the hearts and hands of their forebears and the People were now the guardians of this trust. But the emphasis on the People runs through the film. We are told it was the People and not the state who set up the National Trust in 1895 and it is the People who have the responsibility of protecting the more than 1,000 places and over 150,000 acres held in public trust in perpetuity. The properties are also used by the People, as city-dwellers go to the country to refresh themselves by communing with nature.

The visual images of the film strongly encapsulate the rural myth, as the commentary declares that England has 'some of the loveliest country, the prettiest villages and the largest, ugliest and most vigorous cities in the world'. The implication is that while the cities are necessary and unavoidable, human kind is most at peace and most truly itself if it can escape to the country. Intertwined, then are the threads of tradition, continuity and heritage, on the one hand, and popular use, on the other. Both are themes valuable to wartime projections of Britain and British heritage.

Not surprisingly, Vaughan Williams turned to folk tunes and, on occasion, to popular tunes to create a continuous sound picture, the People's music underscoring the beauty and variety of the People's land.' The film opens with the white cliffs of Dover, the front line against invasion, and then the camera sweeps across the Sussex downs. Vaughan Williams begins with the strains of 'As I Walked out One May Morning' and this is developed into a sweeping pastoral statement, which modulates into a succession of tunes accompanying visual sequences which stress continuity and tradition. Strong chords and solemn ritual music accompany images of the Castlerigg stone circles at Helvellyn in the Lake District; medieval pageant music accompanies shots of the stronghold Bodiam Castle, built by a follower of the Black Prince. Tudor-sounding 'Love Will Find Out' the way accompanies Little Moreton Hall in Cheshire, 'still lived in by the family who built it in the days of Queen Elizabeth'; sturdy, pastoral strains, a Westmorland farm; and the jaunty, folksy 'Chairs to Mend', the village of West Wycombe, a cross-section of the variety of National Trust properties.

The film then gives examples of popular use of the properties. Cyclists scud along country roads to variations on 'Pop goes the Weasel', Boy Scouts hike into the hills to 'John Barleycorn in marchtime', children toboggan down a hillside to 'Boys and Girls Come Out to Play', an angler catches fish to a lilting snatch of 'Rakish Highland Man' and entomologists pursue butterflies in the fens to the wistful, plaintive strains of 'The Springtime of the Year'.

Finally, the Lake District and mention of the Lake poets leads on to inspiring visionary pastoral music, and, as mountaineers ascend the Lake District hills repeated rising phrases finally culminate in surging notes of triumph as they reach the top. The film ends as it began with the white cliffs of Dover, a round tour of the beauties of Britain in just ten minutes and an entrancing, lively and inventive miniature tone poem which cleverly reinforces the messages of the film, messages close to Vaughan Williams's own heart, projecting an England of rural beauty, spiritual peace, open access, continuity, tradition and folk song.

Vaughan Williams's last propaganda assignment was the fifteen-minute documentary film, *Stricken Peninsula* (1945), directed for the Army Film Unit by Paul Fletcher and released by the MoI. It deals with the Allied reconstruction programme for newly liberated Southern Italy, undertaken at a time when the liberation of the North was still not completed.

The film opens with a shot of the ruins of Pompeii and dissolves to the ruins of present-day war-damaged Naples. The narrator outlines the problems faced by the Allies in this area, where because there was no organized resistance to the Fascists there has been a complete collapse of moral and political structures. Each of the facets of the reconstruction work is explained over shots which show it being undertaken.

Reconstruction begins with the clearing of rubble and the digging of graves. In the countryside, farmers recover hidden seed corn, salvage farm machinery and begin to plough and plant even before minefields have been cleared. In the cities, there is no power, light, fuel, transport, food distribution, and the black market flourishes. So the Allies organize soup kitchens and food distribution, relief for the unemployed and a campaign of inoculation against typhus which checks the growing epidemic. Hospital equipment is brought out of hiding and new hospital wards established.

Bridges and railways are repaired. But this is all threatened by lack of power. The Nazis dynamited the main city generator. But an old discarded generator is brought out, refurbished and put into operation, and trolley buses and street cars begin to run again. Fresh fruit and vegetables are brought in from the countryside and sold, but olive oil can only be obtained on the black market. A free press is restored, so that people can read and write whatever they like.

The political process resumes, with free political meetings, trade unions (banned under the Fascists) restored and the workers organizing to rebuild the factories. While workers in the North are sabotaging industry, in the South they are restoring it. Education is being reintroduced, purged of Fascist textbooks and indoctrination, so that the new generation can be instructed in the meaning of liberty. The process of reconstruction is slow and there is an enormous amount to do, but the forces to tackle the job are mobilizing.

The *Documentary News Letter* (*DNL*), keeper of the conscience of the British Documentary movement, reviewed the film, and called it

> one of the more remarkable films to result from Service shooting. Paul Fletcher has examined his subject from a traditional documentary standpoint. Here is no newsreel coverage but an attempt to select and analyse episodes in the story of liberation, and to assemble them into a picture which will not give only the material facts but also the mood and feeling of Italians suddenly fallen between the two stools of Nazism and liberation. Some critics may find the camera dwelling too long on semi-symbolic visuals and there is little attempt at economy of coverage. But such moving episodes as the mass disinfecting of citizens and the clamorous underfed food queues tell us more eloquently than words that the people of Italy may have been liberated but certainly are not yet rehabilitated or even given much opportunity to regain the dignity of free men. The sordid, unhappy scenes are relieved by brighter moments of restored power stations and ploughs taken out once more to the war-scarred fields. But the film leaves us feeling that here is a vast national problem with the full solution still to be found.

Its propaganda value, *DNL* thought, 'salutary and excellent. The realities of war's aftermath presented with considerable artistry.' Of the music, *DNL* said:

> *Stricken Peninsula* is severely handicapped by what in the reviewer's opinion is an execrable musical score by Dr Vaughan Williams. Whatever musical qualities are present achieve no marriage with visuals or commentary. One is conscious only of obtrusive and disagreeable noise intruding between the audience and a moving story.[37]

This is both unfair and inaccurate. Vaughan Williams provides what is in effect a miniature tone poem on the theme of reconstruction. A broad noble theme behind the credits introduces the idea of aspiration and then, over the ruins, bleak, austere music, akin to the second movement of the Sixth Symphony, begun around 1944, sketches the desolation and dislocation left by the war. This modulates into a lively, optimistic march as the reconstruction begins and this reconstruction march returns with variations over each initiative: the repair of the transport infrastructure, the trolley buses running again, the schools reopening. The bleakness returns over scenes of urban desolation but develops over scenes of well-run hospital wards into music of spiritual uplift, akin to the final movement of *Job*. Slow, heavy, threatening chords accompany news of the dynamiting of the power generator but the music then directly echoes the slow and repeated cranking up of the machinery and finally the triumphantly whirring and spinning pistons: a sound picture of a generator being refurbished and brought on stream that recalls the planes revving up in the score of *Coastal Command*. As political meetings revive, preceded by a procession of bandsmen, an orchestrated version of a cheerful Italian folk song is heard. Finally after the light reworking for strings of the reconstruction march over shots of children at play, the score surges back into the spiritual theme from the hospital scenes as the narrator concludes that the forces are mobilizing and the work is underway. The score could, like so much of Vaughan Williams's film music, stand on its own, as an atmospheric and economical but musically sophisticated and multi-layered evocation of the various facets of post-war reconstruction.

Humphrey Jennings was the great poet of the World War Two documentary, his lyrical, richly textured films capturing something of the soul of the nation at war. In his films the propaganda objectives of 'Why We Fight' and 'How We Fight' often imperceptibly merged. Jennings saw England as a family, believed that life had a pattern and a purpose, and in his Festival of Britain film, *Family Portrait*, celebrated the British as a people who loved public pomp and private domesticity. Jennings's love of England centred on three basic principles: his admiration of the common people, his instinctive belief in individuality but always within community (the Welsh miners in *The Silent Village*, the ARP men and WVS women in *Heart of Britain*, the firefighters in *Fires Were Started*), and his love of culture. Gerald Noxon says of Jennings that he had been influenced in his formative years by Shakespeare and Marlowe, Milton and Bunyan, Constable and Blake: 'The works of these men remained in Humphrey's background as a permanent frame of reference. Their kind of Englishness was Humphrey's kind of Englishness.'[38] English music was integral to his films: Handel, Elgar, Purcell, Vaughan Williams; Welsh hymns; popular songs; folk songs; dance band music. He planned a documentary on the London Symphony Orchestra which was never made.

In all this Jennings can be viewed as a soul-mate of Vaughan Williams, who was widely seen to be, in the words of his longtime friend and OUP editor Hubert Foss, 'a great Englishman, essentially English to be ranked alongside

Milton, Shakespeare, William Blake and Thomas Hardy'.[39] Foss's book on Vaughan Williams, published in 1950, is valuable as an indication of the terms in which Vaughan Williams was perceived in the 1940s and 1950s. Specifically Foss sees Vaughan Williams as sharing Milton's 'strong feeling for the English language', 'the remote mysticism' and 'wide imagination' of Blake, the 'humanity, understanding and kindly but incisive humour' of Shakespeare, the attention to human detail and broad philosophical truth of Hardy.[40] More generally Foss relates Vaughan Williams' inspiration to the English landscape, the English language, the English church, English folk song and early music and English life and character: dogged, truthful, open-air, practical, liberal-minded and tradition-loving.[41] Jennings wrote warmly of his admiration of Vaughan Williams's 'absolute humility, humanity – following his own sure company with bravura' and again of 'his creative fire and with it his tenacity and above all his humility'.[42] Vaughan Williams was therefore an obvious collaborator and although they did not work together during the war they came together for *Dim Little Island,* produced in 1949 by Wessex Films for the Central Office of Information, successor of the MoI.[43]

The ten-minute film was intended to tackle 'post war blues', the idea that the country, bankrupt, rationed, depressed after the long cold winter of 1947, was 'going to the dogs'. The film was constructed as a meditation on the past, present and future, by four men, the cartoonist Osbert Lancaster, the industrialist John Ormston, the naturalist James Fisher and the composer Ralph Vaughan Williams.

Lancaster begins by setting out the current view that Great Britain is 'rather a dim little island', 'hopelessly unmusical' and now as always 'going to the dogs'. He examines the painting *The Last of England* (1852) to demonstrate that in 1852 people felt the same, whereas looking back we see it as a time of optimism and expansion. Ormston points out that for nearly a century British shipyards built ships better and cheaper and quicker than elsewhere but the industry was run down before the war reactivated it. James Fisher celebrates the value of wild nature ('It's interesting. We learn from it. It's beautiful, and we refresh ourselves with it. It's fun – we take pleasure in it'). Shots of smoking chimneys and cobbled streets are contrasted with the free expanses of the open countryside. Over scenes of the Pennine Hills, an unaccompanied male voice sings the folk song 'Dives and Lazarus' and Vaughan Williams speaks:

> Listen to that tune – it's one of our English folk tunes. I knew it first when I was quite a small boy, but I realized even then that there was something not only very beautiful, but which had a special appeal to me as an Eng-

lishman. It dates from a time when people, of necessity, made their own music, and when as has been well said – they made what they liked, and liked what they made. I like to think of our musical life as a great pyramid, at the apex of which are great virtuosi and composers of international renown. Them immediately below this come those devoted musical practitioners, true artists who by precept and example are spreading the knowledge and love of music in our schools, our choral societies, our music festivals. Then comes the next layer of our musical structure, that great mass of musical amateurs who make music for the love of it, and play and sing for their own spiritual recreation in their own houses. And then behind that again we have our great tunes which like our language, our customs, our laws are the groundwork upon which everything must stand. So perhaps we are not too unmusical after all. Nevertheless, our music has lain dormant. Occasionally indeed a candle would shine like a good deed in a naughty world. Byrd, Purcell or Arne. And lately the candles have become more numerous (the title pages of scores by Elgar (*Enigma Variations*), Vaughan Williams (*A London Symphony*), Bax (*Tintagel*) and Britten (*Peter Grimes*) are seen). For people have come to find a special message in our music which that of other nations, however skilled and imaginative, cannot give them.

Fisher argues that we must protect our national landscape and resources. Ormston says we can still build ships as well an anyone, 'if we can get supplies and we don't take things too easily'. Lancaster says: 'Doubtless were we a rational race, the spectacle of our present position would overwhelm us. But then we have always been, thank heaven, deaf to appeals to reason' and he cites Dunkirk as an example of a successful act defying rational argument. Vaughan Williams ends his contribution:

> So – the fire is ready. It only requires a match to relight it, to set the whole ablaze. Some great upheaval of national consciousness and emotion. The Elizabethans experienced this and as a result, they produced poetry and music that has never been surpassed. Have we not also experienced lately such a national upheaval? And is this not the reason why, during the late war, those who had never taken music seriously before began to crowd our concert halls from Kensington to Harringay to hear symphony concerts? Today our music which for so long had seemed without life is being born again.

The last words of the film are: 'Who can talk of an end when we are scarcely at the beginning?'

Vaughan Williams's contribution is a succinct statement of the views he had been advancing for many years. Jennings's vision links directly with his. Jennings's little film is constructed as a celluloid symphony in four movements with themes that intermesh: the idea that the country is 'going to the dogs' as an illusion; the strength and viability of Britain's shipbuilding trade and her role as an island race; the beauty and value of nature; the strength and importance of our musical life as representing the soul of the nation. Jennings discovered a ship called *British Genius* of which he gives us a triumphant close-up shot and the film's images tell us that the British Genius consists in the facts that we are good sailors, proud craftsmen, love nature and make our own music – all ideas to which Vaughan Williams could easily and readily respond. The war is seen as a catalyst to promote the national parks, shipbuilding and the revival of musical life, and those ideas intermesh just as the shot of the structure of ship's girders on Tyneside dissolves into the waving reeds of the Mindsmere marshes.

Vaughan Williams's score – a short prelude and occasional musical interludes – consists of orchestrated versions of folk tunes: 'Pretty Betsy', 'The Pride of Kildare' and notably 'Dives and Lazarus', first heard sung by an unaccompanied folk singer, who is then joined by the orchestra in a version which, at Vaughan Williams's mention of great tunes, swells into a solemn and majestic melody. It is similar to, but not exactly the same as, his *Five Variants on Dives and Lazarus*, written ten years before.

As indicated in his contribution to *Dim Little Island*, Vaughan Williams had always been personally devoted to the idea of Elizabethan England. It was to Elizabethan England that the 'English Musical renaissance' turned for an authentic English idiom to combat Germanic domination of music. English folk music was said to be continuous from that period. Elizabethan England was also the age of Shakespeare, the supreme English poet and dramatist, and throughout his career Vaughan Williams set Shakespeare songs and devoted his opera *Sir John in Love* to Falstaff, who like his creator had come – particularly since the nineteenth century – to seem the epitome of Englishness.

But Elizabethan England could also be seen and was used as an analogue of the present. Free Protestant England standing alone against the might of the tyrannical Catholic Spanish Empire leading to the great victory over the Armada in 1588 was seen as a counterpart of England standing alone against Nazi Germany during the 1940s. Elizabethan England was also seen as the first great age of empire, with Raleigh claiming Virginia for the Queen and Drake claiming California for England, an age of seafarers and explorers, when English trading interests stretched from India to Muscovy and the foundations of Britain's sea-borne empire were laid. It was always a period to stir the blood and

Victorians had seen Elizabethan England as a direct precursor of its own age: with a great and long-lived queen presiding over a realm where commercial and maritime expansion were the keys to its preeminence. In 1952 the accession to the throne of a beautiful young queen, Elizabeth II, promoted the idea of the 'New Elizabethan Age', as Empire evolved into Commonwealth and the conquest of Everest by the Hunt expedition, seemed to emphasize Britain's continuing eminence.

In 1955 Vaughan Williams accepted a commission from British Transport Films to provide the score for a short 25-minute Technicolor film, *The England of Elizabeth*, directed by John Taylor, and with an evocative poetic commentary written by the novelist John Moore and beautifully spoken by the actor Alec Clunes. The picture it paints is one Vaughan Williams would have found entirely to his taste. The film (first shown in 1957) constructs the England of Elizabeth as a period of change, development, expansion, exploration and discovery, of sea travel and the defeat of the Armada. It is the first great age of empire with Drake's circumnavigation of the globe epitomizing the overseas expansion ('The East Indies and the West Indies added to the Americas as elbow room for Englishmen'). It is an era of new maps, spices and travellers' tales, bustling, exuberant and optimistic. But it is also an age of spiritual and lyrical inspiration with great poets, notably Shakespeare; the English translation of the Bible produced by Caxton's printing press (represented by majestic quotations from the Book of Job); the creation of the Church of England with its Anglican church music (the Choir of King's College Chapel perform an anthem). At the centre of it all stands the inspirational figure of Elizabeth.

The film stresses that while most of what Shakespeare saw has gone, the spiritual legacy remains, in the songs and anthems and words of Shakespeare and the other great Elizabethans which link the past and the present. Vaughan Williams provided a continuous musical score titled *The Elizabethan Age*. He headed the sections of his score: 'Titles', 'Street Scenes', 'Countryside', 'Tudor Houses', 'Portraits', 'Elizabeth', 'Hatfield', 'Henry VIII', 'Tintern', 'Books', 'Seamen', 'Dance', 'Wedding Procession', 'Country Dance', 'London Theatres', 'Cradle', 'Map', 'School', 'Charlcote Deer Park', 'Road to London', 'Armada', 'Battle', 'Waves', 'Aftermath', 'More Maps', 'Treasures', 'New Houses', 'Yeoman's Cottage', 'Shakespeare Song', 'Shakespeare's Tomb', 'King's College Introduction', 'Conclusion'. But this apparently large medley of subjects masks a greater internal coherence and continuing musical themes run through the film binding the continuing narrative strands: explorers, seamen and merchant venturers; the craftsmen who produce the houses, treasures and maps; Shakespeare, whose life is encapsulated, and Elizabethan poetry; and the life and career of Queen Elizabeth.

The title music is appropriately heroic with drums and trumpets, representing the spirit of the age. After a passage describing the bustle of present-day streets, from which the film urges us to make 'an imaginative leap from our Elizabethan age to theirs', there is a contemplative variation of the brassy march opening, a woodwind rhapsody over scenes of the eternal countryside, stressing the spiritual and rural as counterpart of the public and heroic. The title theme is to run throughout the score as a binding thread, recapitulated briskly and confidently for the Queen but then given a wistful, hesitant variation for her precarious and uncertain youth. There is a bolder variation over portraits of her great soldiers, sailors and explorers. For Shakespeare's life there is a reflective meditative theme which, as the narrator recounts his departure for London, modulates into a version of the main theme, underlining the process by which Shakespeare becomes part of the spirit of the age. The meditative theme returns behind the recounting of his retirement to Stratford but swells into a stately version of the title theme as his legacy is outlined. For Drake's circumnavigation of the globe there is a rollicking shanty-type theme, stirring battle music for the Armada and then tinkling exotic sounds as the trophies and plunder secured on distant voyages are shown. The delicate impressionism of this passage resolves itself into a bold and confident marchlike reworking of the trophies' tune to cover the return of the seafarers and the construction of their grand new houses. Two lively Tudor-style dances, with drums and vigorous violins, represent the popular culture of Tudor England and authentic anthems, sung by King's College Chapel choir, the religious music. The film ends with the death of Elizabeth and a recapitulation of the main theme. This extraordinarily rich, ingenious and inventive score, embracing dances, marches, sea shanties, anthems and rhapsodies, succeeds in encapsulating an entire age. It also represents Vaughan Williams's most complete and coherent vision of England, a nation in its public ceremonial and intimate spiritual sides, a nation of merchants and poets, seamen and churchmen, craftsmen and statesmen, a nation rooted in tradition but looking boldly to the future.

Muir Mathieson constructed a concert suite from the music for *The England of Elizabeth*, which he called *Three Portraits from the England of Elizabeth*, bringing together themes and variations in such a way as to highlight the central threads of the film, the score and Vaughan Williams's vision. The first movement, 'Explorer', functions on a double level, the explorer not just as physical adventurer but spiritual quester, the twin aspects of Christian in *Pilgrim's Progress* and of Scott of the Antarctic. Opening with the triumphant fanfare from the title theme and incorporating the Armada, trophy, returned seafarers' march and Drake's circumnavigation shanty, in mood it moves through the facets of the seafarers' experience: the questing spirit, the exotic destinations, the dogged determination, the triumphant return. The second movement, 'Poet', intercuts the reflective visionary spirit of the seeker after poetic truth, in the Shakespeare theme, with its human inspiration, the people, embodied in lively renditions of 'The Wind and the Rain', with the vigorous drum and violin Tudor folk dance in counterpoint, and 'It Was a Lover and His Lass' which soars grandly at the end of the movement affirming the poet's roots in the human experience. Interestingly, neither Shakespeare song appears in the score on the film, but since Mathieson included them in the suite and also published separately for concert use orchestral versions of the two songs, as *Two Shakespeare Sketches* from *The England of Elizabeth*, they were evidently in Vaughan Williams's original score. The final movement, 'The Queen', establishes Gloriana as Queen and Woman, facing and surmounting the problems of her reign: the majestic introduction with the title theme modulating into the turbulence of the Armada music, the variation on the title theme which speaks of loneliness and isolation, and a grand, sweeping restatement of the introduction, merging the Queen and her age, pageantry, progress and achievement. The fourth theme of the film – the church – does not figure in the suite, as it is represented in the film by contemporary anthems sung by the King's College Cambridge chapel choir.

Perhaps the two most significant elements in Vaughan Williams's vision of England are the pastoral and the visionary. The prime example of English pastoral is *The Loves of Joanna Godden* (1947). The novel by Sheila Kaye-Smith was adapted for the screen by H. E. Bates, directed by Charles Frend partly on location in Romney Marsh and scored by Vaughan Williams. It also featured one of a trio of superb performances by Googie Withers that established her in the late 1940s as one of the finest dramatic actresses produced by British cinema, England's answer to Bette Davis or Simone Signoret. The other two were *It Always Rains on Sunday* (1947) and *Pink String and Sealing-Wax* (1945), both of them also Ealing productions.

Joanna Godden opens in Romney Marsh in 1905 and establishes its heroine (Googie Withers) as a strong-minded, independent woman who despite local conservatism and male prejudice determines to run her late father's farm herself, and in her own way. She refuses a marriage proposal from neighbouring

29   Pastoral England: *The Loves of Joanna Godden* (1947) with Googie Withers.

farmer Arthur Alce (John MacCallum), partly because her father had been pressing the match. She imposes her will, dismissing her shepherd (or 'looker') for disobeying her orders, cross-breeding her sheep and losing three-quarters of them as a result, and ploughing up her part of her land for fodder; all in the teeth of local farmers' opposition. She and Arthur quarrel and he tells her that it is alright to be a woman farmer but she is ceasing to be a woman, which the film defines as being in love. Joanna, seeking love and partly to spite Arthur, becomes engaged to the local squire's son Martin Trevor (Derek Bond). But he is drowned in a swimming accident before the wedding. She realizes too late that she loves Arthur. But Arthur marries her spoiled, selfish younger sister Ellen (Jean Kent), whom Joanna has had expensively educated. Ellen declares she wants 'a good time' and 'lots of nice things', is bored by the farm and farm life. But when Arthur loses his flock to foot and mouth disease and can no longer support Ellen in the manner to which she has become accustomed, she runs away with Squire Trevor. In the crisis, Joanna offers Arthur half her sheep and they join forces as farmers and lovers. So the film ends with the classic British gender compromise. Arthur accepts Joanna being a farmer and she seeks true fulfilment through the love of a good man.

This strong romantic melodrama provides the central core of the film but it also seeks to evoke life in Edwardian Romney Marsh. Director Charles Frend re-creates the rhythms of farming life (ploughing, reaping, lambing, shearing, sheepdog trials); the changes of the season; the haunting beauty of the landscape ('an austere land of windswept distances and scattered communities'); the pattern of community life (marketday, the annual farmers' dinner, the shearing dance, Christmas festivities, Lydd fair). It is these elements that Vaughan Williams responds to and sees as quintessentially English.

Some of the score is just snatches of atmosphere (Arthur leaving angrily after the reading of the will; Ellen waking in the morning; Arthur in his trap; Ellen sketching; Arthur riding). But there are several more substantive and completely characteristic passages. There is a haunting evocation of Romney Marsh. When Joanna describes the Marsh as 'just a lot of old fields and ditches', Martin asks her to look at it with his eyes. Director Charles Frend gives us a passage of pure visual beauty, a lone bird skimming through the marsh sky, the waving grain, a solitary tree etched against the horizon, the pebble beach at Dungeness, the light over the sea, and Vaughan Williams responds to this with shimmering music through which a dark haunting melody runs. There is a brief but highly effective impressionistic passage charting the changing of the seasons from summer to autumn to winter. There is the fulfilment of work on the land in the montages of ploughing, harvesting and rounding up of the rams with music that is purposive, joyous and rhythmic. But while there is work and beauty, there is also cruelty and loss. When Joanna and Martin go swimming at Dungeness, she lies on the beach asleep in the grip of disturbing dreams. He swims out alone to sea and vanishes. The music for this sequence prefiguring Scott features keening female voices, the siren call of the deep water, minatory chords and the musical equivalent of the surge of the water and the howl of the wind. But most chilling is the recurrence of two notes, repeated urgently like a woman's voice calling 'Mar-tin'. The music for the dying of the cross-bred sheep in the cold wind and the burning of the animals killed in the foot and mouth outbreak is grim and dark with that icy sense of bleakness and despair which was so notable a feature of the Sixth Symphony – his major work in progress during these years.

When the film was released, the critics on the whole disliked it. But there was praise for the photography and the score. Dilys Powell in the *Sunday Times* (15 June 1947) thought Vaughan Williams's music 'throughout beautifully suggests the poetic overtones of landscape' and *The Spectator* (27 June 1947) praised 'the sweet, subtle score of Vaughan Williams'. Most reviewers, however, thought the film slow, ponderous and unexciting. Elspeth Grant in the *Daily Graphic* (13 June 1947) thought it 'painstakingly made, excellently photographed – and dull', the *Sunday Graphic* (15 June 1947) opined that 'the director was so bewitched by the animals and vegetables that he had not much time for the humans' and C. A. Lejeune in *The Observer* (15 June 1947) thought 'the human interest is practically nil, and one is sent away with a straight choice between cold and roast mutton'. They all seem to me to underrate the film considerably.

A recording of the highlights from the *Joanna Godden* music was issued after the film's release. The passages preserved were 'Romney Marsh', 'Joanna Godden', 'Sheep shearing', 'Work on the Farm', 'The Fair', 'Martin Drowned at Dungeness', 'Ellen and Harry Trevor', 'Adoption of the motherless lamb', 'Burning of the sheep' and 'Reunion'.[44] But no suite was ever made, published or performed, though it might well have been from the major musical features.

The other aspect of England that regularly inspired Vaughan Williams was the visionary. It was this aspect of the story of Scott of the Antarctic that appealed to him. As the discussion in Chapter 2 demonstrates, Ealing Studios, who were producing the film, laid stress on English character and achievement. But it was perfectly possible for the two aspects to co-exist, as there was always a visionary dimension to the British imperial achievement – and Scott was seen unequivocally as an imperial hero by the public. The finished film was a tribute to gentlemanly Englishness, stressing the quiet determination, understatement, self-deprecating humour and stoical acceptance of defeat that the ethos comprised. Vaughan Williams's music added the visionary dimension.

Ernest Irving, Ealing's musical director, had a clear vision of what the score should do:

> For an epic film on the scale of *Scott of the Antarctic*, I conceive it to be the function of the music to bring to the screen the hidden and spiritual illustration into which the camera, however ably directed, is unable to peer. The essence of heroism in the struggle to reach the Pole, and the sterner, because disillusioned, effort to get back to the base lay in the unbending spirit which endured day after day, hour after hour, mile by mile, yard by yard, unceasing, uncomplaining, unflagging. The camera has a hundred minutes to show these weeks of cracking strain and silent endurance and must portray them in action and dialogue. This is where music can step in as a spiritual ancillary to the spoken word or pictured scene, and the musician should be a composer who works on a scale comparable with the grandeur of the main theme.[45]

Vaughan Williams was his first choice for composer ('There is in my mind no

Imperial hero: John Mills as *Scott of the Antractic* (1948).   **30**

doubt that Vaughan Williams is the greatest living British composer, and in the
rest of the globe I place only Sibelius in the same rank'). Director Charles
Frend and producer Sidney Cole readily agreed. Vaughan Williams was
approached by Irving. Ursula Vaughan Williams recalled:

> He was at first reluctant to commit so much time but Irving was persua-
> sive, and the idea of the strange world of ice and storm began to fascinate
> him. The film studio provided books (notably *The Worst Journey in the
> World*). Pictures of the Scott expedition lay about the house and the work
> was begun. Ralph became more and more upset as he read about the inef-
> ficiencies of the organization; he despised heroism that risked lives unnec-
> essarily, and such things as allowing five to travel on rations for four filled
> him with fury. Apart from this he was excited by the demands which the
> setting of the film made on his invention to find musical equivalents for
> the physical sensations of ice, of wind blowing over the great, uninhab-
> ited desolation, of stubborn and impassable ridges of black and ice-cov-
> ered rock, and to suggest man's endeavour to overcome the rigours of this
> bleak land and to match mortal spirit against elements. For light relief
> there were the penguins and whales. There was to be music not only for
> the polar journey but also for the two women, Kathleen Scott and Oriana
> Wilson, so he had scope for many different kinds of tune.[46]

Vaughan Williams was anxious to have direct discussions with the director, writing to Irving: 'I have very definite ideas and if they do not agree with his it might be rather difficult.' The meeting resulted in complete agreement on style and methods. Irving recalled: 'This was reached after a lively and educative discussion and once having taken the spark, Vaughan Williams proceeded to sketch the entire music for the film, which we received within a fortnight, including many of the important numbers in full score.'[47] Vaughan Williams had been working to a draft script and ahead of receiving the formal list of music cues and timings, which was sent to him after he had already posted his score. But the location shooting for the film was not yet completed and the script was being revised still. Irving recalled that, 'Nearly all the music had to be reshaped' after the final print was assembled, but that, 'This was not so insuperable from the artistic point of view as it might seem, for the music is essentially right in the first place, and all the structural alterations were carried out under the censorship of the original architect.'[48] This resulted in the situation recalled by Ursula: 'the film work, with consultations and visits to the studio to see the pictures, went on all through the year at irregular intervals.'[49] Irving privately advised Vaughan Williams to insist in his contract that any change in the music receive his consent. This was done but Vaughan Williams gave Irving, whom he trusted absolutely, *carte blanche* to deal with the music as he wished. Their correspondence, from which Michael Kennedy prints extracts, shows them debating the music back and forth, discussing such questions as whether or not there should be a prelude, how much of the music would be lost behind dialogue and sound effects, whether a wordless female chorus could be used in the score.[50] Kennedy pays tribute to the role of Irving acting as go-between between Vaughan Williams and Ealing and ensuring that, as far as possible, his wishes were met.

In his autobiography, Irving described Vaughan Williams as 'a great artist – an inspired musician, a humble follower of his art, always ready to learn and seeking to be informed, generous and altruistic, continually planning to help other musicians less fortunately placed then himself'.[51] Irving notes:

> He must have had some of the themes in his mind beforehand, of course, and not all of the music went into the film, but it was all so akin to the thoughts and emotions that stirred that devoted little party of explorers that I was often able to move it about inside the film, applying some of it to incidents for which it was not designed. For instance, the music composed for the main titles – or overture – to the film, exactly fitted the climbing of the glacier and stopped with a shuddering roll on the bass

drum as the party reached the very edge of a fathomless crevasse – one more crotchet would have swallowed up the whole expedition.[52]

It was evidently not just the landscape and the opportunity for musical experimentation that fascinated Vaughan Williams. For the film, as constructed, is almost a secular analogue of *Pilgrim's Progress*. Christian's journey in Bunyan's work was a 'dream', recalling Charles Barr's description of *Scott* as 'dreamlike'. But the incidents, too, of Christian's journey have precise parallels in Scott's. Like Christian, Scott climbs the Hill Difficulty (the Beardmore Glacier), crosses the Valley of Humiliation (finding Amundsen's flag at the Pole), is imprisoned in the dungeon of Giant Despair in Doubting Castle (the storm-bound tent where they die eleven miles from safety). But just as Christian is freed by the key which holds the promise of redemption, the last messages of the explorers talk of their faith in being reunited with their loved ones in the next world. Scott's journey becomes another version of the journey of the human soul, which had long provided Vaughan Williams with inspiration, through the long gestation of his *Pilgrim's Progress* project and dating back as far as his setting of Whitman's *Towards the Unknown Region* (1907), which might almost have been an alternative title for *Scott of the Antarctic*.

Within the film itself there is an obvious religious element, with Oates laying down his life for his friends, Dr Wilson playing 'Abide With Me' on his gramophone and the final letters of Wilson and Bowers, read on the soundtrack and expressing their belief in an afterlife. The final inscription on the cross: 'To strive, to seek, to find and not to yield' could have been Christian's motto in *Pilgrim's Progress*. It is no coincidence that he was working on the opera at the same time as he was developing Scott and the emerging Seventh Symphony. But we cannot wholly divorce the story from the celebration of English character. Let us remember the 'quiet determination' of *Coastal Command*, echoed here in the conduct of the explorers, whose stoical mood recalls that of the RAF personnel in the earlier film, along with the pipe-smoking, boyish japes and sense of masculine camaraderie. It was not all allegory. While working on *Sinfonia Antarctica*, Vaughan Williams referred to it as his *Scott* symphony and in the epigraphs attached to the movements, he deliberately included an extract from Scott's last journal. So Scott is there too, a Pilgrim but a decidedly English Pilgrim. The score for *Scott of the Antarctic* unquestionably represents the peak of Vaughan Williams's cinematic achievement. The film's title music contains the main theme, recurrent throughout the film, and symbolizing human endeavour, struggle both physical and spiritual, the great quest ever onward and upward. It is followed by a prologue, marked by Vaughan Williams 'the terror and fascination of the Pole', over scenes of the Antarctic landscape, eerie, glittering, icy, what Vaughan Williams called his 'Antarctic shimmerings', achieved by the use of glockenspiel, xylophone, vibraphone, celesta, harp and bells, and chanting wordless female chorus, symbolizing the siren call of the Antarctic, the loneliness and wildness of the place, with its ever-changing, treacherous beauty in a kaleidoscopic pattern of wind, snow, storm and cloud formation. After a snatch, barely heard, of the music for Kathleen Scott, behind a shot of her sculpting her husband's bust, and jaunty music for the assembling of the team in London, we get the voyage out to New Zealand and the Antarctic, marked by descriptive musical passages of ice-floes, whales and seals, ships at sea ploughing through the pack-ice, and the immensity of the great ice barrier. The mood of the film is lightened by jolly comic penguin music as they slide and waddle on the ice; the jaunty folk song-like trotting pony theme brings a whiff of the English countryside into the Antarctic waste; and there is a triumphal surge in the music at the appearance of the Aurora Borealis.

As the explorers set out, we get the grim blizzard theme with the keening women's voices and wind effects. The climbing of the glacier employs the slow march theme of the titles, to give a musical equivalent of climbing and plodding. But it is never monotonous, due to the atmospheric weather colouring added and the cumulative effect of the repetition. The main heroic theme follows as they reach the summit.

On the last haul, the regular rhythms of the unending march return with a meditative passage as Scott ruminates on the soundtrack about who to take on the final push. An ominous trombone burst greets the sight of Amundsen's flag. Then there is the long haul back, the rhythms of the march, the howl of the blizzard, the growing sense of despair all captured in the music. After the deaths of Evans and Oates, the music falls silent and there is only the wind and the wordless female chorus. When the remains of the expedition are found, there is a fanfare as the words on the commemorative cross are picked out and the heroic final credits music swells, symbolizing the triumph of the human spirit over death and pitiless nature, another 'thanksgiving for victory' as Dickinson aptly puts it. Indeed it parallels the finale of *Shepherds of the Delectable Mountains* (1921) when the waters of the river of death close over Pilgrim and offstage the trumpets sound.

There was some inevitable cutting and rearrangement. Oriana Wilson's theme was cut and Kathleen's theme reduced to a mere snatch. The polar party departed in silence at the suggestion of director Charles Frend, who also suggested the reprise of the title music on the glacier climb and the elimination of the music composed for the final scene, called 'Only 11 Miles More', in favour of wind and female chorus.[53]

Aside from Vaughan Williams's music, there was also a leavening of popular music in the film. 'The Queen's Birthday March' and 'Will Ye No Come Back Again?' are played by a military band on the quayside as the *Terra Nova* departs, 'Good King Wenceslas' is sung by the expedition at their Christmas party and Dr Wilson plays a gramophone record of Clara Butt's famous rendition of 'Abide With Me' amid the icy polar night.

The score by Vaughan Williams represents the development to final fruition of ideas than can be glimpsed in earlier scores: the glacier music in *49th Parallel*, the drowning of Martin off Dungeness amid wind and women's voices in *Joanna Godden*, itself an effect developed from his opera *Riders to the Sea*.

The story so gripped him that he reworked the film music into his Seventh Symphony, *Sinfonia Antarctica*, which was significantly dedicated to Ernest Irving. The *Sinfonia* was written in five movements and there can be little doubt that they correspond to the phases of the film. The epigraphs he placed at the head of each movement clearly demonstrate that. The first movement, prefaced by an extract from Shelley's *Prometheus*, which he had also inscribed on the film score, universalizes the theme of the film and the symphony, the struggle of Man against Nature:

To suffer woes which hope thinks infinite,
To forgive wrongs darker than death or night,
To defy power which seems omnipotent,
neither to change, nor falter, nor repent:
This … is to be
Good, great and joyous, beautiful and free,
This is alone life, joy, empire and history.

The movement opens with the film's main title theme which becomes the motto theme of the symphony, repeated throughout the first movement. Then comes the prologue from the film. The music for the scenes of the Antarctic is reworked, creating an extraordinary texture of sound, to evoke the heroism of human endeavour against the loneliness and icy desolation of the polar region. The movement ends with the triumphant finale tune from the film.

The second movement, scherzo, with a quotation from Psalm 104 ('There go the ships and there is that Leviathan whom thou has made to take his pastime therein'), represents the sea journey from England to the Antarctic, with ice-floes, ship music, whales and penguin music reworked from the film. The third movement, landscape, with a descriptive passage from Coleridge's 'Hymn before Sunrise in the Vale of Chamouni', uses the iceberg, Ross Island and glacier-climbing music, climaxing in the conquest of the glacier with great peals of triumph on the organ, but drum and cymbal rolls, harp glissandi, wailing flutes, glockenspiel, celesta and piano to stress the nature of the landscape and the weather that they are fighting.

The fourth movement, which according to Dickinson makes no sense, makes perfect sense in the context of the film.[54] The superscription from John Donne's 'The Sun Rising' celebrates the strength of love:

Love, all alike, no season knows, nor clime,

Nor hours, days, months, which are the rags of time.

The movement represents first the recollections of the explorers. It develops Kathleen Scott's theme and the Oriana Wilson theme omitted from the film. The film includes a sequence on the trek back where Scott and Wilson recall their wives in flashback. The movement ends with the music for the death of Oates, whose sacrifice represents a different kind of love – the love of comrades.

The final movement, epilogue, with its quotation from Scott's journal: 'I do not regret this journey; we took risks; we knew we took them, things have come out against us, therefore we have no cause for complaint', represents the fatal last leg of Scott's journey. It opens with a fanfare of human defiance, then moves into the blizzard music and the slow heroic march theme, as the wind and the female chorus assert themselves, until they are all that is left. The explorers have lost their battle but their spirit has conquered, as the first movement indicated.

The film *Scott*, when it was released, received mixed reviews. The photography and the music were universally praised. In a review of the film broadcast on the Overseas Service of the BBC, Roger Manvell said: 'Vaughan Williams has written a great impressionist score, one of the best in my opinion in British film music.' The *Sunday Graphic* (5 December 1948) declared: 'Technically it is almost beyond criticism. The photography is magnificent … The sound (and in particular Vaughan Williams' music) is exactly right.' The *Evening Standard* (2 December 1948) thought 'the camerawork nothing less than superb' and 'the music magnificent'. The *Manchester Guardian* (4 December 1948) thought the music 'fine'. But several critics thought the characters never came alive, that the film itself did not match Herbert Ponting's contemporary film record and that something was missing. John Prebble in the *Sunday Express* (5 December 1948) thought it 'entertaining, sometimes thrilling, but far from great, which is a pity, for it has a noble subject', the *Evening Standard* thought it a 'very good picture' which missed greatness, the *Daily Telegraph* thought it 'did not rise fully either to subject or occasion', and there was a certain amount of damning with faint praise, *Tribune*'s (10 December 1948) 'a worthy essay' being a typical comment. Paul Dehn of the *Sunday Chronicle* thought photography and music 'magnificent', the story marvellous and the film a fitting memorial to the expedition.[55]

Vaughan Williams's final film for Ealing was *Bitter Springs* (1950), the third and final of three Australian productions shot on location in Australia. Superbly photographed on stunning locations and directed by Ralph Smart, it is in effect an Australian Western set in 1900. Australian Wally King and his family purchase from the government the land at Bitter Springs to raise sheep and set off on a 600-mile trek, enlisting as stockmen an indigent English music-hall artist (Tommy Trinder) and his son Charlie, and a Scots carpenter Mac (Gordon Jackson), thereby giving the settlers a truly imperial dimension. Bitter Springs turns out to be the tribal hunting-ground of the Karangani Aborigines. The Kings build a house and uneasily coexist with the Aborigines until after the natives slaughter two of King's sheep, there is a confrontation and John King, Wally's son, shoots and kills an Aborigine. The Aborigines cut off the waterhole and besiege the family, but Tommy, Charlie and the Aborigine stockman Black Jack manage to escape and alert the troopers who raise the siege. A chastened Wally King decides to cooperate with the Aborigines and they are last seen cheerfully shearing sheep together.

The main theme of the family moving into the heart of the continent, encountering natural hazards and danger from the dispossessed Aborigines, is interwoven with the education of the two tenderfoot outsiders Tommy and Mac and the blossoming of a romance between Mac and Emma King. The film was one of a series of post-war Dominions films set in South Africa (*Diamond City*), New Zealand (*The Seekers*) and Australia (*The Overlanders*, *Eureka Stockade* and *Bitter Springs*), extolling the pioneer spirit, and celebrating the heroic period of imperial expansion. For Vaughan Williams it is the optimistic counterpart of *Scott*, a trek with a happy ending, a theme of racial harmony and the triumph of Man over Nature. But this time Vaughan Williams's participation was limited. He provided thematic material which was developed and orchestrated by Ernest Irving. The film's credits read 'Music – Vaughan Williams, music supplemented, arranged and directed by Ernest Irving'. The title music is Vaughan Williams's, an optimistic, bouncy, up-beat march, which Vaughan Williams dubbed 'Irving's March' and of which he wrote to Irving 'What marvels you have done with my silly little tune'.[56] The marvels consist in the fact that the march with variations, recurs throughout the film, faster, slower, grimmer and lighter as circumstances demand. It accompanies the whole of the trek in the first part of the film and returns in martial form as the troopers relieve the besieged farmhouse. Irving reused Vaughan Williams's sheep music from *Joanna Godden* for the scenes of sheep on the move, commenting in his autobiography: 'after all sheep are sheep, and a little change in orchestral colouring will soon flip them over to the Antipodes'.[57] The manuscript score of *Bitter Springs* reveals that other passages in the score were by Irving alone.[58] Particularly splendid is the kangaroo music. When Charlie chases a baby kangaroo and it hops about in, what Irving called its 'little ballet' ending with him leaping into his mother's pouch, the action is set to a rhythmic flute tune. Also Irving's are the music for the cutting down of trees, sawing of wood and building of the house, with the music emulating these sounds; Charlie being taught by an aborigine to throw a boomerang, with the music capturing the flight of the boomerang; and the dramatic music for the burning of the farmhouse, into which the Vaughan Williams march tune inserts itself.

For his last venture into cinema, Vaughan Williams turned again to visionary Englishness. William Blake had always been an influence on Vaughan Williams and he had inspired one of Vaughan Williams' greatest works, *Job: a masque for dancing*, a work Frank Howes called 'wholly characteristic, profoundly English, and unflinchingly modern'.[59] To celebrate the bicentenary of Blake's birth, Guy Brenton wrote and directed a documentary film *The Vision of William Blake* for the Blake Society. The preface declares that Blake (1757–1827), 'poet, painter and visionary, lived unrecognized in opposition to the social and spiritual life of his times. To express his dissatisfaction and torment at this, he invented a personal world and mythology, even a private religion, which this film sets out to explore.' The film, which is narrated by Robert Speaight and with poems read by Bernard Miles, explores his vision by means of his paintings and drawings, a vision dominated by the struggle to recover the lost innocence of childhood, the innocence which allows man to reach up to God. God creates Man from both joy and woe. Eve's sin put Man in Satan's coils and from this came the first murder of Abel by Cain and thereafter evil stalked the world, and there was cruelty, terror and torment, and the final terror of Hell – oneself. But the torment is life-giving, for out of the spirit man can triumph over agony and despair. When the soul is released and joined to God, the earth is torn open and a new world created, in which there is a return to innocence with joy and thanksgiving.

Extracts from Vaughan Williams's *Job* are adroitly used on the soundtrack of the film. But he also composed ten songs for voice and oboe to poems by Blake, which are used in the film. In his published sequence they are: 1) 'Infant Joy'; 2) 'A Poison Tree'; 3) 'The Piper'; 4) 'London'; 5) 'The Lamb'; 6) 'The Shepherd'; 9) 'Ah, Sunflower'; 8) 'Cruelty has a Human Heart'; 9) 'The Divine Image'; 10) 'Eternity'. Of these 9, 4 and 6 are for unaccompanied voice and the rest for voice and oboe. They are dedicated to the singer, tenor Wilfred Brown, and the oboist Janet Craxton, who perform them magnificently in the film. Two things need to be noted. First, Vaughan Williams's sequence which has no particular rhyme or reason is not as good as the sequence in which they appear in the film, which relates directly to the structure and development of the ideas. In the film, the order is 9, 1, 3, 10, 2, 4, 7, 8, 5, 6. But also the musical settings of 1, 2 and 5 are not used in the film, where the director prefers Bernard Miles reciting the poems. So only seven of the songs are used. But the full set remains one of Vaughan Williams's greatest achievements in song. Their austere beauty and piercing purity, with their echoes of folk-song rhythms, reach back to his early musical influences but influences that are distilled into perfect form, at the end of a long and rich career. They celebrate innocence, joy and humanity, man's search for God, as well as recognizing the cruelty, terror and inner Hell with which they coexist, the final crystal clarity of his vision of Man's search for God which *Job*, *Pilgrim's Progress* and other great works have encompassed.

What then can Vaughan Williams's involvement in cinema tell us about him. First, it shows that he fulfilled absolutely his own oft-stated definition of the composer as a citizen, contributing to the life of the nation. He committed 'his skill, his knowledge, his sense of beauty' to the struggle against Fascism in the most populist way possible, by scoring propaganda films. In doing so, he fulfilled exactly the criteria laid down by the Ministry of Information for films about 'why we fight' (*49th Parallel*), 'how we fight' (*Coastal Command*) and 'the need for sacrifice if the war is to be won' (*The Flemish Farm*). His musical projection of the war effort centres squarely on the concept of 'The People's War', the dominant idea of Britain's wartime propaganda policy. In none of the films he scored is there a single individual hero. Throughout, it is the people who are collectively the hero. They contribute as citizens to the defence of democracy (*49th Parallel*, *Coastal Command*, *The Flemish Farm*), in the interests of a shared heritage (*The People's Land*) or to the restoration of civilized values (*Stricken Peninsula*). They do so to the accompaniment of 'The People's Music', as Vaughan Williams draws freely and joyously on hymns, folk songs, marches and dances to celebrate their efforts. After the war he used films to express his personal vision of the nation in a way which would uplift and inspire in the post-war situation. His view was consistent. While celebrating Britain's involvement with her European allies, and her central role in Empire and Commonwealth, his Britain is really England, its true nature, pastoral and visionary, its character, determined, stoical, heroic.

Second, his film music is integral to his general musical development. It is part of the continuing stream of his musical inspiration, resulting in the creation of three orchestral suites, the Second String Quartet, a piano piece, a song cycle and the *Sinfonia Antarctica*. But more centrally, it decisively influenced his musical language. As Hugh Ottaway has perceptively pointed out, the music after *Scott* is different from the music before:

> It would be hard to overestimate the importance of that film score for the composer's further development ... This is partly a matter of colour values, of sheer sonority ... But it goes much deeper than that: the whole substance of the music is modified, so that even when colour provides no obvious clue we can usually tell that a piece is post-*Scott*.[60]

He notes in particular 'i) a freer (sometimes wayward) interaction of contrasting sections, ii) an organic interweaving of ideas in the spirit of "growth"'. All of this is self-evidently the product of the needs and nature of film music.

But in terms of Vaughan Williams's spiritual life, Ottaway also sees Scott as marking a major turning-point, from the acute pessimism of the Sixth Symphony to the final phase of 'tragic but resilient humanism'. The profound and aching pessimism of the Sixth Symphony, which the film evidence suggests can be seen as his war symphony, is balanced in his film output by the recognition of heroism, sacrifice and struggle (*The Flemish Farm, Coastal Command, 49th Parallel*). In *Scott* a balance between the two strands in his 40s work was achieved and was to influence all his subsequent music.

What is particularly striking about the film music is the recurrence of the theme of the journey, the journey as expedition, trek, pilgrimage, mission, escape, a journey that is both physical and spiritual. This is perhaps why the explorer was such a significant figure in Vaughan Williams's world: the explorer explores not just the outer world but the inner self and, through struggle and suffering, eventually returns to God. This is the ultimate theme of Vaughan Williams's work and it is this which relates Scott to his other continuing inspirations Bunyan, Blake, Whitman and Shakespeare. The pilots of Coastal Command, the Belgian airmen, Scott and his comrades, the Australian pioneers, the Elizabethan explorers, all celebrated in Vaughan Williams's film music, all emerge as spiritual analogues of Christian, all like Vaughan Williams himself on their pilgrim's progress.

Notes

1 Hubert Foss, *Ralph Vaughan Williams*, London, 1950, pp. 200–1.
2 John Huntley, *British Film Music*, London, 1947, p. 11.
3 Ursula Vaughan Williams and Imogen Holst (eds), *Heirs and Rebels*, Oxford, 1959, pp. 90–3.
4 Muir Mathieson, 'Music for Crown', *Hollywood Quarterly*, 3 (1948) p. 323.
5 Huntley, *British Film Music*, pp. 56–7.
6 It was subsequently republished in Huntley, *British Film Music* , pp. 177–82 and Ralph Vaughan Williams, *National Music and Other Essays*, new edition, Oxford, 1987, pp. 160–65. Sir Michael Balcon, head of Ealing Studios, conceded the validity of the idea when it was proposed to him by Benjamin Britten, but concluded that it was impractical to implement. Michael Balcon, *A Lifetime of Films*, London, 1969, p. 148.
7 Graham Greene, *The Pleasure Dome*, London, 1972, p. 76.
8 Rachael Low, *Film Making in 1930s Britain*, London, 1985, pp. 125–6.
9 Tony Thomas, *Music for the Movies*, South Brunswick, New York and London, 1973, pp. 26–30.
10 Mathieson, 'Music for Crown', p. 34.
11 Huntley, *British Film Music*, p. 111.
12 Ernest Irving, 'Music in Films', *Music and Letters* 24 (1943), pp. 223–35.
13 Irving, 'Music in Films', p. 229.
14 Ernest Irving, *Cue for Music*, London, 1959, p. 163.
15 Ursula Vaughan Williams, *R. V. W.*, Oxford, new edition, 1992, p. 271.
16 Michael Kennedy, *The Works of Ralph Vaughan Williams*, new edition, Oxford, 1992, p. 300.
17 Ralph Vaughan Williams, *National Music*, pp. 3, 9, 11.
18 Michael Balcon, *A Lifetime of Films*, pp. 48, 61.
19 Jeffrey Richards and Anthony Aldgate, *Best of British Cinema and Society 1930–70*, Oxford, 1983, pp. 99–100.
20 On this phenomenon, see Martin J. Wiener, *English Culture and the Decline of the Industrial Spirit, 1850–1980*, Cambridge, 1981.
21 Ralph Vaughan Williams, *National Music*, p. 23.
22 On Vaughan Williams and Englishness, see especially Wilfred Mellers, *Vaughan Williams and the Vision of Albion*, London, 1989.
23 Ralph Vaughan Williams, *National Music*, pp. 154–9.
24 Ursula Vaughan Williams, *R. V. W.* 239 and Kennedy, *The Works of Ralph Vaughan Williams*, p. 259.

25   On the Ministry of Information and wartime British cinema see Anthony Aldgate and Jeffrey Richards, *Britain Can Take It*, new edition, Edinburgh, 1994.

26   Michael Powell, *A Life in the Movies*, London, 1986, p. 347.

27   For an account of the making of the film and an analysis of it see Anthony Aldgate and Jeffrey Richards, *Britain Can Take It*, pp. 21–43; Powell, *A Life in the Movies*, pp. 346–84 and Kevin MacDonald, *Emeric Pressburger*, London, 1994, pp. 159–82.

28   Huntley, *British Film Music*, p. 57; Frank Howes, *The Music of Ralph Vaughan Williams*, Oxford, 1954, p. 362.

29   Kennedy, *The Works of Ralph Vaughan Williams*, 1964 edn, p. 583.

30   Charles Reid, *Malcolm Sargent*, London, 1968, p. 357.

31   Malcolm MacDonald, *John Foulds*, Rickmansworth, 1975, pp. 47–48.

32   Valerie Pascal, *The Devil and His Disciple*, London, 1971, p. 103. *Saint Joan* was eventually filmed in 1957 by Otto Preminger with a score by Mischa Spoliansky.

33   Foss, *Ralph Vaughan Williams*, p. 172.

34   A. E. F. Dickinson, *Vaughan Williams*, London, 1963, p. 443.

35   *Musical Times*, 86 (1945), p. 285.

36   Dickinson, *Vaughan Williams*, p. 444.

37   *Documentary News Letter*, 5 (1945), p. 77.

38   Aldgate and Richards, *Britain Can Take It*, pp. 228–9.

39   Foss, *Ralph Vaughan Williams*, p. 11.

40   Foss, *Ralph Vaughan Williams*, p. 11.

41   Foss, *Ralph Vaughan Williams*, pp. 49–76.

42   Kevin Jackson (ed.), *The Humphrey Jennings Film Reader*, Manchester, 1993, pp. 146–148.

43   Vaughan Williams denied all knowledge of the film. Kennedy, *Works of Ralph Vaughan Williams* 1992 edn, p. 200, suggests that he may have worked on the film under another title. This suggestion is confirmed by Jackson (ed.), *Humphrey Jennings Film Reader* which indicates that the working title for the film was 'Awful Old England'.

44   Kennedy, *The Works of Ralph Vaughan Williams*, 1992 edn, p. 189.

45   David James, *Scott of the Antarctic: the film and its production*, London, 1948, pp. 144–5.

46   Ursula Vaughan Williams, *R. V. W*, pp. 279–80.

47   James, *Scott of the Antarctic*, p. 145.

48   James, *Scott of the Antarctic*, p. 145.

49   Ursula Vaughan Williams, *R.V.W.*, p. 280.

50   Kennedy, *The Works of Ralph Vaughan Williams*, 1992 edn, pp. 297–300.

51   Irving, *Cue for Music*, p. 174.

52   Irving, *Cue for Music*, p. 176.

53   Dickinson, *Vaughan Williams*, pp. 451–2.

54   Dickinson, *Vaughan Williams*, p. 387.

55   Reviews dated and undated can be found on BFI microfiche *Scott of the Antarctic*.

56   Kennedy, *Works of Ralph Vaughan Williams*, 1964 edn, p. 590.

57   Irving, *Cue for Music*, p. 175.
58   British Museum additional manuscripts 52383a.
59   Frank Howes, *The Music of Ralph Vaughan Williams*, London, 1954, p. 249.
60   Hugh Ottaway, 'Scott and after: the final phase', *Musical Times* 113 (1972), pp. 959–62.

Dickens – our contemporary

n 1965 Jan Kott published the English translation of a book entitled *Shakespeare – Our Contemporary*, stressing the relevance of the Elizabethan playwright to contemporary concerns. This surely is the mark of a great writer: someone who is not only of his own time, addressing the issues and preoccupations of his day, but who also achieves a universal appeal by tackling subjects that remain timeless. Shakespeare did this – and so did Dickens.

It was Dickens more than any other creative artist who captured the Victorian age in all its breadth and variety, spoke to his contemporaries in a way that made him not only respected but loved and has continued to be read and reread, adapted and reinterpreted down to the present. Dickens's contemporary celebrity was due to the fact that he had come to embody the ethos of the Victorian age and to express it eloquently and memorably. As Peter Ackroyd has written:

> He represented the Victorian character, both in his earnestness and his sentimentality, in his enthusiasm and in his sense of duty, in his optimism and in his doubt, in his belief in work and in his instinct for theatricality, in his violence and in his energy. For him life was conflict … it was struggle to maintain a vision of the coherence of the world, a vision of some central human continuity, in this sense it was also a battle against all the self-doubt, anxiety and division which lay beneath the surface of his own nature, just as they dwelt beneath the progressive formulations of nineteenth-century power.[1]

For all his universal appeal, it was recognized that there was something quintessentially English about Dickens. As early as 1850 Dickens was being acclaimed as an English institution. 'He is so thoroughly English,' said one review, 'and is now part and parcel of that mighty aggregation of national fame which we feel bound to defend on all points against attack.'[2] George Orwell pointed to the fact that Dickens

> attacked English institutions with a ferocity that has never since been approached. Yet he managed to do this without making himself hated and, more than this, the very people he attacked have swallowed him so completely that he has become a national institution himself.[3]

This acceptance again derives from the very Englishness of Dickens.

A definition of English character which includes individuality, a sense of humour, a sense of fairplay, stoicism and the stiff upper lip, a capacity for moral indignation, a mistrust of authority, love of home and gardens, sport and animals, a spirit of 'dauntless decency' could equally be given as a summary of the Dickensian ethos.

Dickens was a comic writer of genius, embodying the national sense of humour. He created a gallery of unforgettable characters who testify to that quirky and indelible individuality. He celebrated home and family in a way that appealed to broad public sentiment. His was a pipe and slippers, Sunday roast beef, family Christmas party type of domesticity, undeniably patriarchal but irresistibly warm, comforting and secure. He was deeply sentimental but he wrote from the heart and for an audience which responded. The death of Little Nell reduced such worldly-wise figures as Thomas Carlyle, Daniel O'Connell, Walter Savage Landor and William Charles Macready to tears.[4] He was animated by a deep hatred of cruelty and injustice and in consequence attacked the legal system, the education system and the workhouse system as well as snobbery, selfishness and greed. But he sought not so much major structural change or the radical overhaul of society as the infusion of fairness, humanity and compassion. Dickens had a horror of mob violence (*Barnaby Rudge, A Tale of Two Cities*) and laid his faith in moral reformation along Christian lines (*A Christmas Carol*). This chimed entirely with the tendency of the British to grumble, to mistrust whoever was in authority, to demand fair play for the underdog, but to shy away from revolutionary change. He preferred the application of the Christmas spirit, 'the spirit of active usefulness, perseverance, cheerful discharge of duty, kindliness and forbearance' to each individual, rather than the introduction of the spirit of revolution to society at large.[5] Dickens was neither Socialist nor revolutionary. He believed in the stern treatment of habitual criminals, supported Governor Eyre's brutal suppression of the Jamaica uprising and wanted the perpetrators of horrors against the English during the Indian Mutiny exterminated. He was at the same time both conservative and radical, which is why his appeal transcended party lines.

Dickens's own view of the English was an idealized one. He expressed it in *Household Words* in 1850:

> The English people have long been remarkable for their domestic habits, and their household virtues and affections. They are, now, beginning to be universally respected by intelligent foreigners who visit this country, for their unobtrusive politeness, their good humour and their cheerful recognition of all restraints that really originate in consideration for the general good ... The people in general are not gluttons, not drunkards, not gamblers, nor addicted to cruel sports, nor to the pushing of any amusement to furious and wild extremes. They are moderate ... decent, orderly, quiet, sociable among their families and neighbours.[6]

It is a picture that Baldwin, Orwell and Priestley would have recognized.

Dickens's mastery of melodrama and comedy, his gallery of unforgettable characters, his broad canvas, his social conscience and his sentimentality made a wide appeal to a wide audience, not just in his books but in adaptations of them first for the stage and later for the screen. H. Philip Bolton has traced more than 3,000 separate dramatic adaptations of Dickens between 1834 and 1984 and notes that the dramatic adaptation of his novels and stories has probably been the single most effective means of spreading his fame far throughout the world, and down to the lowest, largest and least literate classes.[7]

In the nineteenth-century theatre, actors and actresses became associated with particular Dickens characters and played them recurrently: W. J. Hammond as Sam Weller, John Martin Harvey as Sydney Carton, Jennie Lee as Jo the crossing sweeper, J. L. Toole as the Artful Dodger and Caleb Plummer. The great actors of the century eagerly seized on Dickens characters to demonstrate their virtuosity. Sir Henry Irving during his long and illustrious career played Nicholas Nickleby, David Copperfield, Bill Sikes, Alfred Jingle, John Peerybingle and Mr Dombey. His Digby Grant in *Two Roses* was directly modelled on William Dorrit and Robert Landry, the hero of *The Dead Heart,* was a blend of Dr Manette and Sydney Carton. His great rival Sir Herbert Tree doubled the roles of Micawber and Peggotty in his production of *David Copperfield* and also played Fagin and John Jasper.

But it was not just on the legitimate stage that Dickens' characters came to life. They came to life on the music-hall stage too. Bransby Williams began to

tour the halls in 1896 with character sketches from Dickens. His first programme included Jingle, Chadband, Quilp, Sydney Carton and Grandfather
Trent. It was a virtuoso quick-change act but its success depended upon instant
recognition by the audience of already well-loved characters. The whole concept is testimony to the English love of a 'character' (that is, individuality).
Over the years he added to his collection and recalled later that the best
received over all had been Daniel Peggotty, Newman Noggs, Barnaby Rudge,
Fagin and Uriah Heep. Interestingly, he alternated his Dickens act with a
Shakespeare act in which he impersonated Hamlet, Shylock, Henry V, Wolsey
and Othello, and he was in demand to do both. In his autobiography he
recalled:

> I little dreamed then that I should be dubbed 'The Dickens Man' all over
> the world. These characters have never failed – never in any part of the
> world. Failure with such characters in the smaller Halls was predicted, but
> the prophets were wrong. These poorer audiences had hearts, and the
> humanity of Dickens gripped them. They knew joy and suffering, and
> recognized it.[8]

Williams toured his Dickens act successfully through the United States,
Canada, Australia, New Zealand and South Africa, attesting to the accuracy of
novelist Stefan Zweig's comment:

> In every village, in every town, in the whole of the British Isles and far
> beyond, away in the remotest parts of the earth where the English speak-
> ing nations had gone to settle and colonize, Charles Dickens was loved.
> People loved him from the first moment when (through the medium of
> print) they made his acquaintance until his dying day.[9]

Williams not only did his music-hall act but in the 1920s took out touring
productions of *David Copperfield, Oliver Twist, Great Expectations* and *Barnaby Rudge*. He transferred easily from medium to medium. He appeared in
four British films, Thomas Bentley's productions of *Hard Times* (1915; as
Gradgrind) and *The Adventures of Mr. Pickwick* (1921; as Sergeant Buzfuz),
and two early sound shorts as *Scrooge* (1928) and *Grandfather Smallweed*
(1928). He appeared on radio, gramophone records and at the age of eighty
played Scrooge in a BBC television production of *A Christmas Carol*.

The cinema took to Dickens immediately, and from the early days of silent
cinema both in Britain and America there were Dickens films. As H. Philip
Bolton points out, it is notable that Dickens was more popular in America
than on the Continent and Scott was more popular on the Continent than in

America. Similarly, Scott appealed to opera composers as a source far more than Dickens. It is evident that Scott's Romanticism chimed with a European and aristocratic sensibility; Dickens's bustling Protestant Anglo-Saxon energy and moralism with that of the middle classes of America.[10] This is so much the case that Americans chose to overlook his virulent attacks on American society in *Martin Chuzzlewit* and *American Notes*, and continued to cherish him as a cornerstone of a common transatlantic culture that persisted until well after World War Two. Bret Harte celebrated this in his poem *Dickens in Camp*, recounting on the occasion of Dickens's death in 1870 a reading of the death of Little Nell round a Western campfire, ending

And on that grave where English oak, and holly,
And laurel wreaths entwine,
Deem it not all a too presumptuous folly -
This spray of western pine.[11]

How did early film-makers condense a Dickens novel into the customary ten-minute running length? Dubrez Fawcett explained:

Take the title of a Dickens story; work some of the best-known incidents into a beginning, a middle and an end: then dress up the players to look like the pictures in the novels. The lettering on the screen would do the rest, and the audience could fill in any blanks from their own stores of Dickensian knowledge.[12]

This again presupposes a detailed knowledge by mass cinemagoing audiences of the story and it must have worked, given the plethora of short versions of Dickens novels that appeared both in Britain and America.

But Dickens had a greater influence than this. It was Eisenstein in a seminal essay in 1944 who argued that D. W. Griffith, the most influential film artist of early cinema and a man who claimed Dickens as his favourite author, had in fact absorbed elements of cinematic technique from Dickens. Eisenstein brilliantly analyses a passage from *Oliver Twist* to show that it is innately cinematic, foreshadowing montage, cross-cutting, close-ups, and that, in its tempo, accumulation of detail, intermingling of aural and visual effects, visualization of characters as slightly larger than life and identifiable by externals of appearance or gesture or verbal mannerism it provides a blueprint for filmmakers.[13] Griffith undoubtedly had a Dickensian sensibility, making an early film adaptation of that paean to domesticity *The Cricket on the Hearth*, and infusing such later films as *Broken Blossoms, Way Down East* and *Orphans of the Storm* with recognizable Dickensian elements.

Dickens's universality became clear as the cinema took him up and each generation reinvented him to make him 'our contemporary'. There were only three Dickens films produced in Hollywood in the 1920s, including Frank Lloyd's fluently cinematic *Oliver Twist* with Lon Chaney as Fagin and Jackie Coogan as Oliver. England produced rather more and here the key figure was Thomas Bentley, 'the great Dickens character impersonator and scholar'. Bentley saw the role of film as illustrating rather than interpreting Dickens and so authentic locations were used, the actors were dressed to emulate the illustrations and chunks of the books literally reproduced. In this vein he directed *Oliver Twist* (1912), *David Copperfield* (1913), *The Chimes* (1914), *Barnaby Rudge* (1913), *Hard Times* (1915), *The Adventures of Mr. Pickwick* (1921) and no fewer than three film versions of *The Old Curiosity Shop* (1914, 1921 and 1934). The first five adaptations were made for Britain's premier pioneer film producer, Cecil Hepworth, himself a keen Dickensian and son of an itinerant lecturer whose star turn had been 'The Footprints of Charles Dickens'. Hepworth was a key figure in the development of a form of 'British heritage cinema', constructed as a deliberate alternative to Hollywood. This has been analysed in detail by Andrew Higson, who characterizes heritage film-making as based on respectable literary sources, shot on location, pastoral in ambiance, usually concerned with the upper classes, shot in a tradition of Victorian picturesque pictorialism and thus slow in pace and cutting, and stately in feel.[14] He singles out the work of Cecil Hepworth as fitting this paradigm. Hepworth himself certainly saw his films as distinctively English, writing in his autobiography that his objective was 'to make English pictures, with all the English countryside for background and with English atmosphere and idiom throughout'.[15] The Dickens adaptations fit this programme precisely.

Bentley's *David Copperfield* (1913), which has survived, begins by stressing its authenticity, announcing itself as 'arranged by Thomas Bentley (the Dickensian character actor) on the actual scenes immortalized by Charles Dickens'. Shot entirely in medium or long shot with no close-ups and few changes of camera angle, it is indeed an illustration of the novel, a static pictorial 'realization' of the book rather than a dynamic dramatization. Three actors play David, the youngest, Eric Desmond (who as an adult and under his real name Reginald Sheffield later became a busy character actor in Hollywood), continually looking at the camera. Murdstone and Heap are played as heavy melodrama villains and only Micawber and Peggotty come across as truly Dickensian characters. Many episodes are omitted (the death of David's mother, David's schoolboy friendship with Steerforth, David's marriage to

Dora, the domestic life of David and Dora), but a lengthy amount of footage is devoted to the stagecoach arriving, the horses being changed and the stagecoach loaded, indicating a desire to emphasise 'quaint' period detail and an 'Old England' feel. It is ironic that although Dickens was a distinctly urban writer, who was most at home in the teeming streets of London, he is being constructed here as a pastoralist, with concentration on scenes of Yarmouth beach, Blunderstone village where David grows up, Highgate village where Steerforth lives, the Wickfields' home at Canterbury and Miss Trotwood's house at Dover which looks more like a suburban villa than a clifftop cottage.[16]

There is no doubt that what audiences in the early decades of cinema responded to most fully was the sentimentality and melodrama of Dickens. Silent screen acting with its repertoire of gestures and postures – despair, joy, invocation, anguish, resignation – recalled directly early stage melodrama acting, when speech was forbidden in the minor theatres and stories were told by a combination of music and gesture. These aspects of Dickens's appeal can be seen clearly in two of the most notable British Dickens adaptations of the period, both of which have survived: Maurice Elvey's *Bleak House* (1919) and Herbert Wilcox's *The Only Way* (1925). Elvey was strongly committed to the projection of Britain on the screen. He told a magazine in 1927 that he had concluded that 'what the world wanted from Great Britain was real British pictures' and in his films he would attempt to depict 'scenes from our history, biography, English life of all classes, and, above all, British character'.[17] A title introduces *Bleak House* by telling us that because there are so many plot strands, the film will concentrate on Lady Dedlock's story. So what we get essentially is *Bleak House* as *East Lynne*, a story which might have been retitled *Lady Dedlock's Secret*. The novel is reduced to a single moral strand, becoming a saga of thwarted mother-love, an 'awful warning' about the dangers of illicit liaisons and illegitimate children, ending with Lady Dedlock expiring at the graveyard where her lover is buried and exclaiming 'it is right that I should die of terror and my conscience'. But virtually all social comment and all the satire on the legal system have been excised, in favour of the melodramas of lawyer Tulkinghorn's investigations and his murder, of Lady Dedlock's exposure, flight and death.

Although there had been stage adaptations of *A Tale of Two Cities* in 1860, 1875 and 1893, *The Only Way* became the definitive version and a theatrical institution. It opened in 1899, was an immediate hit and Sir John Martin Harvey was to play in it 5,004 times between then and his death in 1944. Martin Harvey and his wife constructed a scenario from the novel which was

turned into a script by Reverend Freeman Wills and Canon Frederick Lang-
bridge. It was christened 'The Only Way' because Edward Compton laid claim
to the title *A Tale of Two Cities* as belonging to his recently produced stage version. The play concentrated squarely on Sydney Carton, eliminating both
Madame Defarge – presumably too fierce for Victorian sensibilities – and Miss
Pross. But it added a new character or rather expanded the role of the little
seamstress who died with Carton. She was now introduced at the outset as a
slum waif adopted by Carton and unrequitedly in love with him. She was
christened Mimi after the character in *La Bohème* and was played by Lady
Martin Harvey. This had the effect of redoubling the sentimental element:
Carton is unrequitedly in love with Lucie and dies for her; Mimi is unrequitedly in love with Carton and dies with him. Audiences loved it, as they loved
Martin Harvey's raffishly Bohemian but ultimately noble and self-sacrificing
Carton. Herbert Wilcox filmed *The Only Way* in 1925 and it brought him rave
reviews.[18] He called Martin Harvey 'the finest actor I had directed up to that
time' and Harvey's performance is indeed superb, a miracle of delicate mime
acting, moving and convincing throughout. Wilcox, always a great showman,
arranged a gala opening for the film and persuaded the Home Secretary, Sir
William Joynson-Hicks to appear on the stage of the London Hippodrome to
sing the praises of the film. It was promoted as 'the banner bearer of British
films throughout the world.'

Wilcox opened out the four-act play to include scenes only referred to in the
stage version but familiar to Dickens readers (the release of Dr Manette and his
journey to England; Darnay's Old Bailey trial; the murder of the Marquis St
Evremonde). He restored Miss Pross, played by the beloved comedy actress
Mary Brough, as a very broad comic character who flirts with Mr Lorry, but
not Madame Defarge – Ernest Defarge is, as in the stageplay, the revolutionary villain. It remains, however, a highly effective piece of silent cinema and
captures for us something of the magic of Martin Harvey who remained the
definitive image of Sydney Carton until Ronald Colman eclipsed him in
MGM's sound version.

Where Hollywood in the 1920s had produced only three Dickens adaptations, in the 1930s it produced seven to Britain's two. But then the 1930s was
Hollywood's Anglophile decade with notable screen adaptations of works by
the Brontës, Thackeray, Kipling, Shakespeare and Barrie, as well as Dickens.
The studios sought respectability as well as revenue and saw one answer to this
lying in the dramatization of established Victorian classics. MGM led the way.
But in addition to this strategy, both Irving Thalberg and David O. Selznick,

the leading producers at MGM in the early 30s, came from cultivated Jewish homes where they had grown up with Dickens, Tolstoy, Dumas and others and drew on their fond memories of childhood reading to create works of cinematic art.[19]

The 1930s was also the decade of the Depression. One of the cinema's reactions to that depression was the 'fantasy of goodwill' films notably by Frank Capra and Leo McCarey which proposed as a solution to the Depression an optimistic gospel of all- round kindness and decency, celebrating family, community, good neighbourliness and Christian fellowship. The lavish, star-filled adaptations of Dickens produced at MGM and Universal in this decade were essentially Dickensian 'fantasies of goodwill', brightly lit, cheerful and upbeat.

MGM's versions of *David Copperfield* and *A Tale of Two Cities* have never been surpassed. They are classical products of Hollywood in its heyday, polished, vivid, life enhancing dramas, on which all the departments of the studio were working at the top of their form and in which handpicked casts triumphantly realized Dickens's teeming casts of characters. Their success can be measured by the fact that however many actors have played the roles since, no-one has ever quite equalled Edna May Oliver as Betsy Trotwood and Miss Pross, Basil Rathbone as Mr Murdstone and St Evremonde, Lennox Pawle as Mr Dick, Jessie Ralph as Clara Peggotty, Blanche Yurka as Madame Defarge or Ronald Colman as Sydney Carton.

Both *David Copperfield* and *A Tale of Two Cities* show goodness in action. In *Copperfield* the boy David encounters on his journey through life kindness, help and sympathy from sometimes unexpected quarters (the Peggottys, the Micawbers, Betsy Trotwood and Mr Dick), all affirming Dickens's stated view that 'my faith in the People ... is on the whole illimitable', and more than offsetting the cruelty of the Murdstones, the duplicity of Uriah Heep and the selfishness of Steerforth. *Two Cities* is a classic drama of renunciation and self-sacrifice, duty and redemption, ending with the New Testament promise of eternal life.

Even in Hollywood, authenticity was uppermost in the film-makers' minds. Producer David Selznick and director George Cukor wanted as many English actors as possible in the cast and for the boy David cast a film newcomer, the English Freddie Bartholomew, overruling studio chief Louis B. Mayer's preference for the American Jackie Cooper, who would have been catastrophically miscast. They gave serious consideration to filming it in England but in the end settled for California, though Selznick and Cukor visited England, were taken round the Dickens sites by the Dickens Society and engaged the novel-

Dickensian fantasy of goodwill: *David Copperfield* (1934) with Frank Lawton, W. C.   **31**
Fields and Jean Cadell.

ist Hugh Walpole, then president of the Dickens Society, to turn the adaptation that they had prepared with Howard Estabrook into an acceptable screenplay. Cukor later recalled: 'We photographed Betsy Trotwood's house and the White Cliffs of Dover (but we shot the Dover scenes in California near Malibu, and I have to say *our* cliffs were better – whiter and cliffier).'[20] There is a fundamental truth in this statement. One of Hollywood's abiding strengths was the creation of its own self-contained universe, which contained the essence of the real but transformed into idealization, myth and dreamscape. The first-rate largely British cast was a great help. But controversially Charles Laughton as Micawber was replaced by W. C. Fields, after two days of filming. According to David Thomson, the first rushes of Laughton showed him playing Micawber as a sinister, self-pitying figure more likely to molest David than to befriend him.[21] In my view the casting of Fields was a bold stroke that wholly paid off. The actor had strong linguistic and spiritual affinities with the character and director George Cukor adored and included some of the actor's inspired ad libs, as when during one speech he absent-mindedly dipped his quill pen in his tea and put his foot in the wastepaper basket.[22] The film, which ran for more than two hours, cost $1,069,225 to produce and made a profit of $732,000. Cukor believed – rightly – that the first half of the film was better than the second but gave as the reason – again rightly – that the first half of the book was better than the second.[23] The focus on an innocent young orphan making his way in the world and encountering the best and worst of people had a universal appeal, while the studio located it in a superbly evoked Victorian world that was true to its literary origin.

A Tale of Two Cities (1936) which cost $1.2 million and made only a modest profit nevertheless contained a definitive performance from Colman without his customary moustache, but the film did not overcome the problem posed by the book – and solved by the Marvin Harvey play – that the central character did not appear until twenty-five minutes into the action. Nevertheless, it works triumphantly as a film. Producer David O. Selznick set up a special unit under Val Lewton and Jacques Tourneur to stage the storming of the Bastille, an epic sequence which no other version has equalled; Jack Conway handled the main story with assurance and sensitivity; and Colman's reading of the final, memorable speech, 'It's a far, far better thing I do than I have ever done', still brings a lump to the throat and was voted by readers of the *Sunday Dispatch* in 1940 one of the six most moving fade-outs in film.[24]

MGM also produced the ultimate 'fantasy of goodwill' in *A Christmas Carol* (1938), with Reginald Owen as Scrooge. It is instructive to compare this version with the British version, *Scrooge* (1935), produced by Twickenham Studios and starring Sir Seymour Hicks in the title role. Technically, the American version is superior to the British, highlighting a problem that British films faced in competing with Hollywood. Although Hicks enjoys himself hugely as Scrooge and Donald Calthrop is an appropriately scrawny and put-upon Bob Cratchit, *Scrooge* is disjointed, lacks special effects (most of the ghosts are just voices-off) and despite individually effective scenes fails to build up tension or maintain mood. The Hollywood version is a fine piece of polished studio filmmaking, expertly put together, funny, moving and warm-hearted, with convincing special effects, high key lighting and nice sense of pace and mood. The British version is based in part on J. C. Buckstone's stage adaptation, in which Seymour Hicks had been appearing on stage since the turn of the century, and derived inspiration from Victorian illustrations for the story, notably those of John Leech. It eliminates the Fezziwigs and most of Scrooge's youth, concentrating on the theme of the humanization of his old age. Fascinatingly, it stresses the essential social cohesion of the nation, intercutting between the

Lord Mayor's Christmas banquet and beggars in the street feeding on scraps scavenged from the kitchens. But all join in singing 'God Save the Queen'. In the finale Scrooge joins the Cratchits in church to sing 'Hark The Herald Angels Sing'. So the film's clear message is that monarchy and religion provide the vital underpinnings of society and all will be well if selfish individuals discover the joys of good neighbourliness and are absorbed into the community.

The MGM version, based directly on the book, makes a number of important structural alterations and changes of emphasis, to build up those basic elements of the MGM worldview: the home (extending the coverage of the Cratchit family Christmas), the church (Christmas services) and romance (building up the romance of nephew Fred and his fiancée Bess). Scenarist Hugo Butler 'improves' Dickens by having Scrooge sack Cratchit on Christmas Eve for snowballing him and knocking his hat off. The American version emphasizes youth rather than age, with Fred and Bob Cratchit both given leading roles, made friends, and demonstrating their youthful spirits by sliding on the ice and snowballing. All the darkness in Dickens's original is eliminated and it emerges as a Victorian English equivalent of MGM's popular Hardy Family series of small-town dramas with a plump, genial Bob Cratchit, Fred, Bess, Scrooge and the family Cratchit all celebrating Christmas together at the end.

Paul Davis has plausibly contextualized this film in 1930s America and seeing it as part of the Americanization of *Christmas Carol* with a shift of emphasis particularly appropriate to the decade. He shows how *A Christmas Carol* was less popular in the United States than Britain until the 1930s when it became better known and it was much publicized that President Roosevelt read it out to his family every Christmas Eve. Lionel Barrymore appeared in a radio adaptation of the story every Christmas from 1934 to the early 1950s. It became 'one of the guiding texts of the New Deal', in its Americanized guise, which was, as stressed in the 1938 version, not so much Scrooge's obsession with money as with business. Fred denounces his failure to use his money for constructive purposes. So making money is not bad, how you use it is what is important. So from being seen as an anti-capitalist fable, it becomes a manifesto for capitalism with a caring face, 'an American business ethic of community service'.[25] The Americanization of *A Christmas Carol* was to be completed by Capra in his film *It's a Wonderful Life* (1946), with James Stewart and Donna Reed as modern Cratchits, Lionel Barrymore reproducing his Scrooge as the villainous Henry F. Potter and the Christmas ghosts represented by the Angel Clarence (Henry Travers). It became a regular feature in the Christmas television schedules. The sentimental humanism of Capra and the confident, richly textured, beautifully executed realization of the narrative were both characteristic of the Hollywood studios in their heyday. The Americanization of Scrooge has continued in a film which represents all that is wrong with present-day Hollywood. Richard Donner's *Scrooged* (1988) is a vulgar, coarse and degraded updating of Dickens with the charmless Bill Murray playing Scrooge as a foul-mouthed, crass and self-seeking television executive who after being visited by the ghosts (Christmas Past is a raucous New York taxi-driver; Christmas Present a female fury who keeps slugging him) sees the light. He makes a rambling television confession and promises to turn over a new leaf. The crudity and grossness of the 'comic' proceedings are hitched to a smug sense of political correctness: the Cratchits are black; Scrooge's girlfriend runs a shelter for derelicts and recalls that they used to have 'good sex' (the obligatory ingredient for modern Hollywood well-being) before he became obsessed with his career. It is enough to make Dickens turn over in his grave. But it shows how Dickens continues to be associated with Christmas. The influence of this association is such that MGM interpolated a Christmas church visit for Sydney Carton into *A Tale of Two Cities* and, because there was no Christmas scene in *David Copperfield*, they contrived to include a carol in its title music.

Universal's 1930s Dickensian fantasies of goodwill were both directed by Stuart Walker. Although done with taste and some style, they failed to match up to MGM's. They shared the same characteristic high key lighting, smoothness of execution and evocative art direction. But both stories were reduced to polite and tasteful romantic dramas. *Great Expectations* (1934) eliminated Miss Havisham's terrible death and Pip's snobbish treatment of Joe Gargery, turning Miss Havisham into a crusty old aunt, Estella into a conventional leading lady with none of the necessary icy hauteur and Pip into a breathless juvenile lead. In this version, Magwitch (Henry Hull) is the leading character and the story centres on his benevolence and on the discovery by Miss Havisham and Estella of the value of true love. 'Love is worth all the pain and suffering that comes with it' realizes Estella. The most striking image in the film is Magwitch, arms outstretched against a large stone cross appealing to the boy Pip for help, and looking like Christ crucified. The film then becomes a dramatization of the text 'Love thy neighbour as thyself'. Apart from Francis L. Sullivan giving his first interpretation of Jaggers, a role he was to repeat in David Lean's version, the cast give the impression of being a second-rate American provincial rep company tackling a great English classic (Phillips Holmes as Pip, Jane Wyatt as Estella, Alan Hale as Joe Gargery, Florence Reed as Miss Havisham).

The Mystery of Edwin Drood (1935) is rather better. Claude Rains is excellent as the obsessive, tormented, opium addict John Jasper and there are whiffs of the necessary darkness in the opium den and Jasper's drugged dreams and in the great storm when Edwin disappears. But much of the film involves the brightly-lit triangle romance of Rosa Bud, Edwin Drood and Neville Landless and the investigations of the mysterious Datchery.

The other major 1930s British film was Thomas Bentley's last Dickens adaptation, *The Old Curiosity Shop* (1934) a film that looked archaic beside its Hollywood counterparts. It maintained the style of Bentley's silent Dickens films: rural locations, slow pace, theatrical staging and tableau groupings in a film which resolves itself into a series of what are in effect variety-turns of larger-than-life caricature grotesques (Quilp, Samson and Sally Brass, Codlin and Short, Mrs Jarley's Waxworks, Dick Swiveller and the Marchioness) interspersed with beautifully photographed and idyllic rural scenes. It is a curious undynamic, unintegrated narrative, which in the end resembles a celebration of Priestley's First England, olde- worlde guidebook England, starting as it does with a stagecoach, by now a cliché of biscuit tins and Christmas cards celebrating Merrie England, and then old churchyards, old coaching inns, old country cottages and the old curiosity shop itself, a celebration of a static, timeless, antique England.

The appeal of Dickens in the 1930s to both British and American cinema audiences confirms the truth of Orwell's perception. He wrote in 1939:

> The common man is still living in the mental world of Dickens, but nearly every modern intellectual has gone over to some or other form of totalitarianism. From the Marxist or Fascist point of view, nearly all that Dickens stands for can be written off as 'bourgeois morality'. But in moral outlook noone could be more bourgeois than the English working classes. The ordinary people in the western countries have never entered mentally into the world of 'realism' and power politics. They may do so before long, in which case Dickens will be as out of date as the cabhorse. But in his own age and ours he has been popular chiefly because he was able to express in comic, simplified and therefore memorable form the native decency of the common man. And it is important that from this point of view people of very different types can be described as 'common'. In a country like England, in spite of its class structure, there does exist a certain cultural unity … Nearly everyone, whatever his actual conduct may be, responds emotionally to the idea of human brotherhood. Dickens voiced a code which was and on the whole still believed in, even by people who violate it. It is difficult otherwise to explain why he could be both read by working people (a thing which has happened to no other novelist of his stature) and buried in Westminster Abbey.[26]

32   The unacceptable face of Victorian England: John Howard Davies in *Oliver Twist* (1948).

This passage contains a set of basic propositions and observations which seem to me profoundly and continuously true.

Victorian England, which in the depressed 1930s seemed to represent a lost never-never land of goodwill, had come by the 1940s to stand for something completely different. Immediate post-war Britain is the period of Gothic Dickens. These films came after the Gainsborough melodramas had created a taste for period costume drama but answered the demand of critics for literary respectability and documentary authenticity.[27] Hollywood *film noir* had created a vogue for stories with a visual style of shadows, darkness, chiaroscuro and spiritual bleakness. These two cinematic trends cross-fertilized in the new adaptations of *Great Expectations* (1946), *Oliver Twist* (1948), *Nicholas Nickleby* (1947) and *Scrooge* (1951). Largely stripped of humour and desentimentalized, they restored the darkness to the Dickensian vision and retold the stories in a shadowy, atmospheric, chiaroscuro Dorean London, far removed from the bright, pastoral imagery of 1930s Dickens. Wartime experience and post-war reconstruction aimed at building a welfare state focused attention on getting rid of the evils of Victorian England, and the Dickens novels adapted at that time highlighted the evils of the workhouse and the underworld, the educational system and unreconstructed capitalism. The Beveridge Report had sought to slay the five giants – ignorance, disease, squalor, idleness and want. One of the spirits shows the 1951 *Scrooge* two ragged, emaciated children: 'This boy is ignorance, this girl is want', he says sternly. The other Beveridge evils are amply demonstrated in the films, which taken together construct am image of the Victorian era as something dark, fearful, oppressive and about to be eliminated by the Labour Party's new welfare state.

This post-war period produced the so far definitive screen versions of *Great Expectations* and *Oliver Twist,* directed by David Lean, *Nicholas Nickleby,* directed by Cavalcanti, and *Scrooge,* directed by Brian Desmond Hurst. They all contained performances which have not been matched in cinema since; Martita Hunt's Miss Havisham, Finlay Currie's Abel Magwitch, Francis L. Sullivan's Jaggers, Bernard Miles's Joe Gargery and Newman Noggs, Robert Newton's Bill Sikes, Alastair Sim's Scrooge.

Great Expectations powerfully and sensitively anatomized the class snobbery of a poor boy transformed into a gentleman and embarrassed by his original associates. This is highlighted in key scenes, beautifully played by the participants, of Pip's embarrassment at the visit of the clumsy and well-meaning Joe and at the revelation of his mysterious benefactor's true identity. Dickens, however, was still being seen as peculiarly English. Richard Winnington, the respected critic of the *News Chronicle,* argued on the basis of this and other films the superiority of British films over those of Hollywood, 'in discretion and discrimination and taste' and also in cinematic imagination. He justly linked Dickens, England and British cinema, as interlocking entities.

Dickens has never before been rendered effectively into cinematic terms: now the acceptable adjustment between the realism of the camera and Dickens' robustious enlargement of character is made ... This film could only have been made in England, and a large amount of the visual pleasure is derived from the superlative photography of the Medway saltings and a recognition of the mordant beauty of English weather.[28]

Oliver Twist memorably explored the darker reaches of the Victorian underworld, its burglars, prostitutes, pickpockets and fences. But it ran into trouble in New York where there was fierce opposition from Jewish groups to what was called the anti-Semitic depiction of Fagin by Alec Guinness. Release of the film was held up until 1951 when it finally appeared in America with twelve minutes removed. *Nicholas Nickleby* has suffered by comparison with the Lean films but it is a creditable production which also seeks to restore the darkness of the Dickensian vision, with the horrors of Dotheboys Hall and Ralph Nickleby's suicide graphically depicted.

Nothing could be more unlike the high-key MGM 1938 *Christmas Carol* than Desmond Hurst's 1951 *Scrooge*, a dark Gothic fable, which is a remorseless exposé of heartless capitalism. Fezziwig is the acceptable face of capitalism, explaining that he is in business not just for the money but 'to preserve a way of life one knew and loved ... I have to be loyal to the old ways ... There's more in life than money'. But he goes bust. Fezziwig is replaced by Jorkins, who believes that business is for money-making alone ('Control the cash box and you control the world'), but he embezzles the company's money. He is exposed and driven out, but only so that Scrooge and Marley can take over and hoard money as misers. So the social conscience and generosity of Fezziwig is contrasted with the unprincipled self-aggrandizing of Jorkins and the skinflint miserliness of Scrooge and Marley. Alice, meanwhile, whom Scrooge should have married and did not because of his increasing obsession with wealth, is seen visiting the poor in the workhouse, social conscience again contrasting with self-interested individualism. But Scrooge sees the light and embraces the Fezziwig doctrine at the end.

The 1950s saw the return of a Conservative government, though one which aimed at consensus, in which affluence and full employment led to the slogan; 'You've never had it so good'. The evils of the Victorian age seemed to have been banished by the welfare state and by widespread affluence. The British cinema of the 1950s aimed to recapture the glories of the past, re-creating heroic episodes from World War Two and remaking 1930s successes such as *The Good Companions*. There had not been a 1930s *Pickwick*, though plans to film it had been announced several times. But Noel Langley's *The Pickwick Papers* (1952), with James Hayter, as benevolence personified, toasting 'good will, good hope and good nature', was a veritable 'fantasy of goodwill'. C. A.

Romantic sacrifice: Dirk Bogarde as Sydney Carton in *A Tale of Two Cities* (1958).   **33**

Lejeune in *The Observer* praised it for its 'jolly music, genial acting, the comradeship and adventures of the road and a roaring fire and mug of mulled ale at the end of the journey', emphasizing the prevailing mood of Dickensian jollity.[29] Dirk Bogarde trod in the footsteps of Ronald Colman in Ralph Thomas's 1958 *A Tale of Two Cities* and gave us a romantic, beautifully spoken Sydney Carton, sensitive and self-deprecating. But the production began the trend that has been followed in all subsequent major productions of *Two Cities* and has resulted in the numbing and devitalizing of the story. It is perhaps the influence of television, of which the preferred mode, because of its intimacy as a medium, is naturalism. But Dickens is the opposite of a naturalistic writer.

His was an intensely stylized world, compounded of stage melodrama, Gothic novel, investigative journalism and social reform propaganda, a larger-than-life world teeming with vitality and variety, seasoned with his comic genius, conceived on an epic scale, and peopled with a gallery of larger-than-life characters. To scale down the characters, to stress genuine locations and documentary authenticity, to de-melodramatize the work, is to remove its essence and this is what has happened with successive adaptations from 1958 onwards. A 1980 version of *A Tale of Two Cities* made for American television and directed by Jim Goddard, boasted an unexpectedly stylish and spirited performance from Chris Sarandon in the dual roles of Carton and Darnay, and strong support from a veteran British cast (Peter Cushing as Dr Manette, Flora Robson as Miss Pross, Billie Whitelaw as Madame Defarge, Kenneth More as Jarvis Lorry). However, with its academic fidelity in sets and costumes and naturalistic approach, it emerged as bland. Granada's 1989 version was even worse. With its stately locations, Anglo-French cast and funereal pace, it had an almost dreamlike feel, completely as odds with the energy and vitality of Dickens.

Two Cities is one of the most political of Dickens's novels and it centres on the event which hung over the whole of the culture and thought of the nineteenth century like a thundercloud – the French Revolution. It unleashed the spectre of the world turned upside down, of hallowed institutions and hierarchies shattered, of age-old traditions and privileges dissolved. For some, this heralded the dawn of a brave new world; rather more viewed it with horror as a return to primal chaos. This view has been reinforced by British popular culture which both in fiction and in films has generally lent its support to the aristocrats and against the revolutionaries.

For the Anglo-Saxon world, it is Dickens who indelibly fixed the image of the Revolution as a reign of terror. As befitted a great humanitarian with a hatred of injustice, he was careful to show the excesses of the *ancien régime* in the person of the vicious Marquis St Evremonde, whose carriage symbolically crushes a child of the people beneath its remorseless wheels. But it is the excesses of the revolutionary mob, the meaningless sacrifice of the innocent seamstress and the unrelenting pursuit of Darnay's little child by Madame Defarge that linger longest in the memory. Even more perhaps the presence of such stalwart representatives of the bulldog breed as Jarvis Lorry, Jerry Cruncher and Miss Pross suggests that the excesses of both the *ancien régime* and the Terror are something that happened 'over there', that both are unsportsmanlike, uncivilized and downright un-English. It all derives from the unspoken idea that England had had its revolution in the seventeenth century, had beheaded its king and established a military dictatorship. But it did not take and we had since grown out of all that nonsense, preferring a sensible process of evolution to the irreversible carnage of revolution. Americans have a rather more ambivalent reaction to the French Revolution, but for Hollywood it can serve to highlight the evils of the Old World, which the New World has sought to correct, and the dangers of revolution from which the United States was born but which it has sought ever since to avoid repeating. For in the twentieth century the Bolshevik revolution and the overthrow of the Czars caused the same frisson of terror through the West as did the French Revolution in the nineteenth. It may be more than coincidence then that the major film versions of *Two Cities* came in the 1930s, the era of Stalin, and the 1950s, the height of the Cold War, the French Revolution providing a salutary warning about the dangers of revolutions in general. The 1989 version had a different emphasis and can be seen as a direct response to our membership of the Common Market. This version had a French director and French actors playing the French roles – the ultimate in naturalism. But Dickens's Frenchmen and women were not real Frenchmen and women. They were the products of a very English imagination, and were far better represented from a Dickensian point of view by non-French actors (Basil Rathbone, Blanche Yurka, Mitchell Lewis, Lucille LaVerne) in Hollywood's 1936 version, which was in every way a far, far better film than anyone has done since.

Perhaps the most significant development in Dickensian terms was the beginning of the BBC Sunday teatime serial, which became the flagship of Dickens production in the 1950s and 1960s. Dickens as editor of *Household Worlds*, Dickens as family entertainer, perfectly fulfilled the Reithian image of television, of the family gathered around the wireless or television sharing the culture, a vision based on the premise not of freedom of choice but freedom of access to all that is great. The Sunday teatime serial was the epitome of television as an educational, uplifting, socially cohesive force. In this, television was following a tradition established by radio and carried on in parallel. Each television watching generation saw a new version of *David Copperfield, Great Expectations, Oliver Twist, Nicholas Nickleby, A Tale of Two Cities*. Dickens was constantly remade for television as the technology developed and the medium moved from live performance to videotape to film, from black and white to colour, but it remained on Sundays Dickens the family entertainer rather than Dickens the social critic. Sunday teatime was no place for *Hard Times, Little Dorrit* or *Bleak House*.[30] I grew up in the 1950s watching Peter Wyngarde as

Sydney Carton, Angela Baddeley as Mrs Gamp, Patrick Troughton as Daniel Quilp and was turned into a Dickens reader by watching the television adaptations more than anything else.

The 1960s, affluent, liberated, 'swinging', saw the Victorian era as utterly remote, a picturesque Christmas card/chocolate box/olde-worlde fantasy land full of kitsch bric-à-brac, and the writers of musicals began to plunder the novels for plots, emphasizing the upbeat, entertainment Dickens once again. It began with Lionel Bart's stage musical *Oliver!*, which was a phenomenon. It opened on 1 July, 1960, at the New Theatre, London, and ran for six years in London and for four in America. It was followed by *Pickwick* (music by Cyril Ornadel, book by Wolf Mankowitz, lyrics by Leslie Briscusse), which opened in London on 4 July, 1963, with Harry Secombe ideally cast as Pickwick, and enjoyed a twenty-month run, despite being a 'one-song show' (I'f I Ruled the World'). *The Observer* noted: 'it doesn't feel like Dickens and it doesn't smell like Dickens.'[31] There were subsequently shorter-lived stage musicals: *Two Cities* (1969; music by Jeff Wayne, lyrics by Jerry Wayne), with Edward Woodward as Carton, which notched up only forty-four performances; *Hard Times* (1973), set entirely in the circus ring; and *Great Expectations* (1975; music by Cyril Ornadel, book by Trevor Preston and lyrics by Hal Shaper), which despite a cast including John Mills as Joe Gargery, Leonard Whiting as Pip and Moira Lister as Miss Havisham, never reached the West End but toured in England and Canada.

Oliver! was transferred to the screen with great success by Carol Reed in 1968. With its catchy tunes ('Consider Yourself at Home', 'Food Glorious Food', 'I'm Reviewing the Situation', 'Who Will Buy?'), its exuberant large-scale dance numbers, Ron Moody re-creating his stage role of Fagin as 'lovable scalliwag' and large helpings of heart-tugging sentiment, it became the defining Dickens success of the decade. It was a critical and popular success and won several Oscars. *Pickwick*, although produced on television in 1969, did not reach the cinema screen. But Leslie Bricusse, who wrote the lyrics for *Pickwick*, provided the script, music and lyrics for *Scrooge* (1970), the first colour version of the story and a musicalized one. Directed by Ronald Neame, who had produced David Lean's Dickens films in a very different idiom, it starred Albert Finney, who took over at short notice from an indisposed Rex Harrison. He did one of the character turns he then gloried in but was obviously a young man pretending to be an old one, though Alec Guinness, Edith Evans and Kenneth More as assorted ghosts did well. Although it featured a special-effects sequence of Scrooge taken down to Hell and shown round by Marley's Ghost, the prevailing tone was one of remorseless jollity. In the same spirit, 1974 saw a musical film version of *The Old Curiosity Shop* renamed *Mr. Quilp*, and centring on a larger than life performance from Anthony Newley as Dickens's malign dwarf, Daniel Quilp. Interestingly, *Great Expectations* (1975) was also filmed with Michael York, James Mason and Margaret Leighton but with the songs removed and it emerged as a straightforward, naturalistic telling of the story in colour. The common feature of these musical versions was a devitalization of Dickens, who is sanitized and jollified, and is forever characterized by troupes of well-scrubbed, well-drilled cockney urchins dancing up and down picture-postcard streets. One of the stage phenomena of the 1990s is that there have been large-scale revivals of *Oliver*, *Pickwick* and *Scrooge* (Bricusse's film script turned into a stage musical), a version of *The Mystery of Edwin Drood* constructed as a music-hall evening and a new musical version of *Great Expectations* (music and lyrics by Mike Read), presenting a completely upbeat view of Dickens, which contrasted markedly with the Dickens who was appearing on television.

Dickens came back with a bang in the 1980s and 1990s and it was notable that it was his later, darker novels that the producers seized upon. There can be little doubt that Dickens was now being used as a coded attack on Mrs Thatcher and Thatcherism. Mrs Thatcher famously praised Victorian values, argued that there was no such thing as society and sanctioned the individual pursuit of wealth as the ultimate aim in life. Film-makers turned to Dickens to show the results of such a philosophy. This was in part because of the failure of the contemporary novel to adopt the kind of social canvas that Dickens utilized. It was Angus Wilson who sweepingly, but with symbolic accuracy, suggested that all modern novels were about adultery in Muswell Hill, indicting the narrowness and narcissism of much contemporary fiction. Television had replaced the novel as the primary vehicle for social comment in a world in which 60 per cent of the population never bought a book and 90 per cent of homes had television. For television, Dickens was suddenly vital and relevant. So Granada's *Hard Times* (1977) and the BBC's *Our Mutual Friend* (1976) were followed by the BBC's *Bleak House* (1985) and later the BBC's *Martin Chuzzlewit* and *Hard Times* (both 1994). All of them magnificently realized Dickens's dark vision and, with blazing sincerity and visual power, attacked poverty, exploitation, heartless bureaucracy, inefficient judiciary, sleaze and selfishness. Channel Four showed a complete recording of the RSC's mould-breaking and epoch-making *Nicholas Nickleby*. The first full-scale Dickens novel adaptation on the stage, it took place over two evenings and utilized the entire RSC company, many in multiple roles. It ran triumphantly during 1980 and 1981. The basic idea was to avoid caricature and reducing the book to a succession of turns, but instead to uncover the underlying moral principle of the novel. This it did partly by continuous narration, utilizing Dickens's own words and commentaries on the action, partly by careful social and historical contextualization of the story and partly by deeply felt and truthful ensemble playing, in which David Threlfall as the pathetic Smike and Edward Pether-bridge as a nervously excited Newman Noggs gave unforgettable performances, and Roger Rees turned Nicholas himself, often played as a gentle, well-bred, rather passive hero, into a 'strident, defiant, aggressive defender of truth'. When the play first opened, audiences were ecstatic but critics divided. It was Bernard Levin writing in *The Times* who most effectively captured the intention and effect of the piece when he declared rightly:

> Not for many years has London's theatre seen anything so richly joyous, so immoderately rife with pleasure, drama, colour and entertainment, so life-enhancing, yea-saying and fecund, so ... Dickensian ... It is a celebration of life and justice that is true to the spirit of Dickens' belief that these are the fulcrums on which the universe is moved, and the consequence is that we came out not merely delighted but strengthened, not just entertained but uplifted, not only affected but changed.[32]

While British television was triumphantly producing definitive versions of the later Dickens novels, cinema was on the whole failing to match their magnificence. Television is perfectly placed to adopt the serial form that Dickens originally used and to give far more time to the unfolding of the narrative than cinema can normally allow. *Little Dorrit* (1986), directed by Christine Edzard, sought to gain the space on the cinema screen, by shooting the film at length in two parts, shown on successive evenings. Despite a record assemblage of character actors and wide praise on its first appearance, it is a film which diminishes on each subsequent viewing. Entirely studio-shot, with static camera, flat lighting, naturalistic acting, it is dramatically inert. Apart from the memorable dramatic eruptions of Miriam Margolyes as Flora Finching, it almost never catches fire. A good deal of the publicity was devoted to the fact that furniture and costumes were made to original designs in authentic materials, that Verdi's exactly contemporary music from *La forza del destino* was used as score, and that authenticity was the aim. It was in fact 'heritage film-making' and although 'heritage' has become far too loosely and disparagingly used to apply to anything in costume and often to admirable works (the Merchant-Ivory films, BBC's *Middlemarch*), here the term in its negative sense seemed appropriate to a film which although large in scale and ambition missed the energy and vitality of Dickens completely. *The Mystery of Edwin Drood* (1993), despite a fine central performance by Robert Powell as John Jasper, was a failure for similar reasons. Similarly, two Dickens adaptations, directed by Clive Donner, made for American television but released to British cinemas, *Oliver Twist* (1982) and *A Christmas Carol* (1984), failed to dislodge the David Lean and Brian Desmond Hurst versions from their dominant positions. Both lacked the scale and sweep of the previous versions and the darker tones of Dickens's vision, something which it is possible to achieve in colour – as the BBC's *Bleak House* memorably showed – but which the use of colour often tends to reduce to a numbing visual blandness as here. *Oliver Twist* was reduced to a straight Victorian urban crime thriller, with George C. Scott as a sympathetic, de-Semitized, almost avuncular Fagin (with an impeccable politically correct speech about Jewish persecution), Tim Curry as a very modern nervily psychopathic Bill Sikes and Richard Charles as an impossibly angelic Oliver. Donner, who had edited the 1951 *Scrooge*, also had George C. Scott in his new *Christmas Carol*. Although shot in Shrewsbury and featuring a supporting cast of BBC Dickens veterans (John Sharp, Peter Woodthorpe, Liz Smith, Tim Bateson, Derek Francis), it was compromised by an appallingly cute Tiny Tim, and by George C. Scott's craggily patriarchal Scrooge, more in the Lionel Barrymore warped tycoon mould than the withered miser of Alistair Sim. A characteristically American psychological interpretation of Scrooge is thrown in, based on the parental neglect of Ebenezer and suggesting that Scrooge denied love by his father, turned into a replica of that father, here played by Nigel Davenport and given a much more prominent role than usual. It featured a strongly anti-capitalist message detailing Scrooge's cut-throat business methods and featuring a visit to the homeless and the children, ignorance and want, to point up the message. It led one critic to dub the film 'an anti-monetarist fable', picking up on the Thatcherite context of the remake. The 1990s thus began with two wholly opposing views of Dickens coexisting in the mass media: on the stage, a cheerful, upbeat, all-dancing, all-singing, all's-right-with-the-world musical Dickens, the reassuring, cosy, conservative family entertainer; and on television, the angry, unsparing indictment of social injustice, selfishness and greed, from the radical Dickens, the critic, prophet and preacher. The split directly mirrored the debate about the state of the nation under Thatcherism. It is the multi-faceted nature of Dickens which makes him susceptible of wholly different interpretations and ensures that he remains, like Shakespeare, completely relevant to and in tune with the moods, needs and mindsets of the nation. Whatever the circumstances, he is likely to remain 'Dickens – our contemporary'.

Notes

1   Peter Ackroyd, *Dickens*, London, 1990, pp. 1081-2.
2   Malcolm Andrews, *Dickens on England and the English*, Hassocks, 1979, p. xv.
3   George Orwell, *Collected Essays, Journalism and Letters*, volume 1, Harmondsworth, 1971, p. 455.
4   F. Dubrez Fawcett, *Dickens the Dramatist*, London, 1952, pp. 3-4.
5   Andrews, *Dickens on England*, p. 19.
6   Andrews, *Dickens on England*, pp. 154-5.
7   H. Philip Bolton, *Dickens Dramatized*, London, 1987, p. 3.
8   Bransby Williams, *Bransby Williams by Himself*, London, 1954, p. 41.
9   S. M. Eisenstein, *Film Form*, London, 1963, ed. Jay Leyda, p. 207.
10 Bolton, *Dickens Dramatized*, p. 17.
11 Bret Harte, *Tales of the West, Parodies and Poems*, London, n.d., p. 367.
12 Fawcett, *Dickens the Dramatist*, p. 193.
13 S. M. Eisenstein, 'Dickens, Griffith and the Film Today', *Film Form*, pp. 195-255.
14 Andrew Higson, *Waving the Flag*, Oxford, 1995, pp. 26-97.
15 Cecil Hepworth, *Came the Dawn*, London, 1951, p. 144.
16 *David Copperfield* is analysed in detail in Rachael Low, *History of the British Film 1906–1914*, London, 1949, pp. 236-47.
17 Linda Wood, *The Commercial Imperative in the British Film Industry: Maurice Elvey, a case study*, London, 1987, p. 35.
18 Herbert Wilcox, *25,000 Sunsets*, London,1967, pp. 62-3.
19 Roland Flamini, *Thalberg: the last tycoon and the world of MGM*, London, 1994, p. 19; David Thomson, *Showman: the life of David O. Selznick*, London, 1993, pp. 11-12.
20 Thomson, *Showman*, p. 181.
21 Thomson, *Showman*, p. 181.
22 Patrick McGilligan, *George Cukor: a double life*, London, 1991, p. 102.
23 McGilligan, *George Cukor*, p. 162.
24 Jeffrey Richards and Dorothy Sheridan (eds), *Mass-Observation at the Movies*, London, 1987, p. 200.
25 Paul Davis, *The Life and Times of Ebenezer Scrooge*, New Haven and London, 1990, p. 141.
26 Orwell, *Collected Essays, Journalism and Letters*, volumr 1, p. 503.
27 John Ellis, 'Art, Culture and Quality', *Screen*, 19 (Autumn 1978), pp. 9-49.
28 Richard Winnington, *Drawn and Quartered*, London, n.d., pp. 73-4.
29 Anthony Lejeune (ed.), *C. A. Lejeune Film Reader*, Manchester, 1991, pp. 273-4.
30 The productions are listed in Bolton, *Dickens Dramatized*.
31 Kurt Gänzl, *The British Musical Theatre*, volume 2, 1915–84, Basingstoke and London, 1986, p. 821.
32 Leon Rubin, *The Nicholas Nickleby Story*, London, 1981, pp. 178–9.

12

Dad's Army
and the politics
of nostalgia

As the millennium looms, Britain is undergoing a crisis of national identity, reflected in the stream of 'state of the nation' books and articles, the
questioning of traditional institutions and the general sense of spiritual malaise
infecting all generations. There are three possible directions that the national
identity might take. First, there could be a continued descent into the unrestrained individualism which lay at the heart of Thatcherite philosophy. Francis Fukuyama in *The End of History* (London, 1994) claimed that the collapse
of Communism meant the final victory of liberal democracy and the capitalist
world order in the century-long struggle between rival global systems. By contrast, Alain Minc in *Le Nouveau Moyen Age* (Paris, 1993) argued that the collapse of Communism had put history into reverse. He denied that a single
principle had triumphed but claimed instead that we are entering a world
without coherence, an age with no religion, no ideology, no cultural principles,
a world where there is only the market, and the market is a state of nature.
Lacking rules and principles, it functions merely as a jungle in which the basic
rule is the survival of the fittest. Individual desires, ambitions and goals rule.
That is the recipe for the fulfilment of the reversal of the Perkin analysis which
I suggested at the outset of this study: a return to a situation in which Britain
becomes once again 'one of the most aggressive, brutal, rowdy, outspoken,
cruel and bloodthirsty' nations in the world.

The second possibility is the completion of the Americanization of the
world, a process that has been underway since the beginning of the century,
and which has been variously dubbed the 'Coca-Colonization' or 'Mac-

Donaldization' of the world. These terms were well chosen for they centre on the idea not just of the individual as consumer but as consumer of American products, which when universally desired and pursued lead to the homogenization of the world and the elimination of distinctive national identities.

This has long been a concern of intellectuals, particularly on the Left. In Britain, such influential luminaries as F. R. Leavis, George Orwell and Richard Hoggart have warned of the dangers of Americanization. J. B. Priestley christened the process 'Admass', the mass consumer culture promoted by advertizing. He saw America as its chief advocate and pronounced it as wholly alien to, and opposed to, the kind of decent, tolerant, communal, good-natured Englishness he had so powerfully advocated during the war. As he wrote in 1973;

> The triumphs of Admass can be plainly seen. It operates in the outer visible world, where it offers more and more things – for more and more money of course – and creates the so-called 'Good Life' ... It is easy to understand why there should be this conflict between Admass and Englishness. What is central to Admass is the production and consumption of goods. If there is enough of this – though of course there never is, because dissatisfaction is built into Admass there will be sufficient money to pay for its 'Good Life' ... Now Englishness, with its relation to the unconscious, its dependence upon instinct and intuition ... cannot ignore other states of mind and cannot help feeling that Admass, with its ruthless competitiveness, its idea of man simply as a producer and consumer, its dependence upon dissatisfaction, greed and envy, must be responsible for bad and not good states of mind ... The battle that will decide the future of the English is going on all round us ... Admass could be winning. There are various reasons why this may be happening. To begin with, not all the English hold fast to Englishness. Some important and influential men carefully train themselves out of it ... and a horde of others, shallow and foolish, wander away from it, shrugging off their inheritance. Englishness is not as strong as it was even thirty years ago. It needs to be nourished by a sense of the dignity and possible destiny of mankind ... The *Zeitgeist* seems to be working for Admass. So does most of what we read and what we hear ... Englishness cannot be fed with the east wind of a narrow rationality, a constant appeal to self-interest.[1]

He called for an appeal to restore to people 'their idea of themselves as a family' and 'the chance of behaving better' – the two things being in Priestley's worldview indissolubly linked.

The third possible development is one which would meet Priestley's requirement – a return to the pre-existing ideas of national identity. This is the ultimate objective of the politics of nostalgia. The continuing popularity of *Dad's*

Army is a potent example of that development.

By the late 1960s, television had definitively taken over from the cinema as the mass medium and it is to television thenceforth that we must look for projections of the national image. Cinema's audience had shrunk and its output had fragmented. Increasingly, it reflected and constructed the attitudes and preoccupations of the under thirties and was in consequence increasingly unrepresentative of the nation as a whole. One of the cinema's strategies in this period of shrinking audiences was to turn to television and produce feature-film versions of television successes, particularly that staple of popular viewing, the situation comedy or sitcom. In many cases these cinematizations were artistically unsuccessful, stretching what were naturally intimate, richly textured half-hour 'miniatures' into broader, coarser, more impersonal, more bloated, and less funny ninety-minute rehashes coasting on the affection of audiences for the leading characters. One of the more successful screen transcriptions – though not immune from the problems of stretching – was Columbia Pictures's 1971 film of *Dad's Army*, directed by Norman Cohen.

Dad's Army is one of the phenomena of modern television history. Originally launched as a modest six-part series in 1968, it eventually ran for nine years, ending in 1977 after a total of eighty episodes. It repeated its success in radio adaptations of the television episodes. It inspired a stage version which ran first in the West End of London and then on tour in 1975 and 1976, as well as the 1971 film. Scripts from the series were published. It has maintained its popularity in regular television repeats and both video and audio cassettes have given it a new lease of life.[2] In 1993 a survey reported that Dad's Army was the most popular television comedy show of the past two decades.[3] An official *Dad's Army* appreciation society was launched. In 1995 it became the subject of an arts documentary in the *Omnibus* series. Why does a series about a group of bumbling old men in a Home Guard unit in an out-of-season seaside resort continue to captivate?

On one level, it is the undoubted fact that it is superbly written and played. Within the half-hour format, the writers Jimmy Perry and David Croft, with consistent inventiveness and ingenuity, combined character comedy, verbal routines, broad farce and satire, literally something for everyone, but so deftly done that you could not see the joins. Crucially, it was based in reality, in experience and observation. Jimmy Perry, whose original idea the series was, had served in the Home Guard and provided the inspiration for Private Pike. David Croft, an experienced television producer and former actor, who produced all the episodes, directed many of them, and collaborated on the scripts,

34   Joining up: *Dad's Army* (1971) with Arthur Lowe and John Le Mesurier.

had been an air raid warden before joining the Royal Artillery. He ended the war as a major on General Eisenhower's staff.

In addition to the brilliance of the scripts, a hand-picked cast of talented character actors grew into their roles, continually enriching and deepening them, and provide an object lesson in ensemble playing. Unusually, this series seemed as fresh and inventive at the end of its run as it had been at the beginning, because the writers were writing for the characters as they had evolved. They were a memorable gallery: the pompous and self-important bank manager and platoon commander Captain George Mainwaring (Arthur Lowe) continually sparring with his elegant, insouciant chief clerk, Sergeant Arthur Wilson (John Le Mesurier); the feisty old soldier and local butcher Lance Corporal Jack Jones (Clive Dunn), ever ready to volunteer for anything and continually recalling his military service in Sudan and the efficacy of the bayonet against the enemy; the doom-laden, continually grumbling Scottish undertaker and former naval Chief Petty Officer Private James Frazer (John Laurie); the gentle, amiable octogenarian Private Charles Godfrey (Arnold Ridley), retired to a picturesque country cottage with his two sisters after twenty-five years in the gentleman's outfitting department of the Army and Navy Stores, and plagued by a weak bladder; the ever-resourceful spiv Private Joe Walker (James Beck) and the gangling, accident-prone Private Frank Pike (Ian Lavender) mollycoddled by his protective mother, constantly put down by Mainwaring ('You stupid boy') and with his worldview shaped by comics and the cinema. In addition, there is their arch-enemy, Chief Air Raid Warden Hodges (Bill Pertwee), bullying, loud-mouthed and officious but cowardly.

From the first they were characters, never caricatures, and so it was possible, as time went on to develop serious storylines like the shunning of Private Godfrey when it is discovered he has been a conscientious objector in World War One – it is eventually revealed that he has received the Military Medal for gallantry under fire as a medical orderly. Similarly touching and truthful was the chaste *Brief Encounter* love affair of the unhappily married Captain Mainwaring – whose wife Elizabeth is never seen in the series but remains a formidable presence at the other end of a telephone line. These were three-dimensional characters who became old friends.

Like the great comic creations of Shakespeare and Dickens, these characters took on a life of their own. J. B. Priestley could have been writing about them in anticipation when, in his perceptive volume *English Humour* (1930), he argued that the dominant strain in the best English comic writing was the comedy of character, 'the richest and wisest kind of humour, sweetening and mellowing life for us'.[4] He traces it to the characteristic individuality of the English and says it is best described as 'tender mockery': 'We laugh at those we love...because we have come to know them so well, that certain traits or habits, as familiar to us as their faces, seem peculiarly absurd.'[5]

The two greatest creators of comic characters in English literature were Shakespeare and Dickens. Shakespeare's humour was peculiarly English. Priestley says: 'England and Shakespeare are inextricably intertwined; strands of his weaving run through the fabric of our nation's thought, literature and life.'[6] Wherever his plays may have been ostensibly set, in Italy, Egypt or Illyria, the comic characters were always indisputably English: the 'rude mechanicals' in the Athens woods in *A Midsummer Night's Dream* or Dogberry and the Messina watch in *Much Ado about Nothing*. Shakespeare had his pompous and officious functionaries (Malvolio), his 'stupid boys' (Sir Andrew Aguecheek), his spivs (Autolycus). He even mustered a Tudor Dad's Army as Sir John Falstaff and Justice Shallow recruited their volunteer force in *King Henry IV Part Two*: Mouldy, Shadow, Wart, Feeble and Bullcalf are the ancestors of Jones, Pike, Frazer, Godfrey and Walker. What is crucial about these comic characters is that they are countrymen, rustics and as such represent the state of the Elizabethan nation. The world had changed out of all recognition by the time Dickens was creating his comic characters. They are urban, the denizens of a teeming industrialized world, more than anything else inhabitants of London. But the source of the humour remained constant. Priestley says: 'The humour of Dickens is essentially a humour of character. It is his comic figures we remember first, before we remember the books that contain them.'[7] These characters have become part of a shared memory, constantly revivified in film and television adaptations: Mr Micawber, Sam Weller, Mrs Gamp, Mr Pecksniff, Mr Jingle and the rest. Captain Mainwaring is almost a Dickensian character. It is no coincidence that Arthur Lowe, who played him, also played a memorable Mr Micawber in a television adaptation of *David Copperfield* (1976). By the time we get to *Dad's Army* a further transition has taken place. From the countrymen of Shakespeare and the metropolitan characters of Dickens, the focus has shifted in comedy as indeed in the nation to the suburbs. Although the location is a South Coast seaside town, the characters are indelibly suburban: bank managers, vicars, shopkeepers, retired folk.

Quite part from its place in a hallowed tradition of English comic writing, *Dad's Army* is also rich in resonances from a more recent comic tradition, rooted in the war and in the immediate post-war period. The beloved Liverpudlian comedian Robb Wilton had a classic wartime monologue about the Home Guard which memorably began: 'The day war broke out, my missus looked at me and she said: "What good are you?". I said: "How d'ye mean, what good am I?" She said: "You're too old for the army, you couldn't get into the navy and they wouldn't have you in the air force, so what good are you?".' His solution is to join the Home Guard and with his mates from the *Dog and Pullet* public house, to defy the might of Hitler's onslaught. The Home Guard was thus already a natural source of humour during the war.

Top British box-office star George Formby turned his attentions to the Home Guard in the film *Get Cracking* (1943). There are interesting similarities to and differences from *Dad's Army*. Like *Dad's Army*, the film opens with Anthony Eden's 1940 broadcast announcing the creation of the Local Defence Volunteers (LDV). This is followed by a cod-newsreel history of the LDV and its successor, the Home Guard, narrated by E. V. H. Emmett, familiar to cinemagoers as the voice of Gaumont British News. He stresses the cross-class and multi-national nature of the Home Guard, as we see a peer and his butler, a publican and his customers, a Scot, a Welshman and an Irishman joining up. The central theme of the film is the rivalry of two Home Guard platoons, those

The voice of authority: *Dad's Army* (1971) with Arthur Lowe and John Le Mesurier. **35**

of Minor Wallop and Major Wallop, which is echoed in the rivalry of the Walmington and Eastgate platoons in *Dad's Army*. The rival platoons are both led by tradesmen, Minor Wallop by local publican Sam Elliott (Edward Rigby) and Major Wallop by butcher Alf Pemberton (Frank Pettingell). Formby, who is a garage owner, plays the lance corporal of the Minor Wallop platoon and has one scene trying to instruct a gangling youth, a very 'stupid boy', even more gormless than George usually is, in rifle use. The pub is the Minor Wallop platoon headquarters, the village names are a slang term for beer and George is seen driving a tank with a bottle of beer in his hand, all part of a long-standing association of Beer and Britannia and the traditional depiction of John Bull dining on beer and beef. This contrasts with the Church Hall venue for *Dad's Army* with its Protestant overtones. The rivalry between platoons leads to George being drummed out but he redeems himself by capturing the Major Wallop headquarters and all ends happily when the two platoons are merged. The whole image of the Home Guard is one of muddling through, whimsical ingenuity and dogged individualism, as seen in the difficulty of getting the men together on the same night due to the rival attractions: darts, band practice, courting and the 'pictures'. But the film centres squarely on George, the bumbling, cheerful individualistic Everyman figure, rather than the decided communality of the Dad's Army platoon.

Much of the humour in Robb Wilton's monologue and in Get Cracking derives from the juxtaposition of the day-to-day realities of mundane life and the cosmic implications of world-shattering events. But there is humanity too in the determination of the unfit and the over-age, the misfits and the outcasts to do their bit, part of the long-standing British affection for underdogs and losers. Dad's Army draws on both these sources of inspiration, helped by the location – Walmington-on-Sea – where machine-gun emplacements are to be found in the Novelty Rock Emporium and unexploded bombs land on the Pier Pavilion. J. B. Priestley drew memorably on this contrast in his celebrated BBC wireless postscripts. On Wednesday, 5 June 1940, he broadcast a talk about Dunkirk. He found the whole thing 'typically English', adding 'when I say "English" I really mean British', testifying to the extension of characteristics from one to the other. It was English he thought in its 'folly and its grandeur', in the way it began in 'miserable blunder, a catalogue of misfortunes and miscalculations' and ended as 'an epic of gallantry'.

> We have a queer habit – and you can see it running through our history – of conjuring up transformations ... This is not the German way. They don't make such mistakes ... but also, they don't achieve such epics. There is never anything to inspire a man either in their victories or in their defeats; boastful when they're winning, quick to whine when threatened with defeat – there is nothing about them that ever catches the world's imagination. That vast machine of theirs can't create a glimmer of that poetry of action which distinguishes war from mass murder. It's a machine – and therefore has no soul.

By comparison, what was most characteristically English about it – 'so typical of us, so absurd and yet so grand and gallant that you hardly know whether to laugh or to cry when you read about them' – was the part played in the evacuation not by warships but by little seaside pleasure steamers which seemed to belong 'to the same ridiculous holiday world as pierrots and piers, sand castles, ham-and-egg teas, palmists, automatic machines, and crowded sweating promenades' and which sailed out of that 'innocent foolish world of their – to sail into the inferno, to defy bombs, shells, magnetic mines, torpedoes, machine gun fire – to rescue our soldiers, some of them never to return.'[8]

This memorably evokes the contrast between the domesticity, mundanity, heroic ordinariness of the English and the ruthless, faceless, impersonal military machine of the Germans. It is a contrast, complete with seaside setting, that informs *Dad's Army*. In a subsequent postscript (Sunday, 14 July 1940) Priestley spoke of a recent visit to Margate, as he might have spoken of Walmington:

> Everything was there: bathing pools, bandstands, gardens blazing with flowers, lido, theatres, and the like: and miles of firm golden sands all spread out beneath the July sun. But no people! – not a soul. Of all those hundreds of thousands of holiday-makers, of entertainers and hawkers and boatmen – not one. And no sound – not the very ghost of an echo of all that cheerful hullabaloo – children shouting and laughing, bands playing, concert parties singing, men selling ice-cream, whelks and peppermint rock, which I'd remembered hearing along this shore. No, not even an echo.

There is barbed wire and RAF lorries. 'This Margate I saw was saddening and hateful; but its new silence and desolation should be thought of as a bridge leading us to a better Margate in a better England, in a nobler world.'[9] Priestley also went on duty with his local LDV unit and spoke of that too (Sunday, 10 June 1940). He was speaking of a rural village but his image applies to Walmington-on-Sea. The unit was a cross-section of English rural life – parson, bailiff, builder, farmers and farm labourers – protecting their homes and

> I felt too up there a powerful and rewarding sense of community; and with it too a feeling of deep continuity. There we were ploughman and parson, shepherd and clerk, turning out at night, as our forefathers had often done before us, to keep watch and ward over the sleeping hills and fields and homesteads ... we must face, as our forefathers faced such things in order to enjoy our own again.[10]

Another rich source of wartime humour – sending up bureaucracy, authority and restriction – was exploited by another much loved Liverpudlian, Tommy Handley, in the long-running radio show *ITMA (It's That Man Again)*. Tommy too drew on the comic postcard associations of the seaside by playing the Mayor of Foaming-at-the-Mouth. But he was supported by a rich team of comic characters, each with his or her own catchphrase, from the bibulous Colonel Chinstrap ('I don't mind if I do'), and the cheerful charlady Mrs Mopp ('Can I do you now, sir?') to the seedy peddler of 'filthy postcards' Ali Oop ('I go – I come back'), the mournful washerwoman Mona Lott ('It's being so cheerful as keeps me going') and American tough guy Sam Scram ('Boss, boss, sump'n terrible's happened'). Often they sent up unpopular wartime institutions, satirized as the Ministry of Aggravation and the Office of Twerps.

There are some comparisons with *Dad's Army*, where the officiousness of Captain Mainwaring and Warden Hodges is regularly satirized. Also, all the characters had catchphrases some of which entered the national vocabulary, from Captain Mainwaring's 'Stupid boy' to Jones's 'Permission to speak, sir', 'Don't panic' and of the efficacy of the bayonet, 'They don't like it up 'em', Frazer's 'We're doomed, doomed', Hodges' 'Ruddy hooligans' and Private Godfrey's 'May I be excused?'.

But *ITMA*, which also inspired a feature film spin-off, *It's That Man Again* (1942), has not aged well. Frankly, it is just not funny any more. Fast-paced, mildly surreal in places, it is a string of hit-and-miss gags, atrocious puns, topical references, malapropisms and one-dimensional cartoon characters with catchphrases. What it lacks is precisely that three-dimensional richness of character and realistic base that makes *Dad's Army* live and last.

After the war the great innovation in humour was the Ealing comedies, another source of inspiration for *Dad's Army*. *Dad's Army* is recognizably a late flowering of the Ealing world. We can detect echoes of *Whisky Galore* (1949), in which stuffy pompous Captain Waggett (Basil Radford) and his Home Guard unit, complete with 'stupid boy', seek to prevent the Scottish islanders from looting a wrecked ship of its cargo of whisky, and of *Passport to Pimlico* (1949), in which a determined group of Pimlico shopkeepers, led by the resourceful greengrocer (Stanley Holloway) and a pompous bank manager (Raymond Huntley) declare independence and refight the recent war in miniature against the power of Whitehall. The Ealing comedies with their ensemble casts of character actors, their themes of ordinary people plunged into extraordinary situations and their warm-hearted affirmations of community solidarity provide a clear model for *Dad's Army*.

There is nostalgia, embodied in the use in the television series of popular songs of the period to link the scenes. The series was regularly prefaced by a brilliant period pastiche song, 'Who Do You Think You are Kidding, Mr. Hitler?', recorded shortly before his death by Bud Flanagan, one of the voices closely associated with the war. But it was a nostalgia not so much for the war as a time of shortage, destruction and loss but as a period of shared effort and sacrifice, common purpose and good neighbourliness and justified struggle against a wicked enemy.

But perhaps most of all, despite the presence of John Laurie, as much the token Scotsman of the platoon, as he was in many World War Two movies and briefly Talfryn Thomas as the token Welshman Private Cheeseman, the series

The Home Guard in action: *Dad's Army* (1971) with John Le Mesurier, Clive Dunn, **36**
James Beck, John Laurie, Ian Lavender, Arnold Ridley and Arthur Lowe.

was a celebration of Englishness. But this can be fitted into a wider Britishness. The concept of Britishness as articulated by Linda Colley is fulfilled by *Dad's Army*. There is the Empire, represented by Lance Corporal Jones, who joined the army as a drummer boy at fifteen and served under Kitchener in Sudan, fighting at the Battle of Omdurman, in South Africa during the Boer War, on the North-West Frontier of India and in World War One. He is continually recalling his service in the Empire. One of the television episodes. 'The Two and a Half Feathers' parodies the 1939 imperial epic *The Four Feathers* with Corporal Jones accused of cowardice while in Sudan and eventually revealing that, like Harry Faversham, he has rescued a wounded comrade while disguised as a native. The episode included action footage from the 1939 film, in which coincidentally John Laurie had played the role of the Sudanese leader, the Khalifa. Protestantism is represented by the platoon's headquarters, the Church Hall and the regular appearances as a double act of the vicar, Reverend Timothy Farthing (Frank Williams), an amiable, fussy and dithering Anglican and his devoted and protective verger, Mr Yeatman (Edward Sinclair). Britain's commercial pre-eminence, which led Napoleon to dub the English 'a nation of shopkeepers', is epitomized in miniature by the Walmington platoon: with bank manager Mainwaring, butcher Jones, undertaker Frazer, and in addition, greengrocer Hodges as chief warden. Finally, there is war, not with France but with Germany, though Mainwaring maintains the typically British disdain for the French. He thinks them not much use after lunch ('All that wine and garlic – it's very debilitating. All they know how to do is chase women'). In 'The Captain's Car' Mainwaring to his great embarrassment is kissed on both cheeks by a French general on a visit to Walmington.

The national identity is thus embodied in miniature in the series but so is the national character. Among the many examinations and analyses of Englishness perhaps the most influential was Sir Ernest Barker's *The Character of England* (1947). He identified six common characteristics of Englishness, all of which can be found in *Dad's Army*. First, there is social cohesion but within that cohesion a hierarchy of status that breeds snobbery. That can be found in the solidarity of the Home Guard unit but within it the maintenance of social hierarchy. Much of this hinges on the relationship of Captain Mainwaring and Sergeant Wilson. The writers had the brilliant idea of reversing audience expectations by making Wilson of a higher class than Mainwaring, and providing a continuing and productive theme of tension and rivalry. Mainwaring is lower middle class, the son of a small gentlemen's outfitter, a grammar school boy who has spent his life in Swallow's Bank, working his way up to branch manager at Walmington. He married above himself unhappily – his unseen wife Elizabeth was the daughter of the suffragan Bishop of Clagthorpe. He had served in the army but only in 1919 and has no medals. He is prim, pompous and snobbish but also optimistic, patriotic and utterly fearless. His chief clerk and platoon sergeant, Arthur Wilson, is upper middle class, the great-nephew of a peer, educated at a minor public school, served as a captain in World War One and was decorated but has not achieved as much as Mainwaring because of an early career as a languid man-about-town and ladies' man. This class difference and the tension involved is highlighted in the episode 'Ten Seconds from Now' when the platoon is due to appear on a BBC wireless broadcast to America and the BBC assume that the officer will be upper class and the sergeant a 'Gorblimey guvnor' cockney and have scripted the broadcast as such, leading to great complications. Similarly in 'An Honourable Man' when Wilson is revealed as an 'Honourable', to Mainwaring's fury he is immediately elected to the Golf Club (to which Mainwaring has long aspired), is deferred to by everyone – and in a nice reversal – is awarded the freedom of the city by a Russian visitor who selects him as representative of the workers rather than the bourgeoisie (embodied by Mainwaring).

The second characteristic is the British love of amateurism and mistrust of professionalism, evident in the amateur soldiers of Walmington-on-Sea forever muddling through. The contrast between the dogged amateurism of the British and the ruthless professionalism of the Germans highlighted by Priestley in his postscripts is pointed up at the start of the *Dad's Army* film where the Germans in France with planes, tanks and battalions meticulously plan the Blitzkrieg of England, while in Walmington-on-Sea, after Anthony Eden's 1940 broadcast setting up the LDV, Mainwaring appoints himself platoon commander and makes his dispositions, announcing with no sense of absurdity that he controls the whole of the South Coast from Stone's Amusement Arcade to the Novelty Rock Emporium and setting up a Lewis gun which will cover the whole of the High Street from Stead and Simpson's to Timothy White's. The film reworks the first episode of the television series, 'The Man and the Hour' detailing the creation of the platoon, and then follows the unit through a series of comic misadventures and catastrophes on manoeuvres until at the end they are vindicated and justified by their rounding up of a trio of German parachutists holding the vicar, the mayor and other locals hostage in the Church Hall.

Third, there is the gentlemanly code of conduct – 'good form; the not doing of things that are not done; reserve; the habit of understatement'. This code runs right through *Dad's Army*, honoured in the breach as well as in the observance. Fourth, there is the voluntary habit, 'the old tradition of Englishmen to do things for themselves', on a voluntary basis in free association with others – a perfect description of *Dad's Army*. Fifth, there is eccentricity. Kipling said, 'Allah created the English mad, maddest of all mankind' and Noel Coward equated mad dogs and Englishmen. This madness was really an extreme form of English convention: dressing for dinner in the tropics, making no alteration in daily schedule to accommodate different climate or circumstances. As the American philosopher George Santayana put it, 'England is the paradise of individualism, eccentricity, heresy, anomalies, hobbies, and humours', and in that regard Walmington-on-sea is England in embryo. The Home Guard platoon shows how such a nation of eccentric individualists could be blended together to defend the country in wartime. Last, there is an eternal boyishness. It is this sense of the platoon as overgrown schoolboys, indulging in japes and scrapes, irreverence and incompetence – like those other old boys in *Last of the Summer Wine* – that attracts an audience across the age range from young to elderly.

Critics of *Dad's Army* claim it is a mythic rather than a realistic picture of wartime Britain. But that is not how its millions of fans would see it. Interestingly, sales of *Dad's Army* videos shot up around the fiftieth anniversary of VE Day when the media were saturated in images and memories of wartime Britain. A quarter of a million people converged on Buckingham Palace to salute the Queen Mother, the symbol of the 'never say die' spirit of service and sacrifice that is seen to epitomize Britain at war.

Just as there are millions of people who recall the war as a time of communal effort, when the events and spirit and characters of *Dad's Army* were a reality, there are also millions who recall a time when children were taught to spell and to punctuate, to respect their elders and to cultivate good manners, when graffiti and litter were unknown, when violent crime was simply something you saw on the cinema screen in American films, when people knew the difference between right and wrong and retribution was swift and often final, when the public services functioned efficiently and when community was a meaningful concept implying warm-heartedness, tolerance and good neighbourliness. If this sounds like a combination of *Dixon of Dock Green*, Greyfriars School and *Mrs. Dale's Diary*, it probably is. For this is not a historical picture. Real life in any age is always less neatly defined, more ambiguous and more untidy than it appears in retrospect. My picture is that of a 'Golden Age', a restructuring of the past into an amalgam of myth, reality and ideal. Like all 'Golden Ages', it is just out of reach. It is the world of the day before yesterday, which for some means the 1950s, for others the 1940s and for yet more the Edwardian Age.

But this imagined world is far more significant than the historical reality, because it lives in people's minds, it conditions their responses to the present. It is essentially a reaction to what people see around them. As George Steiner wrote:

> Images and symbolic constructs of the past are imprinted, almost in the manner of genetic information, on our sensibility. Each new historical era mirrors itself in the picture and active mythology of its past... It tests its sense of identity, of progress or new achievement against that past. [11]

Rightly or wrongly many people today perceive themselves to be living in a world in which the rich are getting rich and the poor are getting poorer, a society that is pock-marked by violence, greed and squalor, a culture that is coarse, gross and brutalized, an age in which the public services seem to be inexorably running down. They contrast this with their 'Golden Age'. But its political significance is that it is not just a picture of an idealized past, it is also an image of an imagined future. It sets a list of targets for our elected governors to attain.

It is a great mistake to see nostalgia as a passive, wishy-washy, rose-tinted yearning for the past. Nostalgia is a vital force, passionate, active, committed to the ideal of reviving and preserving the best of the past, not just because it is the past but because it works, it is needed and it is right. For at heart nostalgia is love. To love buildings and see them torn down, to love railway lines and see them ripped up, to love countryside and see it ravaged and despoiled inspires not wistfulness but rage against the Philistines and vandals who put naked profit and brutal functionalism before grace, beauty and social need.

The nostalgiasts are on the march. There has been a potent reaction against the architects and planners who inflicted upon us the concrete megalopolis, with its faceless towers, mugger-haunted subways, and bleak gulag estates, which have stifled individuality and deadened the imagination. But now the identikit city centres of the 1960s are being torn down. In their place are planned low-rise developments of courtyards, alleyways, terraces and squares, distinguished by intimacy and human scale. It is nostalgia for the time in which a house was a home which is inspiring programmes of community architecture, enabling people to have a say in the design of the places where they will live.

It is memories of a formal, disciplined but intellectually productive school system that are creating pressure for reform which will promote literacy, numeracy, articulacy and discipline in our schools. Memories of a peaceful, ordered and structured urban world have led to the return of the community policeman and the appearance of neighbourhood watches.

The much derided 'Hovis' advert view of a Britain of thatched cottages, cobbled streets and 'real butter' is merely convenient visual shorthand for that desire for the best of the past which has led to campaigns for real food, real ale, pure air and lead-free petrol. Wherever you turn, people are looking back to the past and finding things that work. Several cities are reintroducing trams to ease traffic congestion. Our European partners have seen the virtue of expanding the railways to relieve the bulging motorway system. Britain has been much slower to follow suit. But battling nostalgiasts saved the most beautiful railway in England, the Settle–Carlisle line, a miracle of Victorian engineering but also a vital community service.

Mrs Thatcher said: 'There is no such thing as society.' Many agreed with her and act as if there were not. But the VE Day and VJ Day celebrations and the continuing popularity of *Dad's Army* with people of all ages demonstrate that there are many who believe the opposite. Not only is there a society; it has shared memories and shared values. It has an ideal of national identity rooted in tradition, community, tolerance and good nature. As we approach the millennium, battle is joined for the soul of the nation. The future character and identity of Britain will be determined by the outcome of that battle.

Notes

1   J. B. Priestley, *The English*, London, 1973, pp. 240–248.
2   For a detailed account of making of the series see Bill Pertwee *Dad's Army: The Making of a Television Legend*, Abbot and London, 1990.
3   *The Daily Mail*, 12 August 1993.
4   J. B. Priestley, *English Humour*, London, 1930, p. 18.
5   Priestley, *English Humour*, p. 16.
6   Priestley, *English Humour*, p. 164.
7   Priestley, *English Humour*, p. 150.
8   J. B. Priestley, *All England Listened*, New York, 1967, pp. 3–7.
9   Priestley, *All England Listened*, pp. 43–50.
10 Priestley, *All England Listened*, pp. 14–20.
11 George Steiner, *In Bluebeard's Castle*, London, 971, p.13.

Bibliography

Ackroyd, Peter, *Dickens*, London, 1990.

Agate, James, *Around Cinemas* (2nd series), London, 1948.

Aldgate, Anthony and Richards, Jeffrey, *Britain Can Take It: the British Cinema in the Second World War*, Edinburgh, 1994.

Anderson, Benedict, *Imagined Communities: reflections on the origin and spread of nationalism*, London, 1983.

Andrews, Malcolm, *Dickens on England and the English*, Hassocks, 1979.

Balcon, Michael, *A Lifetime of Films*, London, 1969.

Barker, Sir Ernest, *National Character*, London, 1927.

Barker, Sir Ernest, ed., *The Character of England*, Oxford, 1947.

Barnett, Corelli, *The Collapse of British Power*, London, 1972.

Barr, Charles, *Ealing Studios*, 2nd edn, London, 1990.

Barr, Charles, ed., *All Our Yesterdays: Ninety Years of British Cinema*, London, 1986.

Bartlett, F. C., *Political Propaganda*, Cambridge, 1940.

Bartley, J. O., *Teague, Shenkin and Sawney*, Cork, 1954.

Beddoe, Deidre, 'Images of Welsh women', in Tony Curtis, ed., *Wales: the Imagined Nation*, Bridgend, 1986, pp. 237–8.

Berry, David, *Wales and Cinema: the first hundred years*, Cardiff, 1994.

Bluestone, George, *Novels into Films*, Berkeley and Los Angeles, California, 1968.

Bogle, Donald, *Toms, Coons, Mulattoes, Mammies and Bucks*, New York, 1973.

Bolt, Christine, *Victorian Attitudes to Race*, London, 1973.

Bolton, H. Philip, *Dickens Dramatized*, London, 1987.

Bradley, Ian, *The Call to Seriousness*, London, 1976.

Bratton, J. S., *The Impact of Victorian Children's Fiction*, London, 1981.

The British Council, *British Life and Thought*, London, 1941.

Brogan, Sir Denis, *The English People*, London, 1943.

Brown, Geoff, and Aldgate, Tony, *The Common Touch: the films of John Baxter*, London, 1989.

Brown, John, 'The Land Beyond Brigadoon', *Sight and Sound*, 53 (1983/84), pp. 40-46.

Brownlow, Kevin, *The War, the West and the Wilderness*, London, 1979.

Brownlow, Kevin, *David Lean*, London, 1996.

Calder, Angus, *The People's War*, London, 1973.

Carlyle, Thomas, *On Heroes, Hero-Worship and the Heroic in History*, London, 1912.

Cave, Richard Allen, 'Staging the Irishman', in J. S. Bratton *et al.*, eds, *Acts of Supremacy: the British Empire on the stage, 1790–1930*, Manchester, 1991, pp. 62–128.

Chandler, Alice, *A Dream of Order*, London, 1971.

Chapman, James, '*The Life and Death of Colonel Blimp* (1943) Reconsidered', *Historical Journal of Film, Radio and Television*, 15 (1995), pp. 19–54.

Chapman, Malcolm, *The Celts: the construction of a myth*, Basingstoke and London, 1992.

Christie, Ian, ed., *Powell, Pressburger and Others*, London, 1978.

Colley, Linda, *Britons*, New Haven and London, 1992.

Collini, Stefan, *Public Moralists*, Oxford, 1993.

Colls, Robert, and Dodd, Philip ed., *Englishness: politics and culture, 1880–1920*, Beckenham, 1986.

Coward, Noel, *Australia Revisited, 1940*, London, 1941.

Coward, Noel, *Future Indefinite*, London, 1954.

Craig, Cairns, 'Rooms Without a View', *Sight and Sound* 1, n.s. (June, 1991), pp. 10–13.

Crick, Bernard, ed., *National Identities: the constitution of the United Kingdom*, Oxford, 1991.

Cripps, Thomas, *Slow Fade to Black: the negro in American Film, 1780– 1850*, Madison, Wis, 1964.

Cronin, James E., *Labour and Society in Britain, 1918–1979*, London, 1984.

Cross, Gary ed., *Worktowners in Blackpool*, London, 1990.

Curran, James, and Porter, Vincent, eds, *British Cinema History*, London, 1983.

Curtin, Philip D., *The Image of Africa: British ideas and action, 1780–1850*, Madison, Wis, 1964.

Curtis, L. P. Jr., *Anglo-Saxons and Celts*, Bridgeport, CT, 1968.

Curtis, Tony, ed., *Wales: the Imagined Nation*, Bridgend, 1986.

Davis, Paul, *The Life and Times of Ebenezer Scrooge*, New Haven and London, 1990.

Dean, Basil, *Mind's Eye*, London, 1973.

Dick, Eddie, ed., *From Limelight to Satellite*, London, 1990.

Dickinson, A. E. F., *Vaughan Williams*, London, 1963.

Dresser, Madge, 'Britannia', in Raphael Samuel, ed., *Patriotism*, vol. 3, London, 1989, pp.26–49.

Drotner, Kirsten, *English Children and their Magazines, 1757–1945*, New Haven and London, 1988.

Duberman, Martin Bauml, *Paul Robeson*, London, 1989.

Dunne, Philip, *How Green Was My Valley: the screenplay*, Santa Barbara, 1990.

Durgnat, Raymond, *A Mirror for England*, London, 1970.

Dyer, Richard, *Heavenly Bodies*, London, 1987.

Eisenstein, S. M., *Film Form*, London, 1963.

Ellis, John, 'Made in Ealing', *Screen*, 16 (Spring 1975), pp. 78–127.

Ellis, John, 'Art, Culture and Quality', *Screen*, 19 (Autumn 1978), pp. 9–49.

Emerson, Ralph Waldo, *English Traits*, London, 1903.

Fawcett, F. Dubrez, *Dickens the Dramatist*, London, 1952.

Field, H. John, *Towards a Programme of Imperial Life*, Oxford, 1982.

Fisher, John, *Funny Way to be a Hero*, St. Albans, 1976.

Flamini, Roland, *Thalberg: the last tycoon and the world of MGM*, London, 1994.

Foner, Philip, ed., *Paul Robeson Speaks: writings, speeches, interviews, 1918–1974*, London, 1978.

Forster, E. M., 'Notes on English Character', *Abinger Harvest*, London, 1936, pp. 3–14.

Foss, Hubert, *Ralph Vaughan Williams*, London, 1950.

Foster, R. F., *Paddy and Mr Punch*, London, 1993.

Fraser, John, *America and the Patterns of Chivalry*, Cambridge, 1982.

Friedman, Lester D., ed., *British Cinema and Thatcherism*, London, 1993.

Fryer, Peter, *Staying Power: the history of black people in Britain*, London, 1984.

Furhammar, Leif, and Folke Isaksson, *Politics and Film*, trans. Kersti French, London, 1971.

Gänzl, Kurt, *The British Musical Theatre; vol. 2: 1915–1984*, Basingstoke and London, 1986.

Gilley, Sheridan, 'English attitudes to the Irish in England, 1780–1900', in Colin Holmes, ed., *Immigrants and Minorities in British Society*, London, 1978, pp. 81–110.

Girouard, Mark, *Return to Camelot: chivalry and the English gentleman*, New Haven and London, 1981.

Gorer, Geoffrey, *Exploring English Character*, London, 1955.

Greene, Graham, *The Pleasure Dome*, London, 1974.

Gussman, Boris, *Out in the Midday Sun*, London, 1972.

Halliwell, Leslie, *Seats in All Parts*, London, 1985.

Halsey, A. H., ed., *British Social Trends Since 1900*, Basingstoke and London, 1988.

Hardy, Forsyth, *Scotland in Film*, Edinburgh, 1990.

Hardy, Forsyth, ed., *Grierson on the Movies*, London and Boston, 1981.

Harte, B., *Tales of the West; Parodies and Poems*, London, n.d.

Haworth, Don, *Figures in a Bygone Landscape*, London, 1986.

Haworth, Don, *Bright Morning*, London, 1990.

Henty, G. A., *By Sheer Luck*, London, 1884.

Hepworth, Cecil, *Came the Dawn*, London, 1951.

Herman, Gerald, 'For God and Country: *Khartoum* (1966) as history and as "object lesson" for global policemen', *Film and History*, 9 (1979), pp. 1–15.

Heussler, Robert, *Yesterday's Rulers*, Oxford, 1963.

Hewison, Robert, *Culture and Consensus: England, art and politics since 1940*, London, 1995.

Higson, Andrew, *Waving the Flag*, Oxford, 1995.

Hill, John, *Sex, Class and Realism: British cinema, 1956–1963*, London, 1986.

Himmelfarb, Gertrude, *The Demoralization of Society*, London, 1995.

Hodgkinson, Anthony W. and Rodney Sheratsky, *Humphrey Jennings: more than a maker of films*, Hanover and London, 1982.

Hoggart, Richard, *The Uses of Literacy*, Harmondsworth, 1958.

Holmes, Colin, *John Bull's Island: immigration and British society, 1871–1971*, London, 1988.

Holmes, Colin, *A Tolerant Country: Immigrants, Refugees and Minorities in Britain*, London, 1991.

Howard, Ronald, *In Search of My Father*, London, 1981.

Howes, Frank, *The Music of Ralph Vaughan Williams*, Oxford, 1954.

Hughes, Robert, *The Culture of Complaint: the fraying of America*, Oxford and New York, 1993.

Hughes, Winifred, *The Maniac in the Cellar: sensation novels of the 1860s*, Princeton, 1982.

Huntley, John, *British Film Music*, London, 1947.

Irving, Ernest, *Cue for Music*, London, 1959.

Irving, Ernest, 'Music in Films', *Music and Letters*, 24 (1943), pp. 223–35.

Jackson, Kevin, ed., *The Humphrey Jennings Film Reader*, Manchester, 1993.

James, David, *Scott of the Antarctic: the film and its production*, London, 1948.

Jennings, Mary Lou, ed., *Humphrey Jennings: film-maker, painter, poet*, London, 1982.

Jones, D. C., *Social Survey of Merseyside*, Liverpool, 1934.

Jordan, Marion, 'Carry On – Follow that Stereotype', in James Curran and Vincent Porter, eds, *British Cinema History*, London, 1983, pp. 312–27.

Joyce, Patrick, *Visions of the People*, Cambridge, 1991.

Kemp, Philip, *Lethal Innocence: the cinema of Alexander Mackendrick*, London, 1991.

Kennedy, Michael, *The Works of Ralph Vaughan Williams*, 1964 and Oxford, 1992.

Kiernan, V. C., *The Lords of Human Kind*, Harmondsworth, 1972.

Kulik, Karol, *Alexander Korda: the man who could work miracles*, London, 1975.

Lane, Margaret, *Edgar Wallace*, London, 1939.

Lasch, Christopher, *The Culture of Narcissism*, London, 1980.

Leahy, James, *The Cinema of Joseph Losey*, London, 1967.

Legman, Gershon, *Love and Death*, New York, 1949.

Lejeune, Anthony, ed., *C. A. Lejeune Film Reader*, Manchester, 1991.

Lejeune, C. A., *Chestnuts in Her Lap*, London, 1947.

Lejeune, C. A., *Thank You for Having Me*, London, 1971.

Light, Alison, *Forever England*, London, 1991.

Lipscomb, W. P., and R. J. Minney, 'Clive of India', *Famous Plays of 1933–1934*, London, 1934.

Lorimer, Douglas, *Colour, Class and the Victorians*, Leicester, 1978.

Low, Rachael, *History of the British Film*, 7 vols, London, 1948–85.

McArthur, Colin, ed., *Scotch Reels: Scotland in cinema and television*, London, 1982.

McDonald, Kevin, *Emeric Pressburger*, London, 1994.

MacDonald, Malcolm, *John Foulds*, Rickmansworth, 1975.

McGilligan, Patrick, *George Cukor: a double life*, London, 1991.

MacKenzie, John M., 'David Livingstone: the construction of the myth', in Tom Gallagher and Graham Walker eds, *Sermons and Battle Hymns: Protestant culture in modern Scotland*, Edinburgh, 1990, pp.24-42.

MacKenzie, John M., 'Heroic myths of Empire', in John M. MacKenzie, ed., *Popular Imperialism and the Military, 1850–1950*, Manchester, 1992, pp. 109–38.

MacKenzie, John M., *Propaganda and Empire*, Manchester, 1984.

MacKenzie, John M., ed., *Imperialism and Popular Culture*, Manchester, 1986.

MacKenzie, John M., *Scotland and the Empire*, Lancaster, 1992.

McLynn, Frank, *Stanley: sorcerer's apprentice*, London, 1991.

Maltby, Richard, *Harmless Entertainment*, Metuchen, NJ, and London, 1983.

Mancia, Adrienne, and Kardish, Laurence, eds, *Michael Balcon: the pursuit of British cinema*, New York, 1984.

Martin, Bernice, *A Sociology of Contemporary Cultural Change*, Oxford, 1981.

Marwick, Arthur, *Class: image and reality*, London, 1980.

Marwick, Arthur, *British Society since 1945*, Harmondsworth, 1982.

Marwick, Arthur, *Room at the Top, Saturday Night and Sunday Morning* and the 'Cultural revolution' in Britain, *Journal of Contemporary History*, 19 (1984), pp. 127–52.

Mathieson, Muir, 'Music for Crown', *Hollywood Quarterly*, 3 (1948), pp. 323–6.

Mellers, Wilfred, *Vaughan Williams and the Vision of Albion*, London, 1989.

Midwinter, Eric, *Make 'Em Laugh*, London, 1979.

Miers, Sir Henry, 'Some characteristics of Manchester Men', in W. H. Brindley, ed., *The Soul of Manchester*, Manchester, 1929, pp. 33–8.

Mills, John, *Up in the Clouds, Gentlemen, Please*, London, 1980.

Minns, Raynes, *Bombers and Mash*, London, 1980.

Moore-Gilbert, Bart, and Seed, John, eds, *Cultural revolution? the challenge of arts in the 1960s*, London, 1992.

More, Kenneth, *More or Less*, London, 1978.

Morgan, Guy, *Red Roses Every Night*, London, 1948.

Morgan, Prys, 'From a death to a view: the hunt for the Welsh past in the Romantic Period', in Eric Hobsbawm and Terence Ranger eds, *The Invention of Tradition*, Cambridge, 1983, pp. 43–100.

Morley, Sheridan, *Katharine Hepburn*, London, 1984.

Murphy, Robert, *Realism and Tinsel: cinema and society in Britain 1939–48*, London, 1989.

Murphy, Robert, *Sixties British Cinema*, London, 1992.

Naughton, Bill, *On the Pig's Back*, Oxford, 1987.

Naughton, Bill, *Saintly Billy*, Oxford, 1988.

Neville, Richard, *Playpower*, London, 1971.

Newman, Gerald, *The Rise of English Nationalism, 1740–1830*, London, 1987.

Noble, Peter, *The Negro in Films*, London, 1947.

Nuttall, Jeff, *King Twist*, London, 1978.

Orczy, Baroness, *Links in the Chain of Life*, London, n.d.

Ormerod, Frank, *Lancashire Life and Character*, Manchester, 1915.

Orwell, George, *Collected Essays, Journalism and Letters*, 4 volumes, Harmondsworth, 1971.

Ottaway, Hugh, 'Scott and After: the final phase', *Musical Times*, 113 (1972), pp. 959–62.

Pascal, Valerie, *The Devil and His Disciple*, London, 1971.

Peabody, Dean, *National Characteristics*, Cambridge, 1985.

Pearson, Geoffrey, *Swearing*, Oxford, 1991.

Perkin, Harold, *The Origins of Modern English Society, 1780–1880*, London, 1969.

Perkin, Harold, *The Structured Crowd*, Brighton, 1981.

Pertwee, Bill, *Dad's Army: the making of a television legend*, Newton Abbot and London, 1990.

Pines, Jim, *Blacks in Films*, London, 1975.

Pittock, Murray, *The Invention of Scotland: the Stuart myth and Scottish identity, 1683 to the present*, London, 1991.

Poole, Julian, 'British cinema attendance in wartime: audience preference at the Majestic, Macclesfield, 1939-1948', *Historical Journal of Film, Radio and Television*, 7 (1987), pp. 15–34.

Porter, Roy, ed., *Myths of the English*, Cambridge, 1992.

Powell, Dilys, *Films since 1939*, London, 1947.

Powell, Michael, *A Life in Movies*, London, 1986.

Priestley, J. B. *English Humour*, London, 1930.

Priestley, J. B., *Let The People Sing*, London, 1939.

Priestley, J. B., *Our Nation's Heritage*, London, 1940.

Priestley, J. B., *All England Listened*, New York, 1967.

Priestley, J. B. *English Journey*, London, 1968.

Priestley, J. B., *The English*, London, 1973.

Pronay, Nicholas and D. W. Spring, eds, *Propaganda, Politics and Film, 1918–1945*, London, 1982.

Randall, Alan, and Ray Seaton, *George Formby*, London, 1974.

Rapp, Dean, and Charles W. Weber, 'British film, empire and society in the twenties: the *Livingstone* film, 1923–1925', *Historical Journal of Film, Radio and Television*, 9 (1989), pp. 3–19.

Read, Al, *It's All in the Book*, London, 1985.

Reid, Charles, *Malcolm Sargent*, London, 1968.

Richards, Jeffrey, *Visions of Yesterday*, London, 1973.

Richards, Jeffrey, *The Age of the Dream Palace*, London, 1984.

Richards, Jeffrey, *Happiest Days: the public schools in English fiction*, Manchester, 1988.

Richards, Jeffrey, ed., *Imperialism and Juvenile Literature*, Manchester, 1989.

Richards, Jeffrey, 'Ireland, the Empire and film', in Keith Jeffery, ed., *An Irish Empire?*, Manchester, 1996, pp. 25–6.

Richards, Jeffrey, *Stars in Our Eyes*, Preston, 1994.

Richards, Jeffrey, and Anthony Aldgate, *Best of British: cinema and Society, 1930–70*, Oxford, 1983.

Richards, Jeffrey, and Jeffrey Hulbert, 'Censorship in Action: the case of Lawrence of Arabia', *Journal of Contemporary History*, 19 (1984), pp. 153–70.

Richards, Jeffrey, and Dorothy Sheridan, eds, *Mass-Observation at the Movies*, London, 1987.

Robbins, Keith, *Nineteenth-Century Britain: integration and diversity*, Oxford, 1988.

Robbins, Keith, *Nineteenth-Century Britain: the making of a nation*, Oxford, 1989.

Roberts, Elizabeth, *A Woman's Place*, Oxford, 1984.

Roberts, Robert, *The Classic Slum*, Harmondsworth, 1973.

Robertson, James C., *The British Board of Film Censors: Britain, 1896–1950*, London, 1985.

Robeson, Eslanda Goode, *Paul Robeson, Negro*, London, 1980.

Robeson, Paul, *Here I Stand*, London, 1958.

Rockett, Kevin, Luke Gibbons and John Hill, *Cinema and Ireland*, London, 1987.

Rubin, Leon, *The Nicholas Nickleby Story*, London, 1981.

Russo, Vito, *The Celluloid Closet*, New York, 1981.

Samuel, Raphael, ed., *Patriotism; the making and unmaking of British national identity*, 3 vols, London, 1989.

Santayana, George, *Soliloquies in England*, London, 1922.

Seton, Marie, *Paul Robeson*, London, 1958.

Showalter, Elaine, *A Literature of Their Own*, London, 1982.

Sinyard, Neil, *The Films of Richard Lester*, London, 1985.

Sissons, Michael, and Philip French, eds, *The Age of Austerity*, London, 1983.

Slide, Anthony, *The Cinema and Ireland*, Jefferson, NC, and London, 1984.

Smiles, Samuel, *Self-Help*, London, 1911.

Smith, Anthony D., *National Identity*, London, 1991.

Smith, Dai, *Wales! Wales?*, London, 1984.

Smith, Dai, 'Myth and meaning in the literature of the South Wales Coalfield – the 1930s', *The Anglo-Welsh Review* (Spring 1976), pp. 21–41.

Smith, Dai, *Aneurin Bevan and the World of South Wales*, Cardiff, 1993.

Stead, Peter, *Film and the Working Class: the feature film in British and American society*, London, 1989.

Stead, Peter, 'Wales in the Movies', in Tony Curtis, ed., *Wales: the imagined nation*, Bridgend, 1986, pp. 161–79.

Stead, Peter, *Richard Burton: so much, so little*, Bridgend, 1991.

Street, Brian V., *The Savage in Literature*, London, 1974.

Steiner, George, *In Bluebeard's Castle*, London, 1971.

Taylor, Mike, 'John Bull and the iconography of public opinion in England, *c.*1712–1929', *Past and Present*, 134 (1992), pp. 93–128.

Taylor, Philip M., ed., *Britain and the Cinema in the Second World War*, Basingstoke and London, 1988.

Thacker, Christopher, *The Wildness Pleases: the origins of Romanticism*, Beckenham, 1983.

Thomas, Tony, *Music for the Movies*, South Brunswick, New York and London, 1973.

Thompson, F. M. L., 'Social control in Victorian Britain', *Economic History Review*, 34 (1981), pp. 189–208.

Thompson, F. M. L., *The Rise of Respectable Society*, London, 1988.

Thomson, David, *Showman: the life of David O. Selznick*, London, 1993.

Thorp, Margaret Farrand, *America in the Movies*, New Haven, 1939.

Tidrick, Kathryn, *Empire and English Character*, London, 1990.

Tinniswood, Peter, *Uncle Mort's North Country*, London, 1987.

Townshend, Charles, *Political Violence in Ireland*, Oxford, 1987.

Trevelyan, John, *What the Censor Saw*, London, 1973.

Trevor-Roper, Hugh, 'The invention of tradition: the Highland tradition of Scotland', in Eric Hobsbawm and Terence Ranger, eds, *The Invention of Tradition*, London, 1983, pp. 15–41.

Tynan, Kenneth, *A View of the English Stage, 1944–63*, London, 1975.

Vaughan Williams, Ralph, *National Music and Other Essays*, Oxford, 1987.

Vaughan Williams, Ursula, *R. V. M.*, Oxford, 1992.

Vaughan Williams, Ursula, and Imogen Holst, eds, *Heirs and Rebels*, Oxford, 1959.

Vincent, David, *Literacy and Popular Culture: England, 1750–1914*, Cambridge, 1989.

Walker, Alexander, *Hollywood England*, London, 1974.

Walton, John K., *Lancashire*, Manchester, 1987.

Weinbrot, Howard, *Britannia's Issue: the rise of British literature from Dryden to Ossian*, Cambridge, 1995.

Wiener, Martin, *English Culture and the Decline of the Industrial Spirit*, Cambridge, 1981.

Wilcox, Herbert, *25,000 Sunsets*, London, 1967.

Williams, Bransby, *Bransby Williams by Himself*, London, 1954.

Williams, Gwyn A., *When Was Wales?*, Harmondsworth, 1984.

Winnington, Richard, *Film Criticism and Caricatures, 1943–1953*, London, 1975.

Winnington, Richard, *Drawn and Quartered*, London, n.d.

Withers, Charles, 'The historical creation of the Scottish Highlands', in Ian Donnachie and Christopher Whatley, eds, *The Manufacture of Scottish History*, Edinburgh, 1992, pp. 143–56.

Wood, Linda, *The Commercial Imperative in the British Film Industry: Maurice Elvey, a case study*, London, 1987.

Woodruff, William, *Billy Boy*, Halifax, 1993.

Young, G. W., *Victorian England: portrait of an age*, Oxford, 1977.

Index of film titles

General index

14/12.